Sembene

Imagining Alternatives in
Film & Fiction

Sembene

Imagining Alternatives in Film & Fiction

DAVID MURPHY
Lecturer in French at the University of Stirling

James Currey
OXFORD

Africa World Press
TRENTON, NJ

Africa World Press, Inc.

P.O. Box 1892
Trenton, NJ 08607

P.O. Box 48
Asmara, ERITREA

Copyright © 2001 David Murphy

First Africa World Press, Inc. Edition 2001

Library of Congress Cataloging-in-Publication Data

Murphy, David, 1971-
    Sembene : imagining alternatives in film & fiction / David Murphy
    p. cm.
    Includes bibliographical references and index.
    ISBN 0-86543-945-1 -- ISBN 0-86543-946-X (pbk.)
    1. Sembene, Ousmane, 1923---Criticism and interpretation. I. Title.

PN1998.3.S397 M87 2001
843'.914--dc21   2001022361

Published in England by:

James Currey Ltd.
73 Botley Road
Oxford, OX2 OBS

For my parents

Contents

vii

Contents

Film Stills

All stills provided by the British Film Institute

Acknowledgements

This study is based on my doctoral thesis which I completed at Trinity College, Dublin, in 1998. I am indebted to many people for their help and encouragement in preparing this book. I would like to thank Aedín and Paul for their corrections and comments on the original manuscript, which were greatly appreciated. I am grateful to Cécile for correcting the lapses in my French, particularly in the interview with Sembene in the Appendix. I am deeply indebted to Karim for his inexhaustible patience and goodwill in locating documents for me at the Bibliothèque Universitaire in the Université Cheikh Anta Diop de Dakar. I am obliged to Magatte Thiam for arranging the interview with Sembene at Filmi Doomireew. I am also extremely grateful to Sembene himself for finding time in his busy schedule to talk to a young researcher (although, as can be seen in the Appendix, I was made to work for it!). I would like to thank the Trinity Trust for its financial support in purchasing stills from Sembene's films. I would also like to thank the staff of the British Film Institute for their help in obtaining these stills, and I am greatly obliged to Filmi Doomireew for giving me permission to use them in this book. Lynn Taylor of James Currey deserves great credit for making the transformation of the thesis into the book relatively painless (for both parties, I hope!).

I would particularly like to thank two people whose ideas and criticisms have helped to shape this study. Charles Bowao helped me to think about Africa in terms of its modernity, as well as being living proof of that modernity himself. He was also a good friend and guide throughout my stay in Dakar. However, I owe my deepest debt of gratitude to Professor Roger Little who has aided my research on both an intellectual and a practical level during the past few years. His ideas and encouragement have been much appreciated.

Finally, many thanks go to my family and friends (in Ireland, France and Senegal) for their generosity and support, and especially to Aedín for sharing her life with me. Above all though, I would like to thank my parents for their patience and their love. This book is dedicated to them.

The Works of Sembène

Fiction

Le Docker noir, trans. *Black Docker*

O Pays, mon beau peuple!

Les Bouts de bois de Dieu, trans. *God's Bits of Wood*

Voltaïque, trans. *Tribal Scars*

L'Harmattan

Le Mandat with *Véhi-Ciosane*, trans. *The Money Order* with *White Genesis*

Xala, trans. *Xala*

Le Dernier de l'empire, trans. *The Last of the Empire*

Niiwam and *Taaw*, trans. *Niiwam* and *Taaw*

Guelwaar

Films

Borom Sarret

Niaye

La Noire de

Le Mandat/Mandabi

Taaw

Emitaï

Xala

Ceddo

Camp de Thiaroye

Guelwaar

Faat Kine

Introduction

The Senegalese writer and filmmaker Sembene (variously known as Ousmane Sembene and Sembene Ousmane)[1] has always been considered something of an outsider, both as a writer and as an individual. While the vast majority of Senegalese and other African writers are members of an educated elite, Sembene stands out as a self-educated man whose interest in literature was born while he was working as a docker and trade union official in Marseilles. During the 1960s and 1970s, when the literary notion of Negritude, with its essentialist vision of race, was elevated to the status of state ideology by the Senegalese poet/president, Léopold Sédar Senghor, Sembene continued to espouse his radical, Marxist views (the artistic and political disputes between the two men will be discussed at length in Chapters One and Seven). In a

---

[1] There has been much confusion about Sembene's real name. The name which appears on his novels is 'Sembène Ousmane' (sometimes spelt with the 'è', sometimes not). However, this appears to be merely an example of the French practice of placing the surname before the given name on official documents, for 'Sembene' is, in fact, the patronymic (the same process gives us Camara Laye rather than Laye Camara). It has been suggested in some quarters that Sembene has deliberately chosen to have his name placed back to front as a protest against the use of French patronymics for the names of streets in Dakar (this argument is advanced in *Jeune Afrique*, 19 September 1979, p. 71). However, I have yet to find a quote from Sembene to back up this assertion. On a visit to Dublin, in 1993, the artist provided the critic with an escape route out of this confusion by expressing his desire to be known simply as 'Sembene' (with no 'è'). This is the practice which will be followed throughout this study. For a somewhat incomplete biography of Sembene, see Paulin Soumanou Vieyra, *Sembène Ousmane, cinéaste* (Paris: Présence Africaine, 1972). Samba Gadjigo provides a portrait of Sembene, based on a number of the artist's interviews, in 'Ousmane Sembène: les enjeux du cinéma et de la littérature', in *Littérature et cinéma en Afrique francophone: Ousmane Sembène et Assia Djebar*, ed. by Sada Niang (Paris: L'Harmattan, 1996), pp. 110–21. Carrie Dailey Moore (later to become Carrie Sembene) presents some useful information on Sembene's intellectual development (courses he followed while in CGT, writers he met, etc.) in her 'Evolution of an African Artist: Social Realism in the Works of Ousmane Sembene' (unpublished doctoral thesis, Indiana University, 1973).

1

country in which 95 per cent of the population are Muslim, Sembene is an atheist whose work has examined the ways in which temporal and spiritual powers overlap. As becomes clear from these brief examples, Sembene has consistently sought to counter the dominant discourses of his society and I believe that this attempt to *imagine alternatives* stands at the heart of his work. This search for *alternatives* extends to Sembene's choice of media for his work, shifting back and forth from literature to the cinema. In this study, it will be argued that this use of alternative media[2] is closely linked to Sembene's desire to record alternative histories and narratives: the capacity to imagine alternatives is in itself an act of resistance.

As the *fille ainée* of French colonialism in sub-Saharan Africa, Senegal was a prime location for the development of an African literature in French. The site of French trading posts as early as the seventeenth century, the region of Senegambia later became, under the Third Republic, the launch pad for France's conquest of a vast West African empire, which had its capital in the newly built Senegalese city of Dakar. After the conquest, the inhabitants of the original areas of French domination (known as the *quatre communes*) were to continue to enjoy a special relationship with the coloniser. Those Senegalese fortunate enough to have been born in one of the *quatre communes* of Saint-Louis, Gorée, Rufisque and Dakar enjoyed the rights of full French citizenship and were able to vote for a deputy who sat in the *Assemblée Nationale* in Paris. In a complex social and political process, the idea of a Senegalese *nation* was being crystallised at the same time as French domination of the region was nearing completion.

The creation of an educated elite to staff the colonial administration in Dakar and Saint-Louis was to give birth to an African literature in French at the beginning of the twentieth century. The simplistic, assimilationist works of Ousmane Socé Diop and Ahmadou Mapaté Diagne, amongst others, paved the way for more illustrious names to follow: Léopold Sédar Senghor, Birago Diop, Cheikh Hamidou Kane and, the main focus of our study, Sembene. In fact, Senegal is rare among sub-Saharan African countries in that it can genuinely be said to have a *national* European-language literature that consists of a large corpus of work.[3] Within this literature, Sembene's novels (particularly *God's Bits of Wood*, which is undoubtedly his best known work) and short stories occupy an important, if somewhat controversial place, due to his radical Marxist standpoint. Senegal is also one of the few African countries to

---

[2] As well as being a novelist and filmmaker, Sembene has also published some poetry (on a strictly occasional basis) and he adapted his novel, *God's Bits of Wood*, for the stage in 1984. Codou Bop provides a critique of the production of the play at the Théâtre National Daniel Sorano, in Dakar, in 'Les Bouts de bois de Dieu, d'Ousmane Sembene', *Revue africaine de communication*, 5 (March–April 1984), pp. 47–50.

[3] The most comprehensive introduction to Senegalese literature is to be found in Dorothy S. Blair, *Senegalese Literature: a Critical History* (Boston, MA: Twayne, 1984). More recently, Papa Samba Diop has produced a monumental study, *Ecriture romanesque et cultures régionales au Sénégal, des origines à 1992: de la lettre à l'allusion* (Frankfurt: IFO, 1995). The review, *Notre Librairie*, has dedicated special issues to various African national literatures (in French). The issue on Senegalese literature is to be found in *Notre Librairie*, 81 (October–December 1985).

have established a substantial body of cinematic work and Sembene, who has led a dual cinematic and literary career since the 1960s, has played a leading role in its development.

Sembene is the author of ten books, seven of which have been translated into English: *Le Docker noir* (1956), translated as *Black Docker*; *O Pays, mon beau peuple!* (1957); *Les Bouts de bois de Dieu* (1960), translated as *God's Bits of Wood*; *Voltaïque* (1962), translated as *Tribal Scars*; *L'Harmattan* (1963); *Le Mandat* with *Véhi-Ciosane* (1966), translated as *The Money Order* with *White Genesis*; *Xala* (1973), translated under the same title; *Le Dernier de l'empire* (1981), translated as *The Last of the Empire*; *Niiwam* with *Taaw* (1987), translated as *Niiwam* and *Taaw*; *Guelwaar* (1996). He has also made eleven films: *Borom Sarret* (1962) – the film was first shown at the Festival de Tours in January 1963, so it cannot have been made in 1963, as is usually stated; *Niaye* (1964); *La Noire de* (1966); *Le Mandat/Mandabi* (1968); *Taaw* (1970); *Emitaï* (1971); *Xala* (1974); *Ceddo* (1976); *Camp de Thiaroye* (1988); *Guelwaar* (1992); *Faat Kine* (2000).[4]

Although he has long been considered one of Africa's foremost writers and filmmakers, there exist surprisingly few book-length studies of Sembene's work. Hundreds of articles on his films, novels and short stories have appeared in reviews and general studies of African literature and cinema over the past forty years since the publication of his first novel, *Black Docker*, in 1956.[5] However, there have been only two studies devoted to his cinema and a single work devoted to his literature. The lack of in-depth studies of Sembene's cinema, in particular, seems rather unusual. Sembene has won great critical and popular acclaim for many of his films and, although now in his seventies (he was born in 1923), he is still making films which, while they lack the questioning of form and style displayed in his earlier works, *Ceddo*, in particular (1976), remain both popular and politically radical. Indeed, his films have found audiences around the globe. For example, his second last film, *Guelwaar* (1992), which has yet to be widely released in his home country, enjoyed a remarkable success in the United States.

Even if one considers it purely from an historical perspective, it might have been expected that Sembene's films would have been the subject of more full-length studies. Indeed, Sembene's role in the development of the African cinema has been highly significant (he is often hailed as the 'father of African cinema'): he made one of the first films by an African from south of the Sahara (*Borom Sarret*, in 1962), and was the first to make a film in an African

---

[4] Sembene is also reported to have made a film entitled, *L'Empire sonhraï*, for the Malian government in 1962, but it has never been commercially released (if indeed it really exists). Paulin Soumanou Vieyra also notes that Sembene has made two short films (titles not given), one for French and the other for Swiss television, but I have been unable to trace these works. I have also been unable to obtain a copy of *Taaw* which has forced me to omit this work from my analysis. His latest film, *Faat Kine*, premiered in Dakar in May 2000 (I have not seen it yet). Details on the availability of Sembene's films can be found in the filmography at the end of this study.

[5] There also exists a large number of theses examining Sembene's work (the majority of which were written in the United States). Due to the extent of the published material on Sembene's work, I have only consulted a small number of theses. The bibliography contains details of all theses I was able to consult.

3

language (*Mandabi*, in 1968). He is also one of the few African filmmakers who would warrant an entire study for the simple reason that, in a context where it is extremely difficult to find the money to finance a film, he has managed to build up a relatively large body of work, now numbering ten films in all.

The extent of Sembene's cinematic achievement makes the modesty of the critical studies of his films all the more disappointing. Paulin Soumanou Vieyra's *Sembène Ousmane, cinéaste*, which appeared in 1972, is principally a reference book that sets out to lay the groundwork necessary for a complete study of Sembene's cinema, providing scene-by-scene summaries of each of Sembene's films as well as a compilation of reviews of his work. One might have imagined that Françoise Pfaff, writing over a decade later, would have attempted a more ambitious project but her book, *The Cinema of Ousmane Sembene: A Pioneer of African Film*, remains extremely limited in scope and lacks any real critical framework. At one point, she refers to Sembene, the committed Marxist, as a 'humanist trying to reshape Africa', which is indicative of the absence of political considerations throughout her study.[6]

Whatever the limitations of the works dealing with Sembene's cinema, the sole study of his literature is a singularly inept and poorly conceived effort. The very title of Martin Bestman's study, *Sembène Ousmane et l'esthétique du roman négro-africain*, reveals the extraordinary critical approach of attempting to fit a Marxist writer, hostile to essentialist notions of race, into the canon of Negritude. Bestman sets out his goal as that of examining '*la tension toujours croissante entre les deux pôles – tradition et modernisme – qui nous semble être le problème fondamental chez Sembène*' ['the ever-increasing tension between the two poles of tradition and modernity, which I believe to be the fundamental problematic in Sembene's work'][7] and he describes Sembene as a writer who is '*très représentatif de la littérature et de la culture africaines*' ['highly representative of African literature

---

[6] Françoise Pfaff, *The Cinema of Ousmane Sembene: A Pioneer of African Film* (Westport, CT: Greenwood Press, 1984), pp. 158–9. See also Antoine Kakou's *Emblèmes et métaphores d'un conteur: les bases de l'écriture filmique de Sembène Ousmane* (Abidjan: Université d'Abidjan, 1980), a short, modest work that promises, but does not actually deliver, a semiological study of Sembene's cinema. A special issue of *L'Afrique littéraire* was dedicated to both his films and novels, focusing mainly on the cinematic work: *L'Afrique littéraire*, 76 (1985). Sheila Petty has also edited a collection of articles on his cinematic work entitled *A Call to Action: The Films of Ousmane Sembene* (Trowbridge: Flick Books, 1996).

[7] Martin Bestman, *Sembène Ousmane et l'esthétique négro-africain* (Sherbrooke, Québec: Editions Naaman, 1981), p. 10. The translation is mine: throughout the book, all translations from the French are mine unless otherwise specified. Biny Traoré's rambling study, *Aspects socio-politiques et techniques dans le roman africain d'aujourd'hui: l'exemple de 'Xala' de Sembène Ousmane* (Ouagadougou: [n. pub.], 1981) focuses on a single text but it does not provide much critical substance, despite its considerable length (172 pages, to be precise). Clara Tsabedze has recently provided an interesting comparative study of the work of Sembene and the Kenyan novelist, Ngugi wa Thiong'o. See her *African Independence from Francophone and Anglophone Voices: a Comparative Study of the Post-Independence Novels of Ngugi and Sembène* (Frankfurt: Peter Lang, 1994). In the English-speaking world, Pat Corcoran's timely edition of *O Pays, mon beau peuple!*, provided a very useful introduction to one of Sembene's early novels. See Sembène Ousmane, *O Pays, mon beau peuple!*, ed. by Pat Corcoran (London: Methuen, 1986). Another study in French by Anthère Nzabatsinda, *Normes linguistiques et écriture africaine chez Ousmane Sembène* (Paris: Gref, 1998) principally addresses linguistic issues in Sembene's work.

and culture'].[8] The fact that Bestman's main authority on African culture and literature appears to be Léopold Sédar Senghor, a figure who stands at the opposite end of the political and literary spectrum from Sembene, says a lot about the weak intellectual framework of his book, and the distorted vision of Sembene's literature that emerges from it.

In recent years, two collections of articles on Sembene's work, dealing with both his literary and cinematic œuvres, have appeared, both of which apply an altogether more rigorous critical approach than the works mentioned above.[9] One of the most significant contributions of these studies is the fact that they attempt a consideration of both of Sembene's chosen media, for Sembene is not merely a writer who dabbles in the cinema from time to time. He is a novelist *and* a film director (his involvement in the cinema has, unlike that of many writers, not been limited to the writing of screenplays) who has managed to combine both a literary and cinematic career for the past thirty years. However, as one would expect with such collections, these recent studies provide a range of different critical approaches that reflect their authors' varied attitudes and interests rather than a unified theoretical approach to the subject. It is therefore the aim of this study to provide such a unified critical approach to a wide selection of Sembene's films and books (one could never aim at a complete survey when dealing with an œuvre comprising ten books and an equal number of short and feature-length films), in order to come to a better understanding of the precise nature of Sembene's artistic and political project.

The first chapter will set out the critical approach used in this study, attempting to thread a path through the complex ideas of contemporary postcolonial theory. The past decade has seen an explosion in the number of theoretical works dealing with the area of what has come to be known as 'postcolonialism'. Indeed, what is currently termed as postcolonial theory could, in many ways, be considered a branch of poststructuralist theory. The sometimes dizzying arguments of a Homi K. Bhabha or a Gayatri Chakravorty Spivak (who both borrow heavily from the work of Jacques Derrida) display, in fairly equal measure, both the poststructuralists' taste for discourse analysis and their distaste for meta-narratives.[10] Although much of the work produced by poststructuralists/postcolonialists has made a highly significant contribution to the development of postcolonial studies, the 'textual' framework within

---

[8] Bestman, *Sembène Ousmane et l'esthétique négro-africain*, p. 317. For a scathing critique of Bestman's critical approach, see Firinne Ní Chréacháin, 'Sembene Ousmane Incorporated? Bestman's *Sembene Ousmane*: a case-study of hegemonic incorporation in African literary criticism', in *Protée noir: essais sur la littérature francophone de l'Afrique noire et des Antilles*, ed. by Peter Hawkins and Annette Lavers (Paris: L'Harmattan, 1992), pp. 126–40.

[9] See *Ousmane Sembène: Dialogues with Critics and Writers*, ed. by Samba Gadjigo et al. (Amherst: University of Massachusetts Press, 1993), and Sada Niang, ed., *Littérature et cinéma en Afrique francophone: Ousmane Sembène et Assia Djebar* (Paris: L'Harmattan, 1996).

[10] See Homi K. Bhabha, ed., *Nation and Narration* (New York and London: Routledge, 1990) and his more recent *The Location of Culture* (New York and London: Routledge, 1994). Spivak's most influential work is her article, 'Can the Subaltern Speak?', in *Marxism and the Interpretation of Culture*, ed. by Cary Nelson and Lawrence Grossberg (London: Macmillan, 1988). See also her *In Other Worlds: Essays in Cultural Politics* (New York: Methuen, 1987).

which they discuss literary texts seems rather limiting when one is dealing with a literature that, so often, deliberately seeks to be explicitly social and political. To ignore the oppressive reality of international capital and the complex politics of contemporary Senegal in a discussion of Sembene's cinema and literature would, in my view, constitute a failure to engage with certain fundamental aspects of his work. In the case of critics such as Christopher L. Miller, poststructuralism becomes a rather more troubling phenomenon, serving to reinforce essentialist notions of identity in the name of an ill-defined 'ethnicity'. By this most circuitous route, we find ourselves back in the realm of Negritude and its essentialist arguments on race and identity.[11] In the context of this debate on African identity, Sembene's epic novel, *God's Bits of Wood*, with its Marxist vision of a modern, industrialised and assertive Africa, provides a remarkable example of his radical representation of African society. Although this study will seek to 'de-centre' criticism of Sembene's work by shifting the focus from the longer, epic works to shorter, more ironic texts, the analysis of *God's Bits of Wood* in the first chapter will underline the novel's importance both to Sembene's œuvre and to African literature as a whole.

The vast majority of the criticism on Sembene's work has focused on social and political themes. Most of these 'political' critics of Sembene's work have contented themselves with cataloguing the various themes evoked in the course of his novels and films, explaining away their relative lack of interest in aesthetic matters by casting Sembene as a straightforward social realist who is only really worth reading (or watching) because of the social issues that he raises. For example, when critics refer to Sembene's first novel, *Black Docker*, it is almost invariably to mention its socio-political interest as a depiction of the African working-class community in Marseilles. However, the novel is far more concerned with the position of the African artist in relation to his own community. In fact, the novel's obvious flaws stem precisely from Sembene's difficulty in handling the narrative complexity that this *mise en abyme* introduces. The critics' insistence on the documentary value of a novel so clearly concerned with literature and representation serves to underline their relative lack of interest in the 'literariness' of Sembene's work.[12]

One major reason behind this critical approach is that most analysis of Sembene's work is produced by French-language critics of African literature who have, at least until recently, retained a fairly traditional approach to literary criticism, and thus lack the theoretical framework provided by the

---

[11] Christopher L. Miller, *Theories of Africans: Francophone Literature and Anthropology in Africa* (Chicago and London: University of Chicago Press, 1990).

[12] The caricatured portrayal of Sembene as a novelist interested in politics above all artistic considerations is perhaps best exemplified in Martin Bestman's remarks on *Black Docker*. '*Sans se soucier de la forme, l'auteur a voulu, avant tout, apporter un témoignage. Ainsi ce qui sauve* Le Docker noir, *c'est sa valeur documentaire, surtout en ce qui concerne l'acuité de la peinture du monde ouvrier.*' ['Above all, the author wanted to bear witness, without any consideration of artistic form. Therefore, *Black Docker* is redeemed by its documentary value, especially its sharp portrayal of working-class society.'] Martin Bestman, *Sembène Ousmane et l'esthétique du roman négro-africain*, p. 15. The novel has many faults but Sembene's interest in questions of form is unmistakable. This aspect of the novel has been addressed by Andy Stafford in his article, 'Work, Racism and Writing in 1950s France', *ASCALF Bulletin*, 12 (Spring/Summer 1996), pp. 3–13.

6

mainly English-language poststructuralists (a situation which is not repeated in areas other than postcolonial literature, it must be noted).[13] Therefore, one often finds oneself confronted in such works with a dose of aesthetic musing, accompanied by the almost obligatory detour into that favourite theme of critics of African literature, namely the 'tradition versus modernity' debate.

Despite misgivings about certain aspects of the poststructuralist approach, this study has also eschewed a slavishly political critique, choosing instead to adopt a cultural materialist perspective, which seeks to examine the interplay between literary and cinematic 'texts' and ideology. As will be argued throughout this study, Sembene's work is far more complex than the tag of social realist allows (and his work goes well beyond such hackneyed oppositions as that between tradition and modernity). The need for a re-assessment of his work is plainly seen when one notes that, in a recent collection of articles on Sembene's work, which contains a number of interesting critiques, Sembene is still viewed primarily as a politically committed writer who always places didacticism above form: '*Sembène ne brouille pas les limites des genres. C'est un agitateur des consciences, plus enclin à privilégier les fonctions didactiques de l'histoire que les modalités de son écriture, plus enclin à déterrer les épisodes cachés de l'histoire coloniale.*' ['Sembene does not blur the boundaries between genres. He is interested in stirring people's consciences, and he is more concerned with the didactic role of history (for example, unearthing hidden episodes of the colonial era) than with the form of his writing']￼[14] Sembene himself has argued that this notion of 'engagement' (or commitment) as applied to the artist is something of a misnomer. In his view, life itself is a form of commitment: '*chaque fois que je sors dans la rue, je dis que les gens sont engagés. La lutte quotidienne pour améliorer notre société est un engagement. Pourquoi vouloir que l'artiste soit seulement engagé?*' ['each time I walk out into the street, I am aware that people are committed. The daily struggle to improve our society is a commitment. Why do we only speak of the artist in terms of his/her commitment?']￼[15] This argument serves a double purpose: firstly, it attempts to do away with the category of the 'committed writer' by describing 'engagement' as a universal condition; secondly, and consequently,

[13] There are many examples of this generalist approach to African literature. A purely random sample of such works would include: Jacques Nantot, *Panorama de la littérature noire d'expression française* (Paris: Fayard, 1972); Robert Pageard, *Littérature négro-africaine* (Paris: Le Livre africain, 1972); Jingiri J. Achiriga, *La Révolte des romanciers noirs de langue française* (Ottawa: Editions Naaman, 1973); Gervais Havyarimana, *Problématique de renaissance et évolution du roman africain de langue française, 1920–1980* (Louvain-la-Neuve: Publications Universitaires de Louvain, 1992). Even the highly respected Senegalese critic, Mohamadou Kane, remained trapped within the limiting opposition between tradition and modernity. See his *Roman africain et tradition* (Dakar: Nouvelles Editions Africaines, 1982). For a critique of the work of African literary theorists in particular, see Noureini Tidjani-Serpos, *Aspects de la critique africaine*, 1 (Lomé: Editions Haho; Paris: Editions Silex, 1987), pp. 7–13. A useful overview of many of the debates within African criticism can be found in *Le Critique africain et son peuple comme producteur de civilisation* (Paris: Présence Africaine, 1977). Although it was published over twenty years ago, the issues raised in the book remain highly contentious.

[14] Sada Niang, 'Introduction', in Niang, *Littérature et cinéma en Afrique francophone*, p. 10.

[15] Mohamadou Kane et al., 'Comme un aveugle qui retrouve la vue', *Le Soleil* [Dakar], 10 July 1981, p. 4.

he seeks to distance himself from the negative image of the 'committed writer' who writes worthy, committed but fundamentally dull works. For Sembene, the artist is a craftsman, and an essential part of his craft is ensuring that his story is well made, otherwise he will simply not attract a public:

> *Je dis que toutes les œuvres quand elles sont trop engagées |...| ne sont que des marques, des cicatrices sur le corps de l'histoire, le tissu de l'histoire. Mais il y a des œuvres qui dureront éternellement. Est-ce que ces œuvres ont été conçues à partir d'un engagement, d'un défoulement, d'une propagande ou seulement d'une création littéraire? Je n'essaie vraiment pas de me situer au niveau de l'engagement et des missions. J'ai un travail très important pour ma société, pour ma communauté. Mais il ne s'agit pas seulement d'écrire pour le Sénégal, il s'agit d'écrire au-delà du Sénégalais, pour toute la planète |...|. Le degré de la littérature ou son expansion pose pour moi beaucoup plus de problèmes que la littérature de pancarte.*[16]

I believe that works of art that are too committed [...] leave only marks or scars on the surface of history, on the fabric of history. But there are works which will last forever. Were these works conceived out of a sense of commitment or out of a need for self-expression? Were they conceived as propaganda or solely as literary creations? I really don't consider myself in terms of commitment or missions. I have a very important job to do for my society, for my community. But it doesn't mean I write solely for the Senegalese. I write for a public beyond my country, for the entire planet [...]. The state of literature and the struggle to bring it to a wider audience are more pressing concerns for me than the development of a 'literature of political slogans'.

The question of form will therefore be addressed as a key element in Sembene's challenge to the dominant discourses of his society.

In order to illustrate the recurring structures within Sembene's work, the chapters in this study have been organised in pairs. Chapters Two and Three will act as an introduction to the problematisation of form and content within Sembene's books and films respectively. In Chapter Two, the strategy of structuring his work around the notions of silence/discourse and absence/presence will be examined in detail in relation to the collection of short stories, *Tribal Scars*, and the novella, *White Genesis*, two works that have received relatively little critical attention. These works, with their self-conscious problematisation of the notions of representation and discourse, will be presented as paradigms of Sembene's literary approach since independence. As was mentioned above, this constitutes a re-focusing on Sembene's work, deliberately neglecting longer, more epic texts such as *L'Harmattan* and *God's Bits of Wood*, which have always been the main object of critics' attention.

In keeping with Sembene's practice of using alternative media, Chapter Three will shift the focus to Sembene's cinema, analysing his film, *Le Mandat*, which was adapted from Sembene's novella of the same title (another example of using alternatives). The film is of particular interest as it was the subject of a polemical critical debate concerning Sembene's portrayal of life in the African city. It therefore provides a useful vehicle for exploring the notions of representation and resistance as they are worked out in his films. The manner in which Sembene explores the nature of his society's rituals in the film will be

[16] Ibid.

8

argued to be a practice repeated in all of his cinematic work. Later chapters will seek to continue the process of looking at Sembene's use of alternative media by examining a selection of both his films and novels in relation to a number of themes.

Chapters Four and Five deal respectively with the investigation of male and female roles within Senegalese society. Chapter Four is devoted to Sembene's most commercially successful film, *Xala* (once again adapted from one of his own books), which is also one of his most critically acclaimed. A bruising satire of the African bourgeoisie, the film uses the metaphor of male sexual impotence to denounce the role of this class in the neo-colonial exploitation of Senegal. Following on from this, Chapter Five investigates the manner in which Sembene challenges the standard representations of both male and female roles within African literature and society, moving away from the idealistic images of Negritude to a far more complex vision of gender in African society. Finally, Chapters Six and Seven address the questions of colonialism and neo-colonialism respectively, seeking alternative histories to those proposed by the former empire and those proposed by the dominant discourses of the neo-colonial order. These themes are not exhaustive, but rather symptomatic, and are proposed in order to set up a framework in which further research may be carried out.

Above all, it is hoped that this study will serve to problematise the relationship between art and politics, both in relation to Sembene's work, and also to African literature and cinema in general. By steering a path between the discourse analysis of the poststructuralists and the simple enunciation of social themes which so often passes for criticism in relation to Sembene's art,[17] it will be attempted to combine elements of discourse theory with a political consideration of his work. Sembene's radical representations of African history form an alternative, oppositional discourse and, in the context of the 'weak' states of modern Africa, they play a highly political role in questioning the legitimacy of the dominant discourses in his society.

---

[17] Sembene is wary of the explicitly political nature of much of the criticism of his work. In a personal interview with Sembene, he claimed that *'les critiques africains veulent faire la révolution par procuration'* ['African critics want a revolution by proxy'], a charge he also levels against 'radical' African intellectuals, in general. Interview carried out at Filmi Doomireew, Dakar, 30 November 1995 (see Appendix).

1

Imagining Africa

The nature of the colonial encounter in Africa, which saw the military and technological superiority of European culture allow the dominant European powers of the nineteenth century to impose their will upon African states and kingdoms, unable to match such prowess in these fields, understandably led to a polarisation in representations of the coloniser and the colonised. To borrow a phrase from the Marxist critic, Aijaz Ahmad, the African and the European became each other's 'civilisational Other',[1] with the cultural differences between imperial and colonised cultures taking centre stage in debate about the colonial world. This emphasis on the cultural conflict between coloniser and colonised has often resulted in an essentialisation of identity, and has tended to deflect attention from conflicts *within* colonised cultures themselves (or indeed within colonising cultures).[2] Identity politics do have a concrete historical value but

---

[1] Aijaz Ahmad, *In Theory: Classes, Nations, Literatures* (London and New York: Verso, 1992), p. 96. Ahmad uses this phrase in relation to the well-known essay, 'Third-World Literature in the Era of Multinational Capitalism' by the American Marxist critic, Fredric Jameson, whom Ahmad accuses of casting the Third World as the 'civilisational Other' of the First World. Ahmad argues that the prevalence of the coloniser versus colonised mindset has so dominated the postcolonial debate that even a Marxist such as Jameson describes 'Third World Literature' (a term which Ahmad refuses to accept) as being primarily concerned with the creation of 'national allegories'. Jameson's definition of these 'national allegories' as negotiations of the relationship between the individual and the collective is rightly dismissed by Ahmad as being ridiculously general, and just as easily applicable to a vast array of writers in the so-called 'First World'. The fact that Jameson uses Sembene's explicitly *social* satire of the African bourgeoisie, *Xala*, as one of his main examples of the 'national allegory' merely serves to reinforce Ahmad's criticism. Fredric Jameson, 'Third-World Literature in the Era of Multinational Capitalism', *Social Text*, 15 (1986), pp. 65–88.

[2] In his novel, *God's Bits of Wood*, Sembene examines the conflict between coloniser and colonised through the prism of the 1947–8 West African railway strike, casting the struggle between the two groups primarily in social rather than cultural or racial terms. This novel will be examined in greater depth below.

10

the systematic attribution of an inherent set of values to an entire race is in itself a distinctly ahistorical act. One does not need to share Ahmad's unstinting faith in Marxism to agree with his statement concerning the theoretical options made available to the critic by the Marxist approach: 'Like all political positions which are ethically viable, the Marxist one also closes off certain possibilities and opens up certain others. In choosing such a position, one chooses the closures, certainly, but one also chooses the potentialities.'[3] Accordingly, this study will adopt a materialist approach, eschewing essentialist notions of race and identity (under the various names of 'ethnicity', 'tradition' or 'endogenous knowledge')[4] and attempting to open up the possibility of examining the conflicts within colonised and neo-colonial societies (in the case of this study, it is the particular case of Senegal which will be of principal interest).

Marxist theory has often been caricatured as dogmatic and simplistic, accusations that no doubt hold water in a large number of cases. However, it should not be forgotten that there exists a large body of Marxist-inspired work that rejects the schematic economic determinism of what has become known as 'vulgar Marxism'. Antonio Gramsci and Georg Lukács, two of the greatest Marxist theorists of the twentieth century, were deeply interested in the means by which the bourgeoisie sought to establish its hegemony over the rest of society, teasing out the complex links between the economic and the social/cultural.[5] Sembene himself has attempted to combine Marxism with a very deliberate attention to such issues as culture and gender. Similarly, this study will combine a materialist analysis of Senegalese society (politics, the economy, gender, culture, ethnicity) with an examination of the modes of literary and cinematic representation of that society. It is hoped that the discussion of Sembene's novels and films will thus be perceived in relation to the wider social discourses of which the literary and the cinematic form a relatively minor part.[6]

The question of 'African identity' has been inscribed in African literature in French since its very beginnings. The earliest examples of this literature saw writers such as Bakary Diallo and Ahmadou Mapaté Diagne focus on the problem of African assimilation into European culture in works that were largely deferential in tone towards their colonial masters.[7] In a later development within

---

[3] Ahmad, *In Theory*, p. 219.

[4] I have chosen to place what I consider to be some of the more problematic terms of the postcolonial debate within inverted commas when they are referred to for the first time. Subsequent references to these concepts will only be placed in inverted commas or italicised if it is necessary to problematise them within a given argument.

[5] Antonio Gramsci, *Selections from the Prison Notebooks*, ed. and trans. by Quintin Hoare and Geoffrey Nowell Smith (1971; London: Lawrence & Wishart, 1995). Georg Lukács, *History and Class Consciousness*, trans. by Rodney Livingstone (London: Merlin Press, 1971).

[6] I have in mind here Aijaz Ahmad's criticism of Edward Said for his use of Foucault's theories to discuss the discourse of Orientalism almost uniquely in terms of high European literature. See Ahmad, *In Theory*, pp. 159–219. The book criticised by Ahmad is of course Said's *Orientalism* (1978; London: Penguin, 1995).

[7] See Bakary Diallo, *Force-Bonté* (1926; Paris: ACCT/Nouvelles Editions Africaines, 1985) and Ahmadou Mapaté Diagne, *Les Trois volontés de Malic* (1920; Paris: Editions Kraus, 1973). See also the work of Ousmane Socé: *Karim* (1935; Paris: Nouvelles Editions Latines, 1948) and *Les Mirages de Paris* (1937; Paris: Nouvelles Editions Latines, 1964).

Francophone Africa, the Negritude school of writers took on board the standard colonial depiction of the African as being a more primitive and sensual creature than the European, and used it to assert a distinctive African identity in the face of the coloniser's domination of African society. Negritude never constituted a coherent movement as such. Indeed, the writer most often credited with coining the term, Aimé Césaire, in his *Return to my Native Land*, saw it mainly as a means of expressing solidarity between oppressed black communities around the world, not as a means for defining some essential black nature.[8]

However, Negritude is associated primarily with the work of one man, the Senegalese poet, Léopold Sédar Senghor, who developed a complex and rather convoluted racial theory which was inspired principally by the work of the German anthropologist, Léo Frobenius, who was given to vague, essentialist declarations about the nature of 'African civilisation':

> *Quiconque s'approche |du style africain| au point de le comprendre tout à fait reconnaît bientôt qu'il domine toute l'Afrique, comme l'expression même de son être. Il se manifeste dans les gestes de tous les peuples nègres autant que dans leur plastique, il parle dans leurs danses comme dans leurs modes d'existence, leurs formes d'État et leurs destins de peuple. Il vit dans leurs fables, leurs contes de fée, leurs légendes, leurs mythes.[9]*

Anyone who masters the study of [African style] will be aware that this style dominates all of Africa. It is the expression of its very being. It reveals itself in the gestures of all negro peoples as well as in their arts. It is expressed in their dances as well as in their lifestyles, their political systems and in their very destiny as a people. It lives in their fables, their fairy tales, their legends, their myths.

Senghor's racial theories spoke of black and white 'civilisations' as being complementary but essentially opposite in nature. His notion of an emerging black world bringing its sensuality to leaven the dry, rational dough of white 'civilisation' resulted in his formulation of a *civilisation de l'universel*, a new world order in which each race would play its own particular and unchanging part. This essentialism of both black and white natures was given its most succinct formulation in Senghor's 1939 essay, 'Ce que l'homme noir apporte' ['What the black man brings'], where he declares that 'l'émotion est nègre, comme la raison hellène' ['emotion is black, just as reason is hellenic'].[10] The irony of a

---

[8] See Césaire's denial of the claim that he is a 'a prophet of the return to the ante-European past' in his *Discourse on Colonialism*, trans. by Joan Pinkham (1955; New York: Monthly Review Press, 1972), pp. 22, 29. For an account of the differences between Senghor's and Césaire's conceptions of Negritude, see Maryse Condé, 'Négritude Césairienne, Négritude Senghorienne', *Revue de littérature comparée*, 48, 3–4 (July–December 1974), pp. 409–19. The critic, Benita Parry, has sought to stress the essentialist nature of many of Césaire's pronouncements on black identity. Although I would agree with many aspects of her problematisation of Césaire's thinking, I feel that this is carried out at the expense of Césaire's liberation theory. Equally, Parry plays down the committed revolutionary stance of Frantz Fanon in stressing certain of his early pronouncements on black identity. See Benita Parry, 'Resistance Theory/Theorising Resistance', in *Colonial Discourse/Postcolonial Theory*, ed. by Francis Barker, Peter Hulme and Margaret Iversen (Manchester and New York: Manchester University Press, 1994), pp. 172–96.

[9] Léo Frobenius, *Histoire de la civilisation africaine*, trans. by Dr H. Back and D. Ermont (1936; Monaco: Le Rocher, 1987), p. 20.

[10] See Léopold Sédar Senghor, *Liberté 1: Négritude et Humanisme* (Paris: Seuil, 1964), pp. 22–38.

French-educated African, the first to be awarded the prestigious *agrégation*,[11] praising the essentially primitive and sensual nature of all Africans, and indeed, of all black people, is obvious and illustrates the arbitrary nature of the construction of any racial identity. Indeed, the association of race and colour has been increasingly challenged by contemporary science.

The whole project of Negritude came under attack by a younger generation of Africans in the 1970s. Young African philosophers, such as Paulin J. Hountondji, Stanislas Adotévi and Marcien Towa, were particularly keen to criticise the notion of a specifically African ontology and philosophy.[12] In the work of the Senegalese historian Mamadou Diouf, Negritude is presented as having adopted a museum curator's approach to African 'tradition', treating it as an object of historical curiosity rather than as a living and vibrant mode of being:

> *Le retour aux sources de la négritude est, en effet, un exercice intellectuel; traduire cet exercice sur la scène politique pour légitimer une démarche se résoud, dans la pensée de Senghor, par l'acceptation de la parole du griot et du récit des traditions orales comme n'exprimant qu'un ensemble de valeurs. Expression logée dans le rythme, car 'les mots sont chants, incantation, parce que rendus à leurs premières vertus premières de rythme et fabulation, parce qu'ils sont images rythmées'. Rythme consubstantiel à l'image qu'il accomplit, en 'unissant dans un tout le signe et le sens, la chair et l'esprit'. Il n'y a ni anecdotes ni 'tranches de vie'. Seules les images ont leur valeur exemplaire. Le rôle historique du poète allait de soi dans ce contexte.[13]*

Negritude's return to origins is in fact an intellectual exercise. For Senghor, this exercise has a concrete political goal, namely to legitimise Negritude. This is achieved by presenting the traditional oral tale and the words of the *griot* solely as the expression of a set of values. The expression of these values is rooted in rhythm because 'words are chants, an incantation, words used primarily for their values of rhythm and fabulation, for words are rhythmic images'. Rhythm and image are one for they 'unite the sign and the meaning, the flesh and the spirit'. There are neither anecdotes nor 'slices of life'. All that remains is the exemplary value of the image. In this context, the historic role of the poet is self-evident.

Diouf effectively argues that Negritude, in its Senghorian form, serves purely to provide a reservoir of 'traditional' images for the poet-president with which to cobble together a composite image of a set of African values. In the

---

[11] For a biography of Senghor, see Armand Guibert, *Léopold Sédar Senghor* (Paris: Seuil, 1969).

[12] See Marcien Towa, *Essai sur la problématique philosophique dans l'Afrique actuelle* (Yaoundé: CLE, 1971) and especially his *Léopold Sédar Senghor: Négritude ou servitude?* (Yaoundé: CLE, 1971); Stanislas Adotévi, *Négritude et négrologues* (Paris: Plon, 1972); Paulin J. Hountondji, *Sur la 'philosophie africaine': critique de l'ethnophilosophie* (Paris: Maspéro, 1977). The main focus of their attacks were the works of the 'ethnophilosophes' which grew out of the premises of Negritude. We may consider R. P. Tempels' infamous study *La Philosophie bantu* as one of the founding texts of 'ethnophilosophie'. Other influential works in this school would include Alexis Kagamé, *La Philosophie bantu comparée* (Paris: Présence Africaine, 1976); Youssouph Mbargane Guissé, *Philosophie, culture et devenir social en Afrique noire* (Dakar: Nouvelles Editions Africaines, 1979); and Alassane Ndaw, *La Pensée africaine – recherches sur les fondements de la pensée négro-africaine* (Dakar: Nouvelles Editions Africaines, 1983). Kwame Anthony Appiah gives a remarkable analysis of the African philosophical debate about identity and tradition in his study, *In My Father's House: Africa in the Philosophy of Culture* (London: Methuen, 1992), pp. 135–71.

[13] Mamadou Diouf, 'Représentations historiques et légitimités politiques au Sénégal (1960–1987)', *Revue de la Bibliothèque Nationale* [Paris], 34 (1989), p. 16. The passages quoted by Diouf are from Senghor's *Liberté 1*, pp. 174, 211.

process, the very real African 'values' and 'traditions' that were still held dear by the majority of Africans are neglected and marginalised. For Diouf, Senghor's Negritude was merely the literary side of a bourgeois nationalist political movement that sought to establish a narrative of the Senegalese nation (a process also adopted by African leaders in other countries) stretching back into the mists of time while at the same time refusing any value to traditional African values in the modern political process:

> *La vision intellectuelle de la classe dirigeante sénégalaise est claire. Elle rejoint le discours nègre de Senghor, discours qui dépasse les frontières du Sénégal. Elle circonscrit un espace d'exercice du pouvoir, un pouvoir moderne qui n'a nul besoin des traditions historiques anciennes. La démarche est celle de la création d'une nouvelle logique sociale d'intégration nationale.*[14]

> The intellectual vision of the Senegalese ruling class is evident. This vision is closely aligned with the black discourse of Senghor, a discourse which goes beyond the frontiers of Senegal. This intellectual vision delimits a space in which power is exercised. This power is entirely modern and has no need for ancient historical traditions. This process creates a new social logic designed to bring about national integration.

This link between the search for an 'authentic' African identity and the politics of bourgeois cultural nationalism will be examined in greater detail below (including a more detailed discussion of Senghor and Negritude in Chapter Seven).

Negritude was an ideology that was confined to Francophone Africa. In a polemical battle that ironically paralleled centuries of similar battles between their old colonial masters, Anglophone African writers accused the Negritude school of a typically French shabby logic in glorifying an image of the African that had been created by the coloniser. Wole Soyinka, one of the most virulent critics of Negritude, was particularly incensed at the way in which the essentialisation of racial identity portrayed the African as irrational:

> [Negritude] accepted one of the worst blasphemies of racism, that the black man has nothing between his ears, and proceeded to subvert the power of poetry to glorify this fabricated justification of European cultural domination. Suddenly we were exhorted to give a cheer for those who never invented anything, a cheer for those who never explored the oceans. The truth, however, is that there isn't any such creature.[15]

Soyinka views Negritude as the attempt by an educated African elite, caught between the world of the coloniser to which they would never fully belong, and the world of the African masses to which they no longer fully belonged,

[14] Diouf, 'Représentations historiques', p. 16.
[15] Wole Soyinka, *Myth, Literature and the African World* (1976; Cambridge: Cambridge University Press, Canto edition, 1990), p. 129. Soyinka would appear to be here criticising the section in Césaire's *Return to my Native Land*, which runs:

> Heia for those who have never invented anything
> those who never explored anything
> those who never tamed anything

Aimé Césaire, *Return to my Native Land*, trans. by John Berger and Anna Bostock (1939; London: Penguin, 1969), p. 75.

to define an African identity.[16] However, Soyinka's argument is not that any attempt to define racial identity is misguided but that Negritude misses out on that which *is* authentically African. Even in his most famous attack on Negritude where he quips that 'the tiger does not speak of his tigritude',[17] Soyinka is implying that there is an authentic 'Africanness', not the one to be found in the poetry of an African elite but in the reality of the lives of the African masses. While Soyinka accepts that the colonial period has produced a new set of realities, he remains convinced that African society has a distinct and unchanging set of values, and that after independence there 'must come a reinstatement of the values authentic to that society, modified only by the demands of a contemporary world'.[18]

Soyinka's 'authentic native' and Senghor's 'sensual African' are simply two sides of the same essentialist coin. In his introduction to *Myth, Literature and the African World*, Soyinka's voice almost seems to merge with that of Senghor: 'Man exists [...] in a comprehensive world of myth, history and mores; in such a total context the *African world*, like any other "world" is *unique*. It possesses, however, in common with other cultures, the virtues of *complementarity*.'[19] The 'African world' and the 'European world' are separate and although they may have something to learn from each other, certain 'authentic' values will always be in place.

Both Negritude and nativism form an integral part of an African cultural nationalism that developed into a powerful force in the nationalist drive for independence, which was taking place throughout Africa in the post World War Two period. The anti-colonialist nationalist movements relied on a Manichean structure that demonised the coloniser and which exalted an idealised version of the colonised people's pre-colonial past, a past that the nationalist movement claims to be able to restore to the 'nation'. As Edward Said has pointed out, 'all nationalist cultures depend heavily on the concept of national identity, and nationalist politics is a politics of identity: Egypt for the Egyptians, Africa for the Africans, India for the Indians, and so on.'[20] In the face of domination by Europe and its belittling of African culture and history, the African nationalist movements began to glorify the past and to see in it a unifying structure around which to organise anti-colonial resistance. However, the dogma of European superiority was simply replaced by the equally limiting dogma of an authentic African identity. The most impassioned theorist of decolonisation, Frantz Fanon, described this move in the following terms:

---

[16] Soyinka, *Myth, Literature and the African World*, p. 135.

[17] For Senghor's response to Soyinka's criticism see the essay, 'Qu'est-ce que la négritude?', in Senghor's *Liberté 3: Négritude et civilisation de l'universel* (Paris: Seuil, 1977), pp. 100–1.

[18] Soyinka, *Myth, Literature and the African World*, p. x.

[19] Soyinka, *Myth, Literature and the African World*, p. xii (my italics). It is ironic to note that one of Soyinka's most vociferous detractors, the Nigerian critic, Chinweizu, attacks him for being a Eurocentric writer who is alienated from the authentic values of Africa. One of Chinweizu's African literary icons is, equally ironically, Léopold Sédar Senghor. See Chinweizu, Onwuchekwa Jemie and Ihechukwu Madubuike, *Toward the Decolonization of African Literature* (London: Kegan Paul, 1980).

[20] Edward Said, *Culture and Imperialism* (1993; London: Vintage, 1994), p. 322.

'The unconditional affirmation of African culture has succeeded the unconditional affirmation of European culture.'[21] Replacing the systematic valida-
tion of all things European with a blind support for all things African may
have been historically necessary during the fight for independence but this
does not legitimise it as a coherent philosophical system. As one African
philosopher has recently put it: '*l'ethnocentrisme "occidental" n'a pas plus de prix que
l'ethnocentrisme "africain" et vice versa. On ne saurait critiquer l'un comme fait historique
pour légitimer l'autre comme idéal historique.*' ['"Western" ethnocentrism is no more
valid than "African" ethnocentrism and vice versa. You cannot criticise the
former as an historical fact while legitimising the latter as an historical ideal.'][22]

Much of the contemporary debate concerning postcolonial literature deals
with the question of nationalism. Since the Second World War and its horrific
demonstration of the destructive forces that nationalist ideologies could
unleash upon the world, nationalism has become the subject of many intensely
critical sociological and political studies, which have sought to show that all
nations are artificial constructs, not mythical entities waiting to be reborn.[23]
Both in Europe and in Africa the nationalist writer looked towards the peasant
as the ideal representative of the nation, as he was seen to be in touch with the
land, and thus with the mythical past of the nation. The drive at the heart of
nationalist ideology to manufacture a continuity between a glorious past and
its renewal in the near future led to what Eric Hobsbawm and Terence Ranger
have described in a highly influential study as 'the invention of tradition'.[24]
Hobsbawm dismisses nationalist claims of authenticity and unbroken tradition:

> We should not be misled by a curious, but understandable, paradox: modern
> nations and all their impedimenta generally claim to be the opposite of the novel,
> namely remoted [sic] in the remotest antiquity, and the opposite of constructed,
> namely human communities so 'natural' as to require no definition other than self-
> assertion. Whatever the historic or other continuities embedded in the modern con-
> cept of 'France' and the 'French' – and which nobody would seek to deny – these
> very concepts themselves must include a constructed or 'invented' component.[25]

A prime example of this nationalist desire to 'invent tradition' in the context of Senegal would be the attempt by some recent Senegalese historians to
define Islam as the authentic religion of the nation. The historian, Amar Samb,
is not alone in claiming that as the first known ruler of what is now Senegal
was a Muslim, it follows that Islam is an integral part of 'Senegalese identity':

> *L'histoire du Sénégal commence sans doute avec l'existence du royaume Tekrûri dont le premier
> souverain est Waar Diaabé mort en 1040. C'est à partir de là que les événements prennent leurs*

[21] Frantz Fanon, *The Wretched of the Earth*, trans. by Constance Farrington (1961; London: Penguin, 1969), p. 171.

[22] Charles Z. Bowao, '"Désethnologiser": réouverture du débat Hountondji-Diagne', *Bulletin du CODESRIA*, 1 (1995), p. 16.

[23] See Eric Hobsbawm, *Nations and Nationalism since 1780* (1990; Cambridge: Cambridge University Press, Revised Canto edition, 1995).

[24] Eric Hobsbawm and Terence Ranger, eds, *The Invention of Tradition* (1983; Cambridge: Cambridge University Press, Canto edition, 1992). See also Benedict Anderson, *Imagined Communities: Reflections on the Origin and Spread of Nationalism* (London: Verso, 1983).

[25] Eric Hobsbawm, 'Inventing Traditions', in Hobsbawm and Ranger, *The Invention of Tradition*, p.14.

cours, que l'homme sénégalais se définit sans jamais se séparer de l'Islam dont on peut dire qu'il est aussi une religion traditionnelle pour ce pays.[26]

Without doubt, the history of Senegal begins with the birth of the realm of Tekrúri, whose first ruler, Waar Diaabé, died in 1040. It is from this point onwards that events take their course, that the Senegalese define their own identity. Islam has always been an integral part of this identity and one could argue that it is, in fact, a traditional religion within our country.

Islam and the nation were born together so who would dare to separate them? Once Islam has been shown (however tenuously) to be *the* religion of the nation, the intervention of Islamic leaders on the political scene is given a *de facto* legitimacy. The essential interests of Islam are the essential interests of the whole nation: '*l'essentiel est que cette intrusion dans la chose politique se fasse dans l'intérêt supérieur de toute la nation.*' ['the main point is that this intrusion into the political realm is carried out in the interest of the entire nation'].[27]

Although one can recognise in such accounts of Senegalese history an attempt to counter standard Western biases against Islam,[28] the fact remains that the historical processes by which Islam came to be the dominant religion in Senegal (and most of West Africa) are simply glossed over, as Senegal and Islam are presented almost as mythical lovers whose destiny was to have their millennium-old courtship sanctified in marriage on the advent of Senegalese independence. Samb's declaration that Islam is *the* religion of the nation because '*ce sont les ancêtres et l'histoire qui l'ont voulu*' ['it is our forefathers and history that willed it so'],[29] effectively denies history in favour of the manifest destiny of the nation. The first 'king of Senegal' may indeed have been a Muslim but there is no proof that his people were. In fact, Islam's hold on the 'Senegalese' was, by and large, limited to elements of the ruling classes until the middle of the nineteenth century. Mamadou Diouf has shown that the rewriting of Senegalese history which places Islam at the centre of colonial resistance is, in fact, a very recent development that reflects the ever-growing importance of Islam within contemporary Senegalese society:

Réintroduire les marabouts dans la nouvelle histoire anti-coloniale nécessitait l'élaboration de nouvelles représentations. Que faire des héros traditionnels, plus particulièrement Lat Joor, héros national, et Alboury N'diaye? On annexe leur combat à la logique islamique en faisant fi des conflits et des oppositions, ainsi que de la collaboration des communautés musulmanes avec le pouvoir colonial. Pour éviter d'avoir affaire à leur vie, on utilise leur mort pour les convertir.[30]

Including marabouts in the new anti-colonial history required the development of new representations. What should be done with traditional heroes, and in particular, Lat Joor [or Dior], the national hero, and Alboury N'diaye? Their struggles are simply annexed by this Islamic discourse despite all the contradictions, and despite the collaboration of Muslim communities with the colonial powers. By avoiding the

---

[26] Amar Samb, 'L'Islam et l'histoire du Sénégal', *Bulletin de l'IFAN*, série B, 33, 3 (1971), pp. 463–4. See also Assane Sylla, *La Philosophie morale des Wolof* (Dakar: Sankoré, 1978), pp. 43–62.

[27] Samb, 'L'Islam et l'histoire du Sénégal', p. 491.

[28] For the most comprehensive overview of European representations of Islam, see Edward Said's *Orientalism*.

[29] Samb, 'L'Islam et l'histoire du Sénégal', p. 502.

[30] Diouf, 'Représentations historiques', p. 18.

reality of their lives, their deaths are used to convert them to the cause of Islam.

My purpose in criticising Samb's version of history is not to contradict the incontrovertible fact that Islam is now the dominant religion in Senegal (over 90 per cent of the population in the 1988 census),[31] nor do I wish to deny the positive role that Islam has played in Senegalese society. However, in essentialising Islam's role in his society, Samb transforms Islam's present status in Senegal from an historical fact into an historical ideal.[32] In this view, Islam is no longer simply the dominant religion at this particular historical moment but rather we are led to believe that its privileged position has been and always will be guaranteed (a version of history that Sembene strongly contests in his film, *Ceddo,* which will be discussed in Chapter Six).

Many postcolonial critics have lamented the tendency for young Third-World nationalisms to follow in the footsteps of their older European ex-masters in creating a narrow nationalist discourse, and, in the case of such despotic leaders as Bokassa in the Central African Republic and Idi Amin of Uganda (and unfortunately too many other cases to mention), recreating some of the horrific violence caused by the excesses of European nationalisms. Influential postcolonial theorists, such as Homi K. Bhabha and Christopher L. Miller, have shown themselves deeply hostile towards nationalism in all its forms. As the British critic Neil Lazarus has written, 'nationalist discourse – both metropolitan (i.e. colonial) and anticolonial – emerges variously in the writing of these and other theorists as coercive, totalising, elitist, authoritarian, essentialist and reactionary.'[33]

I would agree with Lazarus in arguing that to reject wholesale the process of decolonisation, which this attack on anti-colonial nationalism effectively does, seems to be a case of throwing out the liberationist baby along with the nationalist bath water, for the broad coalitions that comprised the nationalist movements of the colonised world did in fact manage to free their peoples from direct colonial rule. Control of the newly liberated states may soon have passed into the hands of an African elite willing to keep the old colonial machine turning to the profit of the Western powers, but this merely points out the failings of the anti-colonial movement: it should not be allowed to provide a condemnation of the liberationist aims of many of those involved in the fight for independence. The critic, Tim Brennan, has summed up the dilemma facing those involved in anti-colonial nationalist movements in the following terms:

> It is not that people, or the artists who speak for them, can imagine no other affiliations [i.e. other than the nation-state], but that the solutions to dependency are

---

[31] For an analysis of some of the 1988 census results, see Bachir Diagne's 'L'Avenir de la tradition', in *Sénégal: Trajectoires d'un État,* ed. by Momar Coumba Diop (Dakar: CODESRIA, 1992), pp. 281–3. See also Makhtar Diouf, *Sénégal, les ethnies et la nation* (Paris: L'Harmattan, 1994).

[32] Roland Barthes's analysis of the mythologising aspect of European colonialist discourse could here be equally applied to much of the discourse surrounding Islam in Senegal. See 'Grammaire africaine', in *Mythologies* (Paris: Seuil, 1957), pp. 137–44.

[33] Neil Lazarus, 'Disavowing Decolonization: Fanon, Nationalism and the Problematic of Representation in Current Theories of Colonial Discourse', *Research in African Literatures,* 24, 4 (1993), pp. 70–1.

only collective, and the territorial legacy of the last two hundred years provides the collectivity no other basis upon which to fight dependency.[34]

The African states came into existence at a time when the nation-state, under the sanction of the United Nations, had become the Western-inspired norm, and they inherited European-defined states over which they had to exert their control. As Leonardo A. Villalón has pointed out in a recent study of Senegalese society, states may collapse, as the examples of Somalia and Liberia have recently shown, 'but the important fact is that they do not consequently disappear; the re-emergence of these states as juridical entities is virtually assured by the international system, regardless of their empirical status'.[35] The nation-state is simply an historical reality with which the African anti-colonial movements were forced to reckon.

The criticism of nationalism found in the works of Bhabha and such like-minded critics as Gayatri Chakravorty Spivak has provided a highly useful commentary on the limits of nationalist ideology.[36] Bhabha's inquiries into the questions of identity, exile and nationhood have been particularly interesting. Both Spivak and Bhabha are essentially poststructuralist critics who are extremely wary of totalising meta-narratives. Spivak's work has drawn attention to the processes by which the colonial text's construction of the 'subaltern' is repeated in the nationalist text. Equally, Bhabha argues in his 'Of Mimicry and Men' that the hegemonic discourse of colonialism produced a native Other that is, as he puns, 'almost the same but not white'.[37] However, as Neil Lazarus notes, such arguments about the 'derivative'[38] nature of nationalism run the risk of becoming dismissive of the very active resistance involved in national liberation movements.[39]

Certain poststructuralist critics have even gone beyond Spivak's and Bhabha's scepticism concerning notions of representation and have denied the whole possibility of speaking on behalf of others. This conceptual relativism, which is at the heart of much post-Foucauldian/poststructuralist thought, has led some critics to abandon the anti-colonial nationalist project in favour of a vaguely defined 'ethnicity', which is no more nor less than the return of the search for the 'authentic' African. This process is exemplified in the work of

[34] Tim Brennan, 'The National Longing for Form', in Homi K. Bhabha, ed., *Nation and Narration* (New York and London: Routledge, 1990), p. 58.
[35] Leonardo A. Villalón, *Islamic Society and State Power in Senegal* (Cambridge: Cambridge University Press, 1995), pp. 22–3.
[36] See Bhabha's 'DissemiNation: Time, Narrative and the Margins of the Modern Nation', in *Nation and Narration*, pp. 291–322, and Gayatri Chakravorty Spivak, 'Can the Subaltern speak?', in Cary Nelson and Lawrence Grossberg, eds, *Marxism and the Interpretation of Culture* (London: Macmillan, 1988), pp. 271–313.
[37] Homi K. Bhabha, *The Location of Culture* (New York and London: Routledge, 1994), p. 89.
[38] See Partha Chatterjee's discussion of the 'derivative' nature of anti-colonial nationalist discourse in his *Nationalist Thought and the Colonial World: A Derivative Discourse?* (London: Zed Books, 1986). Chatterjee's criticisms of nationalism lead him towards a defence of 'local knowledge' and 'ethnicity'.
[39] Neil Lazarus, 'National Consciousness and the Specificity of (Post)Colonial Intellectualism', in Francis Barker et al., eds, *Colonial Discourse/Postcolonial Theory*, pp. 197–220.

Christopher L. Miller who, in his *Theories of Africans*, discusses the dilemma facing the Western critic of African literature in the following terms:

> What options are really open to a Western reader of non-Western literature? Claiming a break with his/her own culture and critical upbringing, can he/she read the other, the African, as if from *an authentically* African point of view, interpreting African experience in *African terms*, perceiving rather than projecting?[40]

Miller's basic point that the Western reader must be sensitive to differing cultural values when dealing with African literature is no doubt a useful reminder to all Western critics of the dangers of imposing a Western framework on non-Western societies. However, to posit an 'authentic' African world that is totally foreign and incomprehensible to the Western reader is another matter entirely.

On one level, Miller's call for more attention to be paid to the particularities of African culture (which he defines as 'ethnicity') is perfectly understandable and is a process that has been adopted to a large extent within this study. It is clear that Miller's call for the privileging of 'ethnicity' is, in part, a reaction against the vulgar Marxism/Fanonism of certain critics of African literature, most notably Gugelberger's *Marxism and African Literature* with which Miller takes issue at considerable length.[41] Gugelberger's Marxism is distinctly monolithic in form and his claim that issues of class must always take precedence over social issues betrays little awareness or interest in the interaction between culture and politics within Africa. However, it is probably Gugelberger's unwarranted and incredibly general demand that 'Third World Literature must come to terms with its inherent Fanonian nature' that rankles most with Miller,[42] as Fanon, and to a lesser extent Amilcar Cabral, are the main targets of Miller's ire. Essentially, Fanon and Cabral are accused of suppressing the 'local' values of ethnicity in favour of grandiose Marxist universals. Fanon is found guilty by association for the excesses of the regime of Sékou Touré in Guinea and his liberation theories are cast as totalising and absolutist. As Miller so dramatically puts it, 'Fanon's response to local resistance is to call out the firing squad.'[43]

It is not necessary to dwell on the extremely partial nature of Miller's account of both Fanon's and Cabral's ideologies, as this has been convincingly argued by Neil Lazarus elsewhere.[44] However, it is worth pausing momentarily to consider the implications of Miller's dismissal of the explicitly Marxist conceptions of the national liberation movements espoused by both Fanon and Cabral. Fanon is far from being the Eurocentric Marxist that Miller paints him to be, perceiving the process of the people's radical education under the

[40] Christopher L. Miller, *Theories of Africans: Francophone Literature and Anthropology in Africa* (Chicago and London: University of Chicago Press, 1990), p. 1 (my italics).

[41] Georg M. Gugelberger, ed., *Marxism and African Literature* (London: James Currey, 1985). See also Emmanuel Ngara's *Art and Ideology in the African Novel: a Study of the Influence of Marxism on African Writing* (London: Heinemann, 1985).

[42] Gugelberger, *Marxism and African Literature*, p. xiv.

[43] Miller, *Theories of Africans*, p. 50.

[44] Lazarus, 'Disavowing Decolonization', pp. 69–98.

leadership of the Marxist intellectual as part of a dialectical process in which the intellectual learns the values of the people.[45] If Fanon underestimates the value of African culture (of which he had very little first-hand experience outside North Africa), it is because he wrongly believes that it has been almost totally wiped out by the process of colonisation.

Amilcar Cabral makes no such mistake about the survival of African culture. However, despite several references to what he believes to be an African essence, Cabral counsels against a blanket acceptance of the values of existing cultural practices: 'it is important not to lose sight of the fact that no culture is a perfect, finished whole. Culture, like history, is an expanding and developing phenomenon.'[46] It is clear from the liberation theories of Fanon and Cabral that anti-colonial nationalism can just as easily bear the weight of revolutionary as of reactionary elements. In this context, Aijaz Ahmad argues that both the poststructuralist and the 'Third-Worldist' vision of nationalism are inherently flawed:

> What role any given nationalism would play always depends on the configuration of the class forces and sociopolitical practices which organize the power bloc within which any particular set of nationalist initiatives become historically effective. That position cuts against both Third-Worldist nationalism and poststructuralist rhetorical inflations, and implies at least two things. It recognizes the actuality, even the necessity, of progressive and revolutionary kinds of nationalism, and it does not characterize nations and states as coercive entities *as such*.[47]

Giving a Marxist turn to Tim Brennan's contention that the nation is the only form through which colonised peoples can fight dependency, Ahmad argues that, in the modern context of the global market, socialist struggle within the boundaries of individual nations is the only possible response to economic imperialism:

> To the extent that contemporary imperialism's political system takes the form of a hierarchically structured system of nation-states, it is only by organizing their struggles within the political space of their own nation-state, with the revolutionary transformation of that particular nation-state as the immediate practical objective, that the revolutionary forces of any given country can effectively struggle against the imperialism they face concretely in their own lives.[48]

It will be argued below that Ahmad's conception of socialist struggle within the individual nation state is particularly relevant to the work of Sembene.

Returning to Miller's espousal of 'ethnicity', it would seem that it is simply part of a far wider trend in much contemporary poststructuralist theory.[49] The

[45] Fanon, *The Wretched of the Earth*, pp. 85–118.
[46] Amilcar Cabral, 'National Liberation and Culture', in *Return to the Source* (New York and London: Monthly Review Press, 1973), p. 50.
[47] Ahmad, *In Theory*, p. 11 (stress in original).
[48] Ibid., p. 317.
[49] Another well-known champion of the rights of ethnicity is the novelist and critic, V. Y. Mudimbe. See his *L'Odeur du père: essai sur les limites de la vie et de la science en Afrique noire* (Paris: Présence Africaine, 1982), and *The Invention of Africa: Gnosis, Philosophy and the Order of Knowledge* (London: James Currey, 1988).

philosopher Paulin J. Hountondji, who was once a leading critic of the notion that there is a specifically African philosophy,[50] has now come full circle and has become the champion of what he calls '*le savoir endogène*' ['endogenous knowledge'].[51] The old terms of 'tradition' and 'modernity' may have been dropped but they are still easily recognisable lurking behind the terms 'endogène' and 'exogène':

> *On appellera donc 'savoir endogène', dans une configuration donnée, une connaissance vécue par la société comme partie intégrante de son héritage, par opposition aux savoirs exogènes qui sont encore perçus, à ce stade au moins, comme des éléments d'un autre système de valeurs.*[52]

'Endogenous knowledge' can thus be taken to mean a knowledge lived and experienced by a particular society as an integral part of its heritage. Such knowledge stands in opposition to exogenous knowledge which is perceived, for the moment at least, as part of a different value system.

From this hypothesis, Hountondji encourages the search for an African science ('ethnoscience') and an African epistemology ('ethno-épistémologie'), which are contrasted with a specifically Western science and epistemology. Once again, the West and Africa are given radically opposed and mutually exclusive identities, and we find ourselves faced with the cultural stand-off between coloniser and colonised that Aijaz Ahmad had described as the main stumbling block in the examination of social conflict *within* African societies.

The Congolese philosopher, Charles Bowao, has pointed out the problem with such an essentialisation of culture in his polemical attack on Hountondji:

> *Il n'y a pas de science occidentale, pas plus qu'il n'y a de science africaine, de même qu'il ne saurait y avoir d'ethnoscience en général. Car, ce qui fait la science, c'est moins le lieu géographique ou historique de sa production, que l'universalité établie de sa démarche et de ses résultats. Une science valable exclusivement pour une ethnie, un peuple, un continent ou que sais-je encore, n'en est véritablement pas une.*[53]

There is no Western science nor is there an African science. In fact, there could never be such a thing as an ethnoscience because what makes a science is not really the historical or geographical site of its production but the universality of its procedures and its results. A science that is only valid for one ethnic group, one people, one continent, is not truly a science.

At the heart of Bowao's criticism is an acceptance of, what seems to me, to be the indisputable fact that there is no such thing as an authentic, isolated African world. It is simply impossible to deny the alterations that took place in African society during the course of a century of European colonisation. In a fascinating essay, Terence Ranger has written of the ways in which African monarchical power in Uganda was strengthened by British ideas on the nature of 'traditional' African society. In Ranger's thesis, elements of African tradition are shown to have been 'invented' as a result of the negotiation of power between coloniser and colonised: 'The invented traditions of African societies

---

[50] See Hountondji's *Sur la 'philosophie africaine': critique de l'ethnophilosophie.*
[51] See his *Les Savoirs endogènes: pistes pour une recherche* (Dakar: CODESRIA, 1994).
[52] Hountondji, *Les Savoirs endogènes*, p. 17.
[53] Bowao, '"Désethnologiser"', p. 17.

22

– whether invented by the Europeans or by Africans themselves in response – distorted the past but became in themselves realities through which a good deal of colonised encounter was expressed.'[54] Equally, Mamadou Diouf's essay, 'Représentations historiques et légitimités politiques au Sénégal (1960–1987)' ['Historical Representations and Political Legitimacy in Senegal (1960–1987)'], describes the manner in which historical tradition in Senegal has been modified and rewritten in rhythm with the shifting balance of power from the colonial era to the rise of Islam in modern Senegal.[55] In this light, to speak of the Western and African 'worlds' as entirely different systems is a nonsense. One may deplore the nature of European influence on Africa but one cannot deny the reality of that influence. Even the African perception of what is 'authentic' and 'traditional' in their society is shown by both Ranger and Diouf to have been influenced by the colonial encounter.

To split the world into polarised camps (the technological West versus the traditional, primitive Third World), from whatever political motivation, is to engage in what Edward Said has termed a 'rhetoric of blame' that produces nothing but continuing confrontation and hostility.[56] The West's meeting with Africa has produced a new reality for both sides of that encounter, thus making a nonsense of Miller's plea for the privileging of 'local knowledge'.[57] There is no 'authentic' African world in Miller's sense of the term (just as there is no 'authentic' Western world), nor is there an 'authentic African point of view'. Charles Bowao's critique of 'African philosophy' could here be equally applied to Miller's view of African literature and the role of the Western critic:

> On ne saurait parler de philosophie africaine qu'en tant que pratique (ou tradition) de la philosophie en Afrique, peu importe qu'elle porte sur l'Afrique ou qu'elle soit l'œuvre d'un Africain ou non. Au demeurant, au nom de quelle extraversion culturelle peut-on nier la sensibilité africaine à un Sénégalais spécialiste de la philosophie américaine, ou encore de la logique de Boole; et ne point la reconnaître à un Français qui fait la preuve de son excellence dans la maîtrise des réalités africaines?[58]

One can only speak of African philosophy in terms of the practice (or tradition) of philosophy in Africa. It is irrelevant whether a work has Africa as its subject or whether it has been written by an African or not. For a start, in the name of what theory of cultural extroversion can one deny an African sensibility to a Senegalese specialist of American philosophy or even of the logic of Boole? Conversely, how

---

[54] Terence Ranger, 'The Invention of Tradition in Colonial Africa', in Hobsbawm and Ranger, *The Invention of Tradition*, p. 212.

[55] Diouf, 'Représentations historiques', pp. 14–23.

[56] Said, *Culture and Imperialism*, p. 19.

[57] Miller, *Theories of Africans*, p. 50. One of the main problems with cultural relativism is that practices which would be deemed totally unacceptable if carried out by the coloniser are defended simply because they are a part of 'ethnic' culture. In this way, even the caste system can be defended. Assane Sylla, quoting from a Wolof proverb which is startlingly close to the standard European defences of the colonial system, claims that those who are socially oppressed are simply getting what they deserve: *'il est légitime de faire supporter à quelqu'un ce qu'il accepte de supporter.'* ['it is legitimate to make someone endure what they accept to endure.'] Sylla, *La Philosophie morale des Wolof*, p. 142. For Sembene's attacks on the caste system, see *White Genesis* and *The Last of the Empire*.

[58] Bowao, '"Désethnologiser"', p. 18.

can one refuse to recognise the African sensibility of a French expert in African society and culture?

Although it may be considered extremely unfashionable to quote an analytical philosopher in defence of one's case in the current climate of debate within literary theory, I would like to mention briefly the work of the philosopher, Donald Davidson, for a number of reasons. Firstly, I believe it would be a useful exercise to note the presence of certain epistemological concerns in the work of an analytical philosopher, as such work is often caricatured as absolutist and totalising by many poststructuralist critics. Secondly, and more importantly, Davidson's ideas on conceptual schemes directly address the problem of interpreting radically different cultures.

Davidson argues that the notion of conceptual relativism is simply untenable. Examining the cases for both total and partial failure of translation from one scheme to another, he concludes that neither argument can be proven: the former, because if a conceptual scheme were so radically different as to preclude the possibility of translation to a different scheme, one would be in the position of being able to say nothing at all about it (let alone finding an argument for the existence of radically different conceptual schemes); the latter, because we are theoretically obliged to accept a common conceptual framework in order to get the whole project of translation off the ground in the first place. Accordingly, we do not have the conceptual tools to prove that conflicting views between people arise from a difference in concepts, rather than from simple differences in opinion. Therefore, one cannot prove that there are radically different conceptual schemes, but nor can one prove that there is one totalising scheme which serves all of mankind. Davidson argues that the way around the relativist impasse is to abandon the dualism of 'scheme' and 'reality', and, while accepting the limits of language, to attempt to engage with the real world:

> Given the dogma of a dualism of scheme and reality, we get conceptual relativity, and truth relative to a scheme. Without the dogma, this kind of relativity goes by the board. Of course, truth of sentences remains relative to language, *but that is as objective as can be*. In giving up the dualism of scheme and world, we do not give up the world, but re-establish unmediated touch with the familiar objects whose antics make our sentences and opinions true or false.[59]

Partha Chatterjee has taken issue with Davidson's appeal for a 'charitable' reading of other cultures, claiming the whole notion of 'charity' to be a discredited bourgeois humanist concept.[60] Whatever misgivings one may have about Davidson's use of the term 'charitable', I feel that his approach is far more enabling than that of the poststructuralists. Rather than focusing on that which one cannot know, he seeks to set out the criteria by which one can gain knowledge. Poststructuralist critics in general have sought to reveal the manner in which so-called objective knowledge has been implicated in discourses of

---

[59] Donald Davidson, Chapter 13, 'On the Very Idea of a Conceptual Scheme', in his *Inquiries into Truth and Interpretation* (Oxford: Clarendon Press, 1984), p. 198 (my italics).

[60] Chatterjee, *Nationalist Thought*, pp. 11–12.

power, including the discourse of empire. In *The Invention of Africa*, V. Y. Mudimbe makes numerous references to Foucault's critique of the totalising discourses of the social sciences in *The Order of Things*, in order to back his call for an understanding of Africa on ethnic grounds.[61] Although it has been extremely useful to uncover the links between knowledge and power, the debunking of all knowledge in which some poststructuralists engage turns the whole academic process into a mere intellectual game whose codes and structures can be revealed only by the superior readings of the poststructuralist theorist. I find myself in complete agreement with David Harvey's assessment of the dangers of the poststructuralist/postmodernist approach:

> Postmodernist philosophers tell us not only to accept but openly even to revel in the fragmentations and the cacophony of voice through which the dilemmas of the modern world are understood. Obsessed with deconstructing and delegitimating every form of argument they encounter, they can end only in condemning their own validity claims to the point where nothing remains of any basis for reasoned action.[62]

The stinging critique of Western society produced by poststructuralism/postmodernism over the past number of years (in many cases, a totally valid criticism, it must be said) has created a disillusionment with the West that appears to have led certain critics to rally to the cause of ethnicity. It is difficult not to read into Miller's espousal of 'ethnicity' a nostalgia, common among certain Western and African academics, for the passing of the 'traditional' world. In this view, what is being contested is not so much the failings of the anti-colonial nationalist movements as the blandness and uniformity of late twentieth-century culture. Typical of this trend within cultural criticism is the work of the French historian, Yves Person (who was not a poststructuralist but whose arguments are very close to those of Miller), most notably in his book on Samory (or Samori) Touré, a celebrated African ruler who built up a vast empire in West Africa, which he defended for seventeen years against the colonial powers at the end of the nineteenth century. Person sees Samory as a symbol of the resistance of 'traditional' Africa to the modern world (a symbol which Person sees as deeply relevant to contemporary Africa) and we are told in the introduction that

> *la lutte de Samori doit rappeler à l'Afrique d'aujourd'hui que la décolonisation politique n'a aucun sens si le grand mouvement d'uniformisation qui pousse le monde vers l'entropie, c'est-à-dire la mort culturelle, ou l'état non-humain de la 'méga-ethnie', se poursuit sous la direction d'agents africains.[63]*

Samori's struggle should remind today's Africa that political decolonisation means nothing if the vast movement which is pushing the world towards entropy, that is

---

[61] Mudimbe, *The Invention of Africa*. Michel Foucault, *The Order of Things: an Archaeology of the Human Sciences* (London: Routledge, 1989).

[62] David Harvey, *The Condition of Postmodernity* (1989; Cambridge, MA, and Oxford: Basil Blackwell, 1992), p. 116.

[63] Yves Person, *Samori: la renaissance de l'empire mandingue* (Paris: ABC; Dakar: Nouvelles Editions Africaines, 1976), p. 18. One can see a similar attitude in the work of the Senegalese novelist, Aminata Sow Fall. In her novel, *L'Appel des arènes* (Dakar: Nouvelles Editions Africaines, 1993), the musings of the teacher, Niang, present the engagement with modernity as the loss of ethnic identity (p. 72):

to say cultural death, or the inhuman state of the 'giant ethnic group', is continued under the guidance of African leaders.

It seems appropriate here to return to Eric Hobsbawm's notion of the 'invention of tradition' and the distinction that he makes between genuine and invented traditions: 'the strength and adaptability of genuine traditions is not to be confused with the "invention of tradition". Where the old ways are alive, traditions need be neither revived nor invented.'[64] For a tradition to survive, it must be seen by the community in question to be serving a practical purpose in their day-to-day experience. Human communities are subjected to all sorts of social, economic and political pressures. Therefore, a viable tradition (namely one that can provide a framework for dealing with contemporary reality) is a tradition that is constantly reinvented and renegotiated by the community. Souleymane Bachir Diagne analyses this process brilliantly in his essay, 'L'Avenir de la tradition' ['The Future of Tradition']. Diagne dismisses attempts by the Senegalese government in the 1980s to draw up a *Charte culturelle nationale* as doomed to failure because cultural values are not decreed but are the result of 'évaluations' made by the people themselves. Diagne provides a far more dynamic conception of tradition:

[...] le système sénégalais a changé dans sa texture même, en trente ans depuis la mise en place d'un État souverain. Être attentif, dès lors, au mouvement de la société civile sera comprendre que l'identité de la tradition ne peut être une identité de répétition. Après tout, dans son sens premier, 'tradition' signifie ce qui est digne d'être transmis pour être en principe de comportements qui répondent à des conditions et à des temps nouveaux.[65]

[...] the Senegalese system has changed its very texture in the thirty years since the foundation of a sovereign state. Therefore, being attentive to the movements within civil society involves a recognition that traditional identity cannot be an identity based on repetition. After all, the primary meaning of 'tradition' is that which is worthy of being transmitted and which meets the needs of a new era.

Sembene's position in relation to the questions of tradition and identity is rather a complex one. His Marxism causes him to reject the notion of an ahistorical, immutable African identity, along with the standard framework that opposes tradition with modernity, and which is seen in much of African literature and criticism. One Marxist critic has even gone so far as to suggest that questions of identity are overlooked in Sembene's work because 'the identity crisis is an essentially petty-bourgeois disease. No peasant has ever lost

---

[63] (cont.) *Le désordre qui bouleverse le monde a pour cause l'aliénation collective [...]. Chacun refuse d'être soi-même et se perd dans l'illusion qu'il peut se tailler un manteau selon sa propre fantaisie [...]. Le mal est universel [...]. Personne ne sait plus à quoi s'accrocher. L'idéal n'existe plus, mais la course vers les ténèbres. L'homme perd ses racines et l'homme sans racines est pareil à un arbre sans racines: il se dessèche et meurt.*

The disorder which is disrupting the world is the reason behind this collective alienation [...]. We are all denying our true selves and fooling ourselves that we can become whatever we want [...]. This is a worldwide problem [...]. There is nothing left to hang on to. Idealism has disappeared. All that is left is the headlong race into darkness. Man is losing his roots and a man without roots is like a tree without roots: he will dry up and die.

[64] Hobsbawm, 'Inventing Traditions', p. 8.
[65] Diagne, 'L'Avenir de la tradition', pp. 295–6.

sleep over whether having an electric light and running water would impair his authenticity.'[66] However, to claim that the question of identity has simply been dreamt up by the bourgeoisie to keep the peasants in their place is to indulge in a vulgar Marxism that is simply not reflected in Sembene's work. He is highly sensitive to the role played by tradition in the lives of African people. For example, Fa Keïta and N'Deye Touti in *God's Bits of Wood* are both made to call their own identity into question. However, their identity crises are brought about through the turmoil of colonial politics and the polarisation lying at the heart of it: Fa Keïta because he realises that the strike is a departure from 'traditional' patterns of behaviour, and N'Deye Touti because she realises that her wholesale adoption of middle-class 'Western' attitudes has caused her to side with the bosses in the strike, betraying her own people and her own class. It is not the adoption of 'Western' attitudes *per se* that Sembene sees as culturally alienating. It is the reasons behind such a move that interest him: N'Deye Touti apes the West because she is ashamed of her people; Bakayoko accepts certain 'Western' practices in order to empower his people in the face of new social realities. Thus, it becomes clear that Sembene does not ignore the issues of identity and tradition in favour of a purely economic examination of African society. However, unlike those who believe in an African essence, Sembene situates the notions of identity and tradition within an historical dynamic in which social, economic, political and cultural considerations can all be taken into account.

Both of Sembene's novels written immediately prior to French West African independence, *O Pays, mon beau peuple!* (1957) and *God's Bits of Wood* (1960), are infused with the optimism of the independence movement, and they attempt to deal with some of the issues facing an increasingly urbanised and industrialised Africa. In these novels, the anti-colonial movement is portrayed as being profoundly radical. Independence, for Sembene, was not a question of reviving a mythical African past, nor should it simply involve a transfer of power from white to black hands (for if the colonial system was corrupt and unjust, changing the colour of those in charge would hardly change matters). Independence was seen as the first step on the road to the creation of new, egalitarian African societies. Sembene's Marxism thus sets him apart from many of those involved in African literature in the 1950s and reveals a fundamental difference in the political and social visions of those writers who saw themselves as speaking out on behalf of African society.

Frantz Fanon, who shared Sembene's Marxist convictions and belief in the radical nature of the independence movement, was greatly interested in the role of the artist in the fight for independence. In *The Wretched of the Earth*, Fanon discusses what he sees as the three stages in the development of the colonised writer.[67] He describes the first stage as one of assimilation, that is to

[66] Fírinne Ní Chréacháin, 'Sembene Ousmane Incorporated? Bestman's *Sembene Ousmane*: a case-study of hegemonic incorporation in African literary criticism', in *Protée noir: essais sur la littérature francophone de l'Afrique noire et des Antilles*, ed. by Peter Hawkins and Annette Lavers (Paris: L'Harmattan, 1992), p. 135.

[67] Frantz Fanon, *The Wretched of the Earth*, chapter 4, 'On National Culture', pp. 166–99.

say, imitating the styles and language of the coloniser (see, for example, the novels of Ousmane Socé with their highly deferential manner towards all things French). The second stage is one of recollection, whereby the colonised artist distances himself from the coloniser's culture which, in turn, leads him to celebrate the 'black culture' of his own people. Fanon is obviously here talking about the Negritude school of writers. Fanon saw this second stage as a rarefied, elitist position with the colonised artist assuming an emotional attitude towards 'black culture', finding universal truths even in its most banal details.[68]

Although critical of the ideology of Negritude, Fanon nevertheless welcomes it historically as a necessary step on the road to independence (a point that Sembene is also willing to concede).[69] Fanon argues that as the coloniser readily used the argument that blacks were backward and had no culture worth speaking of, it was only natural that the justification of black culture would become an important part in the process of seeking independence. In their celebration of native traditions, Negritude writers were basically saying that if blacks had a rich and elaborate culture in the past, then they should be allowed the freedom to develop that culture in an independent Africa.

It becomes clear from Fanon's analysis of the colonial situation that the questions of independence and national culture are inextricably linked (for African independence, despite pan-Africanist rhetoric, in effect meant the independence of individual African states). However, as Fanon points out, rhetoric about 'la culture négro-africaine' and the Romantic figure of the African, in touch with nature and the world of sensuality, will not be of much help in the actual struggle for independence or in the building of new African societies. This leads us to the third stage in the development of the colonised artist, whom Fanon urges to awaken 'the people' from their lethargy and lead them to revolution. Those who lead the people must themselves become one of the people in order to create a new society:

> The problem is to get to know the place that these men mean to give their people, the kind of social relations that they decide to set up and the conception that they have of the future of humanity. It is this that counts; everything else is mystification, signifying nothing.[70]

Sembene's writing would definitely belong to Fanon's third category and Sembene has always been keen to stress the importance of the African writer in waking the consciousness of the people to social issues. His work is a conscious effort to give voice to Fanon's 'wretched of the earth', the dispossessed of African society whom he saw as excluded from the literature of the Negritude school. In a 1981 interview, he spoke of this desire to write about a different Africa from the one found in the majority of pre-independence African literature:

Je n'ai pas vu dans ces œuvres, les ouvriers, mais des évocations d'une Afrique mystique sous le

---

[68] Ibid., p. 181.
[69] An example of Sembene's views on Negritude can be found in G. D. Killam, ed., *African Writers on African Writing* (London: Heinemann, 1973), p. 149.
[70] Fanon, *The Wretched of the Earth*, p. 189.

bananier, le cocotier, le fruit mûr qui tombe et on bouffe. Je me suis dit, non! non. Il y a une Afrique debout, une qui ne pleure pas sur son passé.[1]

These works had nothing to say about the workers. They were simply evocations of a mystical Africa, where people sit under the banana tree or the coconut tree and eat the fruit that falls from the branches. I said to myself, no! No! There is an Africa that is defiant, one that doesn't cry over its past.

Thus, one can see that at the heart of Sembene's work is a clear desire to question the received ideas on African identity, to discuss issues simply ignored by the dominant discourses of his society, and to draw the reader's attention to the question of representation.

A text vital to an understanding of Sembene's artistic project is his paper, *Man is Culture*, which was presented to an American university audience in 1975.[2] From the beginning, he not only declares his belief in the political nature of all art, but claims that the Romantic Western image of art as decoration is unknown in West Africa:

Where I come from art is not adornment. The word 'art' does not exist in any of the languages of West Africa. On the other hand, *Man* is the symbol of art. He himself is art. (*MC*, p. 1; stress in original)

Culture is far from an abstraction. In fact, it is shown to be an integral part of everyday, lived experience, thus firmly placing it in an historical context, not in the realm of essences and cultural authenticity.

Sembene is also keen to denounce the myths of the colonial ethnographer who sought to portray the colonised world as backward and inferior to Europe:

Much has been said and written about the fetishism of Blacks, their animism, their superstition, as if similarities did not exist in the history of the Greeks. All people practice fetishism. They all have objects which give a concrete form to their beliefs. (*MC*, p. 2)

Sembene argues that this view of African culture was used by the Europeans as an excuse for the slave trade. He claims that the scale of the plight facing Africans during this period was so great that the only method of survival was to seek refuge in the community, elaborating a culture which would express their communal suffering and pain:

Among the people trapped between the Ocean and the Sahara, living in isolation, fetishism and animism prevailed. Spiritualism was re-structured at each stage. Contrary to what one might think of that period, this attitude was not an evasion into the past; it was an act of self-defence. For existence was considered a calamity at that time and in reality, it was. (*MC*, p. 4)

In Sembene's history even the practice of animism is interpreted as an element of popular resistance to European domination (this 'radicalisation' of animism will be examined in relation to *Xala* in Chapter Four).

[1] Mohamadou Kane et al., 'Comme un aveugle qui retrouve la vue', *Le Soleil* [Dakar], 10 July 1981, p. 5.
[2] Ousmane Sembene, *Man is Culture/L'Homme est culture* (Bloomington, IN: African Studies Program, 1979). The 6th Annual Hans Wolff Memorial Lecture (5 March 1975). This is a dual-language text. Further references to this work (hereafter *MC*) will be given in the body of the text.

Imagining Africa

However, unlike many versions of African history, Sembene's does not content itself with simply attacking European brutality in Africa while overlooking the role of Islam and the tribal chiefs.[73] As Sembene shows in his story 'Tribal Scars or The Voltaique' (examined in Chapter Two), Africans were involved as middle-men in the slave trade: 'We must remember that tribal struggles were an occasion to acquire slaves. For a long time, the slave was a medium of exchange between indigenous traders and Europeans' (*MC*, p. 3). And what of the trans-Saharan slave trade which began centuries before the European slave trade and which continued well after the latter had been abandoned? Islam, just as much as Christianity, is shown by Sembene to have been a colonising force in black Africa: 'Each representative of the revealed religions assumed for himself the divine right to guide this lost race to the *Divine Light*' (*MC*, p. 4; stress in original).

It is possible to read into Sembene's criticism of Islam a pining for an 'authentic' African past. One traditionalist Senegalese critic has declared that '*son combat ou sa prise de conscience* [i.e. *des héros de ses romans*] *prend la forme d'une tentative de renouer avec une pureté originelle*' ['the struggle or the awakenening [of the heroes of Sembene's novels] is part of an attempt to rediscover an original purity.'].[74] However, nothing could be further from the truth. What Sembene denounces in his history of Africa is oppression, not the loss of some ill-defined African purity.[75] He accepts that, at certain stages of West African history, Islam has been a symbol of revolt, firstly in its stand against the abuse of power by the traditional African chiefs,[76] and secondly in its opposition to the slave trade, and subsequently the European scramble for Africa at the end of the nineteenth century.[77] However, Sembene sees the rise of Islam fundamentally as the replacement of one oppressive power by another, with the repression of black African culture as an inevitable result:

> In the name of Islam a ferocious opposition was waged against colonial penetration and Christianity. But the victory of the new lords of Islam was nothing more than the substitution of one monarchy for another. The ancient practices diminished in importance. All that remained were phrases devoid of meaning. (*MC*, p. 5)

Sembene does not claim that Islamic culture is inherently inferior to the culture that it replaced. It is the manner in which cultural change takes place that interests him. Aimé Césaire wrote on the notion of colonisation as a means of cultural exchange in his *Discourse on Colonialism*:

[73] For examples of such standard attacks on Europe, see Samb, 'L'Islam et l'histoire du Sénégal', pp. 461–2, and Sylla, *La Philosophie morale des Wolof*, pp. 43–62 and pp. 138–42.
[74] Bassirou Dieng, 'La Tradition comme support dramatique dans l'œuvre romanesque de Sembène Ousmane', *Annales de la faculté des lettres et sciences humaines de Dakar*, 15 (1985), p. 142.
[75] Sembene does not go along with Soyinka who argues that Islam is not an 'authentic' African religion, and who sets up an 'authentically' African spirituality as the 'true' African religion (see Soyinka, *Myth, Literature and the African World*, pp. 76–96). Sembene simply sees Islam as part of contemporary West African reality.
[76] See Cheikh Tidiane Sy's essay, 'Ahmadu Bamba et l'Islamisation des Wolof', *Bulletin de l'IFAN*, série B, 32, 2 (1970), pp. 416–18 for an account of the marabouts' uprising of 1681–3.
[77] See the story of Lat Dior and his conversion from *ceddo* to *talibé* in Vincent Monteil, 'Lat Dior, Damel du Kayor (1842–1886), et l'Islamisation des Wolofs', *Archives de sociologie des religions*, 16 (1963), pp. 77–104.

But then I ask the following question: has colonization really *placed civilizations in contact?* Or, if you prefer, of all the ways of *establishing contact*, was it the best? I answer *no.*[78]

The basic point here is that colonisation is about domination, not cultural exchange. Sembene would argue that one cannot condemn European domination in Africa and exalt Islamic domination as a benign influence. As mentioned earlier, much has been made by West African historians of Islam's 'authenticity' as an African religion. However, Sembene refuses this argument, and Islam's current predominance in West Africa is presented as the result of an original Arab conquest, followed by the gradual spread of the religion through both *jihad* and the erosion of the power of the tribal chiefs. He does not criticise Islam as a religion but denounces the manner in which it sought to destroy the rituals and practices of black African culture. The important thing for Sembene is to challenge the dominant discourse in his society, which would have Islam seen as *the* national religion with the less pleasant aspects of its rise to power simply glossed over or rewritten.

Sembene celebrates the survival of certain elements of black African culture as a symbol of African resistance to domination. However, he refuses to fall into the trap of Negritude with its blind celebration of all things African:

> If the demand for the ancient culture was a just cause, the servile imitation of it checks progress. The obligation to do today as the ancestors did is a sign of intellectual deficiency. What is worse, it reflects a lack of control over daily life. (*MC*, p. 9)

Africa in the late twentieth century is faced with a reality totally different from that in which its cultural traditions were formed. Instead of being swamped by this new state of affairs, Africa must adapt itself as quickly as possible: 'It is not a question of refusing modernity but rather of mastering it and directing it' (*MC*, p. 10).[79] Sembene envisages a new secular African culture, free from ethnic divisions, which will grow out of the present turmoil: 'A new

---

[78] Césaire, *Discourse on Colonialism*, p. 11.

[79] This call to face the challenges of modernity is brilliantly addressed by Charles Bowao:

> *Peut-être vaudrait-il de récuser cet "ethno-idéologisme" en se donnant une vision plus intégrale, donc moins ségrégatiste de la modernité, en la pensant comme mouvement et non comme fin. La modernité se révélerait alors comme une idée régulatrice de l'existence humaine, qui se renouvelle au fil du temps. Être moderne, c'est vivre son époque, mais c'est surtout être au diapason des valeurs contradictoires qu'elle suggère, en action et en pensée. Après tout, modernité est. C'est justement parce qu'elle n'a jamais été et ne sera pas, qu'elle est, simplement, horizon toujours ouvert, quête humaine continuée. Elle puise son dynamisme dans la raison même de l'humain, de l'humanité. La modernité est alors réinvention et non répétition.*

> Perhaps it would be better to challenge this 'ethno-ideology' by proposing a more integrated and therefore less segregational vision of modernity, seeing it as a process and not as an end in itself. Modernity would then be revealed as a regulatory idea for humanity, one which renews itself constantly. To be modern is to live in one's own era but, moreover, it means being in tune with the contradictory values it suggests, both in action and in thought. After all, modernity is. It is precisely because modernity has never been and will not be that it is quite simply the open horizon of a never-ending human quest. Modernity derives its dynamism from humanity itself. Therefore, modernity is reinvention not repetition.

Bowao, '"Désethnologiser"', p. 16. Similar ideas are to be found in Diagne's 'L'Avenir de la tradition'.

African culture is sprouting forth from the political humus. It will bring together the various ethnic groups to make a single people of them. The only sacred aspect it will have will be the respect due to man. For man is culture' (*MC*, p. 11). The only hope for Africa, we are told, is in an egalitarian, socialist future.

This vision of a radical Africa engaging with the challenge of modernity is nowhere more evident in Sembene's work than in his most celebrated novel, *God's Bits of Wood*. The least that can be said of the novel is that it is ambitious. The story of an historical railway strike on the Dakar-Niger line that took place between October 1947 and March 1948 (a strike in which Sembene himself was involved), the novel attempts to capture the scale of the strike, which saw 20,000 men down tools, by constantly shifting between a host of characters across three different cities.[80] However, *God's Bits of Wood* is more than just a realistic narrative. Wole Soyinka has written that the novel 'attains epic levels' and, as is the case with all good epics, 'humanity is re-created'.[81] Indeed, Bakayoko, the driving force behind the strike (and a veritable 'Promethean creation' in Soyinka's view),[82] declares that the old African world is dead and that a new modern society is being created by the strike: 'The kind of man we were is dead, and our only hope for a new life lies in the machine, which knows neither a language nor a race'.[83] The novel depicts the birth of a new society, a society which is bonded together by the common goals and ordeals of the strike.

The difference between Sembene's view of the question of identity and that of the Negritude writers can be neatly examined in the central position of the railway line as a symbol of the spread of modernisation in *God's Bits of Wood*. Camara Laye, in one of the canonical texts of Negritude, *The African Child*, describes an almost idyllic childhood in an African village.[84] The village is presented as an 'authentic' microcosm of African life, where the magic and wisdom of African tradition have been preserved. However, Camara Laye seems completely unaware of the irony of his position as a French-educated intellectual, exalting and idealising a world to which he no longer strictly belongs (if such a 'pure' African way of life still existed, or indeed had ever existed, for him to belong to). Beside this 'authentic' African village lies a railway track which Camara Laye seems to suggest is the *outside* influence of the West, luring his childhood self away from the 'purity' of the African village to the world of Western knowledge in the city.

[80] For a comprehensive overview of the strike see Jean Suret-Canale's essay, 'The French West African Railway Workers' Strike 1947–1948', in *African Labor History*, ed. by Peter C.W. Gutkind, Robin Cohen and Jean Copans (Beverly Hills, CA, and London: Sage, 1978), pp. 129–54. See also the work of Iba Der Thiam on the development of the West African trade union movement: 'La Tuerie de Thiès de septembre 1938, essai d'interprétation', *Bulletin de l'IFAN*, series B, 38, 2 (1976), pp. 300–38; 'Galandou Diouf et le Front Populaire', *Bulletin de l'IFAN*, series B, 38, 3 (1976), pp. 592–618; 'Recherches sur les premières manifestations de la conscience syndicale au Sénégal (1938)', *Annales de la faculté des lettres et sciences humaines de Dakar*, 6 (1976), pp. 87–116.

[81] Soyinka, *Myth, Literature and the African World*, p. 117.

[82] Ibid.

[83] Ousmane Sembene, *God's Bits of Wood*, trans. by Francis Price (London: Heinemann, 1992), p. 76. Further references to this novel (hereafter *GBW*) will be given in the body of the text.

[84] Camara Laye, *The African Child*, trans. by James Kirkup (London: Fontana, 1959).

This image of the railway line as an integral part of the colonial conquest of Africa has strong resonances in Senegal. At the end of the nineteenth century, the building of the railway line from Dakar to Saint-Louis had signalled the downfall of the last *damel* (king) of Kayor, Lat Dior.[85] However, Sembene, unlike Camara Laye, appropriates the image of the railway, using it as a powerful symbol of a changing Africa, increasingly urbanised and growing steadily more aware of its power to challenge the might of its colonial masters. Far from being a symbol of the outside influence of the West, the railway is shown to be that which physically and metaphorically links Africans together.[86] The train, as a symbol of industrialisation, is shown to be in the process of transforming Africa: 'They began to understand that the machine was making of them a whole new breed of men' (*GBW*, pp. 32–3). Sembene argues that technology has nothing to do with race and invites the African to meet the challenges of the modern, industrialised world.[87]

Just as Oumar Faye in *O Pays, mon beau peuple!* was presented as the meeting ground of Western and African culture, so Ibrahima Bakayoko, the militant union leader of *God's Bits of Wood*, is shown to represent black African traditions while still advocating change. Bakayoko's affection for his people is reflected in his qualified respect for the traditions of his land. Before his vital speech at the rally in Dakar, he is approached by an old woman who becomes his adoptive mother when she learns of the death of his natural mother (a gesture that genuinely moves him). Another interesting issue, in this respect, is Bakayoko's acceptance of his marriage to his dead brother's wife. He seems to regard it as his duty to accept his traditional role in this instance but he refuses the whole idea of polygamy and will not take a second wife. Bakayoko's is a selective approach to tradition, only taking on board that which he considers appropriate or relevant to the needs of his age. He is most radical in his support for the increasingly active role of the women in the strike. He approves of the women's decision to march on Dakar, and he shows great respect for their courage and strength. As the men in the novel come to realise, the conditions of the strike have radically changed the role of women in their society: 'And the men began to understand that if the times were bringing forth a new breed of men, they were also bringing forth a new breed of women' (*GBW*, p. 34).

All along the railway line the traditional society (as well as colonial society) and its hierarchical system are being challenged by the advent of new ideas and

[85] Mamadou Diouf examines the role of the railway in the spread of both colonialism and capitalism in northern Senegal in *Le Kajoor au dix-neuvième siècle: pouvoir ceddo et conquête coloniale* (Paris: Karthala, 1990), pp. 263–86. Ahmadou Kourouma's novel, *Monnè, outrages et défis* (Paris: Seuil, 1990), presents a highly ironic image of the railway. In his book, thousands of Africans die attempting to bring progress, in the form of the railway, to the realm of Soba. However, despite the huge loss of life, the train never makes it to Soba.

[86] In *The Communist Manifesto*, Karl Marx makes a similar point about the spread of the railway network in nineteenth-century Europe allowing greater contacts between workers and enabling the formation of nationwide unions. See Karl Marx and Frederick Engels, *Collected Works*, 6 (London: Lawrence & Wishart, 1976), p. 493.

[87] For similar sentiments on the question of technology and race, see Bowao, '"Désethnologiser"', p. 17.

new social conditions. In one of the central episodes of the novel, the trial of
the strike-breaker, Diara, we again see a mixture of the traditional and the
modern. Tiémoko, one of the union leaders, discovers the idea of a trial in a
book by a *toubab*, or a white person, (Malraux's *Man's Estate*) but it is the old
and wise Fa Keïta who pronounces the final verdict. Esteem for the words of
the elders being a fundamental aspect of traditional African society, his words
act as an important marriage of the modern and the traditional: 'A long time
ago [...], before any of you were born, everything that happened happened
within a framework, an order that was our own, and the existence of that
order was of great importance in our lives. Today, no such framework exists.
[...] I think it is the machine which has ground everything together this way'
(*GBW*, p. 94). The whole trial scene serves as an extraordinarily powerful
enactment of the empowering of the colonised, who appropriate the institutions of the coloniser and adapt them to their own political and social aims. As
Wole Soyinka puts it: 'the emphasis of social regeneration is carefully laid on
the intrinsic ethical properties of existing society, their adaptation and
universal relations.'[88] A new and just African society will be born out of the
wisdom of the old African traditions, allied with modern, egalitarian ideas.

The extraordinary power of *God's Bits of Wood* lies in Sembene's ability to
conceive of a complete transformation in the structure of African society, and
the way in which Africans imagine their social relations. Perhaps more than
any other African novel, it succeeds in escaping the binary opposition between
Africa and the West, instead portraying Africans as the masters of their own
destiny. The romanticised notion of a 'pure' African tradition is replaced by
the more historical vision of an African society gripped by social changes with
which 'tradition' must find some sort of accommodation. In the same way as
Fanon's *The Wretched of the Earth*, Sembene's novel manages to capture the
mood of the independence movement in Africa, a time when many radical
intellectuals believed that a social revolution was beginning on the continent,
which would eventually spread to the whole world.

However, if we blindly accept Fanon's and Sembene's view of 'the people'
participating in the liberation struggle in order to pave the way for a socialist
revolution, then the demobilisation of 'the people' after independence, in
virtually all of the newly independent African states, is incomprehensible. In
his lucid study, *Resistance in Postcolonial African Fiction*, Neil Lazarus has argued
that Fanon's vision of a unified mass liberation struggle in Algeria (or elsewhere in Africa) simply does not stand up historically.[89] Effectively, Lazarus
argues that Fanon attributed his own goals and aspirations to the Algerian
peasantry, which was probably at no stage entirely committed to the social
vision of the FLN (Front de Libération Nationale), even when fighting for it.

[88] Soyinka, *Myth, Literature and the African World*, p. 118. Soyinka's view of 'traditional' African
society, although similar to Sembene's in many ways, relies on an idealised version of an
'authentically' African way of life (see his criticism of Islam and Christianity as totally alien
'white' elements in Africa, pp. 61–139). Sembene, however, is far more cautious, praising only
that which he sees as worthy in 'traditional' African society.

[89] Neil Lazarus, *Resistance in Postcolonial African Fiction* (New Haven, CT, and London: Yale
University Press, 1990). See especially chapters 1 and 2.

As the historian Ian Clegg has written: 'The peasants were fighting for what they regarded as their inheritance: a heritage firmly rooted in the Arab, Berber and Islamic past. Their consciousness was rooted in the values and traditions of this past and their aim was its re-creation.'[90] In their commitment to a radical restructuring of African society, both Sembene and Fanon, as good Marxists, view 'the people' as the key to change. However, they both under-estimate the extent to which a profound attachment to social and cultural traditions had survived the colonial era despite the major political and social upheavals that African society had undergone. Instead of becoming the revolutionary force which Sembene and Fanon had anticipated, 'the people' turned out to be a conservative force that settled down into its 'traditional' ways and allowed economic and political power to pass into the hands of the African bourgeoisie. Despite Fanon's misinterpretation of the motivations of 'the people' in the struggle for independence, Lazarus argues that Fanon's integrity is not in question (contrary to what critics such as Miller would lead us to believe, denouncing Marxist discourse as virtually irrelevant and alien to the values of an ethnically defined Africa).[91] Lazarus's view of Fanonian discourse as inclusive and emancipatory is equally applicable to Sembene: 'in this affirma-tive vision lies [Fanon's] power as a theorist of revolution.'[92] Both Sembene and Fanon provide a hopeful social vision that seeks to empower the oppressed and marginalised in their societies. Essentially, they seek to imagine alterna-tives: to give voice to resistance, and to challenge accepted dominant discourses. The value and limitations of their social vision is something I will examine during the course of this study.

Sembene's conception of the role of the artist is as the social conscience of his people. In interviews, he is always keen to stress the independence and integrity of the artist,[93] who he believes must act as the upholder of truth and justice, especially when such values are being swept aside by society. The heroes and heroines of his work embody this spirit of resistance (in the case of the story *White Genesis*, which will be examined in the next chapter, the hero is a *griot*, a storyteller who dares to tell the truth to the hypocritical leaders of his village). This willingness to speak out on sensitive subjects and to challenge the dominant discourses of his society is clearly seen in the closing section of *Man is Culture*:

> Perhaps you would have preferred that I speak to you of the Negro-African ethic, aesthetic, morality, folklore. If that is what you expected, I humbly ask you to forgive me for the disappointment that I have caused you.
>
> I only wished, as a foreigner passing through your city, to speak to you openly and honestly of the problems and preoccupations of my people, without begging for your friendship, and without solliciting your pity. (*MC*, p. 12)

[90] Ian Clegg, 'Workers and Managers in Algeria', in *Peasants and Proletarians: The Struggles of Third World Workers*, ed. by Robin Cohen, Peter C. W. Gutkind, and Phyllis Brazier (London: Hutchinson, 1979), p. 239.

[91] For a criticism of Miller's attack on Fanonian discourse, see Lazarus's essay, 'Disavowing Decolonisation'.

[92] Lazarus, *Resistance in Postcolonial African Fiction*, p. 33.

[93] For an example of this, see Kane et al., 'Comme un aveugle qui retrouve la vue', p. 7.

Dismissing the discourse of African authenticity, and refusing African dependency on the West for the solutions to its problems, Sembene makes the examination of contemporary African society (as well as the history that went into its making) the central concern of his work. As he has put it elsewhere: 'L'Europe est la périphérie de l'Afrique: je dis que l'Afrique est le centre du monde.' ['Europe is peripheral to Africa: for me, Africa is the centre of the world'][94]

The social function of narrative has been a commonplace theme in many recent literary studies. In particular, the parallel rise of both novel and nation in Europe, as well as the manner in which each feeds off the other, is a phenomenon that has been well documented by contemporary cultural critics (most notably the American Marxist Fredric Jameson in *The Political Unconscious: Narrative as a Socially Symbolic Act*).[95] Tim Brennan has argued that 'nations [...] are imaginary constructs that depend for their existence on an apparatus of cultural fictions in which imaginative literature plays a decisive role. And the rise of European nationalism coincides especially with one form of literature – the novel'.[96] One can also see these processes at work in the narratives being created by certain writers from the postcolonial world. However, all writers do not participate in the elaboration of the 'national narrative', and the oppositional writer seeks to develop a counter-narrative that challenges the authority of the 'national narrative'.[97] Homi K. Bhabha has described this process in the following terms: 'Counter-narratives of the nation that continually evoke and erase its totalising boundaries – both actual and conceptual – disturb those ideological manœuvres through which "imagined communities" are given essentialist identities.'[98]

An interesting example of this struggle between 'official' and oppositional narratives can be seen in the case of Bara Diouf's criticism of Sembene's 1968 film, *Le Mandat* (examined in Chapter Three). Writing in *Dakar-Matin* (later to become *Le Soleil*), the 'official' newspaper of the ruling Senegalese Socialist party (then known as the Union Progressiste Sénégalaise), Diouf initially praises Sembene as the '*romancier-cinéaste des petites gens et des déshérités*' ['novelist-filmmaker of the poor and the destitute'].[99] However, he goes on to criticise what he sees as the film's pessimism, which Diouf interprets as an attack on the very process of nation-building:

Il faut qu'Ousmane Sembène se dégage des morales européennes /i.e. le pessimisme moral/ pour adopter la véritable idéologie de pays sous-développé. Nous avons opté pour une morale ouverte qui

[94] Ibid., p. 7. Christopher L. Miller seems to be making a similar claim when he calls for Eurocentrism to be replaced with Afrocentrism (*Theories of Africans*, p. 3). However, Sembene is merely declaring Africa to be the main focus of his attention, not advocating a critical approach to Africa which prioritises 'ethnic' African considerations.

[95] Fredric Jameson, *The Political Unconscious: Narrative as a Socially Symbolic Act* (London: Methuen, 1981).

[96] Brennan, 'The National Longing for Form', p. 49.

[97] It is important to remember that the different sectors of the nation that play a part in the making of the 'national narrative' do not always exist in perfect harmony with one another. For an examination of the tensions between Islam and the Senegalese state, see Villalón, chapter 1, 'Islam in the Politics of State-Society Relations', in *Islamic Society and State Power*, pp. 15–38.

[98] Bhabha, 'DissemiNation', p. 300.

[99] Bara Diouf, '*Le Mandat*, film d'Ousmane Sembène', *Dakar-Matin*, 7 December 1968, p. 1.

intègre nos valeurs négro-africaines et qui participe d'un esprit d'optimisme. Telle est la démarche positive qui nous permet de bâtir une Nation moderne, fondée sur la synthèse dynamique de nos valeurs propres et des valeurs euro-américaines qui sont: la méthode, l'organisation, le travail. Le néo-réalisme sénégalais doit certes dépeindre toutes les fausses valeurs mais chercher également à enrichir ce que nous ne devons pas sacrifier sur le chemin de notre Révolution.[100]

Ousmane Sembène must free himself from European morality [i.e. moral pessimism] in order to adopt the true ideology of an underdeveloped nation. We have chosen an outward-looking morality which expresses our black African values and which expresses a spirit of optimism. It is this approach which allows us to construct a modern nation, based on a dynamic synthesis of our own values and Euro-American values which are: method, organisation, work. Of course, Senegalese neo-realism must depict all the false values within society but it must also seek to enrich those values which we cannot afford to lose on the path towards our Revolution.

Even if one were to accept Diouf's claim that the film's depiction of a society struggling under the double burdens of poverty and corruption is pessimistic (which I do not), it is hard to see what is specifically European about such a point of view. Diouf goes on to argue rather confusedly that the 'true' ideology of an underdeveloped nation is a faith in black-African values, accompanied by a healthy dose of optimism (which must count as one of the more eccentric definitions of ideology). Effectively, what Diouf terms as optimism seems to be a faith in capitalism, the sole problem for 'traditional' society being its integration into the capitalist world system (the *sine qua non* for the establishment of the modern nation), his call for the upholding of certain African values being merely a nod towards the empty rhetoric of Negritude.[101]

However, Sembene does not set up a strict opposition between tradition and modernity in *Le Mandat*. Rather, the film deals with the detrimental effects of the modern capitalist economy on the African community. Ibrahima Dieng, the central character of the film, is just one of the many unemployed trapped in the growing urban sprawl of Dakar. Sembene's argument is that the traditional structures of African society are being torn apart by the capitalist system, and that greed and suspicion are replacing the old, communitarian values. What Diouf declares to be 'our Revolution', Sembene would deem to be the attempt by a neo-colonial elite to preserve its privileged status as middle-men for Western companies.[102]

The bottom line in Diouf's criticism of Sembene is that he does not follow

[100] Ibid., p. 8. The attempt by 'official' narratives to defuse the more problematic elements of oppositional narratives is given a rather comic illustration on the front page of the 1 December edition of *Dakar-Matin* which features a photograph taken at the premiere of *Le Mandat* at the Théâtre National Daniel Sorano in Dakar. The caption claims that the picture shows Sembene in the company of the then Senegalese president, Léopold Sédar Senghor. The message would appear to be that, despite all his criticisms, Sembene remains the friend of the Socialist government. However, in reality, Sembene's support for the government is as illusory as his presence in the photograph where he is notable by his absence.

[101] See Sembene's attack on the African Socialism of the Senghorian regime in his novel, *The Last of the Empire*, trans. by Adrian Adams (London: Heinemann, 1983). This novel will be examined in Chapter Seven.

[102] See Sembene's attack on the African bourgeoisie in his novel, *Xala*, trans. by Clive Wake (London: Heinemann, 1976). The film version of *Xala* will be examined in Chapter Four.

the 'official' party line. Within years of independence, in all too many African states, the newly independent nation had been taken over by *the* national party which banned all opposition parties and declared itself the simple executor of the nation's will. The Senegal of the late 1960s, if somewhat more liberal than many other African states, was sadly no exception to this general rule. The ruling party's need to consolidate its hold on power was all the greater at this particular period following the wave of social protest which had gripped the country in May 1968. In such a context, the voice of the oppositional artist becomes all the more important. The narrative created by the oppositional artist provides an alternative vision to the one provided by the national party, and its leader, the Father of the Nation (with the added irony for Sembene of the head of state of Senegal also being the poet of Negritude). Sembene's films and novels thus play a vital role in the creation of a discourse of resistance that challenges the dominant discourses of his society and their claims to legitimacy. The Anglo-Indian writer, Salman Rushdie, has written of the power of fiction to imagine alternative realities to those proposed by the state:

> Redescribing a world is the necessary first step to changing it. And particularly at times when the State takes reality into its own hands, and sets about distorting it, altering the past to fit its present needs, then the making of the alternative realities of art, including the novel of memory, becomes politicised [...]. Writers and politicians are natural rivals. Both groups try to make the world in their own images; they fight for the same territory. And the novel is one way of denying the official, politicians' version of truth.[103]

Sembene sets about 'redescribing' Africa, challenging the dominant discourses of the state, Islam, patriarchal society, ethnicity. In its place, he proposes a radical Africa, resistant to all forms of injustice and domination. He does not claim that his Africa is more 'authentic' than the one portrayed by others. What he does claim is that his Africa is the Africa of those who are oppressed yet defiant.

The work of the French historian, Michel Foucault, has been at the heart of much contemporary reflection on the question of representation, particularly within the field of postcolonialism. Foucault was fascinated by the relationship between power and knowledge, and his work constantly seeks to examine the ways in which 'discursive practices' create and then exclude and marginalise their 'other'. In *Madness and Civilization: A History of Insanity in the Age of Reason*, he analysed the processes by which madness gradually became attributed with a whole range of negative moral values in the 'classical age' of the eighteenth century. For Foucault, the imprisonment of the insane marked the moment when this social group became the 'other' of 'rational society':

> in the history of unreason, [confinement] marked a decisive event: the moment when madness was perceived on the social horizon of poverty, of incapacity for

---

[103] Salman Rushdie, *Imaginary Homelands: Essays and Criticism 1981–1991* (London: Granta, 1991) p.14. Dominic Thomas analyses 'official' and 'unofficial' narratives from the Congo in his essay, 'Aesthetics and Ideology: The Performance of Nationalism in Recent Literary Productions from the Republic of the Congo', in *Black Accents: Writing in French from Africa, Mauritius and the Caribbean*, ed. by J. P. Little and Roger Little (London: Grant & Cutler, 1997), pp. 123–38.

work, of inability to integrate with the group; the moment when madness began to rank among the problems of the city. The new meanings assigned to poverty, the importance given to the obligation to work, and all the ethical values that are linked to labor, ultimately determined the experience of madness and inflected its course.[104]

Foucault's analysis thus provide a useful framework in which to examine the process of discourse formation, and the ways in which dominant social groups establish their hegemony. However, despite the deeply enabling aspects of his analysis, I would agree with Frank Lentricchia's assessment that, essentially, Foucault's vision of power is both 'metaphysically general and eternally repressive'.[105] Inspired by Nietzsche's ideas on history, Foucault came to see all knowledge as implicated in a process of violence and domination:

> The historical analysis of this rancorous will to knowledge [*vouloir-savoir* in French] reveals that all knowledge rests upon injustice (that there is no right, not even in the act of knowing, to truth or a foundation for truth) and that the instinct for knowledge is malicious (something murderous, opposed to the happiness of mankind).[106]

In his deeply anti-humanist project, Foucault replaces a positivist history of human progress with the nihilistic vision of mankind engaged in a violent combat between oppressors and victims: one may resist power but the overthrow of one system of domination will merely give rise to another.

This study will refuse such a nihilistic approach to the relationship between power and knowledge, arguing instead that it is, in fact, possible to resist the hegemony of social discourses. Although one must not neglect the ability of such discourses to 'co-opt' voices of resistance,[107] to use them as examples of their openness and willingness to allow dissent, this should not be allowed to hide the very real resistance which dominant forces are often obliged to face. It is therefore the aim of this study to chart Sembene's vision of a radical Africa, examining the ways in which his work, both literary and cinematic, disputes the authority of dominant discourses, imagining alternative strategies of resistance. I also aim to show that this desire to create counter-narratives of resistance is not only reflected in Sembene's choice of subject-matter but lies at the heart of a self-conscious reflection in his work on the notions of silence and power, and nowhere is this process more clearly seen in his work than in the collection of short stories, *Tribal Scars*, and the novella, *White Genesis*, to which I shall turn in the next chapter.

---

[104] Michel Foucault, *Madness and Civilization: a History of Insanity in the Age of Reason*, trans. by Richard Howard (London: Routledge, 1989), p. 64. Foucault sets out the most comprehensive overview of his philosophy of history in *The Archaeology of Knowledge*, trans. by A. M. Sheridan Smith (London: Tavistock, 1972).

[105] Frank Lentricchia, 'Foucault's Legacy: A New Historicism?', in *The New Historicism*, ed. by H. Aram Veeser (London: Routledge, 1989), p. 240.

[106] Michel Foucault, 'Nietzsche, Genealogy, History', in *Language, Counter-Memory, Practice: Selected Essays and Interviews*, ed by Donald F. Bouchard, trans. by Donald F. Bouchard and Sherry Simon (Oxford: Basil Blackwell, 1977), p. 163.

[107] Gerald Graff addresses this issue in his article, 'Co-optation', in Veeser, *The New Historicism*, pp. 168–81.

2

The Teller & the Tale

Writing Alternative Histories in
Tribal Scars & White Genesis[1]

There has been a consensus amongst the majority of Sembene's critics that his work, both cinematic and literary, is primarily of interest because of its concern for social issues. This study has no intention of detracting from the force of Sembene's social critique, nor does it seek to conceal his long-standing Marxist values. However, to portray Sembene as a politically engaged social realist with little or no interest in form is to deny much of the force and complexity of his work. I would argue, along with critics such as Mbye Boubacar Cham, that Sembene is an artist who is keenly aware of the dynamics of art and culture, combining traditional African techniques of storytelling with the eye for detail, and the political awareness, of the social realist writer:

> It is this sense of dynamism that enables Sembene to blend the indigenous and the non-indigenous, the traditional and the contemporary, in ways that rejuvenate and push both into relatively new areas of artistic experience while at the same time effectively conveying the basic Sembenian ideal of social, political, and economic justice and freedom.[2]

---

[1] The section of this chapter on *Tribal Scars* has already appeared in a slightly different form, under the title of 'The "architecture secrète" of *Voltaïque*', in J. P. Little and Roger Little, eds, *Black Accents: Writing in French from Africa, Mauritius and the Caribbean* (London: Grant & Cutler, 1997), pp. 157–69. The section on *White Genesis* appears under the title of 'Writing a History of Resistance: Sembene's Conception of the *Griot* in *Véhi-Ciosane*', in the *ASCALF Yearbook*, 3 (1998), pp. 34–42.

[2] Mbye Boubacar Cham, 'Ousmane Sembene and the Aesthetics of African Oral Traditions', *Africana Journal*, 13, 1–4 (1982), p. 38. A number of critics have convincingly argued that Sembene's major epic novel, *God's Bits of Wood*, which is generally considered to be a standard piece of social realism, does, in fact, contain borrowings from the African epic tradition. See Eileen Julien's 'The Democratization of Epic: *Les Bouts de bois de Dieu*', in her *African Novels and the Question of Orality* (Bloomington: Indiana University Press, 1992), pp. 68–84, and Roger Chemain, *L'Imaginaire dans le roman africain* (Paris: L'Harmattan, 1986), pp. 161–4. The Senegalese critic, Alioune Tine, has written a lot on the subject of the 'Africanisation' of Sembene's

Tribal Scars & White Genesis

One of the possible reasons for the critics' insistence on Sembene's social commitment is the fact that most criticism of his literature has focused on the epic and heroic narratives of a number of his early novels. In fact, the early years of Sembene's literary career saw a rapid development and transformation of his style. His first two novels, *Black Docker* (1956) and *O Pays, mon beau peuple!* (1957) were both centred around an individual hero.[3] However, in *God's Bits of Wood* (1960) and *L'Harmattan* (1963), Sembene 'decentred' his work, casting the community, through multiple narratives, as the hero of his novels (although published after *Tribal Scars*, it would appear that Sembene had begun work on *L'Harmattan* as early as 1958).[4]

Sembene was to abandon the grand narratives of these novels in his later works, turning to the novella as his preferred form, adopting a more self-aware, elliptical and ironic style. This chapter will therefore examine the textual strategies used by Sembene in two of his shorter works which have received relatively little critical attention: the collection of short stories, *Tribal Scars* (1962), and the novella, *White Genesis* (1966). In *Tribal Scars*, the whole practice of storytelling is problematised while, in *White Genesis*, it is the role of the storyteller, or *griot*, which is questioned. It will be argued that these works, with their problematisation of the notions of silence/discourse and absence/presence, are paradigmatic of Sembene's literary approach in the period since independence.

Tribal Scars has become one of the canonical texts of African literature. However, it has received a negligible amount of critical attention, and those critics who do discuss the collection have largely confined themselves to an enumeration of the social and political questions addressed by Sembene in his stories.[5] Accordingly, very little consideration has been given to the structure

---

[2] (cont.) literature. His doctoral thesis, 'Étude pragmatique et sémiotique des effets du bilinguisme dans les œuvres romanesques de Ousmane Sembene' (unpublished doctoral thesis, Université de Lyon 2, 1981), is probably the most comprehensive study of this aspect of Sembene's work. See also his article, 'La diglossie linguistique et la diglossie littéraire et leurs effets dans la pratique esthétique d'Ousmane Sembène', in Sada Niang, ed., *Littérature et cinéma en Afrique francophone: Ousmane Sembène et Assia Djebar* (Paris: L'Harmattan, 1996), pp. 82–97. Locha Mateso provides a fascinating study of the issues surrounding the 'orality' of African literature in 'Critique littéraire et ressources de l'oralité', *L'Afrique littéraire et artistique*, 50 (1978), pp. 64–8.

[3] As many critics have argued, there are close parallels between the story of *O Pays, mon beau peuple!* and that of Jacques Roumain's *Gouverneurs de la rosée* (1946; Paris: Editions Messidor, 1992). See especially Victor O. Aire, 'Affinités électives ou imitation? *Gouverneurs de la rosée* et *O Pays, mon beau peuple!*', *Présence Francophone*, 15 (Autumn 1977), pp. 3–10.

[4] Sembene claims to have begun work on *L'Harmattan* 'au moment même du référendum' ['at the time of the referendum']. See Ibrahima Ndiaye, 'La Critique sociale dans l'œuvre littéraire d'Ousmane Sembène' (unpublished master's thesis, Université de Dakar, 1974–5), p. 117.

[5] See, for example, Y.S. Boafo's '*Voltaïque* d'Ousmane Sembène: commentaires et observations', *Présence Francophone*, 15 (Autumn 1977), pp. 11–30, and Daniel Vignal's 'Le Noir et le Blanc dans *Voltaïque* de O. Sembène', *Peuples Noirs/Peuples Africains*, 6, 36 (November–December 1983), pp. 96–115. *Tribal Scars* is virtually ignored in the only full-length study of Sembene's literature, Martin Bestman's *Sembène Ousmane et l'esthétique du roman négro-africain* (Sherbrooke, Québec: Editions Naaman, 1981). Joseph Mbelolo Ya Mpiku declares that the collection marks a real refinement of Sembene's style but devotes only half a page to the work in his sixteen-page essay on Sembene's work. See Joseph Mbelolo Ya Mpiku, 'Un romancier né ex-nihilo', *Présence Francophone*, 1 (Autumn 1970), pp. 174–90.

41

of a collection that I believe ranks as one of Sembene's most complex and experimental works. In examining the 'architecture secrète' of *Tribal Scars* (to borrow Barbey d'Aurevilly's famous comment on Baudelaire's work),[6] I intend to show how the structure of the collection is used to serve Sembene's political aims in investigating the society of independent Senegal, and also to invite the reader of Sembene's work to discover a complexity and self-awareness in his writing that the tag of 'realist writer' has tended to obscure.

Tribal Scars marks a turning point in Sembene's work. Both of his two previous novels, *O Pays, mon beau peuple!* and *God's Bits of Wood*, are infused with the optimism of the independence movement (his earliest novel, *Black Docker*, deals with the African community in Marseilles). They are affirmations of Sembene's belief in the revolutionary potential of the dispossessed in African society to overthrow colonial rule and create just and modern societies. However, despite the moments of resistance and subversiveness that punctuate all the stories in the collection, *Tribal Scars*, which was published in 1962, two years after Senegalese independence, is a far more disillusioned work. Rather than the enfranchising of the dispossessed, independence, in Sembene's view, is seen to have led to the repressive hegemony of the bourgeoisie and the social domination of a stifling, patriarchal Islam.

As was argued in the previous chapter, for a radical writer such as Sembene, independence was not an end in itself. Sharing the Marxist vision of Frantz Fanon, Sembene saw the struggle against imperialism as the first step on the road to a radical restructuring of African society. However, this radical view of the African nationalist movements was proven to be greatly mistaken. After independence, these mass movements, which Fanon and Sembene had hoped would lead to social revolution, soon disintegrated. 'The people' retreated from the political sphere into their 'traditional' way of life and political power was appropriated by the African bourgeoisie.

The disappointment with political developments displayed by Sembene throughout *Tribal Scars* can also be read on a personal level. Sembene had left Senegal in 1948 to live in France, and his early works on Africa were all written from the distance of Europe, giving them, if not a romanticised, then a somewhat optimistic view of the situation in Africa. That is not to deny the powerful realism of his narrative but it could be argued that this protracted absence from his home country, wedded to the optimism of the independence movement, creates a picture of Senegalese society that smoothes over too many vexing problems. For example, the collaboration of El Hadji Mabigué with the colonial authorities in *God's Bits of Wood* and the arrogance and vanity of Oumar Faye's father, the *imam*, in *O Pays, mon beau peuple!* are minor elements in the narrative. However, in the short stories of *Tribal Scars*, many of which appear to have been written during or after Sembene's first trip to Africa in

---

[6] In a letter to Vigny, Baudelaire wrote of *Les Fleurs du Mal* in terms that I think are equally applicable to *Voltaïque*: '*Le seul éloge que je sollicite pour ce livre est qu'on reconnaisse qu'il n'est pas un pur album et qu'il a un début et une fin*' ['the only praise I desire for this book is that it be recognised as having a beginning and an end, and that it is more than a mere album']. Quoted in J.-C. Mathieu, *Les Fleurs du Mal de Baudelaire* (Paris: Classiques Hachette, 1972), p. 49.

over twelve years, in 1960,[7] we are given a much more wide-ranging critique of the role of Islam in Senegalese society, as though the reality of life in Senegal had suddenly been brought home to the writer (see, in particular, the stories, 'The Community', 'The False Prophet' and 'The *Bilal*'s Fourth Wife').

The shift from colonial to postcolonial writing can also be seen in Sembene's use of the short story (a form he had not previously used). The transposition of folk tales into French had been a logical step for the Negritude movement in its attempt to validate African culture, and writers such as Bernard Binlin Dadié and Birago Diop had shown themselves to be great exponents of this form. These tales usually contained examples of traditional wisdom and dealt with issues of morality, often meeting with fantastic episodes along the way.[8] The tales also worked as an expression of the African sense of community with the voice of the narrator often imitating the style of the *griot*, talking directly to the reader, in an attempt to recreate the effect of the direct contact between storyteller and listener in traditional African society.

However, *Tribal Scars* and later collections of short stories, such as Henri Lopes's *Tribaliques*,[9] stand in stark contrast to the earlier folk tales of Dadié and Diop.[10] There is the same economy of means, the same sense of structure and form, a continuing concern with morality, but post-independence stories contain a much greater degree of realism. Mbye Boubacar Cham has described the manner in which Sembene's stories both borrow, and deviate, from the norms of the African folk tale:

> Whereas the traditional oral narrative tends to move linearly toward a resolution in which social order and harmony, disrupted at the beginning, are restored, and reaffirmed, the linear movement of Sembene's narrative ends, for the most part, in a resolution that points to a challenge to, a rejection of, or a struggle against the established social and political order.[11]

This is a far remove from the drama and the highly imaginative dimension of the traditional folk tale. In this realistic world, moral good, of course, does not invariably triumph. Where there was once high drama, all that can be summoned up now is pathos and irony, although these elements are still accompanied by a lingering sense of resistance.

The critic Mary N. Layoun has written that 'the irony of Sembène's texts is distinguished by its structural attempt to allow or gesture to a text/nation/culture that is multivocal'.[12] By taking on the voices of those who are excluded

---

[7] For a brief account of this period in Sembene's life, see Paulin Soumanou Vieyra's *Sembène Ousmane, cinéaste* (Paris: Présence Africaine, 1972), pp. 9–25.

[8] See Dadié's Kacou Ananze stories in *Le Pagne noir* (Paris: Présence Africaine, 1955), and Birago Diop's *Tales of Amadou Koumba*, trans. by Dorothy S. Blair (London: Longman, 1985).

[9] Henri Lopes, *Tribaliques*, trans. by Andrea Leskes (London: Heinemann, 1987).

[10] For a discussion of more recent developments in French-language African fiction, see Clive Wake, 'Negritude and after: changing perspectives in French-language African fiction', *Third World Quarterly*, 10, 2 (April 1988), pp. 961–5.

[11] Cham, 'Ousmane Sembene and the Aesthetics of Oral Traditions', p. 27.

[12] See Mary N. Layoun, 'Fictional Formations and Deformations of National Culture', *South Atlantic Quarterly*, 87, 1 (Winter 1988), p. 60.

or marginalised by society, Sembene's ironic tales of independent Senegal, and his radical representations of the African past in *Tribal Scars*, create a fictional society that is far more democratic than the one that actually exists. The stories are open-ended and invite the reader to interpret them, to fill in the gaps and make connections, to make up his/her own mind.

This playfulness and ambiguity are exemplified by the opening story, 'In the Face of History', which is entitled 'Devant l'histoire' in the French version (the order of the stories in the French version has been completely ignored in the English version). In French, 'histoire' means both 'history' ('Histoire') and 'story' ('histoire'), and this deliberate ambiguity in the title of the story hints at Sembene's highly self-conscious style and immediately involves the reader in the process of deciphering and coming to terms with the ambiguities of the text. The story itself appears rather unremarkable. Three men stand outside a cinema and debate whether they should see the film that is showing. While they are making up their minds, a married couple, known to one of the three men, arrive and get into an argument over whether they too should see the film.

What is the reader to make of such a story? If one starts with the obvious, the story is one of a series of disagreements over the merits (or lack of them) of 'Samson and Delilah. An historical film'.[13] This places us firmly in the realm of culture. The three men cannot decide whether to see the film (a Western art form) or go to see the 'Toucoleur *kora*-player' (a native art form). Equally, the bourgeois married couple are divided on whether to see the film or go to the 'African ballet' (a mixed form of African dance and Western ballet) which found many enthusiasts amongst the supporters of Negritude, most notably Senghor himself. One can imagine that, for this reason alone, Sembene would have perceived the 'African ballet' as a piece of exoticism designed principally for the Western tourist.[14] While that group debate, a well-dressed man, accompanied by his two wives and five children, turn up and do not appear to care what film is being shown. One of the wives merely expresses a desire to see something with a lot of singing and dancing, and her husband's response that the cinema shows only Arab and Indian films would indicate that her desires will be met.[15]

In describing these different cultural attitudes, Sembene reveals his own set of artistic concerns, his constant attempt in his work to get at the underlying

---

[13] See Ousmane Sembene, *Tribal Scars*, trans. by Len Ortzen (London: Heinemann, 1974), p. 21. Further references to this book (hereafter referred to as *TS*) will be given in the body of the text.

[14] The 'ballet africain' was founded by the Guinean poet, Fodeba Keïta. Christopher L. Miller cites Keïta's execution at the hands of Sékou Touré's regime as part of his attack on Fanon. See Christopher L. Miller, *Theories of Africans: Francophone Literature and Anthropology in Africa* (Chicago and London: University of Chicago Press, 1990), pp. 50–67.

[15] Egyptian and Indian films (often referred to as 'films hindous') were very popular in Senegal in the 1960s. Indian films have retained their popularity to this day while Egyptian films appear to have been superseded by the Kung-Fu action films of Hong Kong. Pierre Haffner analyses the popular African taste for such films in his *Essai sur les fondements du cinéma africain* (Dakar: Nouvelles Editions Africaines, 1978). For a discussion of the melodramatic and epic styles used in Indian cinema, see Philippe Parrain, *Regards sur le cinéma africain* (Paris: Le Cerf, 1969; 7e art, no. 48). The issue of cinema in Africa will be examined more fully in Chapter Three.

social and political factors which have formed his society's culture. This desire to link cultural and social issues is obvious from the very first sentence. One of the three men declares to his friends: 'If you see that film, you'll never in your life be able to trust a woman again' (*TS*, p. 18). This is, in effect, all we ever find out about the film but then, of course, when we are told its name, the above reference to trust and male-female conflict (Delilah being the archetypal female betrayer) becomes much clearer.

When the couple, Abdoulaye and Sakinétou, arrive, we are treated to our very own, on-screen (so to speak) battle of the sexes. The three men watch on, following the couple's argument as closely as if they were actually watching a film. When one of them asks what the row was all about, another replies: 'They've lost their sense of balance.' The third man then philosophically claims: 'Just like the country. No balance left' (*TS*, p. 21). The rather comic disagreement and bickering that we see throughout the story is now said to be part of a nationwide malaise; a national, cultural and political uncertainty. In the context of the story, the characters are asked which story or which culture they wish to choose and the result is hesitation and conflict. The educated, French-speaking Abdoulaye and Sakinétou provide us with the first of many male/female conflicts in the book. The three men, one of whom grew up with Abdoulaye, and who is incidentally ignored by the couple (perhaps because he is from a lower class than them, as we are led to suspect), seem listless and cannot make up their minds. In fact, the only person who seems content with his evening out is the well-dressed man who does not care what film he sees. Having two wives and being able to bring them both to the cinema, as well as his five children, indicates that he is a man of means. He is one of the people who have succeeded in this society and he is, consequently, quite content with his lot. Thus, from the start of the collection, we are thrust into a society at a crossroads, in conflict with itself and highly uncertain of the direction in which it is heading. In an ironic final comment the narrator describes the three men walking away, whistling the air to *Soundiata*. The world of epic and its mythical view of the African past literally recede into the distance as the contemporary clash of opposing voices within African society is given voice by Sembene in these stories. The question of culture, enclosed by Negritude within a polarisation between Africa and the West, is here seen to cover a whole range of social issues, most notably those of class and gender.

The final story of the collection is also concerned with the issue of culture, focusing on the vexed question of interpreting African history and traditions.[16] The central question posed by the story is about the source of the tradition of scarification. The young men to whom the question is put by the serious and phlegmatic Saer (the 'Voltaïque' of the story's title) begin to ponder the source and meaning of their society's customs at a very important moment in their

---

[16] For a detailed discussion of the conflict between history and ethnography in 'Tribal Scars or The Voltaïque', see Denise Brahimi's essay, 'L'Anthropologie factice de Sembene Ousmane dans "Le Voltaïque"', in *Images de l'africain de l'antiquité au vingtième siècle*, ed. by Daniel Droixhe and Klaus Kiefer (Frankfurt: Peter Lang, 1987), pp. 203–9.

history. Previously, their discussions had revolved around contemporary politics, such as the break-up of the Mali Federation in August 1960, and the events taking place in the ex-Belgian Congo at roughly the same time. However, this questioning of their own past, of the visible signs on the faces of their fellow Africans, takes on a tremendous importance for them. The narrator remarks that these discussions were so vital to them that 'to hear us, anyone would have thought that the future of the whole continent of Africa was at stake' (*TS*, p. 102). This turns out to be a highly ironic comment as the story will later link the origin of scarification to the whole of Africa, and to the violent events of its history.

It is significant that Sembene writes a story about African history, more particularly about the era of the slave trade, which tells of a conflict between Africans and which is set on African soil. Saer dismisses the interpretations of the young men who turn to the racial and mythical arguments of the colonial ethnographer, which had been so heavily implicated in the colonial project.[17] In Saer's tale, scarification is a practice born from the violence of African history, marks inflicted by an African father on his daughter to save her from black slave-traders. Basically, we are told, Africans have scars because 'they refused to be slaves' (*TS*, p. 116). If we move the context to the Africa of 1962, Sembene's message would seem to be that independence does not simply mean the overthrowing of colonial power but also the overthrowing of social injustice within African society itself.

The critic, Denise Brahimi, has argued that Sembene is attempting, in the title story, to write an African history lived and made by Africans, and not simply blaming the European or using his ethnography to explain Africa's past.[18] Amoo's village is not portrayed as the last remaining vestige of a great African civilisation. In stark, realistic terms, Sembene describes the tragic situation of peasants unable to escape (until Amoo's stroke of genius) from the clutches of the slave trade. These simple people, after Amoo's actions, carry their painful history etched on their faces. In a highly ironic moment, Amoo ponders on the reason why the whites are taking away the slaves, and voices the once common belief that the whites were using the slaves' skin to make boots.[19] The ignorance of the colonial ethnographer's versions of African customs and practices is here returned to the sender. Sembene's story is thus an invitation to Africans to look at their customs and society historically.[20]

---

[17] For an examination of anthropology's role in the colonial project, see Gérard Leclerc, *Anthropologie et colonialisme* (Paris: Fayard, 1972), and Jean Copans, ed., *Anthropologie et impérialisme* (Paris: Maspéro, 1975).

[18] Brahimi, 'L'Anthropologie factice de Sembene Ousmane', p. 205.

[19] For an interesting discussion of African beliefs about the European during the slave trade and the later European exploration of Africa, see Frank McLynn, chapter 15, 'Reputation and Impact', in *Hearts of Darkness: the European Exploration of Africa* (London: Pimlico, 1992).

[20] Borrowing from the work of the black British sociologist, Paul Gilroy, Andy Stafford has argued that 'Tribal Scars or The Voltaique' is a story that examines African history in terms of its 'modernity' rather than as the repetition of a 'traditional' past. See Andy Stafford, '"The Black Atlantic": History, Modernity and Conflict in Sembène Ousmane's "Le Voltaïque"', *ASCALF Yearbook*, 3 (1998), pp. 63–9. See also Paul Gilroy, *The Black Atlantic: Modernity and Double Consciousness* (London and New York: Verso, 1993).

However, Sembene's story is not historical fact. It denies the myths of the ethnographer but presents us with an account of African history that is highly contentious. Sembene himself is well aware of this.[21] In the French version, the narrator of the story finishes with the question, 'Readers, what do you think?' (for some inexplicable reason, the English translator has omitted this crucial line entirely) (*TS*, p. 116). This question is posed not simply at the end of the story but at the end of the entire collection. Therefore, this acts as a problematisation of the collection as a whole. In fact, I would argue that the opening story, 'In the Face of History', with its self-conscious reference to the notions of history and story-telling, and 'Tribal Scars or The Voltaique' with its deliberate invitation to the reader to question what has gone before, act as a framing device for the collection, what I have chosen to call its 'architecture secrète'. The stories in the collection offer competing versions of the same event, often contradicting one another. 'Official', dominant narratives are forced to make room for different interpretations, to allow other, marginalised voices to speak out. Sembene's main aim is to question the discourse of those dominant voices which the *ceddo*, the dispossessed (yet defiant) of African society encounter: the voices of the ruling political class, Islam, patriarchal society, and Eurocentrism (the image of the social category of the historical *ceddo* as they are portrayed in Sembene's film of the same name will be examined in Chapter Six). The irony within the texts thus acts to challenge these discourses, to question their claims to truth. In Sembene's aesthetic and political project, irony and resistance/subversion are seen to go hand in hand.

Sembene carries out this strategy of irony and resistance in relation to all the stories in the collection. Rather than discussing each of these tales, I would instead like to focus on the stories, 'Love in Sandy Lane' and 'The Promised Land', which, in dealing with the themes of political betrayal, and those of exile and the role of women respectively, serve to illustrate many of the thematic concerns of the collection as a whole. Furthermore, I would argue that their positioning within the collection, as second and penultimate stories respectively, serves to reinforce Sembene's framing structure.

'Love in Sandy Lane' is an allegorical tale that deals with the transfer of power into the hands of the African bourgeoisie after independence (this process is also examined in the story that follows it in both the French version and the English translation, 'A Matter of Conscience'). Sandy Lane is a

---

[21] Sembene is more than usually elusive on the source of his information concerning the practice of scarification. In *Man is Culture*, he claims that: 'Originally, scarification and facial markings were signs of the refusal to be deported, to be slaves' (p. 4). During a personal interview with Sembene in 1995, I asked him for further information on this subject and he merely replied that his understanding of the practice of scarification was based on his own personal research (see Appendix). Those references to scarification that I have managed to trace, in a non-exhaustive review of the anthropological material on the subject, interpret the phenomenon as an initiation rite. See Jean Girard, *Les Bassari du Sénégal* (Paris: L'Harmattan, 1984), p. 453. Tracing the origins of such rituals is notoriously difficult, and anthropology has often been accused of producing a static, ahistorical vision of African communities, seeing fixed, immutable patterns where historical processes are at work. Sembene chooses to give a radical interpretation to the practice of scarification, placing the practice within a history of resistance.

friendly street in Dakar where a strong sense of community seems to prevail. The young people, most of whom are unemployed, gather at the ironically titled 'United Nations' Palace', and, once a week, the women meet in order to sweep the street from one end to the other. In fact, Sembene uses the street as a symbol of an almost ideal community where people of highly diverse backgrounds have managed to form a bond for the good of all. The narrator, who clearly identifies with the community, calls the street 'the only one in the town to have such diverse and yet united characters living in it' (*TS*, p. 24).

However, from the very beginning of the story, we are made aware by the narrator of the underlying tensions that exist between the community and El Hadj Mar, an ex-colonial employee who lives in a villa that overlooks and dominates the street, and that acts as a visual reminder of the recent colonial past. El Hadj Mar keeps himself to himself, while still maintaining a watchful, almost prying eye on the people of the street, who refuse to include him as part of their community. Part of the unspoken quarrel seems to be due to the fact that the people of the street had voted 'no' in the 1958 referendum on whether Senegal should keep its contacts with France or effectively become independent, thus giving this rift between neighbours the obvious political dimension of the struggle against colonialism, and subsequently neo-colonialism.

An end to this silent conflict is promised when one of the young men from the street, Yoro, and Kine, the daughter of El Hadj Mar, fall in love. Nothing actually happens as such. The couple do not speak to one another, nor do they ever touch. Their love is silent and is only expressed in fleeting glances or in the music which Yoro plays under his loved one's window. However, the possibility of union between the community and the wealthy El Hadj Mar, which is offered by the love of Yoro and Kine, is dashed by the forces of repression and domination. Top men from the government begin to call on El Hadj Mar and, soon after, Yoro, Kine and other people from the street simply disappear. The narrator does not explain this openly but leads us to suspect that the hand of El Hadj Mar and his government friends is behind it. Now that these nameless men in their big cars have taken control of the country, the young people begin to drift away from the street and the strong bond that held the community together is shown to have been sundered.

Instead of the silence of the young people's love, 'a funereal silence' (*TS*, p. 26) has now fallen over the street, as the people, despite their anger, silently accept the fate that has befallen them. The symbolism of the street's name, with its allusion to shifting sand, becomes abundantly clear as this idyllic community is scattered in the wind, like the sand of the street's surface. The silent love of Yoro and Kine had hinted at what could have been in this independent Senegal. However, instead of a renewed and united society, there is a turn towards neo-colonialism, and Sandy Lane is now said by the narrator to be 'the saddest place in the world' (*TS*, p. 25).

As will have become clear, Sembene is highly concerned with that which is not said, with the silences which surround the events of the story. At one point, the narrator states that the downfall of the people of the street was due to the fact that they did not 'confide in one another' (*TS*, p. 24). The bond between the people is presented by the narrator as something unspoken, as though their consideration for one another were the most natural thing in the world. Their innocence and naïveté lead them to believe that good will always triumph. The union of Kine and Yoro is favoured by a 'conspiratorial silence' on their part because, as the narrator tells us, 'they thought quite simply that if two people loved one another, nothing could be strong enough to stand in their way' (*TS*, p. 25). Sembene seems to be hinting that it is the very inability of the people to articulate, to express their wishes and desires, to protest, which causes them to allow themselves to be dispossessed and disenfranchised (El Hadj Mar too is silent but his is the silence of authority that needs no words to justify its political actions).

It is the narrator of the story who gives voice to their community, who fills in the silences. As the very first line of the story tells us, the street bears no plaque indicating its name. The name 'Sandy Lane' is given to it by the people: it is a name that does not 'officially' exist. The text itself is full of silences as the narrator leaves sentences unfinished, only hinting at the significance of events, expressing a personal sadness and weariness at the tragic fate of the community. By constructing a story around the notion of silence, Sembene is consciously drawing attention to his strategy, employed throughout the collection, of making heard the stories of those who lack the education, the social status or simply the nerve, to speak out, and by extension, questioning the authority of the dominant discourses of his society. Instead of the silence of repression and submission, Sembene encourages open debate and resistance.

The penultimate story (in the translation also), 'The Promised Land', and its companion piece, 'Longing', deal with the issue of emigration to France.[22] They tell the tale of a black maid, Diouana, who follows her white family to France, where she finds herself treated as though she were a slave (ironically, she leaves Senegal just as the country is about to gain self-government in 1958). The France she dreamed of was one which would bring her wealth and happiness. Instead, she is forced to work hard for very little pay (as is the case for most African emigrants), friends of the family see her as an exotic attraction, the children taunt her because of her colour, and her employer, Madame, has no concern for her welfare. Finally, seeing no way out of her situation, she commits suicide.

We are offered several different vantage points on Diouana's death. As the story begins, the police are just arriving at the house to investigate the death of a maid. They question Madame but she cannot see any reason why the maid would do such a thing. When the police suggest that the case might be a

[22] For a discussion of many of the issues involved in the current debate within postcolonialist theory on the questions of exile and emigration, see Homi K. Bhabha's essay, 'DissemiNation: Time, Narrative and the Margins of the Modern Nation' in *Nation and Narration*, ed. by Homi K. Babha (New York and London: Routledge, 1990), pp. 291–322. Aedín Ní Loingsigh deals with notions of exile in relation to two African writers in her article 'Exil et perceptions du temps dans *Le Bruit dort* de Mustapha Tlili et *Mirages de Paris* d'Ousmane Socé', *ASCALF Bulletin*, 16–17 (Spring/Summer 1998), pp. 3–21. Having lived in France for twelve years, Sembene was well aware of the problems facing Africans in Europe, and he examines the question of exile in his first novel, *Black Docker*.

murder, the retired colonel asks who would be interested in killing a negress. The only thing Madame can think of is that Diouana must have been homesick. It is at this point that the narrative takes us back to Africa and the circumstances which led up to Diouana's death. This new account of events, told basically from Diouana's point of view, serves to make us sympathetic towards her and highlights the blindness and stupidity of the earlier comments by both the colonel and Madame.

However, the story does not finish with this more complete account of Diouana's life and death. Instead, we are given two 'official' versions of events. The investigators simply conclude that it was a suicide and file the case, while the newspapers turn it into a *fait divers* on one of the inside pages, stating simply: 'At Antibes, a homesick black woman cut her throat' (*TS*, p. 99).[23] The poem, 'Longing', effectively acts as a response to these versions of Diouana's death. Sembene portrays Diouana as yet another victim of colonialism, as much a slave as those taken by force on the slave ships of the seventeenth century. She becomes a figure to whom all Africans should look. She is 'our sister', 'Goddess of the night', 'gleam of our coming dawns'. In effect, Diouana is a symbol for all that Africa lost under slavery and colonisation. The poem invites Africans to remember those losses and to strive even harder to create a new dawn for Africa. Diouana is now the mother of all Africans. That which was a banal piece of trivia to the coloniser becomes a glowing symbol to the colonised (the death of the Algerian, Chaiba, in the story of the same title is also seen as the symbol of a new dawn for Africa). In this poem, she is no longer the nameless maid of the story's French title, 'La Noire de' (with all its suggestions of anonymity and subjugation, of being someone's *black*). The name, Diouana, omitted by the newspapers and deformed by Madame's sister (she calls her 'Douna'), becomes a refrain for Sembene, a rallying cry to all Africans, returning their personal history to them and restoring the dignity that European arrogance and indifference would deny them. Instead of a European discourse that marginalises and belittles the African, Sembene offers a discourse of resistance, dignity and empowerment.

This defiance of European domination leads us back to the issue of independence and Sembene's disquiet at the nature of the independent African states that were evolving in the early 1960s (more particularly with the case of Senegalese society). The 'architecture secrète' of the collection calls into question the validity of dominant social discourses and highlights the set of priorities and biases involved in the construction of all 'Histoires'/'histoires'. In setting up conflicting versions of events and allowing marginalised voices to speak out and cast doubt on the dominant voices in African society, Sembene is actively seeking to be subversive both politically and in terms of his literature. Politics, religion, history, culture, Eurocentrism are all shown to be

---

[23] Similarly, in *Black Docker*, Sembene presents us with 'official' versions of Diaw Falla's 'murder' of the writer, Ginette Tontisane. The racist bias of the newspaper reports, the judicial system and the scientific establishment (in the person of the psychologist) is counterbalanced by Sembene's intervention on behalf of Diaw Falla, telling the story from his point of view.

open to question, to be both '*discutable et à discuter*' ['debatable and open for discussion'].[24]

The idea of an 'architecture secrète' is not meant to suggest that every story in the collection has a fixed position on which some comprehensive over-arching structure depends. Rather, this 'architecture secrète' gives the collection a beginning and an end, a framework in which to interpret the stories that lie in between. Once we have been alerted to Sembene's structural concern with silence and marginalisation, a story such as 'Letters from France' can be read in a more complex and interesting way. The loneliness of a Senegalese girl, Nafi, living an isolated life far from home in Marseilles, is seen to be reflected in the very form of the story which is told through Nafi's letters, written in secret to an unnamed friend back in Senegal. Nafi's story is literally both hidden and secretive, as those around her either do not want to, or cannot be allowed to, hear it. Sembene is allowing us to read a secret confession, a written cry for help (mirroring the intent behind many of the stories in the collection of giving voice to that which would otherwise have remained silent). Alternatively, the stories 'Her Three Days' and 'The *Bilal*'s Fourth Wife', which deal with women coming into conflict with a male-dominated Islamic society, can be read in the wider context of Sembene's desire to question the authority of the dominant discourses of his society, to question that which those in power wish to be silently accepted as truth.

Sembene's later works have continued to concern themselves structurally with the notion of silence, continuing his project of filling in the silences surrounding discourses of authority or speaking out for the dispossessed who have no voice. For example, his novel, *Xala*, relentlessly works at exposing that which the businessman, El Hadji Abdou Kader Bèye, would like to be kept quiet, and consequently reveals what Sembene sees as the hypocrisy, egotism and impotence of the African bourgeoisie.[25] On the other hand, the novella, *Niiwam*, tells the tale of a poor man whose story is necessarily silent as he takes a bus ride across Dakar, trying to hide from his fellow passengers that the bundle on his lap contains the body of his dead son.[26]

Sembene's concern with the question of form had been evident even in his flawed first novel, *Black Docker*, with its *mise en abyme* of an African writer in Marseilles whose first novel has been stolen by a white French writer. Sembene here draws attention to the struggle of the African writer to tell his own story, to carve out his own history, in the face of white oppression. This process of legitimising the voice of the African, both artistically and socially, is continued in Sembene's following two novels where the characters of Oumar Faye (*O Pays, mon beau peuple!*) and Ibrahima Bakayoko (*God's Bits of Wood*) speak out against the colonial regime and attempt to organise their fellow Africans in resistance against it. Written in the dying days of the colonial era, these early novels turn on the conflict between the coloniser and the colonised

---

[24] Claude Duneton and Jean-Pierre Pagliano, *Anti-manuel de français* (Paris: Seuil, 1978), p. 17.

[25] Ousmane Sembene, *Xala*, trans. by Clive Wake (London: Heinemann, 1976). The film version of *Xala* will be examined in Chapter Four.

[26] Ousmane Sembene, *Niiwam* and *Taaw* (London: Heinemann, 1992).

(while at the same time revealing some of the tensions within African society itself). In *O Pays, mon beau peuple!* and, more importantly, *God's Bits of Wood*, Sembene presents us with his vision of a modern, urban African society discovering the voice of resistance, and overthrowing colonial rule as a prelude to social revolution. The role of the African artist is once again problematised in *L'Harmattan* where the writer, Lèye, abandons poetry in favour of painting in order to be able to gain a more direct contact with the African masses.

However, writing after the demise of French rule in West Africa in *Tribal Scars*, Sembene focuses more clearly on the processes of exclusion and repression within African society itself. The 'black and white' resistance to colonialism is replaced by the portrayal of the more fragmented world of independent African society where the complex subjects of economic, social and religious conflict are fully explored. Forced into opposition by events after independence, Sembene alters his work accordingly, using a smaller canvas (perhaps, a reflection of the break-up of the mass movement which he had hoped would lead to social revolution), going beyond the naturalist/social realist models of Emile Zola and André Malraux which had become his stock in trade,[27] and writing in a far more sparse, ironic and self-conscious style, of which *Tribal Scars* is probably the most daring and accomplished example. *Tribal Scars* thus marks Sembene's entry into literary and political guerrilla warfare with the new regime in Senegal which, by a highly significant twist of fate, was led by Léopold Sédar Senghor, a man at the opposite pole to Sembene both politically and artistically. Marrying form and substance to meet his subversive and provocative ends, Sembene shows his rejection of both the artistic concerns of the Negritude movement and the politics of its chief practitioner (both of which he scathingly satirises in his novel, *The Last of the Empire*). Employing Aijaz Ahmad's terms, evoked at the beginning of the previous chapter, Sembene refuses the limited and limiting opposition between the West and Africa, focusing instead on the interactions between Africa and the West, and, more importantly, on the conflicts *within* African societies themselves. His problematisation of the interlinked notions of storytelling and history-writing in *Tribal Scars* serves to highlight the constructed nature of the dominant discourses within his society, in opposition to which he proposes his own radical, Marxist vision.

■ ■ ■

The problematisation of the whole notion of storytelling in *Tribal Scars* is taken a step further in the novella, *White Genesis*, in which Sembene questions the role of the African storyteller, or *griot*. The modern African writer is often compared to the traditional *griot*, with the purpose of such a comparison

---

[27] Although he has often been compared with both Zola and Malraux, the French writer whom Sembene has most often cited as a model and an inspiration is Roger Martin du Gard, who is best known for his series of novels, *Les Thibault*. Sembene perhaps most openly acknowledges his admiration for Martin du Gard's work in an interview with Mohamadou Kane. See Kane et al., 'Comme un aveugle qui retrouve la vue', *Le Soleil* [Dakar], 10 July 1981, p. 7.

usually being to link the contemporary African writer to a traditional form of African storytelling. As a result, the writer's work is given the stamp of that most problematic of concepts, 'authenticity'. For example, the well known Nigerian critic, Chinweizu, uses the image of the *griot* to posit an 'authentic' form of African storytelling in his anthology of African literatures, *Voices from twentieth-century Africa: griots and towncriers*, in which he declares that the *griot* acts as 'traditional Africa's academy of the humanities'.[28] However, as we shall discover below, the question of which memory and which history the *griot* preserves is far more problematical than Chinweizu's vision allows.[29]

Before turning to *White Genesis*, it would be useful to look at an oft-cited quotation from the 'avertissement de l'auteur' at the beginning of Sembene's novel, *L'Harmattan*, in which he sets out his vision of the role of the African writer, explicitly linking the modern novelist with the traditional storyteller:

> *Je ne fais pas la théorie du roman africain. Je me souviens pourtant que jadis, dans cette Afrique qui passe pour classique, le griot était non seulement l'élément dynamique de sa tribu, clan, village, mais aussi le témoin patent de chaque événement. C'est lui qui enregistrait, déposait devant tous, sous l'arbre du palabre, les faits et gestes de chacun. La conception de mon travail découle de cet enseignement: rester au plus près du réel et du peuple.*[30]

I don't theorise about the African novel. However, I remember that in the so-called classical Africa of the past, the griot was not only a dynamic figure in the tribe, clan, village, but also the chief witness to every major event. It was he who recorded and who, under the palaver tree, recited events and acts before the entire community. My conception of my work is rooted in this teaching: one must remain as close as possible to reality and to the people.

In this passage, Sembene links the standard concerns of the realist writer with the traditional social function of the *griot*. This conception of the artist as someone who holds a mirror up to his society is not presented as something new to Africa but rather as the continuation of a long tradition that has been maintained by the *griot* (or *gewel*, as the *griot* is alternatively known). Effectively, Sembene is here seeking to link his own radical, Marxist ideas to elements of the African past. In invoking this past, he ironically distances himself from the

[28] Chinweizu, *Voices from twentieth-century Africa: griots and towncriers* (London: Faber, 1988), p. xxxiv. Anthère Nzabatsinda makes similar claims about the role of the *griot*, and, more generally, the artist, in Sembene's work in an article entitled 'La figure de l'artiste dans le récit d'Ousmane Sembène', *Etudes Françaises*, 31, 1 (Summer 1995), pp. 51–60. A more recent article by Nzabatsinda focuses solely on the figure of the *griot* in Sembene's work: 'Le Griot dans le récit d'Ousmane Sembène: entre la rupture et la continuité d'une représentation de la parole africaine', *French Review*, 70, 6 (May 1997), pp. 865–72. As in the work of Chinweizu, the *griot* is simply described as the guardian of tradition with no discussion of the questions of the *griot*'s low social caste, his/her financial dependency on the nobility, etc. One of the most intelligent discussions of the various conceptions of the *griot* in contemporary African literature is to be found in Noureini Tidjani-Serpos, 'L'écrivain africain, griot contemporain', *Notre Librairie*, 98 (July–September 1989), pp. 63–7.

[29] In the introduction to their *Contes et mythes wolof* (Dakar: Nouvelles Editions Africaines, 1983), Lilyan Kesteloot and Chérif Mbodj discuss the difference between the epic and the *conte*. The former tell the stories of the nobility, of the reigns of great kings, while the *conte* deals with the daily troubles of the peasant farmer (p. 12).

[30] Ousmane Sembene, *L'Harmattan* (Paris: Présence Africaine, 1963), p. 9.

sentimental view of African history and its *classical* pre-colonial era. Sembene's identification is with the *griot* whom he claims to have been the chief dynamic element in the traditional African village. In fact, in *White Genesis*, Sembene presents the *griot* as the upholder of truth and justice in the face of moral and political corruption. But just how valid are these assertions about the role of the *griot* in African society?

A completely different picture of the *griot* is to be found in Ousmane Socé's *Karim*, where *griots* are presented as being not quite as high-minded as Sembene would have us believe. Far from being the bearers of the truth, they are portrayed as hypocrites who simply sing the praises of the highest bidder. A similar image is to be found in Mariama Bâ's *So Long a Letter* where Ramatoulaye's *griote* is shown to be constantly on the outlook for money-spinning opportunities.[31] Even in Sembene's work, there exist equally negative images of the *griot*. In his film, *Borom Sarret*, a lowly cart driver is persuaded to part with his hard-earned money by a passing *griot* who sings the praises of the cart driver's family line in front of an admiring crowd.

As is often the case with such polarised views, a more balanced picture can be said to lie somewhere between these two extremes of high-minded artist and low-minded hypocrite. The *griot* has played a role in many African societies (although not all, as is often believed) but I would here like to examine his/her position within Wolof society as that is the society principally dealt with by Sembene in his work. Historically, Wolof society was made up of a complex structure of castes and orders.[32] Those of the high caste are called the *géér* while those of the lower caste are called the *ñeeño*, and it is to this latter caste that the *griot* belongs. One's name and one's trade are all the signs necessary for one to be recognised as being of high or low caste. Although many of the structures of Wolof society have undergone profound changes, particularly in the period since independence, this notion of a higher and a lower caste still persists, with all its inherent social prejudices (it remains socially unacceptable for people of different caste to marry each other).[33] In fact, the long-serving Senegalese Prime Minister, Habib Thiam, is a *ñeeño*, and the malicious story in Senegal goes that the Senegalese public can accept a *casté* (a lower-caste person) as the second-highest official in the land simply because they see the Prime Minister as the President's *boy*.[34]

Therefore, being born into a family of *ñeeño*, one is inheriting a whole series of social conventions and restrictions. This is particularly true for the *griot* who

---

[31] Mariama Bâ, *So Long a Letter*, trans. by Modupe Bode-Thomas (London: Heinemann, 1981).

[32] For a comprehensive study of the structures within Wolof society, see Abdoulaye-Bara Diop's *La Société wolof: tradition et changement, les systèmes d'inégalité et de domination* (Paris: Karthala, 1981).

[33] Similar problems of caste are to be found in other West African societies. Christopher L. Miller discusses the complex status of the *griot* within Mande society in his *Theories of Africans*, pp. 79–87.

[34] In his novel, *Le Ministre et le griot*, Francis Bebey tells the tale of a political crisis which erupts when the Prime Minister of the fictional state of Kessébougou, who comes from a family of *griots*, is not invited to the engagement party being thrown by one of his ministerial colleagues because of his status as a lower-caste person. See Francis Bebey, *Le Ministre et le griot* (Paris: Sépia, 1992).

has always occupied an ambiguous position within Wolof society. Charged with the important task of preserving the myths and values of that society by means of the oral tradition, the *griot* is nonetheless looked down upon as a flatterer and a courtier: '*les griots sont enfermés dans leur caste, inférieure à celle des autres ñeeño, à cause de leur fonction méprisée*' ['due to their despised role in society, griots remain enclosed within their own caste, with an inferior status to the other ñeeño'].[35]

In many ways, the *griot* resembles the Renaissance artist, forced to seek patronage from a wealthy noble in order to pursue his work. In the modern period, many *griots* have attempted to find success in the musical field by writing songs about the most powerful Senegalese *marabouts*[36] in the hope of gaining some financial recompense from the objects of their praise. However, this dependence of the *griot* on the purse strings of the wealthy and powerful should not be taken as proof positive that they are simply lackeys to their paymasters. The critic, Mbye Boubacar Cham, has brilliantly described the symbiotic relationship between the *griot* and his 'master':

> The 'gewel' or 'griot' is something of a paradox in Wolof society. He is stigmatized socially because of his profession (the code of noble conduct despises loudness), yet it is this same profession that accords him one of the most important and, indeed, influential positions within Wolof political as well as social circles of power, prestige and wealth. He is socially stigmatized precisely because of his vocation, yet it is this same profession that grants him access to and influence over supposedly social and political superiors who, because of their need to maintain and live up to certain fundamental ideals of their caste or class code of conduct, must, of necessity, retain the services of a gewel. The latter's control over the word and over historical and social knowledge places him in a relationship of mutual dependency with social superiors. He needs their patronage as much as they need his services as artist, communicator, teacher and diplomat. Hence the gewel's own sense of high status, which counters the other socially defined low caste.[37]

Essentially, the *griot* appears to have been used as a safety valve for Wolof society. As a professional manipulator of language, he/she was permitted to say things which 'respectable' people could not.[38]

The oral tradition is still well respected in Senegal, and the stories, songs and proverbs that constitute the *griot*'s repertoire are seen to be of direct

---

[35] Diop, *La Société wolof*, p. 59. Already in the nineteenth century, Abbé David Boilat denounced the immorality of the *griot* in his *Esquisses sénégalaises* (1853; Paris: Karthala, 1984), pp. 313–15. Boilat is equally vitriolic in his descriptions of the *ceddo* (or *thiédo*). There seems little doubt that Boilat's conception of 'traditional Senegalese' society was influenced by the arguments of Islam which was then coming to be the dominant force in Senegal, and which sought to denounce the immoral ways of their fetishist predecessors.

[36] In Senegal, the term, *marabout*, is used to describe both Islamic and animist 'holy men'. For an examination of the figure of the *marabout* in Senegalese literature, see Debra Boyd-Buggs, 'Marabouts-escrocs: désordre religieux et charlatanisme dans le roman sénégalais', *Présence Francophone*, 32 (1988), pp. 85–101.

[37] Cham, 'Ousmane Sembene and the Aesthetics of African Oral Traditions', p. 25.

[38] Denise Paulme has discussed the capacity for the *conte*, as fiction, to broach topics which might otherwise be avoided. See her book, *La Mère dévorante. Essais sur la morphologie des contes africains* (Paris: Gallimard, 1976), p. 11.

relevance to people's everyday lives (although the influence of television and cinema, combined with the breaking up of rural society, is beginning to take its toll). However, the question of which values should be transmitted by the *griot* remains problematic. The ideological nature of much of the debate surrounding the status of the *griot* is well illustrated by recent developments in Senegal. The Senegalese historian, Mamadou Diouf, has described how the former president of Senegal, Abdou Diouf, made use of *griots* during official ceremonies and also on television in order to present his political authority as deriving from, and being sanctioned by, the values of 'traditional' Africa.[39] Attempting to distance himself from the ideology of Negritude espoused by his predecessor, Senghor, President Diouf sought to make himself the champion of a living, 'traditional' Africa that Negritude had essentially by-passed, creating its own myths of the African past. In return for this political favour, the Comité National des Griots pour le soutien à l'Action du Président Abdou Diouf, CONAGRISPRAD, was founded in 1983.[40] The stamp of 'authenticity' provided by the *griot* can thus be seen to be the site of an ideological struggle within Senegalese society. In *White Genesis*, Sembene taps into the image of the *griot* as guardian of a set of moral values. Such values, far from strengthening the position of the regime in power, seek to resist the forces of repression and domination.[41]

The central figure of the story is the *griot*, Dethye Law (and, in a lesser role, his wife Gnagna Guisse). In the European literary tradition, the position of a writer or artist as the central character of a work of fiction has long been used to form a reflection on the very art of writing itself, and I believe that this is precisely what Sembene is inviting us to do in his story. Sembene *writes* about

---

[39] After 19 years in power, Diouf was defeated by his old adversary, Abdoulaye Wade, in March 2000. Wade's election has brought an end to 40 years of one-party rule by the *Parti socialiste*.

[40] Mamadou Diouf, 'Représentations historiques et légitimités politiques au Sénégal (1960–1987)', *Revue de la Bibliothèque Nationale* [Paris], 34 (1989), pp. 19, 22.

[41] The conception of the *griot* as guardian of a set of moral values has been evoked by many traditionalist African writers. One of the best known examples is to be found in Djibril Tamsir Niane's *Sundiata: an epic of old Mali*, trans. by G. D. Pickett, (London: Longman, 1979). See also Camara Laye's *The Guardian of the Word*, trans. by James Kirkup (London: Fontana, 1980). This vision of the *griot* is neatly summed up in Bernard Dadié's 'Le rôle de la légende dans la culture populaire des Noirs d'Afrique', *Présence Africaine*, 14–15 (June–September 1957), p. 165:

> *L'Afrique Noire, faute d'écriture, a en effet cristallisé sa sagesse dans sa littérature orale. Et chaque conteur, chaînon ininterrompu d'un long passé, essaime chaque soir la sagesse des Anciens. Il la confie à ceux qui veulent en profiter et au vent qui l'emportera par le monde, car la sagesse n'est pas un bien que l'on conserve pour soi seul. Et c'est se survivre que de dispenser sa sagesse.*

> In the absence of the written word, Black Africa preserved its wisdom in its oral literature. Each storyteller who spreads the wisdom of the ancestors in the evening is providing an unbroken continuity with the long-distant past. He gives this wisdom to those who wish to benefit from it and he also gives it to the wind which carries it around the world because wisdom is not something to be preserved for oneself. Dispensing one's wisdom is a means of ensuring one's survival.

> However, despite Dadié's impassioned praise of the African *conteur*, it should be noted that the social status of the *griot* is once again ignored. Equally, Niane shows himself to be deeply hostile to those *griots* who have sought to make money from making records. What is being praised, it seems, is the *griot* as he/she used to be.

a storyteller, a man whose role is to maintain the African oral tradition, and, consequently, the values of a whole society. The story is made up in a large part by a series of discussions or debates between the men of the village. These debates are more like chess games, or rather, games of *yothe* (the game played by two of the more independent-minded members of the group), as the men speak in a roundabout fashion of the important issues facing their village, chiefly the case of incest between Guibril Guedj Diob and his daughter, Khar. It is Dethye Law who manages to tease out the truth behind these word-games, to create meaning from the minefield of insinuation and suggestion which make up the discussions. As Dethye Law himself puts it at one point: 'I know the meanings of words'.[42]

Writing at the beginning of a new era for Africa, Sembene invests the traditional *griot* with exactly the sense of justice and integrity that he places at the heart of his own fiction. In this way, Sembene is, in effect, defining himself as a *griot* for contemporary Africa. Santhiu-Niaye, the village where the events of the story take place, is a small, isolated village that is on its last legs, as its people drift away towards the cities. As one era closes and a new one begins, Sembene declares that society needs its storytellers to remind it of its values, and to give expression to the sense of confusion felt by people during such a period of rapid change.

In fact, the urban world presented to us in *The Money Order*, the story that accompanies *White Genesis*, can be seen as an illustration of what happens when a traditional, village-based society is in the process of being transformed into a modern, urban society. As the bonds that had previously joined the community together are slowly broken down, the sole remaining value is money. People no longer trust one another, and language becomes synonymous with deceit and lies. In the words of the main protagonist, the hapless Ibrahima Dieng, 'honesty is a crime nowadays'.[43] However, unlike *White Genesis*, there is no *griot* to create meaning out of this confusion. Indeed, the only *griot* we come across in the story is an impostor, as the 'trickster' figure, Gorgui Maïssa, extemporises at great length on the proud lineage of a young man whose name he has simply overheard while waiting behind him in a queue. From the noble bearer of the truth in *White Genesis*, the *griot* and his art have become just another means of fooling people into parting with their money. In *The Money Order*, Sembene presents a society with no-one to uphold its values or tell its story, except, of course, that in telling this story, Sembene is fulfilling the role of the *griot*. A new society gives birth to a new type of storyteller.

The narrative style of both *White Genesis* and *The Money Order* is very much in keeping with the style of the short stories in *Tribal Scars*. In place of the grand narratives of *God's Bits of Wood* and *L'Harmattan*, there is a far more ironic and elusive narrative voice, which hints at things rather than stating

---

[42] Ousmane Sembene, *The Money Order* with *White Genesis*, trans. by Clive Wake (London: Heinemann, 1972), p. 43. Further references to this story (hereafter *WG*) will be given in the body of the text.

[43] Sembene, *The Money Order*, p. 136.

them straight out. In many ways, this narrative voice imitates the voice of the *griot* in its use of proverbs and its direct addresses to the reader, recreating a bond between the storyteller and his audience. This style is clearly seen, even in the longish introductory section of the story. After the dedication of the story to an unnamed African friend of Sembene, who died in Vietnam, fighting a fellow-colonised people (and whose story prepares us for the introduction of the mad *tirailleur*, or African colonial soldier, Tanor Ngone Diob, later on in the novella), the reader is presented with what seems to be a proverb, which is also used later on (p. 29) in the main body of the text:

> Sometimes, into the most ordinary low caste family, a child is born who grows up and glorifies his name, the name of his father, of his mother, of his whole family, of his community, of his tribe; even more, by his work he ennobles *man*.
>
> More often, in a so-called high caste family which glories in its past, a child comes into the world who, by his actions, sullies his entire heritage, does harm to the honest *man* he encounters and even robs the individual diambur-diambur [i.e. a member of the noble order of Wolof society, not necessarily a *géér*] of his dignity. (*WG*, p. 4; stress in original)

This passage constitutes something of a summary of the events of the story; the lowly *griot* who stands up for the truth, and the respected nobleman who commits incest with his daughter. The reader is presented with the moral of the story before it has even begun, a ploy that is in keeping with oral tradition.

The most important section of the introduction is the final one where Sembene addresses the reader directly. He presents the story as a true one that people wanted to be kept quiet. Once again, as with many of the stories in *Tribal Scars*, we are presented with a story based upon the notion of silence. Sembene uses a tale of incest, perhaps the most vilified crime in all societies (especially when it concerns father and daughter), to look at the breakdown of the traditional African way of life. In the face of the arguments of Negritude and their sentimental glorification of all things African, Sembene invites Africans to make their judgements independently of questions of colour: 'when will we stop acknowledging and approving our actions in terms of the other man's colour, instead of in terms of our *humanity?*' (*WG*, p. 5; stress in original). Sembene sets up his tale as an investigation into the morality of his age, examining the dark corners of his society that the discourse of Negritude wishes to be overlooked, and presenting himself as the narrator of a tale that would otherwise not be told. He rejects the facade of racial and national unity and chooses instead to concentrate on the social conflicts ignored by the discourses of Negritude and nationalism. In the characters of Khar and the child born of her incestuous relationship with her father, Sembene sees hope for a better future, because telling their story is the first step on the road to rectifying the ills in African society, which have brought about their problems. In Sembene's words: 'For out of the defects of an old, condemned world will be born the new world that has been so long awaited and for so long part of our dreams' (*WG*, p. 6). In the process of creating a new society, the act of storytelling, giving voice to hidden conflicts within that society, is shown to be of primary importance.

The notion of silence is put across in the very location of the story. The village is situated in the *niaye*, a barren, sandy region which runs northwards from Dakar to Saint-Louis. A strip of land between the coast and the interior, the *niaye* forms a world apart: it is, in a sense, a no-man's land, an atopia, unfit for human habitation. The village of Santhiu-Niaye is shown to be slowly dying. The descriptions stress the stillness of the village, particularly in the oppressive heat of the noonday sun. In the silent, still landscape, we have a sense of a village existing almost outside of time. This stillness and immobility stand in stark contrast to the rapid decline faced by the village. The young men are leaving for the new urban centres, thus leaving power in the hands of the old men who seek refuge from these troubled times in an extreme fatalism, resulting in an unwillingness to face up to their problems. The young women are left without partners, and their mothers, who realise that this means the death of the village, are both unwilling and unable to speak out: 'Dominated by their men, fearful of today's realities and sick at heart, the mothers said nothing' (*WG*, p. 11). The final image of this opening description of Santhiu-Niaye is of a village separated by dint of caste, even in the physical arrangement of the houses. The villagers live in the same environment, the fate of the individual being tied inextricably to that of the entire community, but they remain separated from one another in so many ways: 'The season's cycle followed its course. The strange character of the niaye bound the people together, yet kept them apart' (*WG*, p. 11). It is these previously unvoiced differences which will come to the surface in the course of the story.

Before turning to the role played by the *griot* Dethye Law in resisting the hegemonic discourses of Santhiu-Niaye, it would be useful to examine how the notions of silence/discourse are played out in relation to some of the other central characters. Ngone War Thiandum, wife of the incestuous Guibril Guedj Diob, is a *guelewar* (more commonly spelt *guelwaar*), a woman born of a noble family, and she is presented to us as the sole member of her family to have maintained some of the dignity and honour of her ancestors. She is very much a woman alone. Her husband has committed incest with her daughter; her son has returned insane from the colonial wars in Vietnam and Algeria. Even her oldest and closest friend, Gnagna Guisse, the *griote* of her family, has drifted away from her since the two of them have married, as their lives are now centred around their husbands and families. Thus, in her moment of crisis, there is no-one to whom she can turn.[44]

As a *guelwaar*, Ngone War Thiandum is overwhelmed with shame at the disgrace that has fallen upon her family. Her knowledge of this incestuous act has not only shaken her faith in her family, but in the whole structure of her society. How could her husband, himself a *guelwaar* of the great Diob family,

---

[44] Ngone War Thiandum's isolation is strikingly visualised in *Niaye*, the film version of the novella. When we first see her, she is peeping through a fence at the village square where the main events of the story take place. As a woman, she is excluded from the power struggles that take place in this public forum and, in her shame, she wishes to keep away from the prying eyes of her neighbours. Sembène thus films her on the edge of her society, visually separated from her fellow villagers.

perpetrate such an act? All her notions of the honour and dignity of her class have disappeared. Even her faith in her God has been shaken: 'Yallah! Forgive Me! But why this act? Why?' (*WG*, p. 14). This questioning of the structures of her society and her faith are born of despair but also hint at an awakening of consciousness that may allow Ngone War Thiandum to overcome the problems she faces. Instead of viewing events in terms of the role laid out for her by her society and her religion, she begins to see them as an individual woman:

> Today's act forced her to question the precepts which, until yesterday, had been the obvious basis of her life. Like a tear, a tiny hole which she unconsciously enlarged, she fell in with her realization – a new step for her – that she could judge events from her own, woman's point of view. (*WG*, p. 15)

However, this new consciousness, instead of empowering her, simply over-whelms her, and causes her even greater pain: 'This new responsibility was a shattering experience for a woman like herself, whose opinions had always been decided for her by someone else' (*WG*, p. 15). Cut loose from the anchors of her religion and her family honour, she decides that she can no longer survive in this new, fallen world, and takes her own life. Her questioning of her society is silenced before it can lead to something positive.

The other main character through whom the notions of silence/discourse are examined is Ngone War Thiandum's son, Tanor Ngone Diob, the mad *tirailleur sénégalais*. Having returned home insane from the colonial wars in Vietnam and Algeria, he parades around the village in his army uniform, living out his military fantasies.[45] Despite the relatively small number of references to Tanor in the story, he is nonetheless a central character.[46] We must not forget that the story takes place during the colonial period and, apart from the commander who comes to collect the taxes right at the end, Tanor is the sole representative of the French colonial presence in Africa. The *tirailleurs sénégalais* (made up of African troops, not necessarily from Senegal, despite their misleading name), with whom he had served, were the principal forces used in the conquest of Africa, and Tanor, in his madness, obviously sees himself as the village policeman, carrying out the coloniser's role of maintaining order. In one highly ironic scene, we are presented with the comic image of Tanor marching into the village at the head of a group of children, and passing under an imitation Arc de Triomphe, made up of palm-fronds. His language is almost exclusively martial and aggressive, with Tanor erupting into real, physical bursts of violence at several points in the story. It is he who chases

[45] In the film, *Niaye*, all of Tanor's appearances on screen are accompanied by a jaunty French tune whistled on the soundtrack (it sounds like 'Auprès de ma blonde, il fait bon').

[46] The figure of the mad *tirailleur* is seen again in Sembene's 1988 film, *Camp de Thiaroye*, in the character of Pays (this film is discussed in Chapter Six). For an examination of the role of the *tirailleur sénégalais* in French-language African fiction, see János Riesz/Joachim Schultz, eds, *Tirailleurs sénégalais* (Frankfurt: Peter Lang, 1989), and János Riesz, 'La "Folie" des Tirailleurs sénégalais: fait historique et thème littéraire de la littérature coloniale à la littérature africaine de langue française', in Little and Little, *Black Accents*, pp. 139–56. Bernard Mouralis provides a fascinating analysis of the notion of madness in African literature in *L'Europe, l'Afrique et la folie* (Paris: Présence Africaine, 1993).

the *navetanekat* (or seasonal worker), who has been wrongly accused of being the father of Khar's baby, from the village. He also carries out attacks on his own family, beating Khar, and murdering his father.[47]

The scene where Tanor carries out the murder is a disturbing one. Obvious distress at the death of his mother becomes mixed up with memories of his time in the colonial army. His father, who had originally signed up Tanor for the army, is stabbed to death with the same efficiency with which Tanor had no doubt killed so many other 'natives' in Vietnam and Algeria. Tanor is a man literally split in two by his experiences in the colonial army. Despite being an agent of colonialism, he is also one of its victims. His confused ramblings serve as a constant reminder of the violence of colonialism and its role in the destruction of the traditional African way of life. In one character, Sembene expresses both the pain and aggression of colonialism: a man whose only means of expression is through violence.

It is in such a context of violence and resigned fatalism that we should examine the role of the *griot*, Dethye Law, who provides the main voice of resistance throughout the story. The scene of his defiant stand against the corruption of those in authority is the village square, where the men meet for their debates. Effectively, what takes place at these meetings is a power struggle to see who will take control of Santhiu-Niaye after the disgrace and subsequent murder of Guibril Guedj Diob. These debates act as a contest for authority in the village. Other events play a vital role in the quest for power by Medoune Diob, Guibril's brother, but these discussions are the site where one gains control over the language of the villagers. Control of language becomes a vital element in the control of power: to hold power, Medoune must silence the dissenting voices and prove himself to be the representative of the 'true' values of African tradition.

In the key debate over the punishment that should be meted out to Guibril Guedj Diob, Medoune Diob carries out the same policy of dissimulation that characterises all the other, smaller rows which take place during the debates. Medoune Diob wants his brother to be executed so that he can inherit his position as village chief, but he cannot declare this out straight, so he is forced to seek legitimacy for this punishment in the *adda*, or traditions of the village. Medoune Diob and his clan argue for the execution of Guibril Guedj Diob by seeking to have strict Koranic law applied to his case. However, Dethye Law and his ally, Massar, refuse to allow Islamic law and the *adda* to be so readily assimilated. Massar, who had lost out in a struggle to become imam with the current holder of that position, contests Medoune Diob's reading of Koranic law and its status in their society.[48] His is a much more liberal view, which is presented as belonging to a secular African tradition:

[47] In *Niaye*, the link between Tanor's murder of his father and the violence of the colonial armies is more openly explored. After the scene of the murder, there follows a dream sequence in which Tanor imagines the village overrun by armoured cars, infantrymen and even parachutists. The spectator is led to reflect upon the links between the violence of the colonial project and the present predicament of Santhiu-Niaye.

[48] Anthère Nzabatsinda maintains that Dethye Law is an alienated figure because he represents Islam in his capacity as *bilal* of the village mosque. The argument that Dethye Law is working

Among us [...] the scriptures are a dead letter. For never in this village, nor in the whole of Senegal, where mosques nevertheless proliferate, not once have the penalties laid down by the holy scriptures been carried out. Go and see the authorities! We respect them and cherish them; that seems to be all. That leaves us the adda, the heritage of our fathers. (*WG*, p. 45)

Dethye Law sees right through Medoune Diob's arguments. Refusing to be dismissed as a *casté*, Dethye Law launches into a defence of his role as *griot*, and criticises the lack of true nobility in those who proclaim themselves to be *guelwaar* (i.e. noblemen) in these modern times:

I ask the assembly's pardon. I know my place in our community. However, one thing is certain. When it is a question of speaking the truth, or of seeking it, there is no nawle [i.e. classes]. It is a known fact that many of my caste have been murdered in the cause of truth. It is true that Guibril Guedj Diob deserves to die. It was the rule of our fathers and of our grandfathers, in the days when the essence of nobility depended on the way one lived, not on self-display. We can call to mind the names of many who put an end to their lives for acts less than the one we are discussing today. They were guelewar, men whose praises were sung by my father and his father, not to give pleasure, but to impress on their hearers the meaning of duty and dignity. Nowadays, people do not conduct themselves in this way. But truth belongs to all times and will do so even after we are dead. (*WG*, p. 43)

Guibril Guedj Diob lacks nobility in not taking his own life over his actions, but Medoune Diob is no better in seeking his brother's life so that he can claim his title. Dethye Law, whose role it is to decipher the meaning of words, recognises that Medoune Diob's cloaking himself in the respectability of tradition and his noble birth is just a ploy in his quest for power, and he refuses to go along with it:

Our inability to recognize the truth does not come from our minds, but rather from the fact that we accord too much consideration to birth and wealth and also, sometimes, because we lack the courage to speak out. Between man and Yallah, I choose Yallah. Between Yallah and the Truth, I am for the Truth. Medoune Diob has something else at the back of his mind. (*WG*, p. 46)

The truth is argued to be the ultimate value for the *griot*, above both God and Man.

It is interesting to note that Dethye Law quotes the words of 'Kotje Barma'[49] in his argument with Medoune Diob. Kocc Barma is an actual historical figure who lived in the kingdom of Kayor, north of Dakar, in the late sixteenth and early seventeenth century.[50] An adviser to the *damels*, or

---

[48] (cont.) *'au service de l'islamisation de son peuple'* ['to convert his people to Islam'] can be rejected for two simple reasons: firstly, as far as the reader is made aware, all of the villagers are Muslims, therefore Dethye Law would be wasting his time in trying to convert them to the religion; secondly, Dethye Law and Massar actively defend the village *adda* against Medoune Diob's arguments for the application of Koranic law. See Nzabatsinda, 'Le Griot dans le récit d'Ousmane Sembène', pp. 869–70.

[49] 'Kotdj' is alternatively spelled as 'Kothie' or 'Kocc'. As the latter has become the spelling most often used in recent times, that is the spelling adopted in this study.

[50] There is a relatively abundant bibliography on Kocc Barma. See Yoro Dyâo and R. Rousseau, 'Le Sénégal d'autrefois. Etude sur le Cayor', *Bulletin du comité d'études historiques et scientifiques de*

kings, of Kayor, Kocc Barma's words and acts have passed into Senegalese folklore to such an extent that proverbs are often introduced by the phrase 'Kocc Barma said', whether this is true or not. The stories concerning Kocc Barma cover a wide range of subjects and, by turns, reveal him as either an arch-conservative or as an oppositional figure.[51]

The ambiguity of the popular image of Kocc Barma is most evident in the oft-cited story of the four tufts of hair.[52] The story goes that Kocc Barma had four tufts of hair on his head, and he claimed that anyone who learned the 'meaning' of each tuft would be able to kill him. The king managed to find out the 'meaning' of each tuft, but before killing Kocc Barma, he asked him to explain each of the tufts to him. The first two, 'love your wife, but don't trust her', and 'an adopted son is not a true son', can only be described as conservative and reactionary (it is Kocc Barma's wife who has betrayed him to the king, and his adoptive son asks him for his clothes before he is murdered because he does not want blood stains on them). However, the final two, 'old people must remain part of the community', and 'a king has no relations', contain an explicitly oppositional message. The wisdom of the elders is portrayed as a counter-balance to the despotic designs of kings, who are willing to kill those around them, including their own family, in order to preserve their grip on power. The story closes with the king recognising the wisdom of Kocc Barma's words, and he promptly promotes him to the position of *lamane* (advisor to the king and leader of the noble community who were given the task of electing the *damels* of Kayor). Truth and justice, the two qualities in the *griot* praised so highly by Sembene, are here shown to be more than a match for the power of the state. Thus, when Sembene has Dethye Law quote Kocc Barma, he is tapping into the tradition of Kocc as a questioner of authority (the figure of Kocc Barma is used in a similar fashion in Sembene's 1992 film, *Guelwaar*, which will be discussed in the final chapter of this study).[53]

The question attributed by Dethye Law to Kocc Barma is 'what one ought to think of old men who marry girls the same age as their daughters?' (*WG*, p. 43). In posing this question, Dethye Law is trying to put Guibril Guedj Diob's crime into the wider context of a society where old men regularly satisfy their pride by marrying girls the same age as their daughters. Medoune Diob and his allies would have the case seen in simple black and white terms,

---

[50] (cont.) *l'A.O.F.* (1933), pp. 269–74, and Bassirou Makhoudia's 'Légendes africaines – Kothie Barma', *Paris-Dakar*, 3 September 1955, p. 4. The short-lived review, *Dèmb ak tey* (published by l'IFAN in Dakar) devoted its second and third editions (1974) to a collection of the various stories concerning Kocc Barma, and to an analysis of his political and philosophical importance. Such is the celebrity of Kocc Barma that the popular Senegalese musician, Youssou N'dour, has recorded a song about him. Further references can be found in the bibliography.

[51] For an interesting analysis of Kocc Barma as both conservative and rebel, see Massaër Diallo's 'Tradition orale et autorité: le cas de Kocc Barma', *Revue sénégalaise de philosophie*, 13–14 (1990), pp. 197–208.

[52] The story exists in many different versions. The version used here is taken from Kesteloot and Mbodj, *Contes et mythes wolof*, pp. 146–51.

[53] Anna Ridehalgh examines the use of the image of Kocc Barma in *Guelwaar* in her article, '*Guelwaar*: the stuff of legend', in Little and Little, *Black Accents*, pp. 171–81.

placing themselves firmly on the side of truth and respectability. However, Dethye Law challenges their self-righteousness by cleverly introducing the words of an historical figure whose very conservatism makes his radical, oppositional claims all the more powerful.[54]

Despite losing the debate, Medoune Diob has Guibril Guedj Diob secretly killed by his son, Tanor. It seems, at first, that this *coup de village* has worked but, more importantly, he is to lose out in his fight for authority in the debates in the village square. Dethye Law claims that he is leaving the village for good which finally stings the independent-minded villagers, particularly Gornaru and Badieye, the *yothe* players, into action and they exclude Medoune Diob from their group.[55] Outside of the debates, where village opinion is formed, Medoune Diob's power simply evaporates. Now that the secular, liberal forces have taken control, there is some hope for the village. Perhaps the road that is to be built across the *niaye* will finally stem the flow of villagers from Santhiu-Niaye (as with the railway line in *God's Bits of Wood*, the road is that which will physically and metaphorically link the village to the rest of the nation: Santhiu-Niaye can no longer exist in isolation). Dethye Law's vision of honesty, truth and equality has won the day.

The story ends in something of a fable-like style. The narrator asks the reader not to ask any question of the villagers if ever they go to Santhiu-Niaye. There is a sense that the telling of this story is a sort of exorcism, and that the pain of past events should now be forgotten. Sembene has told this tale and it is now up to the characters to create something new: 'This story has no other ending: it was a page in their life. A new one starts, which depends on them' (*WG*, p. 73). In the final images of the story, we see Khar and her baby begin their trek towards the city. The child's name, Vehi-Ciosane Ngone War Thiandum (as we learn from the sub-title of the story, 'Vehi-Ciosane' means 'white genesis') is highly resonant. It could be seen to refer to the whiteness/blankness of the *niaye*. Equally, it could be taken to mean that she is a child born of the 'white' colonial era. Whichever it is (perhaps both), a new beginning is what is suggested. Through the articulation of the ills of his society, Sembene seeks to make public that which was previously silent in order to begin the process of constructing a discourse of resistance that may eventually lead to change. Cast in the role of the modern-day *griot*, he presents himself as the defender of the values of his people. Rejecting what he considers to be the self-serving platitudes of the discourses of Negritude and nationalism, Sembene sets his own Marxist agenda and declares that he will write the history of those who are marginalised and oppressed within his society.

---

[54] In a personal interview with the author, he displayed little interest in the figure of Kocc Barma. However, Sembene recognises the respect in which this historical figure is held and he subsequently attempts to adopt him to his own radical cause (see Appendix).

[55] The critic, Patrick Akpadomyne, makes some interesting points on the sexual word play of Gornaru and Badieye in their debates with the imam. They are vibrant, physical characters, unlike the ascetic and other-worldly imam. Patrick Akpadomyne, 'La Parodie et la réécriture chez Sembène Ousmane. Problèmes textologiques', *Neohelicon*, 16, 2 (1989), pp. 211–19.

■ ■ ■

Sembene's desire to replace the *griot* as popular storyteller and guardian of society's values through his literature meets with the inevitable problem of illiteracy within Africa. The simple fact is that the vast majority of Africans can neither speak nor read the European languages that most African writers use in their work. Sembene was highly conscious of this problem at the time at which he was writing both *Tribal Scars* and *White Genesis*. This realisation upon his return to Africa in 1960 that his literature was not accessible to the vast majority of Africans led him to study film-making in the Soviet Union, and, since 1962, he has been engaged in the dual career of both novelist and filmmaker. However, unlike the poet, Lèye, from *L'Harmattan*, Sembene has not completely abandoned literature in favour of the visual arts. Instead, he has adopted a policy of regarding literature and cinema as alternative discourses to be used in accordance with both aesthetic and pragmatic considerations. In fact, Sembene has marked himself out as a distinctive artistic figure by the manner in which he has built up a large body of work in both of his chosen media, now comprising ten books and eleven films.[56]

It is perhaps not surprising that many of Sembene's early films were adaptations of some of his novellas and short stories. Both *White Genesis* and *The Money Order* were adapted for the large screen. The former is called *Niaye* (1964) in its film version while the latter was filmed in both a French and a Wolof version (at the behest of André Malraux, the then French Minister for Culture, who made this a condition for the financing of the film), called *Le Mandat* and *Mandabi* respectively.[37] Such an interplay between literature and cinema has occurred many times in Sembene's career. The short story 'The

---

[56] After the publication of *The Money Order* and *White Genesis* in 1966, it seemed as if Sembene had abandoned his literary career altogether. In the period from 1966 to 1971, he released three feature films, *La Noire de* (which is probably more accurately described by the French term, *moyen métrage*, a medium-length film), *Le Mandat/Mandabi*, *Emitaï*, and a short film, *Taaw*, but did not publish a single book. However, since the publication of *Xala* in 1973, he has moved more readily between literature and cinema. This shifting from one medium to another is often a question of pragmatism. For example, Sembene's satirical film, *Xala* (which will be examined in Chapter Four), was originally conceived as a film but was subsequently rewritten by Sembene as a novel while he was waiting for the finance to be raised to make the film. Finally, after the novel had been published, Sembene rewrote his film script, based on the novel version. Another example of this pragmatism is to be found in relation to the banning of Sembene's next film, *Ceddo*. After Senghor had banned the film, Sembene shifted to the literary form for his next work, *The Last of the Empire*, writing a scathing satire upon Senghor and his government. Aside from the question of choosing the medium best suited to his narrative, Sembene has also made the most of this ability to use an *alternative* art form when political and economic (cinema is an expensive business) circumstances demand it. A number of critics have written of the cinematic quality of Sembene's literature. However, while it may be possible to trace the influence of one form on the other, I believe that such criticism often leads to a reductionist metaphorisation of cinema as literature or vice versa.

[37] For an explanation of the circumstances surrounding the production of the film, see 'Cinéma et littérature: entretien avec Sembène Ousmane', in Peter Hawkins and Annette Lavers, eds, *Protée noir: essais sur la littérature francophone de l'Afrique noire et des Antilles* (Paris: L'Harmattan, 1992), pp. 216–17.

Promised Land' ('La Noire de', in French) (1962) was later to be released in a film version called *La Noire de* (often called *Black Girl*, in English), in 1966, and the novel *Xala* (1973) was adapted to the screen just a year after the publication of the book. Sembene has also adapted his work in the opposite direction, that is, from the screen to the page. The short film, *Taaw* (1970), was published as a novella almost twenty years later in 1988, together with the story *Niiwam* that appears to have had its genesis in an incident taken from Sembene's very first short film, *Borom Sarret* (I am referring to the scene where the cart driver takes a poor man to the cemetery with the body of his dead child). His film, *Guelwaar* (1992), was also transformed into a novel of the same name in 1996.

As the first film to be made in an African language (the language in question is Wolof, which is spoken by a majority of Senegalese), *Le Mandat/ Mandabi* occupies a special place in the short history of African cinema. The film's release was awaited with great expectancy in Senegal and it was to cause quite a stir with a polemical debate breaking out in the local press over Sembene's portrayal of the 'shantytowns' of 1960s Dakar.[58] This ability of cinema to provoke a nationwide debate, pushing certain political concerns to the front of the political agenda (for however short a period) highlights the limits of literature in a continent where literacy rates rarely rise above 15 per cent. Therefore, in the next chapter, I will turn to the film, *Le Mandat/Mandabi*, in order to examine Sembene's political and artistic concerns in his use of cinema as a means of creating a public discourse of resistance, which is, to a large extent, beyond the means of literature in light of the situation in contemporary Africa.[59]

[58] Bara Diouf's criticism of *Le Mandat/Mandabi* was already examined in the previous chapter. See Bara Diouf, '*Le Mandat*, film d'Ousmane Sembene', *Dakar-Matin*, 7 December 1968, p. 1. See also C. V., 'Un film dont on parle et dont on parlera longtemps: *Le Mandat* de Ousmane Sembene', *Bingo*, 195 (April 1969), pp. 41–2.

[59] I was unable to find a copy of *Mandabi* in the course of my research. Understandably, it would appear that most of the available copies in Europe are of the French version. In his *Sembène Ousmane, cinéaste*, Paulin Soumanou Vieyra notes that *Mandabi* is fifteen minutes longer than *Le Mandat* (p.92). However, he does not explain in what ways the two versions differ from one another. While I wish to maintain the notion of the importance of the fact that *Mandabi* was the first feature film in an African language, intellectual honesty dictates that I alert the reader to the fact that it is, in fact, *Le Mandat* which will be analysed in Chapter Three. In order to preserve this balance, I will use the title of both versions, *Le Mandat/Mandabi* in all references to the film.

3
Filming Africa

The Location of an Urban African Discourse in
Le Mandat/Mandabi

The release of *Le Mandat/Mandabi* towards the end of 1968 marked an important point in the development not only of Sembene as a director, but also of
African cinema in general. Much of its fame lies in its ground-breaking use of
Wolof, but one should remember that it was also arguably the first feature film
that Sembene had directed, as well as being his first film in colour (there are a
few short scenes in colour in his 1966 film, *La Noire de*). He had begun his
cinematic career with two short films, *Borom Sarret* (1962) and *Niaye* (1964),
and although his next work, *La Noire de*, had originally been intended as a
feature film, it was later cut to a forty-five minute version, in order to get
around strict French trade union rules governing film production (although a
longer sixty-five minute version does still exist).[1] It should also be noted that
Le Mandat/Mandabi was the first film in which Sembene felt able to do away
with the safety-net of the voice-over in order to relate his story. Therefore, not
only did *Le Mandat/Mandabi* illustrate Sembene's growing maturity as a director
but it also, through its use of Wolof, placed the question of audience firmly at
the front of his considerations.[2] However, before going on to examine the film
in detail, it is important to understand the circumstances which had brought
Sembene to cinema in the first place, and also to trace briefly the development
of cinema in Africa.

[1] For an account of the problems surrounding the final version of *La Noire de*, see Paulin
Soumanou Vieyra, *Sembène Ousmane, cinéaste* (Paris: Présence Africaine, 1972), pp. 82–3.
[2] Alioune Tine has argued that Sembene's decision to turn to cinema, and particularly his use of
African languages in his films, is the logical outcome of his desire to reach a wide African
audience. The africanisation of his French in his novels (what Tine terms their *'oralité feinte'*
['feigned orality']) is a literary attempt at achieving similar ends. See Alioune Tine, 'Etude
pragmatique et sémiotique des effets du bilinguisme dans les œuvres romanesques de Ousmane
Sembene' (unpublished doctoral thesis, Université de Lyon 2, 1981). See also his 'Pour une théorie
de la littérature africaine écrite', *Présence Africaine*, 133–4 (1st & 2nd quarter 1985), pp. 99–121.

Sembene's decision to combine a cinematic career with his, by then, already well-established literary career has been well documented.[3] On returning to Senegal in 1960, after twelve years spent in Europe, he was able to see for himself just how little impact the emergent African literature was having on the illiterate African masses. As a Marxist, it was particularly galling for Sembene not to be able to communicate with the very people that his novels were concerned with and whom he felt it was his duty to represent.

It was while on a subsequent tour of the African continent that he decided that cinema was the solution to his problem. In most interviews, Sembene has described the moment when he decided to turn to cinema in terms of a sort of Joycean epiphany: while sitting in a boat on the Congo river, during the Lumumba era, he had a vision of cinema's power both to describe and to communicate with the masses that he saw everywhere around him. In this vision, Sembene saw the filmmaker as the closest figure to the *griot* in that his/her work combined music, gesture and storytelling, in a communal gathering.[4] Cinema would permit Sembene to reach a much wider audience than his literature and would also serve as a sort of 'evening school', dedicated to the cultural and political education of his people:

> *Force est de constater que la littérature ne mène pas loin. Mais les gens vont au cinéma plus qu'ils ne lisent. Car le cinéma est accessible à tout le monde. J'ai donc jugé plus sage de me tourner vers le cinéma. Avec cette forme d'expression, je suis sûr de toucher la masse. Pour moi, le cinéma est la meilleure école du soir. Il me permet non seulement de faire ce que ne permet pas la littérature, et d'aller plus loin, mais encore de faire parler les gens dans leur propre langue: en l'occurrence le ouolof.[5]*

> One must realise that literature doesn't get you very far. However, people go to the cinema much more than they read. Because cinema is accessible to everyone. Therefore, I decided it was wiser to turn to cinema. This medium would allow me to reach the masses. As far as I am concerned, cinema is the best evening school. It not only allows me to do what cannot be done through literature but also allows me to go further, to let people speak in their own language: that is, Wolof.

However, despite his interest in cinema as a means of communication, Sembene has often declared that he prefers literature to film. He is particularly wary of the immediacy of the image and its power to impose itself on the viewer as truth, leaving no space for reflection :

> *Moi je suis très prudent car souvent c'est trop facile d'être dans une salle de cinéma et de tout gober. Vous ne réfléchissez même pas souvent, vous n'avez pas de recul. Vous avalez, vous avalez et vous sortez et vous n'avez souvent retenu qu'une parcelle. Pour tout cela, je me méfie du cinéma.*

> I am very wary because it's too easy to go to the cinema and to simply swallow

---

[3] See Vieyra, *Sembène Ousmane, cinéaste*, and Françoise Pfaff, *The Cinema of Ousmane Sembene: A Pioneer of African Film* (Westport, Connecticut: Greenwood Press, 1984).

[4] See Mohamadou Kane et al., 'Comme un aveugle qui retrouve la vue', *Le Soleil* [Dakar], 10 July 1981, p. 6.

[5] Siradiou Diallo, '*Jeune Afrique* fait parler Sembene Ousmane', *Jeune Afrique*, 27 January 1973, p. 45. In her thesis, Carrie Dailey Moore cites from a manuscript by Sembene, entitled 'Cinéma: école du soir'. See Carrie Dailey Moore, 'Evolution of an African Artist: Social Realism in the Works of Ousmane Sembene' (unpublished doctoral thesis, Indiana University, 1973).

everything that's laid before you. Sometimes, you don't even think. There's no distance. You swallow everything and when you leave the cinema, you've often only retained a small part of it. That's why I don't trust cinema.[6]

Sembene essentially sees cinema as a powerful force that can be easily abused. The responsibility for the Marxist filmmaker is to use his films to educate as well as to entertain his audience.

Having decided that his future lay partly in cinema, Sembene applied to a number of countries, including France, Poland, Czechoslovakia and the United States, for a grant to study filmmaking but it was eventually the Soviet Union that invited him to study under the well-known Soviet director, Mark Donskoi, at the Gorki studios in Moscow.[7] Upon his return to Africa, he was hired by the Malian government to make a short film, entitled *L'Empire sonhraï*, which has never been shown. While still continuing to write novels and novellas, Sembene has managed to pursue a parallel career in cinema. Having directed seven feature films (including the hour-long cut of *La Noire de*) and three short films since 1962, Sembene is very much a writer *and* film director, not just a writer who sometimes directs films or provides screenplays. He has also made a great effort to bring his films to the people, practising what he calls a 'cinéma forain' (or 'travelling cinema'), going to villages and towns to show his films, and holding debates upon the issues raised by them.

Cinema had a relatively late start in sub-Saharan Africa. It was 1926 before a developed system of distribution was set up. In that year, the *Compagnie Africaine Cinématographique et Commerciale* (COMACICO) established itself in Dakar and was later joined by the *Société d'Exploitation Cinématographique Africaine* (SECMA). These two French companies were to enjoy a virtual monopoly of the cinema market in most Francophone African countries until the 1960s. These companies were able to exploit the popularity of cinema with African audiences and, by the time of independence, Senegal alone had about seventy cinemas, with an enthusiastic and ever-growing audience.[8]

It was this capacity to enthral large numbers of people through a hugely popular artistic medium that attracted Sembene to cinema. Here was the medium that would allow him to convey his social concerns to a wide audience. However, despite the development of African cinema since the 1960s, the fact remains that the vast majority of films shown in sub-Saharan

[6] Kane et al., 'Comme un aveugle qui retrouve la vue', p. 6.

[7] Sembene has stressed the technical nature of his training in Moscow, perhaps as a preventive strike against critics who would search for Donskoi's influence upon his work. Donskoi's brand of social realism may indeed have influenced Sembene but the concern for ritual that is to be found in Sembene's cinematic work is nowhere to be found in Donskoi's cinema. However, one could possibly argue that the ending of Sembene's film, *Niaye*, where the exiled girl, Khar, walks along the beach with her baby, contains echoes of Donskoi's *My Universities*, which finishes with the main protagonist aiding a woman to give birth on the edge of a lake. Both films use images of childbirth and water to suggest a sense of change and promise for the future.

[8] See Paulin Soumanou Vieyra, *Le Cinéma au Sénégal* (Brussels: OCIC/L'Harmattan, 1983) for a detailed account of the different aspects of the Senegalese film industry: distribution, production, etc.

Africa come from foreign cultures – American, French, Egyptian,[9] Indian – leading to what most commentators see as an increased alienation of the African masses. The Tunisian filmmaker, Tahaar Cheriaa, has argued this case in the following terms:

> *L'image que ces spectacles renvoient à l'Africain, du monde, des 'autres' et de lui-même, constitue déjà un élément extraordinairement important de sa conscience et de son inconscient, une présence et une référence de son vécu quotidien particulièrement lourdes de conséquences sur ses relations avec autrui, dans sa propre société comme dans le reste du monde. Le rapport direct entre la 'pédagogie insidieuse' de ces spectacles cinématographiques et la nature – ou plutôt la qualité – du développement des citoyens africains, des sociétés africaines, ne me paraît devoir échapper qu'aux aveugles et à ceux qui ont leurs raisons de refuser à voir.*[10]

The images of the world, of the 'others' and of himself, which these films transmit to the African, constitute an extraordinarily important element of his conscious and unconscious mind. They are an active presence and reference in his daily life and they have a detrimental effect on his relations with others, within his own society and elsewhere in the world. In my opinion, the direct link between the insidious lessons of these cinematic spectacles and the nature – or rather *the quality* – of the development of African citizens and of African societies is invisible only to those who are blind or those who have their own reasons to refuse to see.

Cinema, which Lenin had proclaimed to be the most important of all art forms, is powerful precisely because it communicates specific ideological visions of the world to a vast number of people.[11] Using his metaphor of the cinema as 'evening school', Sembene has argued that it is the role of the African filmmaker to turn the whole cinematic experience into an educational process, replacing the escapist imagery of Kung-Fu movies and Indian melodramas (the staple of modern African cinemas)[12] with a cinema that reflects the reality and concerns of an African public:

> *De toutes les écoles du soir, la meilleure est, chez nous, le cinéma qui réunit plus d'adeptes que n'importe quelle mosquée, église ou parti politique. Or le 'déracinement' de l'Africain commence lorsqu'une Dakaroise veut ressembler à Brigitte Bardot, qu'elle porte une perruque ou des cheveux gonflants. Il y a plus grave: les jeunes Africains s'identifient aux cowboys, aux gangsters, à Jean-Paul Belmondo ou à Marlon Brando. Et cela avec d'autant plus de force qu'ils n'ont pas de héros nationaux auxquels se référer. C'est pourquoi la décolonisation mentale de l'Afrique n'aura lieu que lorsqu'on osera enfin montrer ses réalités propres.*[13]

---

[9] The Egyptian cinema industry is by far the largest in Africa, but its films are often criticised by African directors (from both North Africa and sub-Saharan Africa) as being inconsequential and escapist melodramas. For a discussion between Sembene and the Egyptian filmmaker, Youssef Chahine, on the state of the Egyptian film industry, see Guy Hennebelle, 'Pour ou contre un cinéma africain engagé?', *L'Afrique littéraire et artistique*, 19 (October 1971), pp. 90–1.

[10] Tahaar Cheriaa, *Écrans d'abondance ou cinéma de libération en Afrique?* (Tunisia: SATPEC, 1978), p. 76 (stress in original).

[11] For a discussion of the attitude of the early Soviet governments towards cinema, see David A. Cook, *A History of Narrative Film* (1981; New York and London: Norton, 1990), pp.139–206.

[12] In his *Essai sur les fondements du cinéma africain* (Dakar: Nouvelles Editions Africaines, 1978), Pierre Haffner argues that African filmmakers should attempt to develop an aesthetic based on such popular genres in order to attract a wider public following. However, his arguments have met with little or no response from African filmmakers.

[13] Jean-Claude Morellet, 'Cinéma africain: premiers pas en liberté', *Jeune Afrique*, 26 February–3 March 1968, p. 43.

Cinema is the best type of evening school in our society. Cinema has more disciples than any mosque, church or political party. Now the 'alienation' of the African begins once a Dakar girl wants to look like Brigitte Bardot and starts wearing a wig or a bouffant hairstyle. And what's worse, young Africans identify with cowboys and gangsters, with Jean-Paul Belmondo and Marlon Brando. This identification is all the stronger because they have no national heroes with which to identify. That's why the intellectual decolonisation of Africa will only take place when we dare to represent our own reality on screen.

Over thirty years after Sembene's first film, *Borom Sarret*, was filmed in Dakar, in 1962, the situation of African cinema has not evolved to the extent that African filmmakers would have wished. The launch of the biennial FESPACO (Festival Pan-africain du Cinéma de Ouagadougou), in 1969, and the creation of FEPACI (Fédération Pan-africaine des Cinéastes), of which Sembene is one of the founder members, in 1970, seemed to herald a bright future for African cinema.[14] However, after this promising start, the situation has tended to stagnate. Attempts to nationalise the film industries within African countries have met with mixed success, and what success there has been has usually been confined to the area of distribution, not affecting production, which is by far the most important issue that needs to be addressed.[15] As Sembene himself has put it, African filmmakers engage largely in a process of *mégotage*, scraping around for finance from whatever sources they can find: African governments, the French *Ministère de la Coopération*, European television stations.[16] It may be argued that this is the case for many filmmakers the world over, but perhaps nowhere is the problem as acute as in

[14] Paulin Soumanou Vieyra's *Le Cinéma africain des origines à 1973* (Paris: Présence Africaine, 1975) provides a useful introduction to the early years of African cinema.

[15] There are a number of works dealing with the economic aspects of the film industry in Africa. For a specific look at Senegal, see Vieyra's *Le Cinéma au Sénégal*. See also Pierre Haffner's two-part article for *Le Mois en Afrique*: 'Le cinéma, l'argent et les lois: une situation du cinéma sénégalais en 1981', 198–99 (May–June 1982), pp. 154–66. The sequel is to be found in *Le Mois en Afrique*, 203–4 (December 1982–January 1983), pp. 144–54. A detailed account of Sembene's personal struggle to find the finance for his films is to be found in Claire-Andrade Watkins, 'Film Production in Francophone Africa, 1961–1977: Ousmane Sembene – An Exception', in Samba Gadjigo et al., eds, *Ousmane Sembene: Dialogues with Critics and Writers* (Amherst, MA: University of Massachusetts Press, 1993), pp. 29–36. More general studies of African cinema can be found in Teshome H. Gabriel, *Third Cinema in the Third World: the Aesthetics of Liberation* (London: Bowker, 1982); Jim Pines and Paul Willemin, eds, *Questions of Third Cinema* (London: British Film Institute, 1989); Nwachukwu Frank Ukadike, *Black African Cinema* (Berkeley, CA and London: University of California Press, 1994).

[16] The Mauritanian director, Sidney Sokhona, makes a similar point about the difficulties facing the African filmmaker:

> *Une seule chose peut être commune à tous les cinéastes africains (mis à part les cinéastes gouvernementaux, ou plus exactement les 'griots' du pouvoir), c'est que tous par manque de structures cinématographiques et refusés par les institutions en place, sont à la fois réalisateurs, producteurs, distributeurs, quelquefois même acteurs, en un mot, 'bricoleurs'.*

> The one thing common to all African filmmakers (apart from government filmmakers, or to be more precise, the 'griots' of state power) is that the lack of cinematic structures and government aid forces them to become directors, producers, distributors, sometimes actors: basically, they are DIY men.

Sidney Sokhona, 'Notre cinéma', *Cahiers du Cinéma*, 285 (February 1978), p. 55.

Africa where sources of private capital are so rare. The African bourgeoisie are not renowned for their willingness to invest in business, so it is hardly surprising that they are not willing to fund the work of radical artists who, on the whole, are hostile to the bourgeoisie's very existence as a class. The critic Pierre Haffner has argued that the existence of an African cinema, considering the economic predicament of the continent as a whole, is a worthy achievement in itself. Reflecting on the 1970s, when over 230 African films were made, Haffner claims that: '*la naissance de chacun de ces 230 films est comme une sorte de miracle arraché par la volonté des cinéastes.*' ['the birth of each one of these 230 films is like a miracle brought about by the will of the directors'] [17] Despite misgivings about Haffner's use of the word 'miracle' when applied to the work of a Marxist such as Sembene, one cannot deny the remarkable achievements of African filmmakers in creating such a large and accomplished body of work, and Sembene's films, both in terms of achievement and in number (the fact that Sembene's corpus of work comprises seven feature films and three short films is more than noteworthy in the African context), occupy a central position in the development of African cinema.

In the previous chapter, it was argued that Sembene's literature is far more complex than most critics have made his work appear, and, in this chapter, a similar claim will be made in respect of Sembene's cinema. Usually described as a competent director and good storyteller (simply replace the word 'director' with 'writer' and one has the standard judgement of his literature), Sembene's films are, in fact, far more challenging than such peremptory judgements allow. Pierre Haffner acknowledges this complexity in Sembene's work, even going so far as to describe him as the African filmmaker who has posed himself the most questions over the form of his work:

> *Sembène Ousmane est sans doute le seul cinéaste négro-africain à mettre en question, à chacun de ses films, son langage, son style, sinon sa pensée; cette œuvre est une affirmation progressive, par le cinéma, de l'homme africain, de son geste, de son histoire et de sa situation.* [18]

> Without doubt, Sembène Ousmane is the only black African filmmaker who questions his language and style, if not his ideas, in each one of his films. His body of work represents a cinematic affirmation of African men and women, of their actions, their history and their situation.

Although his work has never been as radically experimental as that of some African directors, most notably his compatriot, Djibril Diop Mambety,[19] Sembene has consistently attempted to find a cinematic form that is both available to a popular African public, and that also contains a serious reflection

[17] Pierre Haffner, 'Situation du cinéma négro-africain', *Le Mois en Afrique*, 184–85 (April–May 1981), pp. 130–1.

[18] Ibid., p. 133.

[19] Djibril Diop Mambety made his directorial debut in 1969 with *Contras City*. He is probably best known for his 1973 film, *Touki-Bouki*, which is often considered to be African cinema's first *avant-garde* work. After a long break from filmmaking, Mambety returned to the world of cinema in 1992 with the highly acclaimed *Hyènes*. The transposition to a Senegalese setting of Friedrich Dürrenmatt's play, *The Visit*, the film is far less experimental than *Touki-Bouki* but it displays all the wit and irony of his earlier works.

on the cinematic means by which his social concerns can best be captured on the big screen. As Mbye Boubacar Cham has argued in an article on Sembene and the Ethiopian director, Hailé Gerima, the ideology of both directors' films is inscribed in the form of the works themselves:

> [...] the ideology embodied in their work does not in any way emerge as a result of moralizing or preaching by the director through mouthpiece characters; rather it emerges primarily from the structure of the film itself and it is the structure of opposites in most of their films that enables them to organize and control shots, sequences and their component elements so that the final product usually becomes a living dramatization of ideology.[20]

If Sembene's literature can best be defined by its structural concern with the notions of silence and language, then, in a cinematic context, it is necessary to supplement these notions with those of absence and presence. It will be argued that Sembene's films engage in the same challenge to the discourses of power within Senegalese society that are to be found in his literature, but that, alongside the questions of who is allowed to speak, and in what context, one must also consider the space occupied by his characters on the screen. At the risk of stating the obvious, literature is an art concerned primarily with language, while the cinema is an art concerned primarily with images. The image is a spatial representation that introduces a different set of concerns from the word-bound literary text. Concerning Sembene's films, it will be argued that the questions of absence and presence, who or what is excluded from, or included in, the images on the screen, play a fundamental role in transmitting his social and ideological concerns.

In *Le Mandat/Mandabi*, it is the magical and elusive power of money that is explored. The arrival of the money order, which has been sent by Ibrahima Dieng's nephew, Abdou, in Paris, has a profound effect on all the characters in the film. The fact that Dieng is obliged to go through a long, arduous and ultimately fruitless quest in order to try and cash the money order serves to lend the very notion of money an almost supernatural quality (the 'quest' ends in failure when the money is stolen by a family relation). This magical aspect of money is reinforced by the fact that the money order has come from the alien and exotic world of France. Indeed, the value of the money order grows increasingly inflated in the minds of Dieng's neighbours and friends who, although they do not know the true amount, convince themselves that it must be an enormous sum precisely because it has come from France, where they assume that Abdou has become a wealthy man (Sembene deflates such romanticised views of life for the African immigrant in France in the sequences where he shows Abdou sweeping the streets against the tourist landmarks of the Eiffel Tower and the Arc de Triomphe). As Pascal Bonitzer has written, it is the absence of the money, the fact that the money order is never cashed, that gives the *idea* of money such an extraordinary presence in the film:

---

[20] Mbye Boubacar Cham, 'Art and Ideology in the Work of Sembène Ousmane and Hailé Gerima', *Présence Africaine*, 129 (1st quarter 1984), p. 81.

[...] jamais l'invisible abstraction de l'argent n'a pris dans un film une telle visibilité. Presque naturellement, sans intervention d'auteur. Parce qu'il est question de mandat, parce que la présence absente du mandat cristallise les désirs, chaque personnage du film, jusqu'au plus infime, se trouve défini par son rapport à l'argent.[21]

[...] never before has the invisible abstract nature of money been so visible within a film. Almost naturally, without any authorial intervention. For the whole film is about the money order. The absent presence of the money order crystallises the desires it provokes to such an extent that every character in the film, even the minor ones, are defined by their relationship to money.

It was argued in the previous chapter that the novella, *The Money Order*, marked a physical and spiritual movement away from the traditional, village-based society described in *White Genesis* to the corrupt and paranoid world of the city, in which money seems to dominate all other considerations. However, Sembene refuses an abstract view of the city as the site of corruption and immorality to be opposed to the ideal and romanticised world of the African village. Rather, he seeks to link inextricably the urban environment to neo-colonial capitalism and the corruption and poverty that it breeds. In *Le Mandat/Mandabi*, Sembene presents Ibrahima Dieng as a product of the values of 'traditional' society but these are shown to be impotent in face of the values of the dog-eat-dog capitalist system, slowly taking control of Senegalese society. As we saw in *White Genesis*, the countryside is not excluded from the effects of greed, with Medoune Diob having his brother murdered so that he can inherit his position. However, the capitalist system is based in the city, the home of the African bourgeoisie. In fact, Sembene has argued that his film seeks to chart the rise of this new social class:

Le vrai sujet du Mandat, *ce ne sont pas seulement les malheurs du héros. C'est la naissance d'une bourgeoisie africaine. Le cousin voleur est un diplômé, un 'Africain d'aéroport', c'est-à-dire un homme habitué à voyager. Cette bourgeoisie s'efforce de vivre comme les bourgeoisies européennes. Mais elle n'en a ni l'esprit d'entreprise, ni la puissance économique. Ces hommes sont des 'Yes men'. En réalité le problème soulevé par le film est politique. Il n'y a plus de Noirs et Blancs, le problème se pose au niveau de la classe.[22]*

The real subject of *Le Mandat* goes beyond the misfortunes of the hero. The film deals with the birth of an African bourgeoisie. The cousin-thief is an educated man, an 'Airport African', someone who is used to travelling. This bourgeoisie tries to live like the European bourgeoisie but it has neither the spirit of entreprise nor the economic clout. They are merely 'Yes men'. To be honest, the real problem raised by the film is political. There are no more Whites or Blacks: the issue is now one of class.

Le Mandat/Mandabi is, therefore, a film about the emergence of Western-style social classes in urban Senegal (the satirical portrayal of the African bourgeoisie in *Xala* will be examined in the next chapter). Questions of racial identity so dear to the hearts of Senghor and his ilk are deliberately ignored as Sembene focuses on the social problems within Africa. He sets out to examine the life of the urban poor in the first decade of Senegalese independence and he discovers people caught in an economic trap from which they can see no

[21] Pascal Bonitzer, 'L'Argent-fantôme', *Cahiers du Cinéma*, 209 (February 1969), p. 58.
[22] Quoted in '*Le Mandat*', *L'Avant-scène cinéma*, 90 (March 1969), p. 149.

escape. In fact, Sembene has argued that the film should not simply be seen as the story of an old man adrift in an ever-changing modern world but rather as the highly political story of

> *un homme qui a deux femmes et huit enfants à nourrir et qui n'a pas l'argent nécessaire. Tout autour de lui un monde s'écroule et il se demande: l'indépendance sert à quoi? Nous assistons au changement du bonhomme et c'est le plus important. Il finit par dire: ou il faut changer le pays ou je dois me changer moi-même en bandit. Le film finit sur cette interrogation. Tout le monde sait que si la France refusait de nous venir en aide, nos États n'arriveraient même pas à payer les fonctionnaires! Ce n'est pas ça la véritable indépendance.[23]*

a man with two wives and eight children to feed, who doesn't have the money to make ends meet. All around him the world is falling apart and he asks himself: what use is independence? The spectator watches this man come to these realisations and that's the most important thing in the film. This man ends up believing that either the country must change or that he himself must change and become a thief. This is the question with which the film closes. Everyone knows that if France refused us financial aid, our states wouldn't even be able to pay their civil servants! That's not real independence.

The rather simplistic opposition between the coloniser and the colonised had hidden a multitude of social conflicts *within* African societies that refused to disappear upon independence from France. Therefore, in *Le Mandat/Mandabi*, Sembene chose to explore these social conflicts *within* post-independence Senegalese society (as he had done in the stories, 'In the Face of History' and 'Love in Sandy Lane', in *Tribal Scars*), and, in the process, succeeded in raising the ire of quite a number of his compatriots.

In one sense, the controversy surrounding *Le Mandat/Mandabi* is difficult to understand. The novella, *The Money Order*, together with *White Genesis*, had won the top literary prize at the Festival Mondial des Arts Nègres in Dakar, in 1966. In fact, the novella has continued to enjoy a high (and non-controversial) reputation, receiving the canonical sanction of becoming only the second of Sembene's works, after *God's Bits of Wood*, to be studied in African schools, and consequently becoming the subject of a number of critical studies for students.[24] However, the film was to stir up a hornet's nest of criticism in the Senegalese press. I believe that it is possible to detect in such criticisms an elitist disdain for cinema as a popular art form, and also a profound distrust of the effects of a radical cinema upon an uneducated public. As Roger Chemain has shown, the portrayal of the ills of the African city had been a recurrent theme in the African novel of the 1950s and 1960s (the African novel as a genre has been largely preoccupied with the city compared to the rural preoccupations of the poets of Negritude).[25] The novella and the film of *The*

---

[23] Ibid., p. 149.

[24] See Annie Moriceau and Alain Rouch, *'Le Mandat' de Sembène Ousmane: étude critique* (Paris: F. Nathan; Dakar: Nouvelles Editions Africaines, 1983), and Madior Diouf, *'Véhi-Ciosane' et 'Le Mandat' de Sembène Ousmane* (Issy-les-Moulineaux: Editions St. Paul, 1986).

[25] Roger Chemain, *La Ville dans le roman africain* (Paris: L'Harmattan/ACCT, 1981). In his influential study *The Country and the City* (London: Chatto & Windus, 1973), the British Marxist critic Raymond Williams discusses the varying images of city and country in English literature from the Renaissance to the twentieth century. In a chapter, entitled 'The New Metropolis'

Money Order present the same story with only minor differences in plot, recounting Ibrahima Dieng's quest in the same tragi-comic style. The fact is that literature remains the preserve of an African elite which saw itself as perfectly capable of understanding Sembene's arguments about the problems facing independent African societies. However, cinema, and particularly the first feature film in an African language, would attract a large, popular audience (it should not be forgotten that the release of *Le Mandat/Mandabi* was an important social event in Senegal), untrained in the ways of critical interpretation, that would merely be disillusioned by Sembene's 'amoral' tale of life for the urban poor in Dakar.[26]

The common denominator in the arguments of these local critics is the questioning of the representation of Africa in the film. In fact, the controversial nature of Sembene's representation of life in Dakar can be seen in the fact that the Senegalese censors thought long and hard about banning *Le Mandat/Mandabi* in the run-up to the film's premiere at the Théâtre National Daniel Sorano in Dakar, until Senghor declared his desire to attend the screening (this counts as one of the rare occasions on which Senghor intervened on Sembene's behalf, although the Senegalese newspapers of the period do not record what Senghor himself made of the film). In an interview with the Senegalese magazine *Bingo* in 1969, Sembene was forced to defend his film against the claim that he had been too harsh in his criticism of Senegalese society, and more particularly, that he had created a false image of Senegal in choosing to depict the *bidonvilles* (shantytowns) on the outskirts of Dakar:[27]

> *La plupart des Sénégalais, ceux que l'on pourrait surnommer les 'nous ne sommes pas comme ça', pensent que le film tend à démontrer que tout le Sénégal est couvert de bidonvilles. Ces gens-là n'ont rien compris au film. Ce ne sont pas les bidonvilles qui nous importent mais les personnes qui y vivent. Les bidonvilles existent, c'est un fait. Pourquoi le nier?* [28]

Most Senegalese, with their refrain of 'we're not like that', think that the film depicts Senegal as a country covered with shantytowns. These people simply haven't understood the film. It's not the shantytowns that interest me but the people who live there. Shantytowns exist, it's a fact. Why try and deny it?

Sembene reacts angrily against the view that to portray the poor neighbour-

---

[25] (cont.)(pp. 279–89), Williams argues that, in the modern period, the colonised world began to enjoy a similar relationship to the Western metropolis as the country had to the city in eighteenth-century England. In the English imagination, the colonies became a place of refuge, escape and, sometimes, salvation.

[26] Bara Diouf's comments to this effect were quoted in Chapter One. His criticism of the film will be examined in greater detail below.

[27] It does not seem strictly accurate to refer to Ibrahima Dieng's home as a 'shanty', as it is quite a solid structure compared to what is usually termed a 'shanty'. What is more, are we to believe that Aram's greedy cousin would be so eager to ruin Dieng in order to be able to buy a mere shanty? In the novella, there is no mention of the word, 'bidonville', in the descriptions of Dieng's neighbourhood. It would seem that in this interview, Sembene merely copied the word used by his interviewer without questioning its validity. Therefore, in the rest of this chapter, instead of the words 'bidonville' and 'shantytown', I propose to use the more cumbersome, but also more moderate, term of 'poor neighbourhood'.

[28] C. V., 'Un film dont on parle et dont on parlera longtemps: *Le Mandat* de Ousmane Sembene', *Bingo*, 195 (April 1969), p. 41.

hoods of the Dakar suburbs is in some way to 'misrepresent' the reality of life in Senegal. For Sembene, these poor neighbourhoods are an inescapable fact of life in his country, and those who seek to deny this reality are merely attempting to take refuge in the image of a 'traditional', rural Senegal in which all signs of social conflict are banished. Later in the same interview, Sembene rejects this notion of an opposition between a corrupt, urban Senegal and an idealised rural community:

Dans Le Mandat, *je ne traite ni du milieu rural, ni du milieu urbain. J'étudie l'évolution d'un individu dans un contexte social donné. L'histoire d'Ibrahima Dieng est celle d'un cas particulier qui, en abordant beaucoup de petites questions, soulève évidemment des problèmes plus généraux. Quant à dire qu'il faut montrer la bonté des Sénégalais, je vous ai déjà répondu sur ce point et ma préoccupation était tout à fait autre. Lors du débat qui a eu lieu au théâtre Daniel Sorano [i.e. à la sortie du film], des spectateurs avaient axé leur critique sur la réaction qu'auraient les étrangers en voyant* Le Mandat. *Ces gens-là voudraient que, pour conserver la légende du Sénégalais, bon, honnête et hospitalier, on masque la vérité.*[29]

In *Le Mandat*, I'm not dealing with either a rural or an urban setting. I'm studying the evolution of an individual in a specific social context. Ibrahima Dieng's story is a particular case which, by addressing lots of little questions, evokes more general problems. As for the idea that I should be depicting the kindness and generosity of the Senegalese, I already told you that I was interested in something different. During the debate in the Daniel Sorano Theatre [i.e. after the film's premiere], some spectators based their criticism on the reaction they thought foreigners would have to the film's vision of Senegal. These people would like to hide the truth in order to preserve the myth of the good, honest and welcoming Senegalese.

Sembene argues that *Le Mandat/Mandabi* is not a film that is primarily concerned with describing urban society. What interests him is the predicament of Ibrahima Dieng in the emerging, capitalist state system, and the telling of his story involves an account of life in the poverty-stricken areas of Dakar (the actual conditions of life for the urban poor in 1960s Dakar will be discussed further below).

In contrast to the critical reaction in Senegal, most French critics (those politically on the left, at least) saw the film as an important step in the development of an indigenous African cinema precisely because of Sembene's representation of the urban poor. However, their arguments are equally centred on the question of the image of Africa being presented by Sembene. Pascal Bonitzer saw *Le Mandat/Mandabi* as the beginning of a 'true' African cinema. For Bonitzer, the birth of African cinema coincides with the death of the 'traditional' African way of life. He argues that the death of such traditions would also mean the death of a certain Western school of filmmaking (Bonitzer makes particular reference to the work of Jean Rouch and *Les Statues meurent aussi* by Marker and Resnais), which was interested in African 'spirituality':

Jusqu'à [Sembene], ce que venait chercher la caméra en terre d'Afrique, c'étaient les ultimes vestiges du Sacré, perdu pour l'Europe [...]. C'est de nous, de l'Europe, de l'Occident, que ces films parlaient. Mais les statues sont mortes, et S. Ousmane veut parler de l'Afrique.[30]

---

[29] Ibid.

[30] Bonitzer, 'L'Argent-fantôme', p. 57.

Before [Sembene], films about Africa were only interested in capturing the last traces of the Sacred, which have been lost in Europe [...]. Such films are about us in Europe and the West. However, now the statues are dead and S. Ousmane wants to speak about Africa.

Essentially, Bonitzer argues that Sembene's cinema eschews the 'spiritual' considerations of the films of Rouch (whose work, in my view, is not nearly as simplistic as Bonitzer would have us believe) in favour of an examination of the concrete problems facing his society. In Sembene's work, Bonitzer argues, Africa becomes an historical and geographical reality, not a site of spiritual pilgrimage.

The main argument put forward by Bonitzer, that Sembene is an artist profoundly interested in the historical rather than the spiritual, is one that has been readily espoused in the opening chapters of this study. However, I believe that it is necessary to examine more closely the notion that the representation of the city and the urban poor is more 'realistic' than the largely rural images which had predominated in previous films dealing with Africa. Could it be argued that Bonitzer and like-minded, left-wing Western critics simply assume that films about rural Africa are more 'traditional' and reactionary than films about the city? Does this criticism locate the city as the sole site of modernity? If this is the case, what should one make of Sembene's film *Niaye* which deals with corruption and greed in a small, rural community? It could easily be argued that the decline of Santhiu-Niaye, recorded in *Niaye*, has as much to do with the advance of modern, capitalist society as the misfortunes that befall Ibrahima Dieng.[31]

Sub-Saharan Africa was one of the last regions of the world to produce its own cinematic images. It is therefore not that surprising that critics applied themselves so readily to the question of the manner in which a 'true' African cinema would differ from other cinemas. For some Western critics, the emergence of African cinema was the source of a grave disappointment. These Western critics did not know exactly what this cinema should be like, but they knew that they wanted it to be radically different from everything that had come before. Michel Ciment's criticism of *Le Mandat*/*Mandabi* is typical in this respect:

> *Ousmane Sembène sacrifie trop à l'anecdote et à un réalisme de surface nourri de gentillesse et d'observation scrupuleuse. Nous attendons autre chose d'un vrai cinéma africain, mais* Le Mandat *fraie peut-être la voie à des œuvres plus mûres, plus combatives et plus personnelles.*[32]

> Ousmane Sembène sacrifices too much to the anecdotal and to a surface realism that is motivated by generosity and scrupulous observation. We expect *something else* from a *truly African cinema*. However, *Le Mandat* might pave the way for more mature, more militant and more personal films.

---

[31] Taking the opposite view to Bonitzer, Pierre Pommier argues that *Niaye* is an 'African film' precisely because of its rural location. By contrast, *Le Mandat* is described as a film made for the '*marché occidental*' ['Western market']. See Pierre Pommier, *Cinéma et développement en Afrique noire francophone* (Paris: A. Pedone, 1974), p. 105.

[32] Michel Ciment, '*Mandabi* [*Le Mandat*], d'Ousmane Sembene', *Positif*, 100–1 (December 1968–January 1969), p. 45 (my emphasis).

Le Mandat/Mandabi

One is immediately struck by the extraordinary cultural arrogance displayed by Ciment in his dismissal of Sembene's film as sub-standard social realism. What does Ciment know of Senegalese culture? What would he reply to Mbye Boubacar Cham's claim that the film is based on the structure of the traditional, 'trickster' narrative[33] (Cham's argument will be discussed in greater detail below)? How will he recognise a 'true' African film if and when it does arrive? As the critic, Serge Daney, has claimed, a certain type of Western critic had been vaguely expecting African cinema to be a non-intellectual, all-singing, all-dancing extravaganza. What room do such views leave for *Le Mandat/Mandabi* and films like it which sought to describe the life of the poor in African cities.[34] The articulate and socially committed cinema represented by Sembene was simply too 'Western' for these critics.

However, there were just as many left-wing, Western critics who readily saw such radical African films as defining the 'true' African cinema. For example, the influential critic, Jean-Louis Bory, who championed Sembene's films in his column in the left-wing *Nouvel Observateur*, saw African cinema in explicitly political terms:

> *Pour tous ces pays, nul doute, le cinéma est une arme. Il doit aider à la lutte commune au tiers monde: prendre conscience d'eux-mêmes, enfin appelés à décider de leur propre destin, en conscience de leurs problèmes politiques et sociaux d'aujourd'hui.*[35]

> Without a doubt, cinema is a weapon for all of these countries. Cinema must aid in the common struggle of all Third World countries: developing a sense of self-awareness, awareness of their own specific social and political problems, now that their destiny is finally in their own hands.

As the possibility of social revolution in the West, which had seemed on the cards throughout the 1960s, faded in the aftermath of the events of May 1968, these critics invested a lot of hope in the radical movements of the Third World. It is therefore not surprising that *Le Mandat/Mandabi*'s tale of the urban poor should meet with such approval from left-wing critics. The city is after all the site of the class struggle through which the revolution would be born.

This belief in the radical power of cinema was not limited to left-wing critics in the West. The mood of revolutionary optimism which accompanied the process of decolonisation saw the birth of the theory of what was to become known as 'Third Cinema'. Taking its name from an influential article by two of the practitioners of Brazilian *cinema novo*, Fernando Solanas and Octavio Getino, 'Third Cinema' stressed the political function of cinema.[36] Those critics who have advocated the theory of a 'Third Cinema' have stressed that 'authentic' Third World films must abandon the structures and thematic

---

[33] Mbye Boubacar Cham, 'Ousmane Sembene and the Aesthetics of African Oral Traditions', *Africana Journal*, 13, 1–4 (1982), pp. 30–2.

[34] Serge Daney, '*Ceddo* (O. Sembene)', *Cahiers du Cinéma*, 304 (October 1979), pp. 51–3.

[35] Jean-Louis Bory, 'La Nouvelle arme du tiers monde', *Nouvel Observateur*, 28 October–3 November 1968, p. 50.

[36] Fernando Solanas and Octavio Getino, 'Towards a Third Cinema', *Afterimage*, 3 (Summer 1971), pp. 16–35. The article was originally published in Spanish in 1969.

concerns of Western cinema. Writing in 1969, Paulin Soumanou Vieyra warned against the dangers of a 'liberal' conception of cinema, stressing the necessity of a strong ideological impulse in African films:

> *Le risque évidemment avec le libéralisme est la multiplicité des tendances qui pour beaucoup peut déboucher sur le commercial au nom précisément de la liberté d'expression. Les cinéastes africains ne cessent de discuter de ces problèmes et de s'interroger sur les voies et moyens de faire du cinéma africain, c'est-à-dire du cinéma authentifiant les réalités africaines. La voie d'un cinéma cosmopolite n'est pas encore prise mais le danger demeure.*[37]

Of course the risk with liberalism is that in multiplying one's influences one can end up with a commercial cinema that must be defended in the name of freedom of expression. African filmmakers continue to discuss such problems and to ask themselves about the best ways and means of creating an African cinema, that is, a cinema which authentically represents African realities. The path to a cosmopolitan cinema has not yet been taken but it still remains a danger.

This ideological imperative is clearly at the heart of Sembene's cinema and he has often stressed the need to move away from the preoccupations of Western cinema, and, more particularly, from its stereotypical images of Africa. However, does this mean that Sembene's work is 'authentically' African? If it is 'authentically' African, should we then consider the films of Idrissa Ouédraogo, which are primarily interested in moral questions, to be somehow less African? Or what of the experimental, *avant-garde* films of Djibril Diop Mambety?

The filmmaker and critic James Potts has noted the tendency within Africa and the West to make sweeping generalisations about the nature of 'black' or 'African cinema'. Not only do such arguments neglect the vast cultural diversity of the African continent, but they also assume that it is possible to create radically different film 'languages'. Side-stepping the debate between theorists over film's status as a 'langue' or a 'langage',[38] Potts takes a much more pragmatic approach. Having worked as a technical adviser on film projects in Ethiopia and Kenya over a five-year period, he was able to experience the problems of filmmaking in Africa first-hand. This leads him to argue that the technical limitations within which African filmmakers are forced to work can be shown to impose an aesthetic on a film far more readily than one can argue that such matters are governed by the director's ethnic origins. Essentially, Potts believes that we do not yet have the theoretical basis to talk about national or ethnic film styles. Instead, he proposes an approach that attempts to negotiate the relationship between the 'universal' and the 'local' aspects of filmmaking:

> I still prefer to think that film-making is a form of universal speech – not so much a 'Visual Esperanto' as a developing visual language with a rich variety of dialects and idiolects which contain both alien and indigenous elements. These elements

---

[37] Paulin Soumanou Vieyra, 'Le Cinéma au 1er festival culturel panafricain d'Alger', *Présence Africaine*, 72 (4th quarter 1969), p. 201. One of the most influential works on the theory of 'Third Cinema' is Teshome H. Gabriel's *Third Cinema in the Third World*.

[38] Christian Metz is the critic who has been most interested in establishing the status of cinema as a *langue*. See his *Essais sur la signification au cinéma*, 1 (Paris: Klincksieck, 1975).

must be studied more closely and made more explicit if genuine intercultural communication is to take place.[39]

Stephen A. Zacks makes a similar point in his discussion of the numerous theories of African cinema. Echoing many of the arguments also expressed in the first chapter of this study, he argues that the starting point for all criticism, whether cinematic or philosophical, must be the rejection of notions of 'authenticity':

> [...] the inevitable charge that African cinema is grounded in constructs or styles supposedly derivative of a Western tradition still too often succeeds in reducing African cultural products to the status of something secondary and servile, subjecting them to the order in which Africa encountered Europe through colonialism. What we identify as authentically African apparently must exclude the European and place itself in opposition to it. But this sort of theory and practice of exclusion and opposition, based on the faulty premise that Europe is the centre and origin of all culture, in advance invalidates any African text as inauthentic, since even the reaction to the other is defined by the limits of the other's discourse. Accepting the terms in which this problem of authenticity is posed is the first point of subjection, as the question is actually nonsensical in most African contexts, returning us to the site of the colonial conflict, with its nearly exhausted colonial oppositions.[40]

These debates upon the nature of African cinema have too often been trapped within a reductive opposition between Western and African culture. As both a director and a writer, Sembene has never sought to hide the influence of Western artists upon his work. Indeed, he has often referred to the cinematic debts he owes to the Italian neo-realists, and also to the work of Bertolt Brecht (in a 1969 interview, Sembene referred to *Le Mandat/Mandabi* as 'un film brechtien'[41]). Sembene has used such models to construct what he sees as a truly radical African cinema. Sembene may regret the lack of social commitment in certain African films but his choice of a political cinema does not prove him to be either more or less of an 'authentic' African filmmaker. What it does make him is a politically aware and ideologically committed filmmaker.

This debate about the cinematic representation of the continent can thus be seen as a continuation of a much wider debate on the nature of the societies that would emerge after African independence. Negritude was the official ideology of the Senegalese state in the late 1960s and its 'literary wing' (principally in the work of Senghor) presented an almost exclusively rural image of Africa. However, Negritude was far more interested in forging a representation of Africa in its own image than in preserving those rural, African traditions that had survived the colonial era. Mamadou Diouf (some of whose arguments have already been discussed in Chapter One) demon-

[39] James Potts, 'Is there an international film language?', *Sight and Sound*, 48, 2 (Spring 1979), p. 81.

[40] Stephen A. Zacks, 'The Theoretical Construction of African Cinema', *Research in African Literatures*, 26, 3 (Autumn 1995), p. 15. It should be noted that, on the same page, Zacks cites the success of Sembene's film, *Guelwaar*, in the United States as an example of African cinema communicating across cultural boundaries.

[41] See Guy Hennebelle, 'Ousmane Sembene: "Pour moi, le cinéma est un moyen d'action politique, mais"', *L'Afrique littéraire et artistique*, 7 (1969), p. 78.

strates this ambiguous side to Negritude by quoting from a 1961 speech by the author Cheikh Hamidou Kane (speaking shortly before the publication of his influential novel *Ambiguous Adventure*) who was a member of Senghor's UPS (Union Progressiste Sénégalaise). Rejecting oral culture, Kane argues for a modern, literate society:

> *L'évidence du sentiment interne que nous avons de nos cultures ne résistera pas à notre entrée dans le cycle du progrès technique;* il faudra, avant de revêtir le bleu de chauffe du mécanicien, que nous mettions notre âme en lieu sûr.[42]

> The internal possession of our cultures will not resist our entry into the cycle of technological progress; *before donning the mechanic's overalls, we must store our souls in a safe place.*

It is clear that Negritude's dedication to the traditions of rural Africa, and the glories of the African past, the praises of which it never ceased to sing, remained limited to the actual recording of the traditions and the events of that glorious past: the African future was envisaged as that of a modern, technological and urban society. It will be recalled from the first chapter that Sembene's novel, *God's Bits of Wood*, had also suggested that Africa's future would lie in the industrialised, urban world. However, Negritude saw the African city in the abstract terms of Senghor's 'civilisation de l'universel', with the development of a city such as Dakar providing Senegal with a base from which to share its 'valeurs négro-africaines' with the rest of humanity. For Sembene, it is the birth of a proletariat, aware of its power and ready to exploit the industrial and technological developments introduced by the West, that lies behind his vision of the city.

The abstract and idealised nature of Senghor's vision of Dakar is neatly illustrated by the preface he wrote for a sociological study of the city, entitled *Dakar en devenir*, at the end of the 1960s.[43] Since its creation as the capital of French West Africa at the end of the nineteenth century, Dakar had grown at a rapid rate, gathering pace after World War Two, with the population reaching approximately half a million people by the mid-1960s (this rapid growth has continued and in the 1988 census the population of the city was estimated at 1.3 million).[44] Given the rate at which the city was growing, it is hardly surprising that the sociologists who wrote the articles in *Dakar en devenir* are keen to stress the need for urgent action to address the situation. In an article entitled 'Urbanisation et santé', several authors warned about the dangers of simply letting the city mushroom to a size for which it was simply impossible for the government to provide services:

---

[42] Quoted in Mamadou Diouf, 'Représentations historiques et légitimités politiques au Sénégal (1960–1987)', *Revue de la Bibliothèque Nationale* [Paris], 34 (1989), p. 16 (stress in original).

[43] M. Sankalé et al., eds, *Dakar en devenir* (Paris: Présence Africaine, 1968).

[44] Alongside *Dakar en devenir*, Assane Seck's *Dakar: métropole ouest-africaine* (Dakar: IFAN, 1970) stands as a key work on the development of Dakar. Statistics giving the details of the latest figures for the population of Dakar and other major urban centres in Senegal can be found in Ralph Uwechue, ed., *Africa Today* (London: Africa Books, 1996; third edition), p.1277. See also Lat Soucabé Mbow, 'Les Politiques urbaines: gestion et aménagement', in *Sénégal: Trajectoires d'un état*, ed. by Momar Coumba Diop (Dakar: CODESRIA, 1992), pp. 205–31.

Le Mandat/Mandabi

Pour que l'infrastructure urbaine rattrape le retard acquis vis-à-vis de l'implantation des habitations, pour éliminer les bidonvilles et les bâtiments vétustes, il faudrait des investissements impossibles à trouver, renouvelés chaque année pendant une trentaine d'années.[45]

If the urban infrastructure were to make up for lost time in the building of homes, putting an end to shantytowns and dilapidated buildings, it would require vast investment that would be impossible to find for the next thirty years.

The shacks of the poor neighbourhoods that so bothered the critics of *Le Mandat/Mandabi* are shown to be the norm rather than the exception (the authors of the article estimated that 70 per cent of people in Dakar were living in wooden dwellings with tin roofs). When we turn to Senghor's preface, we find a completely different vision of Dakar's future:

Que sera Dakar en l'an 2000? La capitale d'un Sénégal entré dans la société industrielle et apportant sa contribution à la Civilisation de l'Universel. Un centre pour le Sous-Groupe des Pays riverains du Fleuve Sénégal. Une mégapolis africaine, recevant, des profondeurs continentales, des biens matériels et spirituels, les transformant et échangeant avec les autres biens et services des autres grands centres du monde, répandant ses savoir-faire, son savoir-vivre, sa sagesse à l'échelle de la planète.[46]

What will Dakar be like in 2000? The capital of a Senegal which has entered industrial society, bringing its contribution to *Universal Civilisation*. A regional centre for the sub-group of countries around the Senegal river. An African megalopolis receiving material and spiritual goods from the interior of the continent. It will transform and exchange these goods for other goods and services from the other major centres of the world, spreading its know-how, its grace and style and its wisdom across the entire planet.

In light of the dire warnings from the experts cited above, one could quite legitimately ask whether Senghor had actually read *Dakar en devenir*. Ever the consummate politician, he stresses his vision of the future, blithely ignoring the facts that do not fit in with his plans. Senghor's vision is essentially defined in racial and nationalist terms. Firstly, he proclaims that the capital city of Senegal will become the flagship of West African commerce and culture. Secondly, Dakar is cast as an illustration of the racial theories of Negritude: '*De Dakar, du socle basaltique du Cap-Vert, l'Africain nouveau s'élancera vers la civilisation pan-humaine.*' ['From Dakar, from the basalt pedestal of Cap-Vert, a new African will soar towards a pan-human civilisation.']'[47] Having fulfilled Senghor's nationalist and racial criteria, Dakar thus seems to be set above any possible criticism.

If we turn to Bara Diouf's criticism of *Le Mandat/Mandabi* (part of which is quoted in Chapter One), we can see that it contains the same ambiguities and evasions as the texts by Kane and Senghor. Unlike the critic from *Bingo*, he does not accuse Sembene of betraying the reality of Senegal in his film. In fact, he openly praises Sembene for the honesty of his portrayal of life in Dakar:

Armé de sa caméra, Ousmane Sembène ne s'est pas contenté de nous livrer les images anachroniques

[45] M. Sankalé et al., eds, *Dakar en devenir*, p. 266.
[46] M. Sankalé et al., eds, *Dakar en devenir*, p. 11 (stress in original).
[47] Ibid., p. 12.

83

et vieillies d'un folklore dont l'Europe est si friande. Il a scruté les âmes, décrit les misérables conditions d'existence, étalé au grand jour les pratiques qui nous rongent comme une lèpre. C'est du cinéma vérité, sans complaisance dans sa rigueur comme dans le pessimisme de son dénouement. On ne peut pas ne pas se souvenir, à la vue du Mandat, *du* Voleur de bicyclettes *de Vittorio de Sica.*[48]

Armed with his camera, Ousmane Sembène was not content to serve us up anachronistic, outdated images from folklore, images which Europe holds so dear. He has examined people's souls, described their miserable existence, and laid out before us the practices which are eating away at us like leprosy. It is a piece of cinéma vérité whose rigour is not lessened by any complacency, as can be seen in the pessimism of its ending. Upon seeing *Le Mandat*, one cannot help thinking of Vittorio de Sica's *The Bicycle Thief*.

This evocation of the work of the Italian neo-realists appears at first to be intended as a positive comment on Sembene's film. However, he goes on scornfully to dismiss what he describes as the absolute pessimism of neo-realism, particularly as he interprets it in *Le Mandat/Mandabi*, which he sees as lacking any moral framework (a groundless charge that will be challenged below). Diouf believes that Sembene's pessimism prevents him from conceiving of a group or party that could bring about change, and it comes as no surprise that the type of party Diouf proposes to play such a role in Africa bears a remarkable resemblance to Senghor's UPS (even if by 1968, the party hardly conformed to his last two criteria): '*dans la dialectique d'Ousmane Sembène, il manque le parti qui doit transformer la société. Evidemment, en Afrique, ce ne peut être qu'un parti à la fois national,* démocratique *et socialiste.*' ['Ousmane Sembène's dialectic omits the party which must transform society. In Africa, such a party must of course be national, *democratic* and *socialist*.']'[49] Portraying Sembene as an opponent of the process of modernisation, and consequently of urbanisation, Diouf seeks to cast the debate on the African urban space in the hackneyed terms of a contrast between tradition and modernity, whereas Sembene would argue that the problems of a city such as Dakar are entirely caused by the ravages of a capitalist system, governed by the West under the compliant eyes of the Senegalese government.

Although Sembene has deliberately sought to represent the problems of the hitherto neglected urban poor in certain of his novels and films, it would be wrong to assume that his work contains an explicit urban bias. His adherence to a Marxist philosophy that places a high premium on the role of the urban proletariat in the class struggle does not mean that he is uninterested in the problems of the Senegalese peasantry. His work has consistently dealt with the questions of oppression and resistance in both an urban and a rural setting. It is true that *God's Bits of Wood* presents the railway workers as an urbanised, proletarian elite, but this is, in part, a recognition of the fact that Senegal was by far the most industrialised region in French West Africa. Senegal's technological advance on its neighbours has led to a situation whereby approximately half of the Senegalese population today lives in urban centres, a remarkable

[48] Bara Diouf, '*Le Mandat*, film d'Ousmane Sembene', *Dakar–Matin*, 7 December 1968, p. 1.
[49] Ibid., p. 8 (my emphasis).

statistic on a continent where close to 80 per cent of people continue to work on the land.[50]

The concern for the urban poor to be seen in *God's Bits of Wood* and *Xala* can be easily counterbalanced by the representation of rural communities in works such as *Niaye*, *Emitaï* and *O Pays, mon beau peuple!* In fact, there is often an explicit link made between the rural and the urban in these works. If *Niaye* records the growing exodus from the countryside towards the cities, then *Xala* recounts the plight of such people when they wash up on the streets of Dakar, forced to beg for their living: the blind beggar arrives in the city after his land has been stolen by El Hadji, while the peasant, who has come to the city to buy food for his fellow villagers, ravaged by the effects of the drought, has his wallet stolen by a pickpocket. Such images provide a stark vision of the fate awaiting many of those who come to the city to seek a better life.[51]

Sembene's first film *Borom Sarret* acts, in many ways, as a mapping out of the African city (in this case, Dakar). Although a short film (it lasts only 19 minutes), it manages to present the spectator with a startling variety of images of life for the urban poor, focusing in particular on the cart driver (the *borom sarret*, that is, the *bonhomme charrette*, of the film's title) whose peregrinations about the city form the basis of the story. Many critics have commented on the almost documentary nature of *Borom Sarret* and particularly on the use of techniques made popular by the Italian neo-realists.[52] The stark contrasts, which form an integral part of the urban landscape, are made evident throughout the film. The cart driver is presented to us as a simple man, trying to scrape a living from ferrying poor people, who do not have their own means of transport, about the city. He is, in a number of senses, a peripheral figure, situated on the outskirts of the city and eking out a living in the margins of society. This peripheral nature is displayed visually by the frequent images of the cars that pass him by on the road (in 1960s Dakar, the car would have been an even greater symbol of wealth than it is today). The cart driver quite literally moves at a different pace from a middle-class Africa that both literally and symbolically leaves him trailing in its wake.

The social chasm that exists between the African bourgeoisie and the urban poor is represented in the very geographical layout of the city. This is

[50] The results of the 1988 census showed that 39 per cent of the Senegalese population live in urban centres. It is now estimated that, at current growth rates, over half the population will be living in towns and cities within a generation. See Lat Soucabé Mbow, 'Les Politiques urbaines', pp. 205–31.

[51] In an article entitled 'Les niveaux de vie' in *Dakar en devenir*, Y. Mersadier argues that the problems created by the rapid growth of Dakar can only be solved by dealing with the problem of migration from the countryside towards the city (pp. 260–3).

[52] Pierre Haffner has described this film as one of the best to have emerged from Africa. However, he believes that it is both too slow and too radical to be a popular success within Africa: 'Borom Sarret [...] ne peut être un film populaire, le public des médinas le reçoit comme une boisson imbuvable et le public des beaux quartiers comme une gifle – l'un et l'autre ne s'empressent de l'oublier.' ['Borom Sarret [...] can never be a popular film: the audiences from the medinas do not find it to their taste, while the audiences from the richer areas view it as a slap in the face – both audiences are keen to forget the film.'] See Pierre Haffner, *Essai sur les fondements du cinéma africain* (Dakar: Nouvelles Editions Africaines, 1981), p. 138.

illustrated when the cart driver is hired by a middle-class customer to bring him to the Plateau (a bourgeois quarter close to the commercial district in Dakar).[53] In place of the hustle and bustle of the poorer areas of the city, we discover sedate, tree-lined avenues that are virtually deserted. This contrast is also represented on the soundtrack where the *xalam* (a traditional Senegalese stringed instrument) of the earlier scenes is replaced with the strains of a piece by Mozart. The cart driver feels out of place and, as we are to find out, he is, from the point of view of the law, a *persona non grata* on the Plateau, where carts such as his are banned. When he is stopped by the police, we are given a visual illustration of the position occupied by the poor in the modern African state. As *borom sarret* hands over his papers, he drops something on the ground. As he bends to pick it up, we see that it is a war medal. However, before his hand can grasp it, the policeman's foot stamps on the medal. As *borom sarret* looks up at his tormentor, we are given a subjective shot of the policeman towering above him. Framed behind the policeman who is writing out a ticket for him, we can see a tall apartment building. For the cart driver, the policeman represents the rich who live in these shiny towers, and the words that he writes in his notebook are incomprehensible to him. When he leaves the Plateau, the music of the *xalam* returns and *borom sarret* comments that: '*Ici, c'est mon quartier. Ici, je me sens bien.*' ['This is my neighbourhood. I feel at home here.'] At this point, the camera turns from the horse and cart, and the spectator is shown the independence memorial at Colobane. The irony of the image is evident: the spectator is invited to ponder on the value of an independence that allows such obvious injustices to continue. The examination of the urban space becomes an examination of the failures of the nationalist movement.

When Sembene came to make *Le Mandat/Mandabi*, another film about urban poverty, he borrowed a narrative form from Wolof oral tradition, that of the 'trickster' tale (the same narrative structure is used in the novella). The archetypal 'trickster' narratives are those concerning Leuk-le-lièvre, the African forefather of the 'Brer Rabbit' character in the tales of the American South.[54] Mbye Boubacar Cham's arguments on the manner in which Sembene adapts such traditional narrative styles to create his own open-ended narratives seem particularly apt in relation to *Le Mandat/Mandabi*. In fact, Sembene's desire to prevent his stories from slipping into folklore and exoticism had almost resulted in the film being shot in black and white, as he believed that audiences (particularly in the West) would become blinded by the vivid colours of the African city and forget about the social and political concerns

---

[53] Assane Seck has shown how the French colonisers displaced the original Lebou settlements at the southern tip of the Cap Vert peninsula in order to begin the construction of Dakar (in the area that has become known as the Plateau). Power and wealth thus became situated in this southern region, and throughout the twentieth century, the poor were pushed further and further northwards. See Seck, *Dakar: métropole ouest-africaine*, pp. 128–32.

[54] For some examples of the tales of Leuk-le-lièvre, see Léopold Sédar Senghor and Abdoulaye Sadji, *La Belle histoire de Leuk-le-lièvre*, (1953; London: Harrap, 1965). See also the story, 'Tours de lièvre' in Birago Diop's *Tales of Amadou Koumba*, trans. by Dorothy S. Blair (London: Longman, 1985).

of his narrative. Cham argues that Sembene's film closely follows, but subtly alters, the structure of the 'trickster' narrative. As in the stories of Leuk-le-lièvre, the protagonist is set a number of challenges with a prize waiting for him at the end of it, but, unlike Leuk, Ibrahima Dieng becomes the victim rather than the perpetrator of deceit, and he fails to obtain his goal (one could also convincingly argue that *Borom Sarret* employs a similar narrative structure, with the cart driver being constantly thwarted in his attempts to make money):

> In the Wolof narrative, the relationship between Protagonist/Trickster and Victims is clearly established and developed with each repetition. In *Mandabi*, it is the relationship between Protagonist/Victim and Tricksters that each repetition explores. Thus, taken together, 'Les Tours de Leuk-le-lièvre' and *Mandabi* reveal a basic set of relationships between Trickster, on the one hand, and Victim, on the other. This becomes, by extension, a relationship between Victimizer–Victim, Have–Have-not, Exploiter–Exploited, a dialectical relationship which characterizes the entire work of Ousmane Sembene [...]. It is within this structure of opposites that Sembene looks at the social and political challenges confronting contemporary Senegalese, and, by extension, African society, just as the structure of opposites in the Wolof narrative provides the framework for the examination of certain aspects of traditional social and political life.[55]

In Sembene's film, the 'universal' tale of clever 'trickster' and hapless victim (itself a gross simplification of the role of such tales in traditional Wolof society) becomes a profoundly social and political story of poverty and paranoia. In the streetscape of the modern African city, the character of the 'trickster' has become an all-pervasive figure. The communal bond has been broken by the impersonal nature of the big city, and the scramble for money, whether amongst the poor who have none, or the bourgeoisie who want more, is the chief concern for people.[56]

Le Mandat/Mandabi is visually structured around the conflict between the rituals of the capitalist world (as well as those of the modern bureaucratic state) and those of the 'traditional' communal order. This concern with ritual is something that has been overlooked by many of Sembene's critics. As with his literature, attention has tended to focus on themes and political issues but with only scant regard for questions of form. However, as we shall see below, Sembene's cinematic exploration of ritual has remained constant throughout his career. In many ways, one could argue that the examination of rituals and cultural signs constitutes the motor of Sembene's cinematic enterprise (this examination of ritual reaches its pinnacle in Sembene's film, *Ceddo*, which is analysed in Chapter Six).

The commercial nature of life in the city is made evident from the opening scene of the film. In what could easily pass for a simple piece of local colour,

---

[55] Cham, 'Ousmane Sembene and the Aesthetics of African Oral Traditions', p. 32.

[56] In many ways, it could be argued that the African city of the 1960s was facing many of the problems faced by major Western cities in the nineteenth century. Writing at the beginning of the twentieth century, the sociologist, Georg Simmel, claimed that the 'modern mind [had] become more and more calculating' in the capitalist metropolis. See Georg Simmel, 'Metropolis and Mental Life', in *The Sociology of Georg Simmel*, trans. and ed. by Kurt H. Wolff (1950; London: Collier-Macmillan, 1964), p. 412.

this opening sequence begins with a low-angle shot looking up at the branches of a baobab tree, while we hear some lively *kora* music on the soundtrack (the *kora* is a twenty-one stringed West African instrument). The camera then pans down to a group of barbers by the roadside, proceeding to move in for a series of close-ups, capturing the movements and gestures of the barbers, which almost seem to be dictated by the music, as they skilfully shave their customers (one of whom is Ibrahima Dieng). However, this beautifully filmed sequence is not intended as a piece of tourist exotica. It is not surprising that Sembene, as a Marxist, and also as a man who had been involved in so many manual occupations (not least the cinema itself), should appreciate the skills involved in the barbers' work. However, Sembene also knows that, for all their beauty and rhythm, the barbers' skills do not come for free. As Dieng rises to his feet after the shave, he plays his part in the transaction by handing over the money he owes the barber for his work. The type of self-gratification in which Dieng likes to indulge requires money and, unfortunately, money is precisely what he lacks.

The centrality of money to the narrative is made even more explicit in the following scene. As Dieng walks away from the barber, the postman passes him by on his way to Dieng's home to deliver the money order. Setting the pattern for the rest of the film, it is Dieng's wives who are left at home to worry about the very real financial problem of putting food on the table each day. When Dieng returns home, a sumptuous meal awaits him, and, while he gorges himself, he is waited on hand and foot by his two wives, one of whom fans him as he eats, while the other disposes of the bones which he spits out into her hand. In a highly comic and ironic sequence, the bloated hero then proceeds to be overcome by a fit of burping (one of the scenes to which some of his rather sensitive compatriots objected). Sembene neatly intercuts this sequence with a shot of Dieng's wife, Aram, nursing a baby (a ploy that he uses again later in the film). Essentially, Dieng is presented to us as a child who cannot look after himself, and this is particularly true when it comes to money. He likes to live the good life but it is simply beyond his means (his love of finery is displayed throughout the film by his magnificent, but comically over-sized, *boubou*). He does not ask where the money has come from for this meal but, before the end of the film, he is to learn that everything has a price.

Just like the cart driver of *Borom Sarret*, Ibrahima Dieng is a man who lives on the periphery of the city.[57] In fact, he is literally a *peripheral* figure in the social and economic scheme of things in this neo-colonial world. He and his neighbours are poor people, forced to live from day to day. They believe that money is something which comes from elsewhere: the banks and businesses of the city centre, the rich homes of the bourgeoisie, and, most notably, from the West (hence the manner in which the value of the money order is inflated when people learn that it has come from France). Therefore, the film is

[57] In the novella, *The Money Order*, Dieng is said to live five kilometres from the 'grande mairie' in Dakar. This means that he probably lives on the very edge of the *Medina*, the *quartier populaire* north of the commercial district.

88

3.1 The hapless Ibrahima Dieng with his wives, Méty and Aram
Le Mandat, Filmi Doomireew – Dakar, Senegal (all rights reserved)

89

marked by Dieng's trips from the periphery to the centre in his quest to cash the money order.[58]

Existing on the periphery means existing outside the spheres in which money freely circulates and Dieng sees the money order as his way out of the poverty trap. He begins the film in debt but still with enough money to pay the barber for his shave. However, his quest to cash the money order drives him further and further into debt. In fact, the more he tries to reach out to money, to integrate himself into the capitalist system, the more it seems to slip away from his grasp. Eventually, it is the corrupt relative, Mbaye, who benefits from the money order. He is the character who is probably the least in need of cash but he is able to use his wealth and his position to cheat Dieng out of his money. It becomes increasingly clear, as the film progresses, that it is money which breeds money. Those who already possess wealth (Mbarka, the shopkeeper, and Mbaye, the corrupt relative) make more money while those who have none remain confined to their position on the periphery.

Dieng's trips to the centre are marked visually by a movement away from the communal, family-based rituals of the periphery to the rituals of the capitalist economy. Essentially, Ibrahima Dieng's life in the *banlieue* is centred around his family and the bonds of the local community (however, as we shall discover below, the dog-eat-dog ways of the centre are increasingly becoming the norm on the periphery). However, in the city, he is simply an anonymous figure, and he cannot count on the ties of family or friendship to bail him out of trouble. This fact is brought home to Dieng on his first trip to the city to have the money order cashed. In what is to be the first of many encounters with unmotivated and unhelpful civil servants, Dieng is treated in a very curt and dismissive fashion by the young post-office clerk. Not only does this young man have no respect for his elders but he tells Dieng that he will have to go through a succession of such interviews in his 'quest' for the documents necessary to cash the money order (Dieng needs an identity card to cash the money order, but, in order to obtain an identity card, he first of all needs to obtain a birth certificate and two passport-size photographs). In a comic coda to this scene, Dieng, who is accompanied by Gorgui Maïssa, is collared by the scribe, played by Sembene, whom he had previously asked to read out his nephew's letter for him, promising payment as soon as he has cashed the money order. In his disappointment, he walks out of the post-office forgetting his promise to the scribe. Despite the picture of Che Guevara on his desk, the scribe's social values do not stretch so far as to allow his work to go unremunerated. A repentant Dieng promises to pay him at a later date, but the scribe is unhappy at this turn in events and he shouts after the pair as they head off: *'Bande de fauchés!'* ['You bums!'] In the city, human contact is fleeting

<hr />

[58] The Zimbabwean writer, Chenjerai Hove, has written of the multiple worlds that exist in African cities, setting the rich apart from the poor, fragmenting the sense of community. See "'First World", "Third World" and "Fourth World" City', in *Shebeen Tales: Messages from Harare* (London: Serif, 1994), pp. 24–32. Alexandre Biyidi, writing under the pseudonym of Eza Boto (which he would later change to Mongo Béti), makes similar points about the African city in his *Ville cruelle* (Paris: Présence Africaine, 1954).

and anonymous, and the ability to pay one's debts is of primary importance.

As this scene demonstrates, the city is also a place in which the written word is used virtually as a means of social exclusion (we saw a similar process at work in *Borom Sarret* above): Dieng's inability to read or write French excludes him from the bureaucratic modern world (his confusion in the French-speaking world is less evident in *Le Mandat* than in *Mandabi* because in the former the dialogue is in French). Ibrahima Dieng simply cannot understand how bureaucracy works. This system of forms and official papers is totally alien to him. In fact, his individual efforts to cash the money order all come to nothing, and it is others who eventually deal with the paperwork: Amath sorts out his problems in obtaining his birth certificate; a man outside the bank takes care of cashing his cheque for him; and, finally, Mbaye goes into the police station alone to obtain the power of attorney (with disastrous consequences). It is Dieng's exclusion from the written word and its codes of power that leads to his downfall.

All of Dieng's dealings in the city are marked by a sentiment of deception and paranoia. Sembene renders this visually by cutting from distance shots of Dieng, lost in the crowded streets of Dakar, to close-ups of his worried face while, on the soundtrack, we hear him thinking despairingly about what his next move should be. He is constantly deceived and disappointed in his expectations and assumptions of what people are supposed to be. The civil servants whom he encounters are supposedly working in the service of the public but they are far from helpful to Dieng, treating him with a mixture of contempt and indifference (a common criticism against bureaucrats in all countries, not merely in Africa). Dieng's bourgeois cousin, Amath, although a much more sympathetic character than the corrupt Mbaye, also fails to live up to his expectations. He does give Dieng some money and he also helps him to obtain his birth certificate but he remains a remote and distant figure. Although willing to help out when pressed, he seems to avoid his poor relations who are constantly in need of financial assistance. Amath can help out with the birth certificate because his friend works in the town hall: although we do not learn of his profession, it is clear that he belongs to the bureaucratic middle-class with which Dieng has so much difficulty. He fails to live up to the standards of family solidarity fostered by Dieng.

These trips to the city gradually succeed in eroding Dieng's faith in the goodwill of his fellow Africans. When he goes to cash the cheque given to him by Amath, a man loitering outside the bank (whose identity we never learn) offers to deal with the matter, explaining that Dieng would not be able to obtain his money without an identity card. Having already had enough of problems concerning identity cards, Dieng readily agrees to this. However, what Dieng takes to be an act of kindness is actually intended as a business transaction: as he leaves the bank, the man is waiting for him and he demands 300 CFA for his part in the deal. At first bewildered by this request, Dieng eventually hands over the money with some reluctance (it amounts to more than one quarter of the cheque's total value: 1,000 CFA). As Dieng wanders off, the camera lingers on the man who pockets the bank notes: in the city, the financial transaction determines the very nature of human relationships.

In the very next scene, Dieng is approached by a woman who asks him for money. Prior to his trip to the bank, he had given money to a woman asking for 20 CFA to enable her to travel home. Obeying Islamic precepts of charity, Dieng sees it as his religious and moral duty to aid the woman (as he hands over the money, he utters the ritual phrase, *'Que tous les malheurs suivent cette pièce'* ['May all misfortunes follow this coin']). However, his experience at the bank appears to have made him wary of strangers and he refuses to give her any cash, claiming that she is, in fact, the same woman who had accosted him earlier. Although this woman physically resembles the one from the earlier scene, Sembene deliberately makes it ambiguous as to whether it is indeed the same person.[59] In this second scene, the woman is carrying a baby, her clothes are a slightly different colour, and her reason for needing the money is completely different. However, the main difference from the prior scene is in Dieng's attitude for he now suspects the motives of all those who approach him in the streets of the city centre (anyone who has visited central Dakar in recent years will know that, if anything, the number of con men who congregate around the banks on the Place de l'Indépendance has grown since Dieng's day). Dieng has come to believe that people cannot be taken at their word, nor can their outward appearance be trusted. He finds himself at sea in a world of paranoia and deceit.

Dieng's most harrowing experience in the city comes after his dispute with the photographer's apprentice. Having come to collect his passport photographs, he is dismayed to discover that they have been ruined due to a technical fault with the photographer's camera. When he demands a refund, a row develops and the young apprentice proceeds to beat up the diminutive Dieng, played by the magnificent Makhourédia Gueye (who also plays the President of the Chamber of Commerce in *Xala* and the king, Demba Waar, in *Ceddo*). After Dieng's bloody retreat, we discover that he has, in fact, been the victim of an elaborate scam: the photographer and his apprentice drink a glass of wine and discuss the perilous nature of their scheme of pretending to take photographs of people, and then simply holding on to the money that they have been paid, claiming a problem with the camera.

Upon his return to the suburbs, Dieng seems to be in total despair, with the money he needs and desires so badly appearing further away than ever. Sembene presents him to us as a broken man: the camera focuses on some blood stains on the ground, around which a small army of ants can be seen swarming, before panning up to a shot of Dieng's bowed head. As the camera moves back slightly, we see that he is sitting on a tree stump, head in hands, dripping blood from his nose on to the ground. He can see no way out of his

---

[59] In his summary of the film, Paulin Soumanou Vieyra claims that: *'Sur le chemin du retour, la même mendiante l'accoste à nouveau, Dieng la reconnaît et furieux lui refuse l'aumône.'* ['On the way back, the same beggar stops him once again. A furious Dieng recognises her and refuses to give her alms.'] Vieyra, *Sembène Ousmane, cinéaste*, p. 89. However, even if Vieyra is correct in claiming that it is indeed the same woman, it remains true that this is not immediately obvious to the spectator.

predicament. When he staggers home, Aram and Méty appear to be taken aback at the fate that has befallen their husband. However, without stopping to find out what has actually happened, the two women proceed to break out into great lamentations about the brutal attack upon their husband which has seen the money from his money order stolen from him. A crowd quickly gathers and news of the 'theft' passes from mouth to mouth. Significantly, one bystander claims that the 'stolen' money order had been worth 100,000 CFA. Such are the financial difficulties in which those on the periphery find themselves that they make the amount of the money order grow to the point where it can solve all their worries: money has come to be an obsession for virtually all members of the community, including those who live on the periphery.

This scene therefore marks something of a turning point in the film, marking the triumph of commercial over communal values. Up until now, we have discussed the dominance of financial considerations in the commercial centre. However, as the film progresses, it becomes clear that the same considerations are coming to dominate on the periphery as well. Aram and Méty flagrantly lie to people about the money order precisely because it has become a source of interest to virtually the entire neighbourhood. The Dieng family had come under intense scrutiny as their neighbours and 'friends' seek to benefit from their windfall. The suburban poor lead such a precarious existence that their sense of community has been reduced to a concern with meeting the needs of one's own family. In this context, neighbours and 'friends' come to be seen as rivals rather than allies in the daily struggle to make ends meet.

Although Ibrahima Dieng is presented to us as a man at sea in the modern, capitalist and bureaucratic world, it would be over-simplistic to view him as the innocent abroad, surrounded by vultures, waiting to pounce on him. His oft-pronounced attachment to the values of a traditional, communal Africa must not be allowed to conceal the fact that he is just as implicated in the deceit surrounding the money order as those who are trying to obtain the money from him. Dieng may rail at an age in which lying has become a way of life, but one must remember that he plans to spend the whole sum of the money order, 25,000 CFA, which his nephew, Abdou, has sent to him, when, in fact, only 2,000 are intended for him (3,000 CFA are intended for Abdou's mother, while the other 20,000 CFA are to be kept safe for Abdou's return to Senegal). Perhaps Dieng genuinely intends to repay the money at a later date but where would he find such a sum when the full total of the money order does not even cover his current debts with Mbarka, the local shopkeeper? The simple fact is that poverty is in the process of destroying the bonds that previously held the community together, and Dieng cannot exclude himself from the consequences of this economic fact. This is brought home in the comic scene where Dieng and his wives oversleep after their heavy meal. The camera pans across from the minaret of the local mosque to Dieng's house, moving in for close-ups of each member of the family soundly sleeping while the *muezzin*'s call to prayer can be heard. The arrival of the money order has allowed Dieng's wives, Aram and Méty, to obtain credit from Mbarka, with which to feed their family: as they sleep soundly after what is probably their first full meal in a long time, it becomes clear that the daily worry of feeding one's family has come to take precedence over spiritual concerns. Money and its promise of physical and material well-being have quite literally distanced the Dieng family from their religion.

This obsession with money creates a feeling of paranoia and suspicion that pervades the film. In this respect, the scene in which Dieng learns of the arrival of the money order serves to set the tone for the rest of the film. The camera films proceedings from a low angle at the far end of the room as Aram and Méty tell their increasingly irate husband that they have used the letter, containing news of the money order, to obtain credit from Mbarka, the shopkeeper (with whom, it would appear, only a financial relationship is possible, despite his claim to be Dieng's friend). The camera angle creates a sense of secrecy, as though they are being spied upon from afar by unknown eyes. As Dieng stresses to his wives, money is something that cannot be talked about in public because one never knows who may be listening. The sensitivity of the whole subject of money is evident in the fact that Aram and Méty have seen fit to go behind their husband's back by going to see Mbarka. While the unemployed Dieng aimlessly passes the time, bemoaning his fate, it falls upon his wives to make sure that there is food on the table every day. The women are forced to borrow and ask for credit wherever they can, without telling their proud but ineffectual husband.[60] Indeed, one of the chief ironies of the film is the fact that money (or rather the lack of it) dominates people's lives yet they are unable to speak openly about their concerns. This evasive style of speech when dealing with money serves to give it even more of a mysterious and powerful aura.

Once the news of the money order has spread, the Dieng household becomes the subject of constant observation. As Dieng leaves Mbarka's shop in the following scene, Gorgui Maïssa is waiting to pounce on him. Once again, the camera follows proceedings from a low angle as Gorgui Maïssa, who towers above Dieng, probes his 'friend' for information about the money order (as was mentioned above, the use of such low-angle shots helps to create a sense of unease and suspicion). As it turns out, Gorgui Maïssa is simply the first in a seemingly endless procession of people who seek aid from Dieng, whom they see as some sort of rich potentate who could solve all their financial woes if only he saw fit to do so. Even when Dieng offers some help, people are not satisfied. Not having any money to meet these incessant demands, he decides to distribute some of the rice which has been sold to him (on credit) by Mbarka, despite the protests of his wives (who, as we saw above, are much more pragmatic than their husband). Three men gathered outside his house comment on the pitiful amount of rice that Dieng has given to one of them, claiming that he had received one hundred kilos of rice from

---

[60] At the end of *Borom Sarret*, it is the cart driver's wife who goes out to earn the money needed to put food on the table. Although it is not stated explicitly, it is understood that she is going to earn this money through prostitution.

Mbarka (Dieng had, in fact, received less than ten kilos of rice). As Dieng leaves his house, we are given a subjective shot from the men's point of view, of the diminutive figure moving off into the distance: his neighbours are constantly watching him and they are unwilling to take his words at face value. Even Dieng's sister, Astou (whose son has sent the money from Paris), does not seem to fully believe him when he says that he is having difficulty in cashing the money order. However, the sense of suspicion that hangs over Dieng finds its most threatening aspect in the character of Mbaye, the relative who eventually steals the money. On a number of occasions, we see him lurking outside Dieng's home, and, as we learn in one of the early scenes in the film, his aim is to force Dieng into selling him the house in order to pay off his debts (he is in league with Mbarka, the shopkeeper, to achieve this end). The notion of the extended family is here shown to have been completely undermined.

This sense of being watched gradually forces Dieng into a spiralling circle of half lies and deceit. He attempts to hide the truth about the money order from his neighbours, suspecting them of coveting his money (a suspicion that proves correct), while his neighbours attempt to conceal their designs by presenting themselves as his friends and allies in his struggle with the bureaucratic powers that be. In many ways, the only thing that distinguishes Dieng from the 'trickster' figure, Gorgui Maïssa, is that Dieng is simply not as good at deception. Essentially, Ibrahima Dieng is a pathetically comic character, who is well-meaning but ineffectual. Sembene uses the recurring joke of showing Dieng constantly pushing up the sleeves of his over-sized *boubou* when he is annoyed: he is the little man up against the world, without the strength of character to stand up to the corruption and deceit that he sees around him, and unable to play the game of deception himself.

As was mentioned above, the scene in which Aram and Méty lie to the crowd about the theft of the money order marks a crucial development in the struggle between communal and commercial values. For the first time, Dieng comes to realise that he is as implicated in the lies and deceit of his age as those around him. After the clamour of the crowd, we cut to a shot of the branches of a baobab tree (which is the national emblem of Senegal) filmed from a low angle, echoing the opening image of the film. The camera circles around the tree, capturing the glint of sunlight through the branches. Sembene here seems to be providing both his hero and his audience with a moment of reflection in the midst of all the lies and deception: has Senegal really become a country where, to use Dieng's words, '*l'honnêteté est un délit chez nous*'? ['Honesty is a crime nowadays'] It should be noted that, at this point, the film's Wolof refrain, written by Sembene, can be heard on the soundtrack, commenting on the story (at one point in the film, we actually hear Méty singing it).[61]

[61] In an interview with Nourredine Ghali, Sembene discusses the use of music in his films. He confirms that he wrote the lyrics to the refrains in both *Le Mandat*/*Mandabi* and *Xala*. However, although he explains the meaning of the lyrics to the latter song, he does not explain the meaning of the lyrics of the song in *Le Mandat*/*Mandabi*, although it is made clear that the song comments on the theme of the film. See Nourredine Ghali, 'Ousmane Sembene. "Le cinéaste de nos jours peut remplacer le conteur traditionnel"', *Cinéma*, 208 (April 1976), p. 90.

The film ends on a rather ambiguous note. Having been betrayed by Mbaye, Ibrahima Dieng appears close to despair. He sits disconsolately on the street beside the sack of rice given to him by Mbaye, and, within seconds, a crowd of women has gathered and begins to empty the rice from the sack (only the arrival of Aram and Méty prevents the whole stock being lost). Confused and defeated, Dieng declares that the communal bond has been broken, and that, from now on, he too will engage in deceit and hypocrisy (the irony being that Dieng has been increasingly involved in lies and deceit as the film progresses). At this point, Bah, the postman, the figure who had set the action of the story in motion through the delivery of Abdou's money order, calls with another letter for Dieng. He 'delivers' a message of hope, telling Dieng, flanked by his two wives, that *'demain, nous changerons tout ça'* ['tomorrow, we'll change all that']. Dieng slowly rises to his feet disbelievingly, and in response to his question, *'moi?'* ['me?'], the postman replies: *'Oui, toi, tes femmes, tes enfants, moi. Nous changerons tout ça.'* ['Yes, you, your wives, your children, me. We will all help to bring about change.']

As most commentators have argued, the postman is given a clearly symbolic role within the film. However, he remains a largely ambiguous figure. At the beginning of the film, neither Aram nor Méty seem to trust him as they think that he can only be bringing bad news: an agent of the government is an enemy of the people in their book. As it turns out, Bah is probably the only public servant in the film who can truly be said to carry out his job in the service of the public. An ordinary man who can read and write (it should be remembered that he knows the truth about the money order when the Dieng family claim it has been stolen) and who knows the misery of those he meets on his rounds, Bah offers a positive vision of the modern state structure. In many ways, his criss-crossing of the city on his rounds could be said to mirror Sembene's mapping out of the urban landscape: both observe the modern city and seek to 'deliver' a message. At first, Bah brings hope in the form of the money order, then, in the final scene, he brings hope in the form of solidarity with Dieng, revealing his problems to be the problems of a whole society. Rather than the individual quick-fix of short-term cash relief offered by the money order, he offers the hope of a better future for everyone.[62]

The ambiguity of Bah's message appears all the more clearly in the closing images of the film. As Dieng, Aram and Méty look at each other questioningly, pondering the meaning of the postman's words, a poor woman, accompanied by two children, arrives looking for aid. They are soon followed by Dieng's sister, Astou, who has come looking for her money, which he will be unable to give to her. Shifting from a medium shot of Dieng and his wives, the camera moves behind them to capture the arrival of these newcomers. The spectator is invited literally to face this situation from the point of view of the Dieng family. What can they do for these people? How can the postman's words of hope and solidarity be given a practical application? This sense of doubt and

---

[62] In the novella, *Le Mandat*, Dieng is said to have lost his job because he had gone on strike. In the light of this fact, it is understandable that he has lost faith in the power of communal action and solidarity.

confusion is conveyed visually and aurally by a sequence of flashbacks in which we once again witness Dieng's problematic quest to cash the money order, and hear the voices of those who had solicited his aid. The sequence closes with his despairing claim that '*l'honnêteté est un délit chez nous*' ['honesty is a crime nowadays']. Will Dieng join the ranks of the cheats and the deceivers or will he show solidarity with his fellow poor on the periphery? The film gives voice to the desire for a more honest, just and egalitarian society but such is the predicament in which people find themselves that they cannot imagine an alternative to the present situation.

In *Le Mandat/Mandabi*, Sembene deliberately sets out to examine the problems of his society from the perspective of people who can see no way out of the problems that face them. As has been argued in previous chapters, it is through the articulation of these problems that he seeks to make public that which was previously silent, in order to begin the process of constructing a discourse of resistance. However, by using the medium of cinema, Sembene is also seeking to locate a discourse of the urban African poor (and consequently of the African bourgeoisie). In a physical sense, he maps out the space in which the urban poor live, their peripheral existence on the outskirts of the city. However, he also seeks to locate the urban poor ideologically. In what appears on the surface to be a highly individualistic, dog-eat-dog world, Sembene hints at the possibility of the formation of a social bond that could bring the poor together rather than pitting them against one another. The money order therefore serves both to divide the poor and to bring them together in their need, but the possibility of communal action, while longed for, never seems attainable. In Sembene's 1974 film, *Xala*, which will be examined in the next chapter, the power of the communal bond becomes a major force in the battle against the neo-colonial world order. In this later film, the urban poor of the periphery take their revenge on the middle-classes who control the financial heart of the city: the revolt hinted at in *Le Mandat/Mandabi* becomes a cinematic 'reality'.

4

The Indiscreet Charm of the African Bourgeoisie?

Consumerism, Fetishism & Socialism in

Xala

One of the most interesting facts about Sembene's satirical film *Xala* is that it managed to achieve that which is so elusive for most African films, that is, popular box-office success within Africa. It finished second in the 1975 Senegalese ratings behind a film featuring the formidable Bruce Lee, the most successful of the Kung Fu kings who still dominate the screens of African cinemas today. On top of this success within Senegal, *Xala* also had a respectable career on the Francophone African film circuit. Far too often, African films never even reach a popular African public, their distribution usually being limited to the French Cultural Centres (the film's non-commercial distribution rights often being bought by the French Ministère de la Coopération), or the African film festivals in Carthage and Ouagadougou. On some occasions, they are never seen at all and remain stored in warehouses gathering dust, as the French-owned distribution companies usually refuse to take a risk on African films, preferring to provide their audience with their tried and tested diet of karate and melodrama.

However, *Xala* was to enjoy a better fate than most African films not only because of its cinematic quality, but also, more practically, because of the favourable climate within the Senegalese film industry. The French company, UGC, had recently taken over the Francophone African distribution circuit from SECMA and COMACICO (whose role was discussed in the previous chapter). The Senegalese government, having nationalised the distribution circuit in 1972, was a dominant partner with UGC in SIDEC, the new national distribution agency. The Senegalese government provided the majority of the company's capital but then somehow managed to negotiate a deal with UGC, which effectively gave their minority partner a veto over all company decisions, thus leaving control of the distribution circuit firmly in UGC hands. The decision to release *Xala* widely in 1975 would appear to have been a token concession in order to appease the Senegalese government, which had set up a government-backed production company, the *Société Nationale de Cinéma* (SNC), in 1974, and *Xala* was one of its first co-productions (made in conjunction with Sembene's company Filmi Doomireew).[1] As both a critically acclaimed film and a genuine popular success within Africa, *Xala* stands as an example of the possibilities for a popular, radical African cinema.[2]

Xala also provides us with an opportunity to compare Sembene's cinematic technique with the one used in his literary work. The close interplay between film and novel, the scenario providing the basis for the novel, which subsequently feeds back into the final film script, allows us to examine the ways in which different aspects of the story are conceived of in their respective literary and cinematic forms. Sometimes we are presented with the same scene, with virtually the same dialogue, in both film and novel but the effects achieved are radically different.

Xala tells the story of El Hadji Abdou Kader Bèye, a Senegalese businessman who is struck down with the *xala* (the curse of temporary impotence) on the night of his wedding to his third wife. As a representative of the African bourgeoisie, El Hadji is clearly presented to us as a symbol of that class's impotence. Sembene defines his conception of the *xala* in the following terms:

> *[...] pour moi, ce n'est pas seulement mon personnage principal, El Hadji Abdou Kader Bèye, qui est atteint de 'xala', mais toute la couche sociale qu'il représente. Ces gens qui détiennent souvent des postes clés sont frappés d'impuissance culturelle, politique et économique, d'impuissance au niveau des origines mêmes de la création. Ces privilégiés ont un rôle négatif. Ils pervertissent le progrès social, inhibent les efforts du peuple vers le progrès, vers la réalisation de ses aspirations au mieux-vivre et détournent les fruits pénibles de ces efforts populaires à leur profit exclusif et contre nature. N'étant que les reflets et les intermédiaires de l'impérialisme, ces parvenus sont incapables de construire le pays. Frappés de 'xala', ils imposent leur impuissance temporaire à l'ensemble du corps de la nation.*[3]

[...] to my mind, it's not only my main character, El Hadji Abdou Kader Bèye, who is suffering from the 'xala'. It is the whole social class that he represents. These people, who often hold vital positions within society, are struck down with a cultural, political and economic impotence, an impotence that saps their creative instincts. This privileged class plays a negative role. It perverts social progress towards its own desire for material wealth. Thus, it prevents the people from

---

[1] For details on SIDEC and the SNC, see Paulin Soumanou Vieyra, *Le Cinéma au Sénégal* (Brussels: OCIC/L'Harmattan, 1983). 1974 was a bumper year for Senegalese cinema with six films being made in all. As Vieyra points out, most of these films were only co-productions in name, with the SNC putting up all the finance. *Xala* is a true co-production, however, with Sembene's Filmi Doomireew providing 40 per cent of the finance.

[2] The critics have been almost uniformly positive in their appraisal of *Xala*. The claim by Khamaïs Khatami that the film is nothing but a 'cathéchisme soporifique' constitutes one of the few negative criticisms of *Xala*. See Khamaïs Khatami, 'Xala: un catéchisme soporifique', *CinémArabe*, 3 (May–June 1976), p. 40. Férid Boughedir, who is a firm admirer of Sembene's cinema, sees the film as one of Sembene's most important works, but he also believes that it is a flawed work. See Férid Boughedir, 'Une parabole des privilégiés', *Jeune Afrique*, 2 April 1976, pp. 56–8.

[3] Tahaar Cheriaa and Férid Boughedir, '*Jeune Afrique* fait parler Sembene Ousmane', *Jeune Afrique*, 2 April 1976, p. 54.

progressing and steals the hard-earned fruits of popular efforts for its own, unnatural ends. Being mere reflections and intermediaries of imperialism, these parvenus are incapable of developing the country. Struck down with the 'xala', they impose their temporary impotence on the whole nation.

We can see that the central metaphor of the *xala* clearly establishes a link between the political and the sexual, focusing on the issue of male impotence. As will be argued below, this problematisation of sexuality is a recurrent theme of Sembene's work (and also of African literature and cinema, in general). Sembene often seeks to challenge male stereotypes of virility, and this is particularly true of *Xala*. His work also raises a whole series of questions about the role of African women. If men cannot be assumed to be the 'natural' leaders of African society, should women take their place? What part do women play in the radical restructuring of African society envisaged by Sembene? In the next chapter, these questions will be addressed more fully when I examine the representation of women in Sembene's work.

As well as introducing the problematisation of sexuality, *Xala* also raises questions as to the status of the supernatural, as El Hadji Abdou Kader Bèye's impotence is, after all, the result of a curse. Although critics have agreed upon the fact that the *xala* is used by Sembene as a metaphor for the impotence of the African bourgeoisie as a social class, there have been widely varying interpretations of the reasoning behind this link between fetishism and politics. Teshome H. Gabriel assumes that the *xala* must be a result of El Hadji's advanced years, or due to some unnamed psychological problems.[4] However, he then goes on to interpret the film working on the contradictory assumption that it is the blind beggar who has placed the curse on El Hadji. In his critique of the novel, *Xala*, Matiu N'noruka claims that the psychologist's interpretation of El Hadji's impotence is the only valid explanation, thus leading him to claim that the blind beggar did not place the curse on El Hadji at all.[5] Not only does N'noruka's reading deny the blatantly symbolic nature of the novel (as well as the film), it is also based on a complete misreading of the conversation between the psychiatrist and Rama's fiancé, Pathé (a scene missing from the film version). Asked by Pathé if he thinks there is a scientific cure for El Hadji's impotence, the doctor replies: 'we are in Africa, where you can't explain or resolve everything in biochemical terms. Among our own people, it's the irrational that holds sway.'[6] In a society where people routinely believe in fetishes and the supernatural, one is obliged to consider such beliefs as a social reality, irrespective of one's own personal opinions on such matters. In both the film and the novel versions of *Xala*, all the characters are seen to

---

[4] See Teshome H. Gabriel, *Third Cinema in the Third World: the Aesthetics of Liberation* (London: Bowker, 1982), p. 78: 'Unfortunately, the weight of El Hadji's fifty years and his psychological makeup prevent him from consummating the marriage.'

[5] Matiu N'noruka, 'Une lecture de *Xala* de Sembène Ousmane', *Peuples noirs/Peuples africains*, 6, 36 (November–December 1983), pp. 57–75. For a similar argument, see Emeka P., 'Le symbolisme de l'impuissance dans *Xala* d'Ousmane Sembene', *Présence Francophone*, 19 (Autumn 1979), pp. 29–35.

[6] Ousmane Sembene, *Xala*, trans. by Clive Wake (London: Heinemann, 1976), p. 47. Further references to this book will be given in the body of the text.

accept the reality of this curse, and their actions are determined by this belief.[7] As a Marxist, it is unlikely that Sembene would adhere to such ideas, but, sensitive to the nature of Senegalese culture, he uses the *xala* as a powerful symbol of popular social resistance to neo-colonialism.[8] He had already used elements of fetishist culture in a similar fashion in the film version of *La Noire de* when, in the closing sequence, Diouana's young brother (who, incidentally, and also rather fittingly, is played by the same actor who plays the blind beggar's guide in *Xala*) doggedly follows his dead sister's ex-boss through the streets of Dakar, wearing the mask that Diouana had brought to Europe with her. The mask and all it represents seem to haunt the Frenchman until he manages to escape from the 'native' district of the city. Equally, in the novel *L'Harmattan*, the murder of the French game warden and the fatal wounding of his African assistant by the hunter, Digbé, are carried out upon the orders of the *marabout*, Bita Hien. In these instances, resistance to European domination is combined with a defence of fetishist practices.

In stressing the symbolic and political nature of Sembene's use of the *xala*, it is not my intention to dismiss real psychological interpretations of impotence. Freud, for example, believed impotence to be one of the main sources of neurosis, seeing in the very notion of impotence a symbol of the general apprehension towards the sexual act in civilised societies.[9] Some critics may argue that the fact that psychological reasons are missing from both film and novel should not be allowed to deter the critic from applying psychological criteria to *Xala* (a position with which I would largely agree). However, applying Western psychological theories to other cultures raises a number of problematic questions. Western literary and film critics are wont to see Oedipal and castration complexes at work in the most unlikely of cases, despite modern psychology's questioning of these ideas. Placed in the West African context, the waters become even murkier, for how can one speak of such problems in non-nuclear families, where the husband often has more than one wife, and where uncles and aunts often occupy as important a role as mothers and fathers? In her analysis of *Xala*, Laura Mulvey seems to warn against the dangers of such a Eurocentric approach when she declares that 'the particular discourse of sexuality, on which Freud's theory of fetishism depends, cannot

---

[7] For a discussion of some of the practices involved in *maraboutage*, see M. Diop and H. Collomb's 'Pratiques mythiques et psychopathologie: à propos d'un cas', *Psychopathologie Africaine*, 1, 2 (1965), pp. 304–22. Particularly interesting for our study of *Xala* is Diop and Collomb's analysis of the close link between sexuality and the spirit world, the *marabout*'s contact with both *djinné* (ambivalent, but generally benign spirits) and *seytané* (evil spirits) usually taking on an erotic form. See also chapter 5 of Vincent Monteil's *Esquisses sénégalaises* (Dakar: IFAN, 1966) for the relationship between Islamic mysticism and African fetishism.

[8] For a satirical and highly comic attack on a 'vulgar' Marxist approach to the question of fetishist practices in Africa, inspired by the Communist regime in Congo-Brazzaville, see the stories, 'L'étonnante et dialectique déchéance du camarade Kali Tchikati' and 'Le procès du Père Likibi' in Emmanuel Dongala, *Jazz et vin de palme* (Paris: Hatier, 1982).

[9] See Freud's 'On the Universal Tendency to Debasement in the Sphere of Love' (1912), in *The Complete Psychological Works of Sigmund Freud: Five Lectures on Psycho-Analysis. Leonardo Da Vinci and Other Works*, 11 (1957; London: Hogarth Press, 1995), pp. 177–90.

be imposed carelessly on another culture'.[10] However, on the very same page, Mulvey goes on to apply a standard Freudian reading to the use of fetishism in the film:

> For Freud, the fetish enables the psyche to live with the castration anxiety; it contributes to the ego's mechanisms of defence; it keeps the truth, which the conscious mind represses, concealed. When the fetish fails to function effectively, the symptoms it holds in check start to surface.[11]

If Freud's theories are not universal, why does Mulvey apply them to *Xala?* Or is she arguing that we should make a distinction between a 'careful' and a 'rash' application of such theories to other cultures?

This debate over the universality of Freudian and other psychological theories has a long history. In their famous study, *Œdipe africain*, based on four years of clinical practice in Dakar (1962-66), Marie-Cécile and Edmond Ortigues argue for the universality of Freud's Oedipal complex.[12] In so doing, they were countering the ideas of, amongst others, the respected anthropologist, Malinowski, who had taken the opposite approach.[13] As the influential postcolonial critic, Bernard Mouralis, has argued in his study, *L'Europe, l'Afrique et la folie*, psychoanalysis has long been the chief methodological tool of anthropologists in their work on African societies.[14] When modern anthropology was born at the close of the nineteenth century, it seemed that the emerging discipline of psychiatry would provide the perfect basis for the anthropologist's 'science of mankind'. However, Mouralis argues (borrowing from Foucault's work) that just as the discourse of reason defined the insane as its 'Other', anthropological discourse cast 'primitive man' as the 'Other' of rational, civilised man. This was perhaps an inevitable outcome of the anthropological approach because, whereas psychiatry is interested in the

---

[10] Laura Mulvey, '*Xala*. Ousmane Sembene 1976: The Carapace that Failed', in *Colonial Discourse and Post-Colonial Theory: A Reader*, ed. by Laura Chrisman and Patrick Williams (London: Harvester Wheatsheaf, 1994), p. 527.

[11] Ibid.

[12] Marie-Cécile and Edmond Ortigues, *Œdipe africain* (1966; Paris: Union Générale d'Editions, 1973). The Haitian-born writer Dany Laferrière deals with stereotypical notions of African male sexuality in an extremely playful fashion in his novel, *How to Make Love to a Negro*, trans. by David Homel (London: Bloomsbury, 1991). Dealing with the issue of the Oedipus complex, he declares: 'I'd like to be a better kind of white. A white without the Oedipus complex. What good is the Oedipus complex, since you can't eat it, sell it, drink it, or trade it for a round-trip to Tokyo? Or even fuck with it (well, maybe so)' (p. 59).

[13] Bronislaw Malinowski, *Sex and Repression in Savage Society* (1927; Cleveland, OH, and New York: World Publishing Co., 1964).

[14] Bernard Mouralis, *L'Europe, l'Afrique et la folie* (Paris: Présence Africaine, 1993), pp.15–74. Certain anthropologists, among them Claude Lévi-Strauss and George Devereux, have made great use of Freudian theories in their work. See Claude Lévi-Strauss, *Structural Anthropology*, trans. by Claire Jacobson and Brooke Grundfest Schoepf (London: Penguin, 1968), and George Devereux, *Ethnopsychoanalysis: Psychoanalysis and Anthropology as Complementary Frames of Reference* (Berkeley and London: University of California Press, 1978). Critics of this anthropological approach have accused its exponents of overlooking historical facts in favour of the fruitless quest for the essential and unchanging modes of thought of indigenous peoples. See Gérard Leclerc, *Anthropologie et colonialisme* (Paris: Fayard, 1972).

individual case, anthropology is the study of social groups. This led to an 'essentialisation' of 'primitive man' who was argued to have his own distinct mental structures.[15] The psychological profile of each individual 'native' thus becomes generalised to fit into a preordained pattern of social and ethnic behaviour.[16]

In an area marked by such methodological confusion, the literary or cinematic critic would do well to exercise a large degree of caution. Therefore, I will argue that standard Western psychological interpretations of impotence cannot simply be applied in an *ad hoc* fashion to cultures very different from those in which such explanations were formulated (explanations which themselves are subject to fierce debate and which have been increasingly challenged within the West). The aim of such an argument is not to posit a separate African psychology, distinct from its Western counterpart, but rather to highlight the dangers of a universalist approach that fails to consider cultural differences. In the absence of a well-argued psycho-analytical approach to African society, I intend to tease out some of the socio-psychological implications of Sembene's use of the image of impotence by referring to a psychological study carried out at the Centre Hospitalier de Fann in Dakar, and co-ordinated by R. Schenkel (Marx's ideas on the notion of 'commodity fetishism' will be examined below). Published in 1971, the study, entitled 'Le Vécu de la vie sexuelle chez les Africains acculturés du Sénégal, à partir de notions d'impuissance et de puissance sexuelle' ['A Study of the Sex Life of Acculturated Africans, based on sexual impotence and potency'],[17] does not hide from the difficulties for the researcher faced with the virtually unexplored area of African sexuality, an area still dominated by European myths of African sexual prowess, particularly the myth of the size of the African male's penis. Deliberately limiting the range of his study to acculturated Africans, Schenkel's analysis has one central (Freudian) question at its heart: *'une restriction ou une répression de la vie sexuelle est-elle nécessaire pour rendre possible une vie communautaire, dirigée par le progrès. En d'autres termes, y a-t-il opposition entre sexualité et civilisation?* ['is the restriction or repression of sexual life necessary for the cohesion of a community that is being governed by progress. In other words, is there an opposition between sexuality and civilisation?'][18] Schenkel admits that the study does not find a satisfactory answer to this question but it still

---

[15] Mouralis cites Lucien Lévy-Bruhl's *Les Fonctions mentales dans les sociétés inférieures* (Paris: Alcan, 1910) to illustrate this argument.

[16] Mouralis notes that even Fanon's work on Africa is torn between a psychological and a socio-political critique of African societies. For his discussion of Fanon's work, see Mouralis, *L'Europe, l'Afrique et la folie*, pp. 131–65.

[17] R. Schenkel, 'Le Vécu de la vie sexuelle des Africains acculturés du Sénégal, à partir de notions d'impuissance et de puissance sexuelle', *Psychopathologie Africaine*, 7, 3 (1971), pp. 313–88. For another analysis of the social significance and magico-religious explanations of impotence in Senegal, see M. Diop et H. Collomb, 'A propos d'un cas d'impuissance', *Psychopathologie Africaine*, 1, 3 (1965), pp. 487–511. Of particular significance for our study of *Xala* is the fact that the case dealt with here is of a sixty-year-old man, taking on a twenty-year-old fourth wife with whom he suffers from impotence.

[18] Schenkel, 'Le Vécu de la vie sexuelle', p. 314.

provides a useful basis for reflection on *Xala*. Precisely what resonance does the notion of impotence have in Senegalese society? Is it becoming a particularly acute problem in this era of rapid social change?

One of the main conclusions that Schenkel draws from the study is that, within Senegalese society, sex is viewed primarily in terms of procreation rather than in terms of pleasure. For many of those interviewed, impotence is closely associated with sterility, the impotent man being someone who is incapable of fathering children. In a society where such a high value is placed on procreation, it is no surprise that impotence is a deeply feared condition:

> *A première vue, on peut dire que c'est la fonction de procréation qui est à l'avant-plan de toutes les préoccupations et que la perte de cette fonction est une menace pour le groupe et pour l'individu qui risque de perdre son image et sa place au sein du groupe. L'impuissance sexuelle est une menace perpétuelle, préoccupante.*[19]

> Straight away, it appears that the procreative function is in the foreground of their anxieties and that the loss of this function presents a threat for both the community and the individual, who runs the risk of losing his status and his position within society. Sexual impotence is a perpetual and worrying threat.

This fear of impotence is heightened by the fact that the husband in a polygamous society is expected to satisfy sexually up to four wives, in a perennial cycle (called *ayé* or *moomé*) in which he is obliged under Islamic law to spend three days with each of his wives. In fact, the polygamous situation is experienced by many men as a daily burden that causes them a great amount of anxiety.[20] The Senegalese man takes on second and third wives in order to fit in with traditional social patterns, but often finds that this places him under a lot of strain.

The most interesting section of the study for our purposes is the analysis of twenty-six real cases of impotence. What ties these cases in so closely to our study of *Xala* is the fact that the patients are from a highly educated background, forming part of the Westernised elite to which El Hadji Abdou Kader Bèye also belongs. Their impotence is closely tied to problems of integration with the majority of the community. The report essentially comes to the same conclusion, although using rather more scientific terms, as the *Badiène* (a matchmaker, in this case the bride's aunt) who declares of El Hadji that he is neither 'fish nor fowl':

> *Ils se sentent affectés dans leur santé et handicapés dans leur vie sociale [...]. Tous, en plus, ressentent une difficulté à s'adapter dans leur vie sociale et familiale. Ce sentiment est vif et ressenti comme insupportable. Nous pouvons parler sans crainte d'une pathologie de l'adaptation.*[21]

> They feel that their health is affected and they feel handicapped in their social lives [...]. Moreover, all of them experience great difficulty in adapting in their social and family lives. This feeling is very strong and is experienced as an unbearable weight. Without fear of exaggeration, we can speak of a pathology of adaptation.

[19] Ibid., p. 331.
[20] Ibid., p. 328.
[21] Ibid., p. 371.

The patients in Schenkel's study identify wholly with the West and are very dismissive of Senegalese society, in the same way that El Hadji surrounds himself with the trappings of the Western bourgeoisie, ostentatiously drinking from bottles of Evian in a drought-ravaged land and clinging to the business-man's status symbol, the briefcase. One must be careful here not to confuse Sembene's position with a traditional Negritude point of view, with its purist vision of an 'authentic' Senegalese/African culture. El Hadji Abdou Kader Bèye is not culturally alienated because he adopts certain Western social practices. One of the most radical figures in the film is El Hadji's daughter, Rama, who drives a scooter, studies languages in university, and has a poster of Charlie Chaplin on her wall. El Hadji sees Western trappings as status symbols that place him above the majority of his compatriots, while Rama simply adopts specific Western practices that she sees as useful. They become a new element of her African identity: she does not use them to vaunt her superiority over her less wealthy compatriots.

The cases of impotence analysed in Schenkel's study reveal a social group that sees itself as caught between two modes of existence. The result of this is sexual impotence, an inability to further one's line, to guarantee the continuity of the social collectivity through the dynastic family. As was mentioned above, El Hadji Abdou Kader Bèye, as a representative of the African bourgeoisie, is presented to us as a symbol of his class's impotence: he and his kind are unable to spawn a new, revitalised African society. In Sembene's view, the African bourgeoisie is a class which is purely parasitic with no productive value whatsoever: it is quite literally sterile.

The linked notions of impotence and sterility are very important themes within African literature and cinema, albeit relatively unexplored by critics.[22] In Sembene's novel *L'Harmattan*, the father's brutality and inability to deal with the society being created in modern Africa, is closely linked to his own sexual impotence. In one of the most important postcolonial texts, Ahmadou Kourouma's *The Suns of Independence*, the central character Fama is unable to father children. Although it is possible that it is his wife who is sterile (female sexuality often being an equally problematic notion in African cinema and literature), the fact remains that he is the last of his line. An African prince, reduced to the state of a pauper in independent Africa, Fama's sterility becomes symbolic of the decline of the old political order throughout the continent. Those who held power in pre-colonial times are dying out: their line is literally coming to an end.[23] In a similar vein, Isidore Okpewho places an impotent traditional chief at the heart of his novel, *The Last Duty*.[24] Chief Toje Onovwakpo has become impotent and he tries to regain his virility by bedding the wife of his rival, Mukoro Oshevire, whom he has had imprisoned on

[22] Ella Shohat and Robert Stam explore the allegory of impotence in relation to three 'Third World' films in their *Unthinking Eurocentrism: Multiculturalism and the Media* (New York and London: Routledge, 1994), pp. 271–9. Alongside *Xala*, they look at Glauber Rocha's *Terra em transe* (*Land in Anguish*, 1967) and Michel Khleifi's *Urs bil Galil* (*Wedding in Galilee*, 1987).

[23] Ahmadou Kourouma, *The Suns of Independence*, trans. by Adrian Adams (London: Heinemann, 1981).

[24] Isidore Okpewho, *The Last Duty* (1976; London: Longman African Classic, 1986).

trumped-up charges. Once again, we see that impotence and social status are presented as inextricably linked concepts: the 'true' leader must be virile and be able to maintain his line. Neither Fama nor Toje Onovwakpo is capable of this.[25]

Apart from direct references to impotence, sexuality in general has been a central theme in African literature and cinema. The main protagonists of countless African novels and films have faced social and cultural problems that have, at least in part, expressed themselves in some sort of sexual trauma. In Djibril Diop Mambety's 1992 film *Hyènes*, a scorned lover comes back to seek revenge on the man who deceived her in her youth. Cheikh Hamidou Kane's Samba Diallo and V.Y. Mudimbe's Nara are both traumatised by failed relationships with white French women.[26] In the case of Nara, the disjointed narrative of his final diary makes numerous references to his feelings of 'impuissance', and we eventually learn that his sexual problems stem from his inability to accept the fact of his own homosexuality. Continuing with the homosexual theme, Raymond Spartacus, the last in Ouologuem's line of long-suffering African peasants, in *Bound to Violence*, appears to reject the notions of fatherhood and the continuation of the family line by engaging in a homosexual relationship with a white Frenchman.[27]

As we saw in the previous chapter, the problem of incest was the central theme of Sembene's *White Genesis* (as well as its film version, *Niaye*). There is also a variation on the theme of incest in Idrissa Ouédraogo's film *Tilaï* in which a son has a sexual relationship with a young girl who had been promised to him before his departure from the village, only to find on his return two years later that his father has married the girl. In Sembene's work, one can see severe social and sexual tensions at work in the series of marital disputes that he records in the stories, 'Her Three Days', 'The *Bilal*'s Fourth Wife', not to mention *Xala* itself, where the marital bond is shown to be under great stress.[28]

---

[25] Pat Corcoran discusses the problematisation of fatherhood in African literature in his essay, 'Fathers and Sons in African Fiction', in J. P. Little and Roger Little, *Black Accents: Writing in French from Africa, Mauritius and the Caribbean* (London: Grant & Cutler, 1997), pp. 83–96.

[26] See Cheikh Hamidou Kane, *Ambiguous Adventure*, trans. by Katherine Woods (London: Heinemann, 1972), and V.Y. Mudimbe, *L'Ecart* (Paris: Présence Africaine, 1979).

[27] Yambo Ouologuem, *Bound to Violence*, trans. by Ralph Manheim (London: Heinemann, 1971). The homosexual theme within modernist writing, as represented by Proust or Gide, is, on the whole, missing from African literature and cinema. Ouologuem's Raymond Spartacus and Mudimbe's Nara are rare exceptions. In his *L'Europe, l'Afrique et la folie*, Bernard Mouralis claims that Clarence's obsession with the king in Camara Laye's *The Radiance of the King*, trans. by James Kirkup (London: Fontana, 1973) contains homosexual overtones (see Mouralis, pp. 183–4). The only homosexual character in Sembene's work, colonel Luc, appears in *L'Harmattan*. An old-fashioned, patriarchal colonialist, he abuses his position in order to give '*libre cours à sa nature d'homosexuel*' ['free reign to his homosexuality'] (p. 55). Homosexuality is here presented as a form of moral deviance: it is almost as though it were a European 'disease' imported into Africa. There is also an instance of transvestism in Sembene's work (although transvestites are not necessarily homosexuals). The character of the transvestite in the film version of *Xala* is portrayed in a comic fashion, ironically commenting on the sexual prowess of El Hadji. The issue of African attitudes towards homosexuality merits further research.

[28] In a story that bears many similarities to the plot of *Xala*, Cheikh Aliou Ndao's *Excellence, vos épouses!* (Dakar: Nouvelles Editions Africaines, 1993) describes the fall of Goor Gnak, a former

Xala

The sociologist, Luc Thoré, has gone so far as to privilege marital relationships as one of the most significant means of gauging social change in Africa:

> *La colonisation, et plus généralement, l'impact de la civilisation technique, ont entraîné des conséquences importantes en ce qui concerne l'institution matrimoniale, parce que celle-ci se situe précisément au point de jonction entre la société globale et la cellule conjugale.*[29]

Colonisation and, more generally, the impact of technological civilisation, have had considerable consequences on the institution of marriage precisely because marriage is situated at the point of contact between the wider world and the family unit.

The family becomes the site for the playing out of a whole series of social dramas affecting African society. What is at stake in such works is the 'conception' (pun intended) of a new Africa, born out of the traumas of both colonialism and neo-colonialism.

In many ways, the process at work in such novels and films is remarkably similar to what Edward Said has called the transformation from *filiation* to *affiliation* in modernist writing. In the period of rapid social change that marked the beginning of the twentieth century in the West, a deep anxiety over the (im)possibility of filiation, of guaranteeing future generations, is seen to be at the heart of modernist concerns (*Ulysses, The Waste Land* and *A la recherche du temps perdu* all serve as powerful examples of this phenomenon):

> Relationships of filiation and affiliation are plentiful in modern cultural history. One very strong pattern, for example, originates in a large group of late nineteenth- and early twentieth-century writers in which the failure of the generative impulse – the failure of the capacity to produce or generate children – is portrayed in such a way as to stand for a general condition afflicting society and culture together, to say nothing of individual men and women [...].
>
> Childless couples, orphaned children, aborted childbirths, and unregenerately celibate men and women populate the world of high modernism with remarkable insistence, all of them suggesting the difficulties of filiation.[30]

Once filiation has become problematic, the search begins for something with which it can be replaced, and this is where Said introduces the notion of affiliation. This acts as a compensation for the loss of the bonds of filiation and attempts to provide a new bond that can serve to link people together. This affiliative bond can take the form of a shared culture, institutions, myths, or, arguably the most powerful bond of the twentieth century, that of radical class-consciousness.

The current period of African history marks an equally traumatic period of social transformation. As was argued above, this has led to a problematisation of filiation. In its place, some writers have focused on the affiliative bonds of a shared African culture, or of an 'authentic' African identity that distinguishes

---

[28] (cont.) government minister, who has lost both his position and his status. This fall is explored primarily through his relationships with his four wives.

[29] Luc Thoré, 'Mariage et divorce dans la banlieue de Dakar', *Cahiers d'études africaines*, 4, 16 (1964), p. 482.

[30] Edward W. Said, 'Secular Criticism', in *The World, the Text and the Critic* (1983; London: Vintage, 1991), pp. 16–17.

Africans from their former colonial masters. In *Xala*, the impossibility of filiation is seen to bring about the possibility of an African class-consciousness, and the overthrow of the impotent, bourgeois regime. In denouncing the impotence of the African bourgeoisie, Sembene is striving to break out of the impasse of Africa's contemporary political and social misfortunes by imagining an alternative social bond around which Africans can organise their lives.

■ ■ ■

Xala is structured principally around the notion of fetishism, presenting the rituals of the African bourgeoisie in all their contradictions. An idealisation of the West is shown to exist side by side with a profound belief in superstition and magic. In a 1974 interview, Sembene showed that he was well aware of these contradictions within his film:

> *La contradiction est que la société africaine actuelle est partagée entre deux fétichismes: le fétichisme technique de l'Europe, la conviction de ces privilégiés qu'ils ne peuvent rien faire sans l'accord de l'Europe et les conseils de ses techniciens d'une part; et d'autre part le fétichisme maraboutique qui fait que sans le secours du marabout toute entreprise serait également vouée à l'échec. La vraie réussite humaine n'est plus alors le fait de l'homme africain, mais plutôt l'heureuse conjugaison des deux bénédictions du technicien européen et du marabout.*
>
> *Ces responsables sont, en fait, aussi loin de la véritable technique européenne que de la vraie tradition et de la spiritualité africaines. Les conseillers techniques européens ne sont ni plus ni moins charlatans que les marabouts. Le recours aux uns et aux autres n'est donc que l'expression de la même impuissance.*[31]

The contradiction lies in the fact that contemporary African society is torn between two types of fetishism: firstly, the fetishism of European techniques, and the profound conviction of this privileged class that it can do nothing without Europe's agreement and the advice of its specialists; on the other hand, there is a fetishism of the marabout, without whose advice any undertaking is doomed to failure. In this situation, genuine human success has nothing to do with the capabilities of Africans, but is rather the result of a happy mixture of the blessings of the European specialist and the marabout.

The truth is that this ruling class is as far removed from genuine European techniques as it is from the genuine tradition of African spirituality. European specialists are no more credible than the marabouts. Having recourse to both is merely the expression of the same impotence.

The theme of fetishism is a long established one in Marxist theory. Marx begins his sweeping analysis of nineteenth-century capitalist society in *Capital* with a discussion of the 'commodity', essentially defining capitalism as the accumulation of commodities. He then proceeds to examine the phenomenon that he terms 'commodity fetishism', that is the quasi-religious process by which value is attached to these commodities. This process by which the 'exchange-value' of commodities is given almost inherent, religious qualities, effectively denying the labour that went into their making, is described by

---

[31] Cheriaa and Boughedir, '*Jeune Afrique* fait parler Sembene Ousmane', p. 55. Sembene expresses similar ideas in his interview with Aly Khary N'Daw: 'Sembène Ousmane et l'impuissance bourgeoise', *Jeune Afrique*, 27 April 1974, p. 20.

Marx as 'the Fetishism which attaches itself to the products of labour, so soon as they are produced as commodities, and which is therefore inseparable from the production of commodities'.[32] Sembene's African businessmen, and El Hadji Abdou Kader Bèye in particular, are obsessed with commodities, with the objects that prove their social status, and which stress their identification with and emulation of the West. However, they are also still in the grip of the supernatural, of the fetishist practices that marked their African upbringing. In such a context, the rituals of the capitalist world and the fetishist world are seen to vie for people's attention: the possession of a briefcase acquires the same ritual status as the possession of a *gri-gri* (i.e. a talisman or charm).

Therefore, in *Xala*, the representation of the various rituals, both 'Western' and 'African', within Senegalese society becomes a means towards an examination of that society's ills.[33] However, such questions have received scant attention from critics. Françoise Pfaff writes of the symbolic and socio-realistic function of each of El Hadji's wives, but there is no attempt to deal with the larger symbolic issues arising from Sembene's representation of his society's rituals.[34] Teshome H. Gabriel is more illuminating on the film's symbolism and his central image of 'a cinema of wax and gold', with a deeper layer of meaning lying beneath the obvious surface meaning, provides a useful framework within which to analyse the film, but it cannot be counted as a meaningful analysis of the film in itself.[35] In a film in which there are so many non-realistic elements, it is essential to examine the way in which these symbolic, ritualistic elements are used within the story.

The three feature films made by Sembene in the 1970s, *Emitaï, Xala* and *Ceddo*, are without doubt his most symbolic, non-realistic works (both *Emitaï* and *Ceddo* will be examined in Chapter Six). Experimenting with form, Sembene moves away from the social realism of earlier films (which still featured various non-realistic elements – witness the scene with the mask at the end of *La Noire de*, or the dream sequences in *Niaye* mentioned above). Following on from Brecht (whose influence Sembene has acknowledged in relation to *Le Mandat/Mandabi*), he seeks to capture the 'realities' of his society through a variety of representational means. Brecht had disagreed fundamentally with Lukács' model of realism, which he saw as needlessly tied to particular forms and conventions. In place of this model, Brecht proposed the following, more fluid conception of realism in his influential essay, 'The Popular and the Realistic':

Our conception of *realism* needs to be broad and political, free from aesthetic

---

[32] See Karl Marx, 'Commodities', chapter 1, section 4, 'The Fetishism of Commodities and the Secret Thereof', in *Capital*, 1, trans. by Samuel Moore and Edward Aveling (London: Lawrence & Wishart, 1974), p. 77.

[33] For a discussion of the use of ritual in the film, see Ogunjimi Bayo, 'Ritual Archetypes – Ousmane's Aesthetic Medium in *Xala*', *Ufahamu* (Journal of the African Activist Association), 14, 3 (1985), pp. 128–38.

[34] Françoise Pfaff, *The Cinema of Ousmane Sembene: a Pioneer of African Film* (Westport, CT: Greenwood Press, 1984), pp. 149–63.

[35] Gabriel, *Third Cinema*, pp. 77–86.

restrictions and independent of convention. *Realist* means: laying bare society's causal network/showing up the dominant viewpoint as the viewpoint of the dominators/writing from the standpoint of the class which has prepared the broadest solutions for the most pressing problems afflicting human society/ emphasising the dynamics of development/concrete and so as to encourage abstraction.[36]

In *Xala*, Sembene lays bare the 'causal network' of his society by setting up a series of rituals whose contradictions reveal the tensions and the fault lines within the African bourgeoisie.

The film's concern with ritual is evident from the opening scenes. In what could be described as a piece of 'epic' Brechtian symbolism, the African businessmen chase the Europeans from the Chamber of Commerce, at the same time removing all the signs of French colonial power. Dressed in traditional African clothes, they place on the steps of the Chamber, amongst other items, a statue of Marianne, the symbol of the French Republic, and a pair of jackboots, symbolising French colonial domination in Africa. The President of the Chamber's speech, which we hear on the soundtrack, makes it clear that this act is being carried out on behalf of the whole nation. In fact, Senegalese businessmen had taken control of the Dakar Chamber of Commerce in the aftermath of the social upheaval of May 1968. Their struggle to gain a larger slice of the economic cake from the French was cast in nationalist terms, turning the issue of control of the Chamber of Commerce from what was essentially an economic issue into a nationalist one.[37]

The first scenes on the steps of the Chamber are shot from a low angle. This is an 'heroic' moment and the crowd, whose viewpoint the camera adopts, looks up at its leaders in respect and admiration. However, what Sembene sees as the true nature of this takeover is shown in the very next scene. The camera has moved back to a high, remote angle as the crowd, in whose name the businessmen had supposedly been acting, are pushed back by the police, led by their white commander.[38] In the space cleared around the Chamber appear Dupont-Durand (the 'representative' Frenchman) and a white companion, both of whom had been ejected from the Chamber in the previous scene. The businessmen's struggle for control of the Chamber had

---

[36] Bertolt Brecht, *Brecht on Theatre: The Development of an Aesthetic*, ed. and trans. by John Willett (London: Eyre Methuen, 1978), p. 109 (stress in original). Brecht's influence on film theory and filmmakers such as Jean-Luc Godard, in the late 1960s and 1970s, is discussed in George Lellis, *Bertolt Brecht, 'Cahiers du Cinéma' and Contemporary Film Theory* (London: Bowker, 1982). An analysis of the various theories concerning film narrative is to be found in David Bordwell, *Narration in the Fiction Film* (London: Methuen, 1985). See also Bill Nichols, *Ideology and the Image: Social Representation in the Cinema and Other Media* (Bloomington, IN: Indiana University Press, 1981) for a discussion of the manner in which ideology can be perceived in the cinematic text.

[37] For a discussion of the aftermath of May 1968 and the lobbying powers of the Senegalese business class, see Pierre Fougeyrollas, *Où va le Sénégal?* (Dakar: IFAN; Paris: Anthropos, 1970), pp. 11–43.

[38] The then Minister for the Interior, Jean Collin, was a Frenchman who had taken on Senegalese citizenship after independence. No doubt due to this, all scenes featuring the white chief of police were cut in Senegal. For a discussion of Collin's career, see Momar Coumba Diop and Mamadou Diouf, *Le Sénégal sous Abdou Diouf* (Paris: Karthala, 1990), pp. 101–14.

4.1 El Hadji celebrates his wedding night
with the businessmen and the ubiquitous French adviser
Xala, Filmi Doomireew – Dakar, Senegal (all rights reserved)

111

needed the support of the people but, now that this has been achieved, the former colonial powers resurface, filling once more, both literally and metaphorically, the space which the people had momentarily occupied. As these two men climb the steps of the Chamber, carrying a number of briefcases, we hear on the soundtrack the continuation of the President's speech (which is clearly a parody of Senghor's notion of 'African Socialism'): '*Nous optons pour le socialisme, le seul vrai socialisme, la voie africaine du socialisme, le socialisme à hauteur d'homme. Notre indépendance est complète.*' [We have chosen socialism, the only true socialism, African socialism, socialism with a human face. Our independence is now complete.][39] The irony of this final line becomes clear as Dupont-Durand and his partner distribute the briefcases, which are full of money, to the members of the Chamber, now dressed in Western suits. For Sembene, this is the reality of Senegalese/African independence.

The symbolism of the scene is carefully laid out for the spectator. Having witnessed the distribution of the briefcases to the various committee members, we finally see the President being presented with his case. The camera moves in for a subjective shot, finally showing us what is contained in the briefcases, that is, bundles of bank notes. Unlike the grins and gasps of his colleagues, the President's reaction is self-restrained. He turns to Dupont-Durand who meekly bows his head. He then looks at the photograph that he has just placed on the wall. As the camera moves in for a close-up of the photograph, we see that it is a picture of the President himself in dignified pose, dressed in black tie with his sash of office over his shoulder. The dignity of the photograph and his demeanour on opening the briefcase contrast dramatically with the hypocrisy of the whole situation. In his speech to the committee, he speaks of '*notre action révolutionnaire*' ['our revolutionary action'] and warns the businessmen to be vigilant because '*nos adversaires n'ont pas désarmé*' ['our enemies have not given up']. The hollowness of such nationalist discourse is evident in the light of what has gone before. The businessmen's so-called revolution was presented in terms of a popular mass movement in the opening section. However, all that has happened is that the former colonial powers have retreated into a murkier, more veiled, but equally powerful form of economic and political control. In a startling image of this neo-colonial situation, we see Dupont-Durand, the symbol of French power in Africa, standing silently but contentedly behind the President when he rises to speak. In the opening scene, he was the enemy but now he has become the President's personal adviser (the character of Monsieur Adolphe plays a similar role in *The Last of the Empire*, which will be examined in Chapter Seven). In this same shot, on the wall behind Dupont-Durand, we see a political map of Africa, a symbol of the European division and control of the continent. In this image, African independence is portrayed, not as a break with the colonial past, but rather as a continuation of European domination in new and more subtle forms.

It becomes clear from this opening section that the film is intent on

[39] For Senghor's ideas on African Socialism', see his *Liberté 2: Nation et voie africaine du socialisme* (Paris: Seuil, 1971), especially the paper entitled 'La Voie africaine du socialisme: nouvel essai de définition', pp. 283–315.

exposing the hypocrisy and corruption that lie behind the rituals and fetishes of the African bourgeoisie. The nationalist celebration that opened the film, with its use of African drummers and bare-breasted female dancers, is just a smokescreen for the real transformation that is taking place. Such references to traditional culture are simply token gestures by those in control who seek to appropriate tradition for their cause. The rituals that are of most significance to the bourgeoisie are those of the capitalist, consumer society. The ritual handing-over of the briefcases is the true commemoration of the businessmen's taking over of the Chamber of Commerce. In fact (as was mentioned above), the briefcases take on a fetishistic quality, such is the nature of the status that accompanies those who carry them (acting as an illustration of Marx's notion of 'commodity fetishism'). El Hadji carries his with him on all occasions and, when he is dismissed from the Chamber at the end of the film, the situation requires the ritual handing-over of his briefcase. It is also a means of identifying the businessmen metonymically. As they arrive at the wedding reception, they are shot from the waist downwards with only their polished shoes, well-pressed trousers and briefcases visible to the spectator.

The wedding reception, which comes directly after this opening sequence, is the longest section of the film, taking up about thirty minutes of screen time. In El Hadji's speech to the committee, the link between the takeover of the Chamber and his wedding is made explicit: '*La modernité ne doit pas nous faire perdre notre africanité.*' ['We must be African as well as modern.'] This is one of the contradictions which was evoked earlier. As a well-respected figure within the community and a wealthy member of the Chamber of Commerce, El Hadji is a social success. Thus, his third wedding becomes a symbol of his social status in both Western and African terms. His claim that '*je suis marié à nouveau par devoir*' ['I have married another wife out of a sense of duty'] can be read in two ways: his third marriage marks him out as a respectable figure within a polygamous society but it also allows him to engage in an ostentatious display of wealth, gauged in terms of his Western consumerist possessions. Writing about the novel version of *Xala* (in terms equally applicable to the film), Pius Ngandu Nkashama has described the ritual value of the *fête* in the following terms: '*c'est autour de la fête que se réalise la prise de conscience, que s'effectue le mimétisme social.*' ['it is through the festivities that the awakening of consciousness takes place and it is also here that we see the reflection of society as a whole.'][40] Nkashama describes the wedding reception in *Xala* as the *fête* of the neo-colonial bourgeoisie, and its sole social function is that of displaying El Hadji's wealth and social standing: '*La fête aura donc été, tout au long de ce roman, le moment le plus pathétique d'une passion douleureuse: la découverte de sa vanité.*' ['These festivities act as the most pathetic moment in the novel which enacts a painful process: the realisation of his own vanity.'][41] Thus, in this long section of the film, El Hadji sets himself up on a pedestal from which he will soon be knocked off in the second half of the film, once he has been struck down with the *xala*.

[40] Pius Ngandu Nkashama, 'La Fête et l'extase dans le roman africain de langue française', *L'Afrique littéraire*, 65–66 (1982), p. 32.
[41] Ibid., pp. 35–6.

Throughout the wedding reception, the camera moves restlessly from one group of people to the next, pausing only momentarily to listen in on conversations or simply to observe events. In keeping with the satirical nature of the film, these *tableaux* are designed to show up the neo-colonial bourgeoisie's hypocrisy and pretension.[42] Such an approach results in an all-out critique of the bourgeoisie, ranging from the trivial to the political and socially vital. If the *tableau* that shows a guest indiscreetly picking his nose arms itself with the more coarse weaponry of satire, the scene in which the *Badiène* runs through the list of El Hadji's presents for his bride (including a television, gold jewellery and, most notably, a car) contains an explicit political and social critique.

Since the works of Juvenal, satire has always striven to work on these two levels. However, in his review of *Xala* in *Positif*, Alain Masson claims that the film's criticisms are both too numerous and too weak to constitute a proper political accusation.[43] By describing the beggars' revenge on El Hadji at the end of the film purely in terms of a 'traditional' theme of vengeance, Masson denies the film the political significance that is its driving force. In many ways, the review is an exemplary case of the pitfalls that await the uninformed Western critic when writing about either African cinema or literature. Having decided that there can be no political rationale behind such a satirical film, Masson allows himself a few fatuous jibes at Sembene's expense, claiming, for example, that one could conclude from the film that polygamy is permissible and viable with two wives, but that having three will lead to rack and ruin. Such an approach not only ignores the very clear links made in the film between El Hadji's social status (and thus by implication neo-colonialism) and his third wedding, but also betrays a fundamental ignorance of West African society. The tension between the first two wives escapes his notice, as do the consequences of urban polygamy, where a husband's wives can be spread out around different parts of the city. The explicitly 'commercial' nature of this third wedding is also passed over unnoticed.

An alternative approach to *Xala*'s satirical style is to be found in Danièle Dubroux's review of the film in *Cahiers du Cinéma*.[44] She argues that the caricatural portrayal of the bourgeoisie is satirical, but nonetheless based on social realities. This image of the African bourgeoisie as a grotesque imitation of their Western counterparts is evoked by Frantz Fanon in *The Wretched of the Earth*:

[42] Jack Kroll favourably compares the wedding sequence in *Xala* with the famous wedding party in Francis Ford Coppola's *Godfather*. See Jack Kroll, 'The World on Film', *Newsweek*, 13 October 1975, p. 52.

[43] Alain Masson, 'Mascarade à Dakar (*Xala*)', *Positif*, 182 (June 1976), pp. 54–6.

[44] Danièle Dubroux, 'Exhibition (*Xala*)', *Cahiers du Cinéma*, 266–67 (May 1976), pp. 72–4. Nourredine Ghali makes a similar point in his critique of the film: '*Les contours des personnages sont dessinés à gros trait. Et le film est si incisif qu'on croirait à la caricature si la réalité n'était en fait plus caricatural que le film.*' ['The characters are drawn in broad strokes. The film is so incisive that we would believe it was a caricature if the reality was not, in fact, more of a caricature than the film.'] See Nourredine Ghali, '*Xala*: histoire symbolique d'une déchéance', *Cinéma*, 208 (April 1976), p. 95.

114

In the colonial countries, *the spirit of indulgence is dominant [l'esprit jouisseur domine,* in French] at the core of the bourgeoisie; and this is because the national bourgeoisie identifies itself with the Western bourgeoisie, from whom it has learnt its lessons. It follows the Western bourgeoisie along its path of negation and decadence without ever having emulated it in its first stages of exploration and invention, stages which are an acquisition of that Western bourgeoisie whatever the circumstances. In its beginnings, the national bourgeoisie of the colonial countries identifies itself with the decadence of the bourgeoisie of the West. We need not think that it is jumping ahead; it is in fact beginning at the end. It is already senile before it has come to know the petulance, the fearlessness or the will to succeed of youth.[45]

For Fanon, Africa has a twofold problem insofar as the bourgeoisie is concerned. Firstly, the national bourgeoisie of the Third World has disenfranchised the masses in whose name decolonisation was supposedly taking place. Secondly, this national bourgeoisie is completely unproductive, dominated as it is by its 'esprit jouisseur' (this image seems particularly apt in relation to the character of El Hadji Abdou Kader Bèye). As the African bourgeoisie rely so heavily on the Western bourgeoisie for their models, they effectively become caricatures of that which they are trying to imitate. In a 1976 interview, Sembene evoked this imitative, 'bastard' nature of the neocolonial bourgeoisie in the following terms:

Les gens que je montre dans mon film ne sont pas vraiment des bourgeois, même s'ils se flattent de s'identifier à la bourgeoisie européenne qui est leur modèle. Ils n'appartiennent même pas à une classe; ils constituent une couche de la population, une catégorie sociale qui se trouve en situation objective de 'privilégiés' indécents. Ces gens qui ont vociféré d'allégresse pour le drapeau, pour l'hymne national etc., et qui, une fois dans la place 'reconquise de haute lutte', se conduisent exactement comme les autres, comme ces anciens maîtres étrangers, ces 'abominables' colonialistes qu'ils dénonçaient à grands cris. Non, ces parvenus ne sont même pas des bourgeois; ils ne sont que la frange périphérique de l'impérialisme.[46]

The people that I show in my film are not really bourgeois even if they flatter themselves by identifying with the European bourgeoisie that acts as their model. In fact, they don't belong to any class; they constitute a section of the population, a social category which enjoys an indecent level of 'privilege'. These people were the first to call for the flag and the national anthem, etc. but, once they are safely ensconced in power they have 'won through a noble struggle', they begin to behave exactly the same as the 'awful' colonists they had so vociferously denounced. No, these parvenus are not even bourgeois; they are just the extreme periphery of imperialism.

As we saw when looking at the opening section of the film, the neo-colonial order dissimulates its true nature by surrounding itself with a series of rituals and fetishes with which it seeks to identify. This world of seeming and appearance is explored throughout the wedding reception with Sembene (through his camera) serving as our guide.

One of the most effective ways in which this theme is examined is through

---

[45] Frantz Fanon, *The Wretched of the Earth*, trans. by Constance Farrington (London: Penguin, 1969), p. 123 (my italics).
[46] Cheriaa and Boughedir, '*Jeune Afrique* fait parler Sembène Ousmane', p. 54.

the use of costume. As was mentioned earlier, the businessmen abandon their African clothes in favour of the Western three-piece suit as soon as they have installed themselves in the Chamber of Commerce. At the wedding reception, all the male guests are in similar Western attire (although the women are often dressed in traditional African style). In this context, the three-piece suit becomes yet another status symbol, distinguishing them from the masses. In a moment of great irony towards the end of the film, the pickpocket, who had stolen money from the peasant who has come to town to buy food for his village, replaces El Hadji in the Chamber of Commerce, wearing the suit and stetson that he has bought with his ill-gotten gains. The difference between thief and businessman is presented as lying purely in the outward appearance (it should be remembered that El Hadji is cast as a thief also: he stole from the blind beggar and he uses the money from the sale of rice intended for the needy to help finance his third marriage). However, it would be wrong to read the use of costume in an over-schematic fashion, presenting those who wear African dress as virtuous and those in Western clothes as corrupt bourgeois. The situation in Africa is far more complex with many poor people wearing Western jeans and t-shirts because they are simply cheaper than traditional African materials. Within the film, the scheming, materialistic *Badiène* is always seen in African dress, while Rama, a radical African student, wears a mixture of Western and African clothes.

The importance of dress is most clearly seen in relation to El Hadji's three wives.[47] Adja Awa Astou, his first wife, is a devout Muslim who wears traditional African dress. A simple, passive, but ultimately loyal woman, she is presented as a figure of both great dignity and great suffering. However, the other two wives stand in stark contrast to Adja Awa Astou. If the latter was El Hadji's first love in the days before his success, then both Oumi Ndoye and Ngoné are merely 'trophies' who serve as symbols of that success. Oumi Ndoye, the second wife, is a sensuous woman who dresses exclusively in Western clothes, going to the wedding reception replete with bouffant wig and low-cut black dress. A wholly materialistic woman, she bullies El Hadji, placing constant financial demands upon him. In the very first scene in which we see her, she pushes El Hadji on to the bed when he tries to lay down the law to her. In fact, it becomes clear that it is she who gives the orders in the household, as she aggressively demands more money from him.

This symbolism in relation to costume is most clearly seen in the character of El Hadji's third wife, Ngoné. She is introduced to the spectator at the wedding reception where she is wearing a Western-style wedding dress. As she arrives, the camera moves in for a close-up of the wedding cake, on top of which we see a plastic model of a white bride and groom. The incongruity of the whole wedding becomes apparent in this one image. Aspiring to Western

---

[47] Masson perceptively describes certain elements of this concern with costume but he makes the absurd claim that the only difference between Adja Awa Astou and Oumi Ndoye lies in their clothes, ignoring the fact that the former is portrayed as a devout Muslim who remains loyal to her husband, while the latter is a sensual materialist whose relationship with El Hadji revolves solely around sex and money. Masson, 'Mascarade à Dakar (*Xala*)', pp. 54–5.

bourgeois standards involves copying the Western marriage down to the last detail, including the white wedding dress, which has no place in either Islamic or African animist/fetishist practices.

However, Ngoné's real value to El Hadji is seen in the bedroom scenes where she lies naked on the bed waiting for El Hadji to consummate their marriage. Ngoné is merely a sexual object that El Hadji has acquired. This is made clear in the scene where the *Badiène* undresses Ngoné on her wedding night. As the *Badiène* gives her advice on how to fulfil her duties as a wife, we see a nude photograph of Ngoné on the wall in the background. Shot in profile, showing Ngoné's bare back and a glimpse of one of her breasts, the photograph acts as a promise of what the marriage is supposed to bring to El Hadji. The eroticised Ngoné of the photograph is the one that El Hadji is marrying. As the *Badiène* finishes speaking, Ngoné turns around and we see her bare breasts which are mostly hidden in the 'tasteful' photograph. El Hadji is about to realise his wish: the image is about to take flesh (until the *xala* strikes, that is). This commodification of Ngoné is evident from the extravagances of the wedding reception and the presents which he lavishes upon her as part of her dowry. Chief amongst these presents is the car. As El Hadji arrives at Ngoné's house finally to consummate the marriage, after he has been temporarily cured by Sérigne Mada, he pauses to kiss the ribbon on the car. El Hadji believes that he will at last be able to enjoy his new possession, but is once again left disappointed because Ngoné is having her period.

If clothes are symbolic of social status, then part of El Hadji's cure for his *xala* must involve a stripping away of his Western business attire. When he goes to visit the 'real' *marabout* Sérigne Mada, he progressively leaves behind his Western trappings. The village is inaccessible by car so he must take a horse and cart rather than his Mercedes. Then, once in the village, he must abandon his business suit for African robes: only at this point is he cured. We see the same process at work in the final scene where he is ordered to strip off his clothes in front of the beggars. El Hadji must be stripped of his material possessions, including his three-piece suit, in order to be cured of the impotence that affects both him and his class

El Hadji's fall is thus the stripping away of the fetishistic signs of his wealth. So obsessed has he become by his *xala* that he lets his business crumble around him. After the President of the Chamber has warned him of the problems that his bounced cheques are causing for the group as a whole, the camera follows him into the lift. We see only half of El Hadji's body in the shot, with his back reflected in the mirror. He seems to be literally losing his substance as his fortunes decline. He is subsequently expelled from the Chamber of Commerce and has his briefcase taken from him. All that is left within it are his failed business plan and the fetish that had been given to him by one of the many *marabouts* whom he has visited. The two modes of fetishism in which he had placed his entire faith are removed from him in one fell swoop.

The closure of El Hadji's shop is treated in highly ironic fashion. The keys of the shop are taken away from him and his Mercedes (which had earlier had its radiator filled with El Hadji's fetish drink, Evian) is repossessed. However, neither the soldiers nor the bailiff know how to drive so they are forced to push the car away. In a country where poverty is widespread, few are those who can offer themselves the luxury of a car, let alone a Mercedes. Equally, in a country where drought had been stalking the land throughout the early 1970s, it is only the rich who can allow themselves to use bottled French mineral water to fill their car radiators. Now that the car has been taken from him, El Hadji is forced to walk through the city, accompanied by his chauffeur, Modu, who is still dressed in his uniform, and carrying a stool, the only item that the bailiff has permitted El Hadji to keep. In a parody of El Hadji's earlier chauffeur-driven journeys through the city, we now see him accompanied by what is, effectively, a 'chauffeur-driven' stool.

As was mentioned earlier, some critics have sought to play down the beggars' role in El Hadji's *xala*, choosing to explain his impotence in purely psychological terms. This latter interpretation of the film relies on a reading of the blind beggar's claim in the final sequence as a sort of *deus ex machina* that simply arrives out of nowhere, an argument which is more understandable when applied to the novel version of *Xala* where the beggars occupy a far more peripheral role. They are referred to in passing in the novel, for example, when El Hadji dreams of the beggar's song after failing to perform sex with Oumi Ndoye (*Xala*, p. 100). Here, the link is made between the beggars and El Hadji's *xala*, but never as explicitly as in the film.

This contrast is perhaps best illustrated by one of the central episodes in both film and novel. The morning after his disastrous wedding night with Ngoné, El Hadji calls the President of the Chamber to his office to ask for his advice on the *xala*. In the novel, when El Hadji reveals the nature of his problem to the President, the beggar's song is suddenly heard: 'The beggar's chant, almost as if it were inside the room, rose an octave' (*Xala*, p. 33). However, in the film, the role of the beggars within this scene takes on a much greater significance. Following the President's question asking him who could be responsible for his *xala*, El Hadji, instead of replying, walks out of his back office to the shop front where he looks out at the blind beggar, whose song can be clearly heard. Returning to his office, he asks for the President to have the police dispose of these 'human dregs'. In this powerful scene, we are given a clue as to the identity of those behind the *xala* and to their motives behind this act. Excluded from independent Senegalese society, the beggars and cripples are reminders of the harsh realities of neo-colonialism. When El Hadji tells the President 'that's not what our independence is about', we are clearly shown that independence, for El Hadji, is something from which only the privileged few are entitled to benefit. As we later discover, El Hadji is directly responsible for the destitution of the blind beggar whose land he had stolen by changing the names on the title deeds, using his Western education in the name of corruption and capitalism (which are synonymous terms within the film). As with Mbaye's theft of the money order in *Le Mandat/Mandabi*, the educated are shown to play on the poor's ignorance of the written word.

In a repetition of the violent imposition of neo-colonial order in the opening sequence, the police arrive and round up the beggars and cripples whom they dump on the outskirts of the city. However, amongst the beggars are two figures who are simply rounded up by the police because they are in the vicinity of El Hadji's shop. The first is the peasant whose money has been stolen by the pickpocket who eventually replaces El Hadji in the Chamber of Commerce. Sembene thus links the plight of the peasantry to that of the urban destitute. The second figure is the young *Kaddu* seller. *Kaddu* was a Wolof-language newspaper on which Sembene collaborated with the Senegalese linguist Pathé Diagne in the early 1970s. A highly political journal (one issue featured Sembene's translation of the *Communist Manifesto*), *Kaddu* sought to promote Wolof, which is spoken by the vast majority of Senegalese, as the 'official' national language, thus replacing French.[48] The young newspaper seller is thus presented as a threat to the neo-colonial order. It should be remembered that the Chamber of Commerce is the one place in the film in which French is spoken at all times. The French language becomes another bourgeois fetish, a symbol of one's social status. This situation is examined in a highly ironic scene where Rama calls to visit her father in his office. He speaks French while she answers him in Wolof. When the camera focuses on El Hadji, we can see a political map of Africa on the wall behind him. When the camera focuses on Rama, we see a map of Africa with no political boundaries on it. As she prepares to leave, El Hadji asks if there is anything she needs. Her reply is simple: 'The only thing is to see Mother happy.' Beyond the immediate reference to the suffering of Adja Awa Astou, her own mother, there is a wider, more symbolic meaning. After she has left the office, the camera lingers on the unified map of Africa. This is the Mother which Rama, the radical student, wants to see happy. She wants Africa to escape from the divided, European-dominated reality shown on the political map of the continent. El Hadji later tries to adopt his daughter's linguistic radicalism when faced with expulsion from the Chamber of Commerce, but it is too late for such gestures.

In having the police round up these various figures, Sembene links together a range of social groups that are disparate in nature, but which are all shown to be the victims of the neo-colonial regime. The political nature of their position within the film is made evident through the lyrics of the beggar's song, which is heard throughout the second half of the film, after El Hadji is struck down by the *xala*. Sembene explained the significance of this song in a 1976 interview:

C'est une sorte de chanson populaire que j'ai écrite moi-même en wolof [...]. C'est l'allégorie d'une sorte de lézard qui est un mauvais chef. Quand il marche devant et vous derrière, il vous tue en disant que vous voulez le mordre. Quand vous marchez à sa hauteur, il vous tue en disant: 'Vous

---

[48] Carrie Dailey Moore provides some useful information on Sembene's involvement in *Kaddu*, including some French translations of articles from the journal. See Moore, 'Evolution of an African Artist: Social Realism in the Works of Ousmane Sembene' (unpublished doctoral thesis, Indiana University, 1973), pp. 170–5. Pathé Diagne's ideas on the question of African languages can be found in his *Langues africaines et impérialisme: africophonie et modernité* (Dakar: IFAN, 1976). Pierre Dumont's *Le français et les langues africaines au Sénégal* (Paris: Karthala, 1983) provides a useful overview of the status of African languages within Senegal in the period since independence.

voulez être mon égal'. Quand vous marchez devant lui il vous tue en disant: 'Vous voulez profiter de ma chance'. La chanson dit qu'il faut se préoccuper de ces chefs qui ressemblent à cet animal et s'en débarrasser. Elle se termine à peu près ainsi: 'Gloire au peuple, au règne du peuple, au gouvernement du peuple, qui ne sera pas le gouvernement d'un individu![49]

It's a sort of popular song that I myself wrote in Wolof [...]. It's an allegory about a lizard who is a bad leader. If he were to lead and you to follow, he'd kill you, claiming that you wanted to bite him. If you were to walk alongside him, he'd kill you, claiming that: 'You want to be my equal.' If you were to walk in front of him, he'd kill you, claiming that: 'You want to replace me.' The song says that we must keep an eye on leaders who behave like this lizard and get rid of them. The song ends something like this: 'All glory to the people, to the reign of the people, to the government of the people, which can never be the government of one individual!'

The beggar's political folk song contrasts sharply with the other music in the film. In the opening sequences, the traditional drummers and dancers are used as a piece of local colour to brighten up the businessmen's celebration. At the wedding reception, there is the constant sound of the Afro-Caribbean music being played by the band. In the 1960s and 1970s, this style of music was very influential in Africa, acting to the detriment of more traditional forms of African music.[50] Therefore, in the film, the music acts as another sign of the bourgeoisie's social status. In many ways, the political struggle that takes place in the film is reflected by the contest between this jaunty Afro-Caribbean music and the beggar's song. Despite the momentary return of the Afro-Caribbean music after El Hadji's temporary cure from Sérigne Mada, it is eventually the beggar's song that wins out.

The lyrics of the beggar's song give a specific political context to the beggars' presence within the film (although the fact that the lyrics are not translated in the sub-titles leaves the meaning of the song completely opaque for the non-Wolof speaker). Although, in the novel, the beggars only appear in occasional references, in the film, their presence, and equally their absence, is presented much more forcefully. Immediately after the businessmen arrive at the wedding reception (identified metonymically by their briefcases) we catch our first glimpse of the beggars watching on, kept at a safe distance from the house by the presence of two policemen (the beggars are not present at the reception in the novel). As El Hadji arrives, he disdainfully scatters some coins on the ground for the beggars to collect. However, a menacing-looking policeman prevents them from collecting one of the coins by placing his foot upon it (in an act similar to that of the policeman who stands on the cart driver's medal, in *Borom Sarret*). Totally destitute, the beggars are completely dependent on the charity of the bourgeoisie, whom they follow around in hope of aid. In this scene El Hadji obliges, no doubt in an attempt to maintain

[49] Nourredine Ghali, 'Ousmane Sembene. "Le cinéaste, de nos jours, peut remplacer le conteur traditionnel"', *Cinéma*, 208 (April 1976), p. 90.

[50] In reaction to the influence of Afro-Caribbean music, a number of leading Senegalese musicians, including the highly influential Youssou N'Dour, began to develop a form of music known as *mbalax*, which blended 'foreign' music with 'traditional' Senegalese, drum-based music. A highly evocative, fictionalised account of the contemporary Senegalese music scene is given in Mark Hudson's novel *The Music in my Head* (London: Jonathan Cape, 1998).

the image of the respectable, wealthy Muslim, which is a major factor behind his third marriage.[31] However, the policeman, who is portrayed as working specifically for the bourgeoisie, has no time for such pretences, and openly takes from the poor.

El Hadji is not so charitable the following day when he has the President of the Chamber order a police wagon come to remove the beggars from outside his shop. In preceding scenes, we have seen cripples, lepers and beggars converge on the area, seemingly drawn by the blind beggar's song, which is a recurrent presence on the soundtrack. They are rounded up and taken to the outskirts of the city but they are not absent for long. Significantly, we next see them after the question of who has put the *xala* on El Hadji comes up again. After Oumi Ndoye's visit to his office, El Hadji seems convinced of her guilt, but the real perpetrators become visible in the very next scene. Led by the blind beggar and his young helper, the beggars and cripples limp and crawl their way back from the edge of the city, as their song is once again heard on the soundtrack. El Hadji and his class want these people to be excluded from their society, to be hidden from view. However, the camera shows them constantly reappearing to remind those in power of their existence, and, more pragmatically, because the city is the site where they gain their income. As indicated by the stories of the blind beggar and the peasant whose money is stolen, the destitute from the countryside eventually wash up in the city, scratching a living from the charity of those who have brought about their predicament. In neo-colonial regimes, the poor and the destitute are a constant presence.

A number of commentators have evoked a link between the ending of *Xala* and that of Luis Buñuel's *Viridiana* (1961).[32] While both films have a beggars' revolt as their climax, there is a dramatic contrast between the political significance of these scenes within the two films. *Viridiana* is an anti-clerical work and the scene in which the beggars hold an anarchic feast in the mansion is filmed as a clear parody of Leonardo da Vinci's *The Last Supper*. The Rabelaisian behaviour of the beggars, which finally subsides into obscenity and violence, is used to symbolise man's fallen state, contrasting sharply with Viridiana's piety. *Viridiana* is a film that must be viewed in the context in which it was made in Franco's Spain, the film acting as a scathing critique of the pious hypocrisy of that regime.

The beggars' revolt in *Xala* performs a completely different function. As we have already seen, the film gives the beggars a distinct political role. Far from the anarchic, squabbling figures presented in *Viridiana*, Sembene's beggars show tremendous solidarity with one another. Great significance is given to the two scenes where they eat together. As they return to the city, after being

---

[31] Aminata Sow Fall deals with the issue of Islamic conceptions of charity in her novel, *The Beggars' Strike*, trans. by Dorothy S. Blair (London: Longman, 1981). In fact, her tale of a strike by beggars, refusing to seek charity from the Muslim faithful, who are thus unable to meet their religious duties, would appear to be an Islamic reply to Sembene's film/novel.

[32] Alain Masson compares *Xala* unfavourably with *Viridiana*. Masson, 'Mascarade à Dakar (*Xala*)', pp. 54–6. Although he does not mention *Viridiana* by name, Louis Marcorelles describes the finale of Sembene's film as being reminiscent of Buñuel's style. See Louis Marcorelles, 'Le ciné-livre de Sembène Ousmane', *Le Monde*, 6 March 1975, p. 17.

carried away by the police, the beggars stop to eat at a roadside canteen. The camera attentively follows the hands distributing the food and drink, making sure that everyone gets his share (it should also be noted that the beggars pay for what they eat, which constitutes another factor distinguishing them from Buñuel's 'freeloaders'). In a society where the communal, ritual aspect of eating is so strong, the sense of community that emanates from the beggars' meal is highly significant. It is a far cry from the lavish extravagances of the wedding reception, where the ritual of the feast has been completely appropriated by the neo-colonial bourgeoisie and its commodity fetishism. This ritual of the communal meal is repeated in the final part of the film when the beggars burst into Adja Awa Astou's home to confront El Hadji. They eat his yoghurts and drink his soft drinks but they do not mindlessly destroy El Hadji's belongings (a distinct contrast to the riotous behaviour of Buñuel's beggars). We must remember that the words of the blind beggar's song are constantly heard in the background during both of these scenes, reminding us of the political nature of their acts.

The combination of fetishism and social revolt in the beggars' punishment/cure of El Hadji is another of Sembene's radical interpretations of African tradition. As Laura Mulvey has argued, the idea of an 'uncivilised' African fetishism played an important part in the European justification of colonialism.[53] The word derives from the Portuguese word *feitiço*, which means witchcraft, and it became a term applied by the Portuguese to all African beliefs and practices that they could not understand. Effectively, fetishism was used as conclusive proof by Europeans that Africans were mentally inferior. Hegel, for instance, uses it as a damning instance of African barbarism and savagery in his *Lectures on the Philosophy of World History*.[54] Europe was also able to turn African fetishism to its own economic advantage. As the European economic system developed, European traders were able to profit from Africans' inflated evaluation of certain objects, buying goods in return for what were mere trinkets to European eyes.

In *Xala*, Sembene dismisses the notions of backwardness attached to fetishism: all cultures are seen to have their own rituals and fetishes. As he argues in *Man is Culture*:

> Much has been written about the fetishism of Blacks, their animism, their superstition, as if similarities did not exist in the history of the Greeks. All people practice fetishism. They all have objects which give a concrete form to their beliefs. (*MC*, p. 2)

The neo-colonial bourgeoisie depends on an amalgam of Western technical/commodity fetishism and African, 'supernatural' fetishism. However, the majority of the *marabouts* in the film who claim to possess supernatural powers are merely charlatans. Alongside these figures, the film presents a more 'honest' version of fetishism, as witnessed by the powers of Sérigne Mada and the blind beggar. Just after the blind beggar has claimed that he can cure El Hadji's *xala*,

---

[53] Mulvey, '*Xala*. Ousmane Sembene 1976: The Carapace that Failed', pp. 521–4.
[54] Georg Wilhelm Friedrich Hegel, *Lectures on the Philosophy of World History. Introduction: Reason in History*, trans. by H. B. Nesbitt (1830: Cambridge: Cambridge University Press, 1975), pp. 173–90.

we see a shot of the figure on the head of his stick against the background of the clear, blue sky, giving the impression that it is moving by itself, and therefore presenting the beggar as a supernatural figure. However, just as the bourgeoisie's fetishism contained both Western and African elements, so does that of the beggars. Their curse on El Hadji is cast in the name of an embryonic class-consciousness that sees El Hadji as its enemy. A supernatural act the curse may be, but it has its source in human actions, as both Sérigne Mada and the blind beggar proclaim: 'What one hand has done, another can undo.' When the beggars spit on El Hadji's naked body (a ritual which does not exist in Senegalese tradition), they are spitting out the anger of all those who are socially excluded from Senegalese society. The film ends with a freeze frame on El Hadji as we continue to hear the sound of the beggars spitting at him. The spectator is left to ponder on the meaning of this political and supernatural act, merged into one.

Sembene's use of rituals and fetishes forces the spectator (particularly the Senegalese spectator to whom the film is primarily addressed) to examine the values attributed by his society to certain objects. Laura Mulvey puts this in the following terms:

> Sembene makes use of the language of cinema, its hieroglyphic or pictographic possibilities, and creates a text which is about the meaning of objects as symptoms. His use of cinematic rhetoric is the key to *Xala*. The form of the film engages the spectators' ability to read the signs that emanate from colonialism and its neo-colonialist offspring.[55]

Xala presents a society where the signs of consumerism, fetishism and socialism are shown to intermingle, creating new social meanings. Dealing with rituals known to his Senegalese audience, Sembene then proceeds to put them into new configurations. His 'socialist fetishism' proved highly popular with Senegalese film audiences, and obviously touched on a sore point with the Senegalese government which ordered ten cuts to the film before allowing it to be released (thus creating the paradoxical situation whereby foreign audiences, who were secondary to Sembene's thinking, are the only ones who are able to see the film in its entirety).[56] With *Xala*, Sembene finally proved that African cinema could both be politically engaged and achieve popular acclaim.

Xala also produced a profound questioning of notions of male sexuality: El Hadji Abdou Kader Bèye's impotence can be read as a symbolic commentary not only on his class, but on notions of masculinity in general. As was argued above, Sembene's work has commented on the 'impotence' of African men in general, not simply those who make up the neo-colonial bourgeoisie. By questioning the status of African men, Sembene effectively challenges traditional African notions of the family, and also of the structure of society. This examination of male sexual and social roles in his work is necessarily accompanied by a thorough examination of the representation of African women, and it is to this subject that I shall turn in the next chapter.

---

[55] Mulvey, '*Xala*. Ousmane Sembene 1976: The Carapace that Failed', p. 527.
[56] For a list of these cuts, see Ghali, 'Ousmane Sembene. "Le cinéaste, de nos jours"', p. 86.

5

Mothers, Daughters
& Prostitutes

In many ways, to write a separate chapter on the representation of women in
Sembene's work is to fly in the face of Sembene's view that the status of
women in African society is inextricably linked to cultural, political and
economic issues. Previous chapters have already illustrated Sembene's keen
interest in exploring the role of women within a polygamous, Muslim society.
Chapter Two described Ngone War Thiandum's *prise de conscience* as she comes
to question the values to which she had adhered throughout her life, and
Chapter Four discussed El Hadji Abdou Kader Bèye's third marriage in terms
of consumerism, with the youthful Ngoné acting as El Hadji's gift to himself
on acceding to the Chamber of Commerce. However, it is useful to take a
more detailed look at the ways in which Sembene represents his female
characters in order to understand better Sembene's vision of an egalitarian,
socialist Africa.

The previous chapter dealt with the theme of impotence as a metaphor for
the inability of a male-dominated African society to face up to the problems of
the neo-colonial world. To a large extent, the dynamic role attributed by
Sembene to many of his female characters can be seen to be a corollary of this
male impotence. Indeed, it is often the female characters who are obliged to
replace their menfolk as the providers for the family. As in the cases of the
films, *Borom Sarret* and *Le Mandat/Mandabi*, described in Chapter Three, it is the
wives who ensure that there is food on the table at the end of the day, despite
all the frantic but ultimately futile efforts of their husbands.[1] This chapter will

---

[1] At the end of *Borom Sarret*, the cart driver's wife hands over the baby to her husband, leaving
him with the words, *'Je promets qu'on va manger ce soir.'* ['I promise that we'll have food on the
table this evening.'] In a clear echo of these words, Ibrahima Dieng's wife, Méty, states, upon
receiving the money order, that *'aujourd'hui, on mangera'*. ['Today we'll eat']. Throughout his
work, Sembene consistently stresses the pragmatism of the majority of his female characters.

124

therefore discuss the manner in which Sembene uses the dynamism of certain female characters to counterbalance this male impotence, casting women as a potent force within African society. A clear example of Sembene's attitude to these issues is to be found in a 1991 interview in which he rails against Africa's reliance on Western handouts for its survival. The process of decolonisation is argued paradoxically to have produced a dependency mentality rather than an independent, assertive Africa. Seeing this as an example of the failure of the men of his generation, Sembene declares: '*Moi, je dis toujours si j'étais une femme, je n'épouserais pas un Africain. Il faut épouser un homme, et non pas un infirme mental.*' ['I've always said that if I was a woman, I'd never marry an African. A woman seeks to marry a man, not someone who is mentally ill.']² What conclusions are we to draw from such an attitude? Does Africa need dynamic women simply because its men are doing such a poor job or is the liberation of women to fill more powerful roles a necessary condition for the creation of an egalitarian society? These are some of the main issues this chapter aims to address.

The role that feminism should play in postcolonial literary theory is an issue that has exercised the minds of many leading postcolonial critics. Third World critics, in particular, have been keen to problematise the notion of sisterhood and to challenge the assumptions made by Western feminists about women from the Third World. Chandra Talpade Mohanty goes so far as to claim that Western feminism, in its writings on the postcolonial world, has created the 'Third World Woman'.³ This argument is echoed in the work of the highly influential critic Gayatri Chakravorty Spivak who has argued that Western feminist criticism recreates the norms of imperialism by placing the individual, female European subject at the centre of its preoccupations.⁴ In this context, the notion of sisterhood has been treated with suspicion and its universal claims dismissed. In its place, it has been proposed that the oppression of women be investigated through the analysis of male domination in specific social contexts.

Another major issue facing feminist critics has been that of where to place feminism within the postcolonial debate. Can feminism and neocolonialism be dealt with separately? Should gender or racial issues take precedence? In her book, *Feminism and Anthropology*, Henrietta L. Moore has examined the manner in which recent feminist anthropological studies have attempted to study the complex relationship between race, gender, history and culture (not always in a satisfactory manner).⁵ Most feminist critics have concluded that

² Firinne Ni Chréacháin, 'Si j'étais une femme, je n'épouserais jamais un Africain', *Peuples noirs/Peuples africains*, 14, 8 (March–April 1991), p. 88.

³ See Chandra Talpade Mohanty, 'Under Western Eyes: Feminist Scholarship and Colonial Discourses', in *Third World Women and the Politics of Feminism*, ed. by Chandra Talpade Mohanty, Ann Russo and Lourdes Torres (Bloomington: Indiana University Press, 1991), pp. 51–80.

⁴ Gayatri Chakravorty Spivak, 'Three Women's Texts and a Critique of Imperialism', *Critical Inquiry*, 12, 1 (1985), pp. 43–61.

⁵ Henrietta L. Moore, *Feminism and Anthropology* (Oxford: Polity Press, 1988). For a discussion of gender issues specifically in relation to African literature, see *Unheard Voices: Women and Literature in Africa, the Arab World, Asia, the Caribbean and Latin America*, ed. by Mineke Schipper and trans.

decolonisation and women's liberation are inextricable issues, and that a feminist approach must therefore be one that deals with political, economic and cultural issues. As Sara Suleri has argued, the real challenge facing feminist critics is that of thinking out the complex relationship between gender, race, history and culture described by Moore in her work.[6]

As one would expect from a Marxist, Sembene's approach to feminist issues has attempted to negotiate a path through the questions of gender, class and race/culture. Highly dismissive of Western feminism, which he sees as a liberal, bourgeois movement that focuses on the rights of the individual, Sembene advocates an African feminism that will examine women's role in African society from a Marxist perspective. As he put it in a 1976 interview:

> [...] il y a bien entendu un problème indéniable: celui de la polygamie, que nous combattons. Il y a un problème, mais le problème est clair puisque l'infériorité de la femme est visible. Mais la solution, nous ne la trouvons pas dans la conception de la famille en Occident car cette famille ne produit qu'une déchéance de l'individu. En fait, le problème ne doit pas se poser en termes de sexe mais en termes de classes.[7]

> [...] of course, there is one undeniable problem against which we are fighting, that of polygamy. This problem is obvious as the inferiority of women is clearly visible. However, we don't believe that the solution is to be found in the Western conception of the family because that type of family only produces the degeneration of the individual. In fact, the problem should not be posed in terms of gender but in terms of class.

For Sembene, the liberation of women can only be achieved through economic and social change. Women must be liberated as a social group, not as individuals, in order to bring about real change in African society.

However, the Senegalese critic, Mohamadou Kane casts the debate over the role of women within the African novel as a conflict between conservatives and liberals, with the former emphasising the will of the group, and the latter putting forward the rights of the individual. Even Tioumbé, the radical schoolteacher of Sembene's *L'Harmattan*, is said to have rebelled against her family because of an *'éveil de l'individualité'* ['awakening of her individuality'].[8] In his over-schematic division of the African novel between the traditional and the modern, representing the group and the individual respectively, Kane casts the question of women's emancipation in purely individualistic terms. In fact, the whole issue of women's role in society is forced to take second place to Kane's vision of a generational conflict between the traditional and the

---

[5] (cont.) by Barbara Potter Fasting (London and New York: Allison & Busby, 1985), pp. 19–68.

[6] Sara Suleri, 'Woman Skin Deep: Feminism and the Postcolonial Condition', *Critical Inquiry*, 18, 4 (Summer 1992), pp. 756–69. For a radical rethinking of the relationship between feminism and social change, see Maria Mies, *Patriarchy and Accumulation on a World Scale* (London: Zed Books, 1986). For a specific consideration of African women's status within the capitalist world order, see Fatou Sow, 'Femmes africaines, emploi et division internationale du travail', *Présence Africaine*, 141 (1st quarter 1987), pp. 195–226.

[7] Nourredine Ghali, 'Ousmane Sembene. "Le cinéaste, de nos jours, peut remplacer le conteur traditionnel"', *Cinéma*, 208 (April 1976), p. 89.

[8] Mohamadou Kane, *Roman africain et tradition* (Dakar: Nouvelles Editions Africaines, 1982), p. 385.

modern: '*c'est par le biais du thème de la femme que le conflit des générations trouve sa plus remarquable illustration.*' ['it is through the theme of women that the generational conflict is given its most noteworthy illustration.']⁹ This is precisely the type of reductionist argument that Sembene has dismissed throughout his career. Female emancipation brings about a growing individual consciousness, but this does not necessarily mean that all group values will subsequently be cast aside. The example of Tioumbé, which Kane cites in his argument, proves the point. Rebelling against her tyrannical Catholic father and his submissive adherence to colonial rule, she joins the *Parti* and campaigns for the 'no' vote in De Gaulle's 1958 referendum. Her *prise de conscience* leads her to reject the traditional organisation of African society but it does not turn her into an alienated, Western-obsessed liberal. As a Marxist, she argues for a new social bond within Africa based on the values of Marxism.

The limited and limiting view of the world that separates the traditional/ African from the modern/Western (which has been so convincingly denounced by Aijaz Ahmad) is perhaps best illustrated in relation to traditionalist notions of what constitutes the woman's role in African society. Much of the resistance to change in the status of women comes from the assimilation of the notion of female emancipation with rampant Westernisation. In the nationalist atmosphere of many postcolonial states, preserving institutions such as polygamy is seen as an act of resistance against outside forces. This dichotomy between nationalist and feminist considerations in Third World Muslim countries is astutely analysed by Fatima Mernissi. Although her analysis is based on the countries of the Middle East, I feel that it is equally applicable to the Muslim states of West Africa:

> Women's liberation is directly linked to the political and economic conflicts rending modern Muslim societies. Every political setback generates a new necessity to liberate all the forces of development in Islamic nations. But paradoxically, every political setback inflicted by infidels generates an antithetical necessity to reaffirm the traditional Islamic nature of these societies as well. The forces of both modernity and tradition are unleashed in a single stroke and confront each other with dramatic consequences for relations between the sexes.¹⁰

Effectively, what Mernissi is describing is the rather perverse situation whereby the rapid changes within postcolonial societies create, at the same time, both the need for the emancipation of women and conservative reaction to change that aggressively defends the status quo, proclaiming that the subjugated position of women forms an integral part of the immutable identity of the community.

One of the most controversial issues concerning African women is that of genital mutilation (an issue that Sembene has only dealt with in passing in *O Pays, mon beau peuple!*). Routinely condemned by the West, this practice is defended by many Africans in the name of 'cultural authenticity'. In those societies where it is practised, female excision appears to have the same social

⁹ Ibid., p. 375.
¹⁰ Fatima Mernissi, *Beyond the Veil: Male–Female Dynamics in Modern Muslim Society* (London: Al Saqi Books, 1985), p. 11.

value as male circumcision but it has none of the attendant health benefits of male circumcision, and, in fact, carries serious health risks, sometimes resulting in death.[11] The defence of excision is not carried out solely by men but also by women, who, as we shall see below, are often the most fervent supporters of the very practices that keep them trapped within certain social roles. For example, Joséphine Guidy Wandja has defended genital mutilation as a valuable initiation process. She argues that Western criticism of excision is a result of 'ethnocentrism': '*Si l'excision est condamnée aujourd'hui vigoureusement, c'est parce que la science vient d'accorder au clitoris un rôle dans la sexualité féminine.*' ['Excision is vigorously condemned purely and simply because science has attributed a role to the clitoris in defining female sexuality.'][12] Essentially, Western critics of excision are here accused of imposing Western notions of sexuality on Africa. Guidy Wandja's subtext appears quite plain: the 'sexually liberated' West has produced a decadent society in which the sexual act has ceased to be primarily a matter of procreation, and has become a question of mere pleasure, in turn creating a society which suffers from severe sexual problems, including increased numbers of rape victims. However, the bias evident in her polemical diatribe against the 'decadent' West leads one to wonder whether she is even aware of the existence of similar problems in Third World countries. In India, for example, there exists a powerful women's movement against rape, the summary despatch of female children, and the general exploitation of women. In the blinkered view of commentators such as Guidy Wandja, any Western criticism of genital mutilation is disqualified in advance as a result of the 'ethnocentrism' of a morally corrupt society.

A very different approach to these issues is to be found in the work of the Association of African Women for Research and Development (AAWORD), based in Dakar. Although they criticise the paternalistic/maternalistic approach of those in the West who sensationalise the question of genital mutilation, presenting themselves as modern-day civilisers saving Africa from its own barbarism, these female African academics argue against the passive and defensive reactions of Africans to such criticisms from the West. These women believe that Africans must learn to criticise their cultural practices constructively. AAWORD is firmly opposed to genital mutilation and all forms of exploitation of women, but it believes that such matters can only be fruitfully examined in light of a consideration of the poverty and ignorance bred by the plight of African countries in the neo-colonial world order. In its policy document from 1978, AAWORD argued its case on the issue of excision:

> On the question of such traditional practices as genital mutilation, African women must no longer equivocate or react only to Western influence. They must act in

[11] For some harrowing accounts of the process of excision, see Awa Thiam, *Black Sisters, Speak Out: Feminism and Oppression in Black Africa*, trans. by Dorothy S. Blair (London: Pluto Press, 1986), pp. 57–87. For a fictionalised account of genital mutilation (which is followed by a rape), see Ahmadou Kourouma, *The Suns of Independence*, trans. by Adrian Adams (London: Heinemann, 1981).

[12] Joséphine Guidy Wandja, 'Excision? Mutilation sexuelle? Mythe ou réalité?', *Présence Africaine*, 141 (1st quarter 1987), p. 57.

favour of the total eradication of all these practices, and they must lead information and education campaigns to this end within their own countries and on a continental level.[13]

Rather than arguing for an absolute right to cultural difference as does Guidy Wandja, groups such as AAWORD seek to find ways of improving women's lot by improving their education and their general standard of life. In this view, the liberation of women must be both economic and social.

Several African governments have tried to defuse feminist protests by holding an annual *Fête de la femme* or by appointing a token woman to the cabinet to deal with women's affairs. In her study, *Black Sisters, Speak Out*, Awa Thiam quotes from a speech by the then Senegalese Prime Minister Abdou Diouf on the occasion of the first *Journée de la femme sénégalaise* in 1972: '*Vous avez refusé la tentation d'un féminisme stérile consistant à vous poser en rivales envieuses et complexées de l'homme pour vous poser noblement en partenaires égaux.*' ['You have refused the temptation to adopt an aggressive, sterile feminism, which sets you up as the envious rivals of men, full of complexes.'][14] Thiam rejects the hypocrisy of Diouf's stance, interpreting his words as a justification for the maintaining of the status quo:

> Decoded, the message of this quotation, which has not actually been stated, is 'Refuse the temptation of feminism.' After this injunction, the prime minister of Senegal continued, ' ... so that you can assume your position nobly as equal partners'. Moral considerations apart, we would like to know what this equality comprises. How is it translated into concrete terms? By the appointment of a few women as deputies, by admitting a tiny minority of women to public office, by the absolute right of husbands to exploit any number of wives, or by polygamy instituted to the detriment of women?[15]

Sembene parodies such half-hearted measures in his political satire, *The Last of the Empire*, in which the ironically titled female *Ministre de la condition féminine* is presented as a stooge for the government, and also as yet another sexual conquest for the Machiavellian Mam Lat Soukabé. A similar parody is to be found in Henri Lopes's short story 'The Esteemed Representative' in which the eponymous deputy delivers a speech on the subjugated position of women

---

[13] See chapter 22, 'A Statement on Genital Mutilation', in *Third World – Second Sex: Women's Struggles and National Liberation*, ed. by Miranda Davies (London: Zed Books, 1983), p. 219.

[14] Thiam, *Black Sisters, Speak Out*, p.12. A former Senegalese Minister for Culture has elsewhere written of the central role played by African women in the civic, moral and religious life of their communities. However, no mention is made of their absence from the political life of their communities. Significantly, what Seck regards as the fundamental role of women is their capacity for silent suffering. Women are here seen as an active, but silent and unquestioning force in society: '[la femme africaine] *incarne la dignité du groupe, par sa capacité de résistance silencieuse et méprisante devant la force aveugle et l'injustice, et aussi par sa capacité de donner sans réserve et parfois dans la souffrance*'. ['[African women] embody the dignity of the social group through their silent and disdainful resistance to blind force and injustice, as well as through their boundless ability to give, even though they themselves might suffer.'] See Assane Seck, 'Préface', in A. Raphaël Ndiaye, *La Place de la femme dans les rites au Sénégal* (Dakar: Nouvelles Editions Africaines, 1986), p. 5.

[15] Thiam, *Black Sisters, Speak Out*, p. 12.

in Africa, then returns home to order his wife and daughter around, before going out to spend the night with his mistress.[16]

Within nationalist pre-independence African literature, two main models of African womanhood were proposed: the mother and the beautiful young woman/virgin. Negritude produced countless examples of these two figures but I would here like to focus on works by two of the writers most closely identified with Negritude: Camara Laye's *The African Child* and Léopold Sédar Senghor's poem, 'Black Woman'.[17] As was argued in Chapter One, *The African Child* is a highly romanticised vision of an idyllic African childhood. One of the key texts of Negritude, the book describes an African society governed by Islam, the supernatural and the family. Within this society, the narrator's mother plays a vital role in the transmission of values from one generation to the next. It is the mother who tells the story of the father's *génie*, the snake. She herself seems to possess supernatural powers, as is witnessed by the magic charm that protects her from the crocodiles that abound in the river where she goes to collect water for the family. These supernatural powers serve to heighten the image of the mother, giving extra significance to the more usual values associated with motherhood: caring for and nurturing the child, providing for his/her material welfare. As Arlette Chemain-Degrange has put it:

> *La mère de la petite enfance de ces sociétés rurales et patriarcales rêvées a un rôle par ses connivences avec les forces surnaturelles. Elle fait respecter les règles du groupe et connaît les mystères et l'origine du clan. Elle sait enraciner l'enfant dans sa famille et dans son ethnie.*[18]

The idealised mother of these rural, patriarchal societies has a strong role to play in the education of young children through her association with supernatural forces. It is she who maintains respect for society's rules and who knows the mysteries and origins of the group. The mother roots the child within the family and the ethnic group.

This idealised vision of the mother in African societies can be readily seen in Mineke Schipper's study of a wide range of proverbs, concerning the role of women, from various African communities, in which the sole universally positive representation of the female is that of the mother (one could easily find such negative images of women in proverbs from many corners of the globe; however, the point is not to condemn Africa, but rather to understand how gender differences are constructed *within* African societies).[19]

The Negritude vision of the mother presents her as a link to the ancestral world, the values of which she incarnates. As the person responsible for beginning the process of transmitting the values of her society to the next generation, the mother, in effect, perpetuates the situation whereby women

---

[16] Henri Lopes, *Tribaliques*, trans. by Andrea Leskes (London: Heinemann, 1987), pp. 32–41.

[17] For an examination of the role of both the mother and the beautiful young woman in the pre-independence African novel, see Arlette Chemain-Degrange, *Emancipation féminine et roman africain* (Dakar: Nouvelles Editions Africaines, 1980), pp. 51–157.

[18] Chemain-Degrange, *Emancipation féminine*, p. 54.

[19] Mineke Schipper, *Source of All Evil: African Proverbs and Sayings on Women* (London: Allison & Busby, 1991), pp. 37–41.

occupy a largely submissive role.[20] However, within the spheres of action left open to them by tradition, women do exercise a certain amount of power. This leads the narrator of *The African Child* to conclude that the independence of mind shown by his mother is proof of his society's respect for those who stand up for themselves, thus dismissing any notions of an inherently inferior social status for women:

> In our country, custom demands a deep-seated independence, an innate pride. One only oppresses those who allow themselves to be oppressed. My father would never have dreamed of bullying anyone, least of all my mother. He had great respect for her, as did everyone, including our friends and neighbours. I am sure that this was due to my mother's strong-willed character and also to the supernatural powers that she possessed.[21]

Although the narrator's mother does come across as an independent-minded character, it is hard to see how this alters the fact that this independence remains confined to the sphere of action which is socially determined to be that of a mother. We have already discussed in Chapter One the specious nature of many of the arguments put forward by those who defend oppressive social practices in the name of a 'local knowledge' that is set against the universal claims of what is perceived as a Western value system. To argue that those who are dominated and oppressed within a given society are simply those who allow themselves to be oppressed is to cast aside all social, cultural and economic criteria in favour of an argument based on individual character. It should be recalled that similar arguments were used in the West to justify both slavery and colonisation, which were deemed necessary because of Africans' inherent inferiority and their incapacity to govern themselves.

Above all, the image of the mother in *The African Child* functions as a symbol for Africa. In the nationalist struggle for independence, the image of 'Mother Africa', preserving the values of the pre-colonial society that independence would once again restore to the continent, was particularly powerful. This duality between the personal and the political is clearly seen in Laye's dedication of the book to his own mother (in a language that clearly echoes that used by Senghor in 'Black Woman'):

> Black woman, woman of Africa, O my mother, I am thinking of you[22]

Before referring to her directly as his mother, she is both the generic black and African woman. Therefore, the rest of the dedication must be read as referring to both his real mother, Daman, and to 'Mother Africa'. They nurtured him, taught him the ways of the world, cared for him and loved him. Now that the

[20] Mamadou Diawara has written about the meagre literature that exists on African women as a source of history. See his article, 'Women, servitude and history: the oral historical traditions of women of servile condition in the kingdom of Jaara (Mali) from the fifteenth to the mid-nineteenth century', in *Discourse and its Disguises: The Interpretation of African Oral Texts*, ed. by Karin Barber and P. F. de Moraes Farias (Birmingham: University of Birmingham, Centre for West African Studies, 1989), pp. 109–37.

[21] Camara Laye, *The African Child*, trans. by James Kirkup (London: Fontana, 1959), p. 58. I have used my own translation here as Kirkup's translation of this passage is extremely poor.

[22] Ibid., p. 5.

young boy has grown up and is living far away in Paris where he is writing this book, he longs to be back home with his two loving mothers. Trapped in the modern, urbanised world of Paris, he longs for the traditional ways of his homeland:

> O Daman, Daman, you of the great family of blacksmiths and goldsmiths, my thoughts are always turning towards you, and your thoughts accompany me at every step. O, Daman, my mother, how I should love to be surrounded by your loving warmth again, to be a little child beside you.
>
> Black woman, woman of Africa, O my mother, let me thank you; thank you for all that you have done for me, your son, who, though so far away, is still so close to you![23]

The image of the mother thus plays a key role within Negritude, acting as both a personal and a political symbol of the ancestral African past.[24]

In contrast to the idealised mother, the young black woman/virgin, while still representing the traditional values of the African community, is presented as a symbol of the flowering of a new, independent Africa. As Arlette Chemain-Degrange has put it: '*La jeune fille a pour mission de sauvegarder la pureté africaine et les valeurs anciennes malgré une timide évolution.*' ['Despite a minor evolution in her role, the young girl's principal mission remains that of safeguarding African purity and traditional values.'][25] Referring to the African novel, Chemain-Degrange argues that the figure of the young woman acts as a yardstick for judging the moral climate of society. In Abdoulaye Sadji's *Nini, mulâtresse du Sénégal*, Nini's moral depravity seems all the more serious because of her inability to meet the ideal standards of femininity that society desires of her.[26] Another favourite theme of Negritude, that of the corrupting influence of the city (here with regard to the corruption of women), is explored in Ousmane Socé's *Karim*, where the women characters seem solely intent on bleeding their potential suitors of as much money as they can. As was already argued in Chapter Three, Negritude never did manage to create a positive vision of the African city.

In Senghor's poem 'Black Woman', we are presented with the archetypal Negritude vision of the young black woman.[27] Senghor's 'black woman' is described through a series of rural images: 'savannah stretching to clear horizons', 'ripe fruit', 'high up on the sun-baked pass [...], I come upon you, my Promised Land': she is a simple, rural beauty. In keeping with the typical Negritude practice of inverting the denigrating colonial discourse on Africa, proudly

---

[23] Ibid., p. 5.

[24] Sembene dedicated his novel, *Black Docker*, to his mother. However, unlike Camara Laye, Sembene addresses the irony inherent in dedicating a book to an illiterate person: 'This book is dedicated to my mother, although she cannot read.' This acts as a neat reflection of the different concerns of the two artists in their respective works: in *The African Child*, Camara Laye is interested in creating an idealised vision of Africa, while Sembene's novel seeks to uncover social conflicts.

[25] Chemain-Degrange, *Emancipation féminine*, p. 101.

[26] Abdoulaye Sadji, *Nini, mulâtresse du Sénégal* (1954; Paris: Présence Africaine, 1988). A profoundly moralising tale, *Nini* is also a work that persistently veers towards racism and misogyny in its account of its heroine's debauched and feckless life.

[27] See 'Black Woman', in *Léopold Sédar Senghor: Prose and Poetry*, selected and trans. by John Reed and Clive Wake (London: Heinemann, 1976), pp. 105–6.

wearing as a badge of identity that which the coloniser had seen as savage and barbaric, Senghor describes his ideal African women as naked, dark and animal-like. He alternatively refers to her as both 'naked woman, black woman' and 'naked woman, dark woman', and, in true *Song of Solomon* style, her sensuality is constantly stressed:

> Firm-fleshed ripe fruit, sombre raptures of black wine, mouth
> making lyrical my mouth.

She is also said to have an immense grace and calm:

> Oil that no breath ruffles, calm oil on the athlete's flanks, on
> the flanks of the Princes of Mali
> Gazelle limbed in Paradise, pearls are stars on the night of
> your skin

Despite its claims to represent the *authentic* African woman, the poem is, in many ways, an imitation of the genre of Renaissance poetry which sought to depict the ideal woman, setting its object of attention upon a pedestal. This desire to create an image of the woman that will last after she has turned to dust (one of the central themes of Renaissance poetry) is seen in the final stanza:

> Naked woman, black woman
> I sing your beauty that passes, the form that I fix in the Eternal,
> Before jealous Fate turn you to ashes to feed the roots of life.

In a Senegalese landscape that lacks the ephemeral roses so dear to the hearts of the Renaissance poets who have obviously influenced Senghor, the vision of the ideal woman is Africanised by reference to darkness, drum rhythms, ancient kingdoms, and the other favourite tropes of Negritude (the poem contains deliberate echoes of the *Song of Solomon*, and its idealisation of the beauty of the Queen of Sheba). Senghor's young African woman is thus presented as an ideal by which to set the standards of African femininity.

■ ■ ■

Sembene's work provides a far more complex vision of African women, questioning the 'traditional' roles of both mothers and daughters. Perhaps the best illustration of the manner in which Sembene modifies and counters Negritude's assumptions about motherhood is to be found in the short story, 'The Mother'. In keeping with the ironic tone of many of the stories in *Tribal Scars*, 'The Mother' announces itself as a tale about the kings of long ago. One could almost believe it to be a standard Negritude tale of the grandeur of the African past, as the narrator lists the ceremonies and artifacts surrounding the all-powerful monarch. However, behind the people's submissive adherence to monarchical rule there lies a deep-seated resentment towards the king's despotic power: 'There were [servants] to sing his praises and to dance for his entertainment. All cherished a desire to see him burnt alive, for he was not a God but a despot with the power of life or death over his subjects' (*TS*, p. 35).

133

The king's despotism finds particular expression in his seeming desire to possess sexually all the young women of the kingdom. Thus, the king's oppressive regime is cast almost entirely in terms of the domination of women.

Resistance to the despotic monarch comes in the form of a mother whose daughter has been kidnapped by the king. In her desire to spare her daughter from the fate that has befallen so many other girls, the old woman stands defiantly before the king and launches a verbal attack upon him. In this tirade, the king's lack of respect for women, and particularly for the figure of the mother, is seen to represent a fundamental lack of humanity on his part:

> Sire, by the look of you, anyone would think that you have no mother. From the day you were born until now, you have contended only with women, because they are weak. The pleasure you derive from it is more vile than the act itself. I'm not angry with you for behaving in that way. Because you are a man and because a woman is always a woman, and so Nature wills it. I'm not angry with you for you do have a mother, and through mothers I respect every human being. Son of a king or of a slave, the mother bears a child with love, gives birth in pain, and cherishes the rending of herself in the utmost depths of her senses. In her name I forgive you. Hold women in respect, not for their white hairs but for the sake of your own mother in the first place and then for womanhood itself. It is from woman that all greatness flows, whether of the ruler, of the warrior, the coward, the griot or musician. In a mother's heart, the child is king. All these people around you have a mother, and in their time of grief or of joy she sees but her child. (*TS*, p. 36)

The language used does not greatly differ from Camara Laye's dedication to his mother in *The African Child*. The mother is presented as a figure who loves and cares for her children, and the very fact of motherhood is presented as a common bond of humanity within society. The old woman does not challenge men's superiority over women but she does challenge the king's right to abuse this power. His disrespect for women is cast in terms of a disrespect for motherhood, and thus as a fundamental disrespect for his fellow human beings.

While keeping largely to the vision set out by Negritude, Sembene politicises the role of the mother by making her responsible for the overthrow of the despotic king (in a striking echo of Kocc Barma's role in the overthrow of the equally despotic Daou Demba). It is in this politicised context that we should read the 'hymn' to African women at the end of the story:

> Glory to all, men and women, who have had the courage to defy slanderous tongues. Praise to all women, unfailing well-springs of life, who are more powerful than death. Glory to you, coolies of Old China and the tagala-coye of the Niger plateau! Glory to the wives of seamen in your everlasting mourning! Glory to thee, little child, little girl already playing at being the mother.
> The boundless ocean is as nothing beside the boundless tenderness of a mother. (*TS*, p. 37)

The story contradicts Camara Laye's vision of an African society where men and women live in total harmony, complementing each other's good points. Women may possess certain maternal traits that distinguish them from men, says Sembene (a concept with which many feminists would not necessarily agree), but this does not prevent them from taking decisive and even aggressive social actions. Taking the tenderness and loving of a mother as a given, Sembene often proceeds to put his mother figures into situations where these feelings are forced to express themselves through explicitly social or political action. In *God's Bits of Wood*, the respected old woman, Ramatoulaye, reflects upon a situation whereby the men are no longer able to play the traditional breadwinner of the family, leaving it up to the women to show initiative and direction. Due to the exigencies of the strike, the women are simply obliged to take on more aggressive and assertive social roles:

> When you know that the life and the spirit of others depend on your life and your spirit, you have no right to be afraid – even when you are terribly afraid. In the cruel times we are living through we must find our own strength, somehow, and force ourselves to be hard. (*GBW*, p. 69)

Unable to feed their families, which they see as one of their primary functions, the women are obliged to step outside their traditional roles. When the women ask themselves where Ramatoulaye has discovered her newfound force and courage, they find their answer 'beside a cold fireplace, in an empty kitchen' (*GBW*, p. 74).

Equally, in the story, *Taaw*, the mother, Yaye Dabo, finds herself pushed into radical action by the weight of circumstances. Threatened with repudiation by her husband Baye Tine, who has just chased their son, Taaw, along with his pregnant girlfriend, from the house, Yaye Dabo finally reacts, pushing over her husband and repudiating him as he lies prostrate on the ground before her:

> Well, it is I who repudiate you, and in front of these witnesses here. Leave this house. Keep your trousers, they're all you have here. In front of the men you act the part of the husband. But when it's just the two of us, you are as limp as this old cloth. In this house, anything that stands upright is thanks to me. You no longer have a wife here.[28]

Defying custom and tradition, Yaye Dabo repudiates her husband and becomes head of her household. The first thing she does is to invite Taaw and his girlfriend to live with her. Her instinct as a mother is shown to be stronger than the demands of social conformity.

An interesting example of Sembene's representation of the young African woman is to be found in another story from *Tribal Scars*, 'The Promised Land', and particularly in the accompanying poem, 'Longing' (a more complete analysis of the story is to be found in Chapter Two). Presented as a victim of European colonialism, Diouana, whose death had seemed so insignificant to the Europeans in 'The Promised Land', becomes a symbol of African resistance against oppression, and of the day of independence that is not far away (Diouana's suicide occurs in June 1958, two years before *les indépendances*). Sembene employs a language remarkably similar to Senghor's images of rural landscapes and the abundance of the land:

---

[28] Ousmane Sembene, *Niiwam* and *Taaw* (London: Heinemann, 1992). Further references to this novella will be given in the body of the text.

Diouana, proud African girl,
You carry to your grave
The golden rays of our setting sun,
The dance of ears of fonio,
The waltz of the rice-shoots.
(*TS*, p. 100)

However, unlike Senghor's 'black woman', Diouana represents an Africa emerging from colonialism. She is not an idealised African woman, representing the values of Negritude, but a symbol of a liberated Africa. Rather than producing a prescriptive vision of the role allotted to African women, Sembene effectively transforms the suffering of an individual African woman into an incident of political significance for all of Africa. In the final stanza, 'our sister' Diouana becomes 'our Mother Africa':

Diouana,
Our sister,
Light of the days to come,
One day soon
These forests,
These fields,
These rivers
This land,
Our flesh,
Our bones
Are ours alone.
Image of our Mother Africa,
We lament over your sold body,
You are our
Mother,
Diouana.
(*TS*, p. 101)

Although the image of a feminised Africa remains, Sembene's vision of 'Mother Africa' is here used as a stark anti-colonial statement (in the manner of some of the poetry of David Diop[29]). The fact that Diouana is a maid who is overworked and neglected by her French bosses gives the use of the image of 'Mother Africa' a social dimension missing from the images of Negritude. Once again, the African woman is placed firmly within the political arena.

Sembene's work features a whole array of radical young women. Tioumbé, the radical schoolteacher in *L'Harmattan*, is a Marxist who revolts against her Catholic father, going so far as to confront him physically (Tioumbé's mother is scandalised by such behaviour: as we shall see below, mothers and daughters in Sembene's work often find generational barriers between themselves[30]). In *Xala*, El Hadji's daughter Rama is portrayed as a student radical, who is engaged in the fight for the promotion of Wolof in Senegal and who has

---

[29] See David Diop, *Hammer Blows*, trans. by Simon Mpondo and Frank Jones (London: Heinemann, 1975).

[30] In *God's Bits of Wood*, the most important example of generational conflict between women is that between Niakoro and her granddaughter, Ad'jibid'ji.

obvious Marxist sympathies (in the film version of *Xala*, we see a photograph of Amilcar Cabral, the Marxist leader of the PAIGC independence movement of Guinea-Bissau, on her bedroom wall). Rather than representations of some idealised form of African femininity, Sembene's young women represent the possibilities open to African women in the future. A startling example of this is to be found in *God's Bits of Wood* where Ad'jibid'ji, the adoptive daughter of the strike leader Ibrahima Bakayoko, dreams of one day becoming a train driver, following in the footsteps of her father. Ad'jibid'ji, the girl who can speak French, as well as Bambara and Wolof, and who possesses a keen intelligence, offers a stark contrast to the standard Negritude images of the African woman who is presented as beautiful, simple and graceful, but never as bright, intelligent and dynamic.

The obvious concern within Sembene's work to challenge accepted conceptions of the African woman is perhaps best illustrated in the character of the princess, Dior Yacine, in his 1976 film, *Ceddo* (this film is analysed in greater depth in Chapter Six). Kidnapped by the *ceddo*, or outsiders, who intend to use her as a bargaining chip with her father, who is increasingly coming under the sway of the imam and his Muslim disciples, the princess is at first presented to us as a haughty, arrogant noblewoman who sees herself as superior to the *ceddo*. Later in the film, after her arrogance has failed to impress her captor, Sembene presents the princess as seductress. Emerging naked from the sea, she appears, as if in a vision, to tempt the *ceddo* but he does not seek to take advantage of his prisoner.[31] She then shows a rebellious and cunning side to her character by attempting to grab one of the *ceddo*'s arrows while he drinks from the gourd that she has given him. The princess is eventually freed by two warriors sent by the imam, who has now taken over the reins of power after the suspicious death of the king. Effectively, a coup d'état has taken place and Islam is the new state power. After the *ceddo*'s death,

---

[31] Some critics have taken issue with Sembene's use of a nude scene in his depiction of the princess. For example, Mireille Amiel has argued that: '*la princesse Dior est vraiment belle mais Sembène Ousmane se sert de sa nudité comme les pires auteurs français se sont servis naguère de celle de Brigitte Bardot.*' ['Princess Dior is truly beautiful but Sembène Ousmane uses her beauty in the same fashion as the worst French directors treated Brigitte Bardot.'] See Mireille Amiel, '*Ceddo –* Ousmane Sembène', *Cinéma*, 249 (September 1979), p. 93. Another critic (who prefers to remain anonymous) widens the attack on Sembene's use of nudity to the scenes featuring Aram in *Le Mandat* and Ngoné in *Xala*. See Un patriote sénégalais S KH SY, '*Ceddo ou le poids des mystifications en Afrique*', *Peuples noirs/Peuples africains*, 12, 2 (November–December 1979), pp. 37–46. I have already examined the purpose of the nude scenes in *Xala* in Chapter Four. In *La Noire de*, we see Diouana naked in the bath after her suicide. One could argue that Sembene deliberately uses this scene to refuse publicly the pornographic representation of the African woman: her nudity is deliberately presented in a non-erotic fashion. The very short nude scene in *Le Mandat/Mandabi* is used to poke gentle fun at the piety of Ibrahima Dieng as he finds himself embarrassed on coming across his wife bathing in the courtyard of the family home. To suggest that any of the nude scenes is intended to exploit women is a patent nonsense. Would one make a similar claim about the nude scene featuring a youthful Guelwaar, escaping the wrath of his lover's husband, in Sembene's most recent feature film? Sembene claims that he was asked to include 'erotic' scenes in *Le Mandat/Mandabi* by his French producers, but he refused. See Jean-Claude Morellet, 'Cinéma africain: premiers pas en liberté', *Jeune Afrique*, 26 February–3 March 1968, pp. 42–3.

the princess has a vision in which she hands a gourd of water to the *ceddo* returning from a day's hunting. The sense of loss that she feels after his death is presented through the act of providing a visitor with water (an act of great ritual importance in the drought-ravaged region of Senegambia), which she had earlier subverted in her attempt to kill the *ceddo*. Although one cannot deny that this image of the princess kneeling before her brave 'dream-husband' presents a submissive picture of women, it should also be noted that this act represents a belated rallying to the cause of the *ceddo* in their fight against Islam. Upon returning home, the princess refuses to endorse the new regime, and, in an act of political defiance, she shoots the imam. In the course of the film, the princess has moved through the stages of arrogant noble-woman, seductive temptress, to the final scene where she becomes a focus of resistance to the domination of Islam. As we shall see below, much of Sembene's criticism of Islam stems from the social status that it allocates to women, particularly through the institution of the polygamous marriage.

Sembene's desire to provide alternative images of African women, to give voice to their stories, has been a constant in his work since *God's Bits of Wood*. (In both *Black Docker* and *O Pays, mon beau peuple!*, the female characters are relegated to a marginal position within the text, the action concerning them being limited to the domestic sphere which, contrary to his later works, is presented as an entirely separate space to the social sphere.) In many ways, his project is similar to that of Awa Thiam in her remarkable sociological study, *Black Sisters, Speak Out*. A compilation of interviews with women from various parts of Africa, the introduction to Thiam's book clearly sets out her objective as that of liberating the female African voice:

> Black Women have been silent for too long. Are they now beginning to find their voices? Are they claiming the right to speak for themselves? Is is not high time that they discovered their own voices, that – even if they are unused to speaking for themselves – they now take the floor, if only to say they exist, that they are human beings – something that is not always immediately obvious – and that, as such, they have a right to liberty, respect and dignity?[32]

In many interviews, Sembene has expressed his belief that men and women play complementary roles. However, the problem is that men do not want to give up their privileged status to allow a more dynamic role for women. Sembene claims that it has always been men who have criticised women. In order for things to change, it is thus necessary to allow women's criticisms of men to be heard:

> *L'homme et la femme sont deux pouvoirs qui se complètent. Nous ne sommes pas meilleurs, nous ne sommes pas pires. Nous pouvons avoir un regard critique sur la femme, mais est-ce que nous*

---

[32] Thiam, *Black Sisters, Speak Out*, p. 11. A revealing example of the submissive role that women play in African society is to be found in a collective interview carried out by Thiam in Guinea, involving seven men and eight women, including Thiam herself (see pp. 30–40). Throughout the course of the interview only two of the women actually speak out, even when explicitly asked to do so by Thiam and a number of the men. One would be hard pressed to find a clearer example of the sense of inferiority experienced by many African women.

5.1 Princess Dior returns to confront the imam
Ceddo, Filmi Doomireew – Dakar, Senegal (all rights reserved)

nous sommes jamais demandé quel est le regard critique que l'épouse passe sur son mari quand elle voit son ventre grossir, sa chair devenir flasque, alors que lui joue à la virilité avec les poils qui poussent autour des oreilles? Est-ce que nous nous sommes posé cette question? Voilà le problème. Les femmes aussi ont droit à un regard critique.[33]

Men and women constitute two complementary powers. Men are neither better nor worse than women. We can be critical of women but we have never asked ourselves what a woman thinks when she sees her husband's stomach grow fat and flabby, while he still plays the role of the virile man, not noticing that there are hairs growing out of his ears. Have we asked ourselves this question? Here lies the problem. Women have the right to be critical as well.

Needless to say, one may question Sembene's ability, as a man, to capture the concerns of African women.[34] However, one may equally question the images of African women presented by well-respected African women writers. Despite the praise heaped upon it, Mariama Bâ's impressive debut novel, *So Long a Letter*, remains the expression of the concerns of middle-class African women and displays little of Sembene's concern for the economic aspect of the female condition.[35] Christopher L. Miller intelligently draws attention to Mariama Bâ's problematisation of the act of storytelling in making her novel a one-way correspondence (the novel consists of a single letter that is never sent, as the addressee is due to arrive the day after the letter's completion).[36] The novel's form thus highlights the difficulty for women in gaining access to literacy and in developing an arena of public discourse. However, Sembene had similarly highlighted this difficulty in his story 'Letters from France' in *Tribal Scars*. Nafi's secret correspondence is a form of empowerment, allowing her to voice her concerns and to maintain a symbolic contact with her home country. Sembene is also well aware of the importance of female literacy in the modern world.

Another Senegalese woman novelist, Aminata Sow Fall, often appears to have little concern for the question of female emancipation. Essentially a traditionalist and a firm supporter of Islam, she is extremely suspicious of all that she perceives as Western influence. In her novel, *L'Appel des arènes*, she paints a satiric and somewhat cruel picture of the Westernised Diattou and her attempts to wear short skirts in an imitation of the female Western professional:

---

[33] Mohamadou Kane et al., 'Comme un aveugle qui retrouve la vue', *Le Soleil* [Dakar], 10 July 1981, p. 7.

[34] One critic has gone so far as to claim that Sembene's concern for his female characters is only skin deep: '*Avec Sembène, la révolte des femmes est vue avec les yeux qui maintiennent le statu quo, voilés qu'ils sont par les larmes de la compassion phallocratique.*' ['Sembene views women's rebellion through eyes that maintain the status quo, even though they are veiled with the tears of phallocratic compassion.'] See Vieux Savané, 'La Femme dans l'univers romanesque de Sembène Ousmane', *Tribune africaine: revue trimestrielle d'analyse et d'opinion*, 1 (1983), p. 49.

[35] Mariama Bâ, *So Long a Letter*, trans. by Modupe Bode-Thomas (London: Heinemann, 1981).

[36] For Miller's discussion of Mariama Bâ's work as well as that of other Senegalese women writers, see his *Theories of Africans: Francophone Literature and Anthropology in Africa* (Chicago and London: University of Chicago Press, 1990), chapter 6, 'Senegalese Women Writers, Silence and Letters: Before the Canon's Roar', pp. 246–93. See also Susan Stringer's recent study, *The Senegalese Novel by Women: through their own eyes* (Frankfurt: Peter Lang, 1996).

[...] elle provoquait des sourires éloquents lorsqu'elle ôtait sa blouse et que se ballotaient ses grosses fesses rebelles à toutes les crèmes amincissantes, sous une jupe très courte qui mettait à nu ses mollets bourrés de cellulite. Sa petite taille n'était pas pour arranger les choses.[37]

[...] she used to bring a knowing smile to everyone's lips when she took off her coat, revealing her fat bottom, which was resistant to all slimming creams. Her bottom would roll around in a tight mini skirt that exposed her cellulite-laden calves. Her thin waist didn't help matters.

Although Sembene often has harsh words to say about women who blindly imitate Western fashions (witness his descriptions of Oumi N'Doye in *Xala*), nothing in his work approaches such a vitriolic portrait which, if it were written by a man, would understandably be considered by many people to be misogynistic. Despite the fact that he works on somewhat essentialist notions of femininity, Sembene's representation of African women manages at least to open up the terrain and to give voice to a wider range of concerns than was touched on by the preceding generation of African writers.

The main prism through which Sembene looks at the status of women within African society is that of the institution of polygamy. As was argued in the previous chapter, Sembene uses the family as a site for the playing out of the social turmoil affecting contemporary Africa. In many of his films and novels, we are confronted with conflicts between husband and wife/wives. This picture of marital strife stands in stark contrast to the vision of perfect male and female complementarity imagined by Camara Laye in *The African Child*. Many critics have written of Sembene's willingness to reveal the problems faced by women within Senegalese society,[38] but none of them makes the very basic point that Sembene is recording a startling social reality in his tales of marital breakdown. Far from being an exaggeration on Sembene's part in order to push home his feminist viewpoints, the fact is that, for many years now, Senegal has experienced a remarkably high divorce rate. In a 1960/61 study carried out in Pikine, a satellite town of Dakar, Luc Thoré discovered that 44.5 per cent of all marriages ended in divorce.[39] This elevated figure was not a result of Thoré choosing a location where there was a well-educated, Westernised elite. Indeed Thoré specifically chose Pikine as a location because peasants leaving the countryside often chose to settle there on moving to Dakar. This allowed him to examine how people who had recently left the traditional, rural milieu were adapting to modern, urban life. Part of the reason behind such a high rate of divorce was the ease with which a divorce could be obtained. Marriage was purely a religious affair, requiring no simultaneous civil marriage, nor did the state even keep a register of marriages. Under Islamic law, divorce takes the form of a repudiation (the Arabic term

[37] Aminata Sow Fall, *L'Appel des arènes* (Dakar: Nouvelles Editions Africaines, 1993), p. 96.

[38] Edris Makward, 'Women, Tradition and Religion in Sembene Ousmane's Work', in *Faces of Islam in African Literature*, ed. by Kenneth W. Harrow (London: James Currey, 1991), pp. 187–99. Jarmila Ortova, 'Les Femmes dans l'œuvre d'Ousmane Sembène', *Présence Africaine*, 91 (3rd quarter 1969), pp. 69–77; and Chemain-Degrange, *Emancipation féminine*, pp. 287–310.

[39] Luc Thoré, 'Mariage et divorce dans la banlieue de Dakar', *Cahier d'études africaines*, 4, 16 (1964), pp. 530–2.

for divorce is *talak*, meaning 'repudiation'), which can take several forms. Thoré argues that people in the Senegalese urban centres were simply growing more independent, often rejecting family-imposed marriages by divorcing the family's chosen partner after a number of years and subsequently marrying a partner of their own choice.

Such was the extent of this divorce culture that the government introduced a *Code de la famille* in 1972.[40] This new family code, which finally came into force in 1974, did away with simple repudiation, deciding that a divorce could only be granted by the courts. However, under the new legislation, the judge is obliged to grant a divorce if repudiation (and hence a breakdown in the marriage partnership) has occurred. This legislation has failed to halt the rate of divorce. In a survey carried out by Abdoulaye-Bara Diop, he found that 36 per cent of the men questioned had been divorced at least once. Therefore, one can readily discern the obvious pressures which a modern capitalist society is placing upon the traditional Senegalese marital structure. Far from the representation of a traditional African family structure, the polygamous marriage is being increasingly disrupted by radical changes within African society, and this is the situation that Sembene attempts to capture in his work.

Despite the prevalence of these marital and social problems, polygamy remains commonplace in Senegal, especially amongst the Wolof. In the same survey by Abdoulaye-Bara Diop mentioned above, it was found that 45.4 per cent of the heads of family in Wolof areas were polygamous (28.6 per cent is his figure for Senegal as a whole).[41] Diop found that men were generally in favour of polygamy, viewing it as something of a status symbol to have more than one wife (a phenomenon recorded by Sembene in both *Xala* and the short story, 'The *Bilal*'s Fourth Wife'). Women are generally against polygamy, seeing the only benefit for themselves as that of having another woman to help them with the heavy household tasks. For Sembene, polygamy is basically the means by which men institutionalise their superiority over women.[42]

One of the claims most often made about Sembene's treatment of women in polygamous marriages is that they are portrayed as victims. Arlette Chemain-Degrange argues that, after *God's Bits of Wood* with its vision of a radical, emancipated African woman, Sembene shied away from such an optimistic view of the female condition within Africa, deciding instead to focus on the

[40] For an analysis of the situation concerning divorce in contemporary Senegal, see Abdoulaye-Bara Diop's *La Famille wolof: tradition et changement* (Paris: Karthala, 1985), pp. 201–42. Diop also analyses the changing attitudes towards marriage and polygamy (see pp. 81–199). Kenneth Little examines the status of African women in the new urban centres in his two works, *African Women in Towns* (Cambridge: Cambridge University Press, 1973), and *The Sociology of Urban Women's Image in African Literature* (London: Macmillan, 1980).

[41] Diop, *La Famille wolof*, pp. 183–99.

[42] Fatima Mernissi argues that the polygamous marriage is an attempt by Islam to control active female sexuality, which is considered as a potentially destructive force. The heterosexual unit is feared as a threat to the man's devotion to Allah, and hence to Islam itself. See Mernissi, *Beyond the Veil*, p. 8. While Mernissi's ideas may hold some validity as a theoretical understanding of the original basis for polygamy under Mohammed, it certainly denies the modern-day reality in both North and sub-Saharan Africa, whereby polygamy institutionalises male hegemony.

harsh day-to-day realities faced by women.[43] Although I would agree with Chemain-Degrange that there is a move away from the epic, emancipatory narrative in Sembene's work following *God's Bits of Wood*, her argument ignores the resistant role played by many of Sembene's female characters from later works (Tioumbé, in *L'Harmattan*, and Rama, in *Xala*, stand out as two of the most obvious examples). However, Chemain-Degrange is correct in claiming that many of the female characters in Sembene's later work find themselves unable to rebel against tyrannical husbands. As was argued above, such is the hegemonic status of the social discourse concerning women that many women are not simply dominated *by* men but actually feel themselves to be inferior *to* men. Even in *God's Bits of Wood*, Sembene's most radical expression of female emancipation, we find that Assitan, the wife of the strike leader, Bakayoko, is a submissive, repressed figure. In portraying such characters, Sembene is once more dealing with the notions of language and silence. The very fact that these women either do not see any alternative to their own inferior position, or are unable to express their true feelings of anger and revolt, makes it all the more important that their stories be told.

Two of Sembene's most interesting female characters are also two of the most resigned. Ngone War Thiandum in *White Genesis* is a proud noblewoman but she is also a devout Muslim who has always obeyed her husband. However, after her discovery of the terrible act committed by Guibril Guedj Diob, she is shaken out of her certainties. Crying out to Allah, she cannot understand how this fate has befallen her as she has always been a loyal, obedient wife:

> I remained a wife and a mother without complaining, without blaming the infidelities of my husband. I was submissive to my lord, my master after you, Yallah, my guide in this world, my advocate in the next, according to your teaching. I only rested when my lord rested. My voice never rose above his. In his presence, I always kept my eyes on the ground. Astafourlah! Perhaps not every day, Yallah. I have always obeyed him, knowing that I was obeying your will. Yallah! Forgive me! But why this act? Why? (*WG*, p.14)

Unfortunately, her *prise de conscience* overwhelms her rather than liberating her and she takes her own life (at least showing more respect for her noble upbringing than her disgraced husband).

The second character is Adja Awa Astou in *Xala*, who is presented to us as the model of the good Muslim wife. Her life is governed by the dictates of Islam and she silences any dissent she feels internally, silently and resignedly overcoming her jealousy at her husband taking a second wife: 'By an act of will, she had overcome all her feelings of resentment towards the second wife. Her ambition was to be a wife according to the teachings of Islam by observing the five daily prayers and showing her husband complete obedience' (*Xala*, p. 23). Both Awa and Ngone War Thiandum are traditional Muslim wives who do not challenge their position in society. Rather than glorifying this fact, Sembene displays his admiration for such women, while attempting to voice the concerns that they keep silent.

---

[43] Chemain-Degrange, *Emancipation féminine*, p. 298.

One of Sembene's clearest examinations of the constraints that polygamy places upon women is to be found in the story 'Her Three Days' which tells the tale of Noumbe, wife of Mustapha. When the story begins, Noumbe is excitedly preparing for *her three days* (or *ayé*), meaning the three days when her husband is due to stay with her as part of the constant rotation between wives within polygamy. Noumbe is the third wife, but now she has been superseded by a younger, fourth wife, and is no longer the main object of her husband's attentions. Sembene describes her lavish preparations for her husband's arrival as she desperately seeks to regain his former attentions. She bathes in henna and dresses herself in her finest clothes to try and arouse the passion which he once had for her, but Mustapha fails to appear.

This is one of the main points in Sembene's critique of polygamy. A wife is obliged to cater for her husband's every need but when a husband grows tired of his wife, he simply finds himself a younger woman. He is obliged to take care of her financially but her emotional needs are never addressed. When Mustapha finally arrives, Noumbe flies into a rage that her husband finds completely irrational and unjustified. He and his friends pour scorn on women's attempts to organise themselves, with Mustapha sarcastically declaring that if women want independence 'they can go out to work then' (*TS*, p. 53). However, the patriarchal social structure that supports polygamy dictates that women remain in the home, so financial independence is obviously the main problem facing those women who wish to break free from the hold of men.[44] In the face of the overwhelming domination of her husband, Noumbe's revolt is limited to a temper tantrum during which she breaks a few plates but, more importantly, the story records her *prise de conscience*. Her revolt may lead to nothing more than a few broken plates but, in telling the story, Sembene voices a form of resistance that could not find expression in her own words.

One of the most interesting aspects of the story is the visit of the second wife who comes to gloat over the fall of her former rival. This visit highlights one of the main obstacles to female solidarity. Dependent on their husbands for their economic well-being, wives of the same husband often engage in a battle to become his *favourite*, with all the benefits which that entails. In this situation, women become rivals rather than allies. Noumbe comes to realise that what is happening to her now is the same as what she had done to the second wife:

> The visit [of the co-wife] meant in fact: 'You stole those days from me because I am older than you. Now a younger woman than you is avenging me. Try as you might to make everything nice and pleasant for him, you have to toe the line with the rest of us now, you old carcass. He's slept with someone else [i.e. the new wife] – and he will again. (*TS*, p. 48).

[44] In *Taaw*, Yaye Dabo is obliged to set up a stall in the market in order to make ends meet. This gives her an element of financial independence from her tyrannical husband (Salimata, in Kourouma's *The Suns of Independence* also runs her own stall). The growth in women's participation in the commercial sector is noted by one of the contributors to *Dakar en devenir*. See Mme. D. Aguessy, 'La Femme dakaroise commerçante au détail sur le marché', in *Dakar en devenir*, ed. by M. Sankalé et al. (Paris: Présence Africaine, 1968), pp. 395–421.

Rather than creating a dialogue between women living under the same conditions, polygamy often creates a situation whereby women use lies and deceit to gain an advantage over their rivals.

We see the same process at work in *Xala*. As El Hadji's first two wives, Awa and Oumi N'Doye, discuss their husband's third marriage, Oumi N'Doye's jealousy is plain to see. However, Awa is quick to remind her that what is happening to Oumi now is what had happened to Awa herself upon El Hadji's marriage to Oumi N'Doye:

> 'It is Yay Bineta who is your rival. I have never entered the fray. I am incapable of fighting or rivalry. You know that yourself. When you were a young bride you never knew I existed. I have been the awa [i.e. the first wife] for nearly twenty years now, and how many years have you been his wife, my second?'
>
> 'Seventeen years, I think.'
>
> 'Do you know how many times we have met?'
>
> 'To tell the truth I don't,' admitted Oumi N'Doye.
>
> 'Seven times! During the fifteen or so years you have been the second wife that man, the same man, has left me every three days to spend three nights with you, going from your bedroom to mine. Have you ever thought about it?' (*Xala*, p. 21)

Awa's final remark brings home the distance that separates her from Oumi. They share the same husband but they know nothing of each other. They never meet again in the story, not even when El Hadji goes bankrupt. They literally have nothing to say to one another.

In addressing the issue of conflict between women themselves, Sembene reveals one of the main obstacles to their emancipation. Imbued with a sense of their own inferiority, women often become paralysed before male domination. When Ouhigoué attempts to stand up to the tyrannical Joseph Koéboghi in *L'Harmattan*, she awakens bitterness in her co-wives who fear that their husband will take out his anger on them. A similar reproach is made to Yaye Dabo in *Taaw* when she repudiates her husband, Baye Tine. Sembene here faces up to the reality that as much support for polygamy and male domination comes from women as from men. It is this internal resistance that he is expressing in such incidents.

However, polygamy is not portrayed as a uniquely divisive institution for women. Aram and Méty, the co-wives of the hapless Ibrahima Dieng in *The Money Order*, stand by each other and hold the family together during their husband's fruitless quest to cash his money order. Equally in *Taaw*, there is shown to be a strong bond between the wives of Baye Tine, as well as the other women of the compound. On several occasions in the story, we see the women laughing and joking with each other, mainly about the shortcomings of their husbands. In a comic illustration of the *regard critique* on men that Sembene wishes to express, the bawdy and boisterous Aminata describes how she deals with her husband during her *ayé*. One of four wives, she receives her husband only every nine days, and, despite his desire to use his time with her to convalesce, Aminata will have none of it:

> When the poor wretch gets to me, he's in a bad way. I fix him up well the first night. But the other nights, I make him pay for my troubles. I milk him dry. And

even when it's siesta time, he does it. Nobody eats my rice just to go to sleep. (*Taaw*, p. 97)

However, Aminata is not merely a comic character. She is also imbued with a keen political sense. In response to Yaye Dabo's pessimistic remarks about the future, she replies that she sees a cause for hope in the turmoil created by the ever-growing urban sprawl around Dakar:

> Yaye Dabo, you are saying things that we, as women, do not like to hear. The tomorrow of our children, you must ask the men about that. Look at the suburbs! Who knows where it starts? Or where it will end? All the ethnic groups in the country can be found here mixed up together. Famine and drought do not only drive whole families from the villages, they also destroy and dislocate the community, and break up family unity. Urbanisation and the development of commercial centres push the have-nots out into the suburbs. And here, amongst us, we have some of the better-off poor, as well as the most destitute poor. Tomorrow, it is from these neighbourhoods that the leader, or the leaders, the real ones, will come. (*Taaw*, p. 99; I have used the word 'neighbourhoods' instead of the translator's 'townships', which gives a false impression of the area in which the women live)

Aminata's declaration that questions about the future should be put to the men betrays an acceptance of patriarchal values, but the climax of the story where Yaye Dabo repudiates her husband suggests a questioning of this position. As she wakes up on the first morning after her 'revolutionary' action, Yaye Dabo reflects on the change that has taken place in her life: 'The warm dawn brings her the conviction that never again will she be a woman of the past. Strangely, she feels that she is putting into motion a whole new world' (*Taaw*, p. 110). Is she the leader who Aminata predicts will emerge from the suburbs? Will the women who had previously been supportive of each other stand by Yaye Dabo who has broken such a strong social taboo by humiliating her husband in public? Will Yaye Dabo's actions provide an example for her fellow women? The story simply leaves us to ponder on these questions.

The most startling example of female solidarity is to be found in *God's Bits of Wood*. All tensions between co-wives are progressively forgotten as the women take on an increasingly dynamic role. Their first run-in is with the water-seller whose water they steal out of pure necessity, as they have no money and the colonial authorities have switched off the supply to the local water pumps. Born of necessity, this solidarity between women eventually results in the political consciousness that leads to their march from Thiès to Dakar in support of their striking menfolk. They even create the song that becomes the strike's anthem.

However, as was argued above, in most cases, Sembene portrays individual acts of female rebellion against polygamy in his work. Yaye Dabo's revolt in *Taaw* has already been discussed above, but an equally interesting example is to be found in the short story, 'The *Bilal*'s Fourth Wife'. The eponymous central character of the story is a highly respected elder of the community and *bilal* (i.e. the caretaker) of the local mosque. Despite his advanced age, Suliman decides that he would like a fourth wife, a young girl, in order to end on a high note, so to speak. This is the same motivation that guided El Hadji Abdou Kader Bèye, in *Xala*, to marry the youthful Ngoné. However, unlike El Hadji, Suliman is not marrying a passive girl with nothing to say for herself. Indeed, Yacine, the girl he marries, is described by the narrator of the story as 'a tomboy, a hard worker' (*TS*, p. 11).

There is one other similarity with the story of *Xala*. As one could reasonably expect in a marriage between a man who is 'past middle-age' (*TS*, p. 8) and a girl of twenty, there exists a chasm between the sexual appetites and capabilities of both parties. Effectively, after fathering one child by her, Suliman becomes impotent, which causes Yacine to take a lover by whom she has a child. Inevitably, this leads to a breakdown in the marriage, with Yacine returning to her parents' home. As Yacine has left the conjugal home (and committed adultery) she would normally be considered the guilty party in the divorce, which means that her family would have to repay the huge dowry they had received from Suliman (something which her family simply cannot afford to do).

During the divorce case, Yacine challenges the discourse of male hegemony within Islam by contesting some of the chief tenets of Islamic family law. Before a massed crowd of the curious and the learned, Yacine refuses to repay the dowry. If Suliman was willing to pay out such a large sum in order to obtain a pristine virgin, she argues that repayment of the dowry should be accompanied by *repayment* of her virginity: 'I will only agree on condition that Suliman gives me back my virginity' (*TS*, p. 16). This response throws the Islamic experts into turmoil with some arguing in Yacine's favour and others against. However, this is just a prelude to the coup de grâce that comes when Yacine refuses to hand over her first child to Suliman. All the Islamic scholars stand against her, except for the independent-minded Froh-toll who questions the absolute right of the father to gain custody of the children. His basic point is resumed in the final lines of the story: 'There can always be doubt as to who is the father of a child. But never as to who is the mother' (*TS*, p. 17). In a fashion similar to that of 'The Mother', Sembene sings the praises of motherhood against the rights of the domineering male. Yacine's questioning of the Islamic laws concerning marriage disputes Islam's claims to absolute truth and argues a female case against a male-dominated institution.[45]

Yacine is simply one of a number of Sembene's younger female characters who are unafraid to break with their traditional roles. Through these characters, the polygamous marriage loses its status as the social norm and alternative lifestyles, including a life outside of marriage altogether, become viable options. Tioumbé, in *L'Harmattan*, has a profession (she is a teacher) as

---

[45] Birago Diop's story, 'A Judgment', tells a similar tale, in which a husband is tricked by the imam of the holy village of Maka-Kouli into admitting, after much denial, that he has, in fact, repudiated his wife. It is interesting that such a challenge to male authority is to be found in a 'traditional' tale. It shows that Sembene is tapping into a tradition of dissent within his society, not simply acting as the mouthpiece for a 'Western' ideology as some critics would argue. See Birago Diop, *Tales of Amadou Koumba*, trans. by Dorothy S. Blair (London: Longman, 1985), pp. 8–14.

well as carrying out various tasks on behalf of the *Parti*. This does not preclude her from emotional attachments (although, in keeping with the tone of Sembene's first two novels, the domestic and the political are cast as entirely separate spheres). She is in love with another militant of the party, Sori, with whom she leads the life of a couple, outside of marriage. Her mother Ouhigoué, a passive and obedient woman, cannot understand her daughter and is scandalised when she finds her in bed with Sori: '*Tu te prostitues. C'est tout. Ton père a raison de dire que tu es perdue comme l'eau du fleuve. Et si tu étais une chèvre, j'aurais déjà eu un troupeau de chèvres?* ['You are prostituting yourself. It's as simple as that. Your father is right to say that you are as lost as the water in the river. If you were a goat, I'd already have a herd of goats on my hands by now.'] (*Harmattan*, p. 308). An older generation of women simply cannot come to terms with the way their daughters are choosing to lead their lives.

A similar example of the radical young woman is to be found in the character of Rama in *Xala*. A student radical, she too is seen to have lost none of her femininity. Indeed, the scenes in the novel where we see her playfully talking with her boyfriend Pathé are some of the very few 'love' scenes in all of Sembene's work. They intend to get married but they envisage their relationship as that of equals, and they exclude the possibility of Pathé taking any further wives. Rama, although close to her mother, is still seen by Awa to be shameless and impudent. She categorically refuses Rama's offer to speak to El Hadji about his impotence as she believes that no woman, especially not a daughter, has the right to talk about such issues with a man.

Perhaps the most scandalous of Sembene's liberated women by traditional standards is Penda, in *God's Bits of Wood*. She is referred to as a 'whore' by the haughty Awa, and simply described in the *dramatis personae* at the beginning of the original French version of the novel as a *femme de mauvaise vie*. Whether she is a prostitute or not, Penda is a woman who definitely leads an active sexual life outside the institution of marriage, which casts her as an immoral and degenerate person in the eyes of the local community (in Sembene's film and novel, *Guelwaar*, the eponymous hero's daughter Sophie is a prostitute who provides for her family from her earnings).[46] However, she comes to play a vital role in the strike. The union leaders ask her to distribute the food because the men could find themselves accused of favouritism towards their own spouses if they were in charge of the distribution. As a fiercely independent woman, Penda is well able to deal with any disputes that arise. She emerges as one of the key figures in the strike and it is she who announces the women's decision to march from Thiès to Dakar:

> I speak in the name of all of the women, but I am just the voice they have chosen to tell you what they have decided to do. Yesterday we all laughed together, men and women, and today we weep together, but for us women this strike still means the possibility of a better life tomorrow. We owe it to ourselves to hold up our

[46] The Senegalese woman writer, Ken Bugul, describes her descent into the world of prostitution in Belgium in her autobiographical novel *Le Baobab fou* (Dakar: Nouvelles Editions Africaines, 1982). Jean-François Werner examines sexual behaviour and attitudes in the suburbs of Dakar in his *Marges, sexe et drogues à Dakar: enquête ethnographique* (Paris: Karthala/ORSTOM, 1994).

heads and not to give in now. So we have decided that tomorrow we will march together to Dakar. (*GBW*, p. 187)

Throughout the strike, Penda displays her worth to the community and gains the respect of those who had previously been hostile to her. However, her social rehabilitation remains incomplete as she is shot by soldiers upon the women's arrival in Dakar. Interpreting her death is quite problematic. Until that moment, the story seemed to be saying that her choice of sexuality did not preclude her from an active participation in her society. However, she is murdered along with Samba N'Doulougou, father of Maïmouna's twins. In this context, their deaths can be read as the sacrifice of two sexual sinners, atoning for their sins in death. Perhaps, more than all else, these two deaths are symptomatic of Sembene's taste for having a tragic fate befall his heroes in his early novels: Diaw Falla is sentenced to life imprisonment; Oumar Faye is murdered by unnamed assailants (suspected to be representatives of the colonial authorities); and *God's Bits of Wood* has its *dramatis personae* dramatically reduced in numbers by the end of the novel.[47]

It was argued in Chapter One that the power of *God's Bits of Wood* lies in its attempt to rethink the social relations of an entire community, and the participation of women in the construction of the new Africa is stressed throughout the novel. The strike sees the birth of a new African woman, alongside the new African man: 'And the men began to understand that if the times were bringing forth a new breed of men, they were also bringing forth a new breed of women' (*GBW*, p. 34). The little girl Ad'jibid'ji, who is virtually the mascot of the strike, plays a vital role in the structure of the novel, which opens and closes with scenes featuring her (although there is a short epilogue after her final scene). Defending her ambition to follow in her father's footsteps and become a train driver, she quotes Bakayoko to Fa Keïta: '*Petit père* says that men and women will be equal some day' (*GBW*, p. 97). Ad'jibid'ji thus acts as a symbol of a future egalitarian Africa that has overcome all social and sexual oppression. The women's participation in the strike gives them access to areas previously denied to them. Women speak at the trial of Diara, and Penda addresses a meeting to announce the women's decision to march to Dakar. The strike places women firmly in the social and political sphere (even the *évoluée*, N'Dèye Touti, casts off her romantic, Western-inspired dreams of bourgeois domestic bliss to help her fellow Africans).[48]

Throughout his work, Sembene has attempted to open up the representation of African women to include more dynamic and aggressive female characters. Delving back into history, he produces a record of female resistance in stories such as 'The Mother' and in films such as *Ceddo* and *Emitai* (both of which will be discussed in the next chapter). Even *God's Bits of Wood* is linked to female heroism in the African past by Maïmouna's singing of the *Legend of Goumba* (a legendary warrior woman). Sembene has also tried to suggest possible future avenues for the development of male-female

---

[47] Alice Walker satirises the literary genre in which the hero/heroine is sacrificed in her novel, *Meridian* (1976; London: Women's Press, 1982).

[48] World Wars One and Two had a similar liberating role for European women.

relationships within Africa. In the stories *Taaw*, 'The *Bilal*'s Fourth Wife' and 'Her Three Days', we are presented with a complete breakdown of the traditional polygamous marriage. Despite the fact that many women find themselves unable to establish an equal footing with their husbands, Sembene provides us with many examples of those who do. In fact, in the cases of Yaye Dabo (*Taaw*), Yacine ('The *Bilal*'s Fourth Wife') and Penda (*God's Bits of Wood*), we are presented with characters who choose to lead a life outside the institution of marriage. When one also considers the dynamic role of young women such as Tioumbé (*L'Harmattan*), Rama (*Xala*) and Ad'jibid'ji (*God's Bits of Wood*), it becomes clear that Sembene sees the increased participation of women in the decision-making within African society as one of the keys to change. The impotent, male-dominated society must give way to a more egalitarian society produced by the overthrow of all sexual and social repression.

To attempt a response to the question which I posed at the beginning of this chapter, Sembene's conception of women's role in his society does rest in part on his disappointment with the men of his generation, but this does not mean that Sembene does not believe that the emancipation of women is a necessary goal in itself. Ultimately, he adheres to the argument that men and women are complementary figures, and he believes that a monogamous system based on equality and respect is the way forward. His work thus acts as a means of giving voice to the concerns of women, and as an attempt to imagine a new set of male-female relationships. As he put it in a 1981 interview:

> *Le rôle de la femme va s'intensifier de plus en plus. Il s'agit maintenant de voir comment les femmes vont assumer ce rôle. Vont-elles imiter les femmes européennes pour dire qu'il faut coûte que coûte l'égalité, ou il faut coûte que coûte une compagne tout le long du chemin de l'existence? L'homme doit cesser de trop se vanter de son rôle de mâle. Même dans la civilisation chrétienne, la monogamie n'a rien résolu, et pourtant c'était l'idéal.*[49]

Women's role in society will grow more and more important. It's just a question of what women intend to achieve through this role. Are they going to imitate European women, claiming that they want equality no matter what the cost? Or are they going to decide that, no matter what the cost, they need a companion throughout their lives? And men must stop boasting about their masculine superiority. Even in Christian societies, the supposedly ideal solution of monogamy has not resolved these problems.

Such an attitude may provoke criticism from both traditionalists and feminists alike but the fact remains that, of all modern African writers, Sembene has been the most consistent in his questioning of the status of women and he has produced a range of female representations which take us far beyond the African women originally imagined by Negritude.

[49] Kane et al., 'Comme un aveugle qui retrouve la vue', p. 7.

6
Dis-membering Empire,
Re-membering Resistance

The Memory of Colonialism in
Emitaï, Ceddo & Camp de Thiaroye

Denouncing the crimes of colonialism has been one of the major themes of contemporary French African literature. From the rather timid protests against colonial abuses in René Maran's *Batouala* (1921) to the violent critiques of empire in the works of the Cameroonian novelists Mongo Béti, *Ville cruelle* (1954), written under the name of Eza Boto, and Ferdinand Oyono, *Houseboy* (1956), one can note a clear attempt to counter imperial accounts of the colonial enterprise.[1] African cinema has been no less concerned with this theme: Gillo Pontecorvo's remarkable account of the Algerian war of independence, *The Battle of Algiers* (1966), has become the classic of the genre. More recently, Med Hondo's *Sarraounia* (1986) and Flora Gomes's *Mortu Nega* (1987) have presented narratives of resistance to French and Portuguese imperialism respectively. This chapter will examine the three films by Sembene (*Emitaï, Ceddo, Camp de Thiaroye*) in which he focuses on the issue of West Africa's colonial past. I will argue that in these films Sembene challenges the claims of colonial discourse, proposing his own discourse of resistance in its place: effectively, Sembene 'dis-members' the discourse of empire, and 're-members' a discourse of resistance.

However, before turning to the films, it is necessary to examine the nature of the French imperial discourse against which Sembene is reacting (the nature of the Islamic discourse that he challenges in *Ceddo* will be examined below). As many commentators have pointed out, European colonisation in Africa (and in other parts of the globe) remained a relatively haphazard process, governed by political contingencies, until the 1880s.[2] Indeed, the French

---

[1] René Maran, *Batouala*, trans. by Barbara Beck and Alexandre Mboukou (London: Heinemann, 1972); Eza Boto, *Ville cruelle* (Paris: Présence Africaine, 1954); Ferdinand Oyono, *Houseboy*, trans. by John Reed (London: Heinemann, 1966).

[2] There exists a huge body of literature on European imperialism. Some of the most

151

showed themselves hostile to the process of colonisation when the French Prime Minister Jules Ferry began to co-ordinate a systematic programme of colonial expansion in the early 1880s, 'acquiring' Tunisia in 1881, and, during his second ministry later in the same decade, beginning the colonisation of Indo-China. Both of his governments were toppled by a broad coalition of anti-colonialist forces who opposed the government's policies for vastly different reasons: monarchists distrusted Republicanism, nationalists believed the country would be better served seeking to regain its territories of Alsace and Lorraine (lost to the Germans in the defeat of 1870), while liberals believed that foreign conquest was simply too expensive.[3]

However, by the 1890s, public opinion had rallied to the imperial cause. As the conquest of Africa became a military reality, colonialism simply became an accepted part of the political landscape. In her study of French colonial literature, Martine Astier Loutfi has argued that the French taste for the exotic, which had been growing throughout the nineteenth century, paved the way for an acceptance of the conquest of foreign cultures. She claims that the work of exoticist writers, such as Pierre Loti and Ernest Psichari, effectively conflated the notions of the 'colonial' and the 'exotic' in the public mind:

> *Dans tout ceci, ce qui frappe, c'est le contexte presque exclusivement évocateur de découvertes et de pittoresque, dans lequel sont placés les pays conquis. Les romanciers de l'exotisme ont puissamment contribué à ce mouvement, ils ont présenté au public des images de ces pays, sans admettre, ou même soupçonner, les déformations fondamentales que le système colonial faisait subir aux mondes qu'ils découvraient et à leur propre vision.*
>
> *L'équivoque s'observe d'ailleurs au niveau du mot, et même là, elle n'est pas sans conséquence. 'Colonial' est souvent employé comme un synonyme d''exotique' ou de 'tropical' [...].*
>
> *Le fait ne présente pas seulement un intérêt documentaire. L'interchangeabilité des notions 'exotique', 'tropicale', 'coloniale' étendait énormément les usages courants du mot et du système colonial. Lié à une référence géographique ou climatique, il appartient désormais à la nature même des régions évoquées: la colonisation est normalisée, intégrée.*[4]

The most striking aspect of these novels is that the conquered territory is always described in evocative, picturesque terms. These exoticist novelists played a vital role in this whole shift in thinking. They presented the public with such images without ever admitting, or perhaps even suspecting, the fundamental changes which were being imposed on these societies, and on their vision of them, by the colonial system.

This equivocal position can be seen in relation to the words these writers use: 'colonial' is often used as a synonym for 'exotic' or 'tropical' [...].

---

[2] (cont.) influential texts are V.G. Kiernan's *The Lords of Human Kind: Black Man, Yellow Man, and White Man in an Age of Empire* (1969; London: Hutchinson, 1988), Philip D. Curtin, ed., *Imperialism* (New York and London: Harper & Row, 1971), and D. K. Fieldhouse, *The Colonial Empires: A Comparative Study from the 18th Century* (1966; Houndmills: Macmillan, 1991).

[3] Raoul Girardet examines the evolution of ideas on colonialism in France in his monumental study *L'Idée coloniale en France, 1871–1962* (Paris: La Table Ronde, 1972). The history of French anti-colonialism in the run-up to the First World War is discussed by Charles Robert Ageron in *L'Anticolonialisme en France de 1871 à 1914* (Paris: Presses Universitaires Françaises, 1973).

[4] Martine Astier Loutfi, *Littérature et colonialisme: l'expansion coloniale vue dans la littérature romanesque française, 1871–1914* (Paris and The Hague: Mouton, 1971), p. 46. Alec G. Hargreaves provides an equally illuminating account of the French literary representation of colonialism in his *The Colonial Experience in French Fiction: A Study of Pierre Loti, Ernest Psichari and Pierre Mille* (London: Macmillan, 1981).

This fact is not merely an historical curiosity. As the terms 'exotic', 'tropical' and 'colonial' become interchangeable, the way in which colonialism is understood is also modified. Linked to geographical and climatic considerations, colonialism becomes a fundamental feature of the regions under discussion. In short, colonialism becomes normalised and integrated into the fabric of society.

To achieve the colonisation of approximately one quarter of Africa as the French were to do between the conquest of Algeria, begun in 1830, and that of Morocco in 1912, involved the destruction of African towns and villages, and the massacre of many thousands of Africans.[5] However, in the aftermath of the conquest, French rule in Africa simply became a fait accompli to be justified by any reasoning other than that of the rule of force, which was what had in fact prevailed in Africa in the late nineteenth century. Following the doctrine of 'what we have we hold', even the Radicals, who had been among the fiercest critics of Ferry's colonial policies while in opposition, maintained and defended France's growing empire when they themselves took office.

One of the main motivations of French imperialism had been the desire to emulate and to outdo the British who had a much more long-established empire. Towards this end, the French stressed the *mission civilisatrice* that they claimed was at the heart of their colonial conquests. The main aim of such arguments was to indicate the superiority of the French Empire over its English counterpart: the French were the native's friend whereas the English were mere profiteers. This attitude is captured by Victor Piquet in his *Histoire des colonies françaises*, which was published in 1931, no doubt to cash in on the excitement generated by the Exposition Coloniale held in Paris in that same year. According to Piquet, 'Le Français colonise avec son cœur; il aime les indigènes: *il est donc tout à fait désigné pour réussir auprès des populations autochtones.*' ['*The Frenchman colonises with his heart; he loves the indigenous people*: this explains his successful relationship with the local population in the colonies.']6 Instead of the violence of colonial conquest and the domination of one society by another, we are presented with the image of a paternalistic France taking care of the interests of its African children. This paternalistic love is what distinguishes the French from the cold and distant English (they are so despicable in Piquet's eyes that they are not even worthy of being named):

Notre attitude vis-à-vis de l'indigène est essentiellement différente de celle de tel peuple qui a pour les 'natives' un éloignement de principe. Quiconque a vu des troupes de différentes nations exercer des occupations simultanées ou successives, pendant et après la guerre n'en saurait douter. Le Français est familier et si confiant qu'il oublie de redevenir ferme quand il le faudrait.[7]

Our attitude towards the indigenous person is fundamentally different from that of a certain people who, out of principle, maintain a distance between themselves and the 'natives'. Anyone who has seen troops from different nations occupying conquered territories, during or after the war, would be left in little doubt in this

---

[5] For accounts of the arduous and bloody battles that accompanied European colonialism in West Africa, see B. Olatunji Oloruntimehin, 'Senegambia – Mahmadou Lamine', in Michael Crowder, ed., *West African Resistance* (London: Hutchinson, 1971), pp. 80–110.

[6] Victor Piquet, *Histoire des colonies françaises* (Paris: Payot, 1931), p. 327 (emphasis in original).

[7] Ibid., pp. 327–8.

regard. French troops are so familiar and easygoing that they fail to show the necessary firmness when it is called for.

The aim of such an argument is to occult the violent nature of the colonial project in the stages of both conquest and occupation. The forces of domination and resistance are not seen to be at work in the relationship between coloniser and colonised. Instead, we are presented with harmonious images of a unified, if paternalistic colonial world:

> *Il est parfaitement exact que, même en opérations militaires et même en pays jaune, on voit le jeune Français sympathiser avec les indigènes,* avec les habitants paisibles, s'entend. *Lors de l'expédition de Chine de 1900, des Européens très divers se sont plu à le constater: c'était toujours le soldat français que l'on voyait prendre sur ses genoux les bébés chinois et jouer avec eux, sous le regard confiant des parents.*[8]

> Even during military operations and even in Asian countries, it is noticeable that the young French soldier associates readily with the indigenous peoples (*with the peaceful inhabitants, let it be understood*). During the 1900 expedition to China, various European observers were happy to relate that it was invariably the young French soldier who was to be seen with a Chinese baby bouncing on his knee while the parents looked on contentedly.

That such idyllic scenes were probably to be found in the territories occupied by the French is not in question. However, as Piquet himself admits, sympathy with the 'native' is only possible when dealing with 'the peaceful inhabitants'. Piquet does not say what the French thought of those who were not so happy to see a foreign power invade their country. As Philip D. Curtin has argued, despite French rhetoric about assimilation (i.e. turning the colonised into Frenchmen), their actual policy of association was far closer to the British policy of indirect rule:

> Difference in emphasis [...] should not be allowed to obscure the basic similarity of Indirect Rule and Association. Both were variants of the idea of trusteeship in which conversionism was minimal. Both Indirect Rulers and Associationists were suspicious of religious missions, and both doubted that the values and standards of Western civilization were universally applicable. Both expected a period of imperial tutelage that would extend far into the future.[9]

There may have been those in Europe (especially within the Church) who believed passionately in Europe's mission to 'civilise' Africa, and particularly to convert Africans to Christianity, but no European government saw assimilation as a viable option, either politically or economically. Colonialism was about the domination of foreign cultures and the perpetuation of that rule.

During the conquest itself, the excesses of certain colonial commanders occasionally managed to awaken the metropolis from its largely indifferent attitude towards the process of empire-building that was allegedly being carried out in its name. One of the most infamous *bavures* of the colonial army (a *bavure* being the French Establishment's version of the British 'unfortunate error') took place towards the end of the era of conquest in 1899. The two French

[8] Ibid., p. 327 (my emphasis).
[9] Curtin, *Imperialism*, p. xxiii.

154

commanders Voulet and Chanoine led one of three military columns to take control of Northern Chad, which had been attributed to France in an Anglo-French agreement in 1898. In their search for plunder, Voulet and Chanoine not only ravaged the new territory but also areas already under so-called French 'protection'. When the army sent out another column to track them down, Voulet and Chanoine, who by now had completely lost their regard for military discipline and had a virtual mutiny on their hands among their own troops, ordered their artillery to fire on the pursuers. This episode created a tremendous scandal in France, which the French military was keen to play down as much as possible.[10]

The whole Voulet-Chanoine affair is highly instructive in our understanding of the manner in which colonialism is sanitised by the coloniser, most notably by the colonial army. For the French army, the actions of Voulet and Chanoine were exceptional, constituting a mere *bavure*. Those French people who did criticise such atrocities were protesting against actions that they saw as demeaning the conception they had fostered of France's position within the world. As Martine Astier Loutfi has argued, anti-colonialism *within* Europe was concerned primarily with European issues:

> *Le colonialisme avait transformé [l'univers de l'homme blanc] en un gigantesque domaine dont il était l'unique habitant, où il avait la satisfaction ou l'angoisse de ne plus entendre que l'écho de sa propre voix. Les critiques de l'impérialisme n'ouvraient pas un dialogue, elles continuaient un monologue, sur un ton moins triomphant.*[11]

> Colonialism had transformed [the white man's universe] into a vast domain of which he was the sole inhabitant. Within this domain, the white man could enjoy the satisfaction or suffer the anguish of hearing only his own voice. The critics of imperialism were not engaging in a dialogue. They were continuing a European monologue in a less triumphant tone.

What was missing from the anti-colonial debate within France were the voices of those who were enduring European oppression. For the colonised, the atrocities of a Voulet or a Chanoine were not mere *bavures*: they were perceived as symptomatic of the violent and oppressive nature of colonialism. In his *Discourse on Colonialism*, Aimé Césaire cites, amongst others, de Montagnac and Bugeaud, two of the conquerors of Algeria, who make no attempt to prettify the nature of colonial conquest.[12] For Césaire, colonialism is an inherently savage business. The coloniser treats the colonised as a beast but, in the process, he loses his own humanity. This is what he is attempting to demonstrate in his use of such graphic quotes on the nature of colonial conquest:

> For my part, if I have recalled a few details of these hideous butcheries, it is by no means because I take morbid delight in them, but because I think that these heads of men, these collections of ears, these burned houses, these Gothic invasions, this steaming blood, these cities that evaporate at the edge of the sword, are not to be

---

[10] For a contemporary account of the Voulet-Chanoine affair, see Paul Vigné d'Octon's *La Gloire du sabre* (1900; Paris: Quintette, 1984).

[11] Loutfi, *Littérature et colonialisme*, p. 137.

[12] Aimé Césaire, *Discourse on Colonialism*, trans. by Joan Pinkham (1955; New York: Monthly Review Press, 1972), pp. 18–19.

so easily disposed of. They prove that colonization, I repeat, dehumanizes even the most civilized man; that colonial activity, colonial enterprise, colonial conquest, which is based on contempt for the native and justified by that contempt, inevitably tends to change him who undertakes it; that the colonizer, who in order to ease his conscience gets into the habit of seeing the other man as an animal, accustoms himself to treating him like an animal, and tends objectively to transform himself into an animal. It is this result, this boomerang effect of colonization, that I wanted to point out.[13]

Effectively, Césaire's argument in *Discourse on Colonialism* amounts to a challenge to the coloniser's version of the imperial project. He is engaged in a fight for the 'memory' of colonisation.[14]

Two of the films that will be discussed in this chapter, *Emitaï* (1971) and *Camp de Thiaroye* (1988), are centred around so-called *bavures*, committed by the colonial army in Senegal. *Emitaï* is based on a number of massacres that took place in Casamance in southern Senegal in 1942. The army had been sent in to requisition rice and, in a number of incidents, opened fire on the villagers when they refused to reveal where they had hidden their foodstuff. *Camp de Thiaroye* is based on an incident that took place at the Thiaroye demobilisation camp, just outside Dakar on 1 December 1944.[15] Over 1,000 *tirailleurs sénégalais* (African infantrymen), including many ex-POWs, the first to be sent home from Europe, were housed in the Thiaroye camp while awaiting repatriation to their countries of origin (despite their name, the *tirailleurs sénégalais* were, in fact, drawn from all over the French Empire in Africa). However, a dispute arose with the French military authorities over the full payment of demobilisation premiums and the soldiers refused to obey their commanders, temporarily taking hostage the head of the French West African army. In an act of brutal retribution, the camp was attacked by the French army, who killed thirty-five *tirailleurs* and wounded hundreds of others. Neither the events in Casamance nor the appalling repression at Thiaroye have ever been officially recognised by the French state or military authorities. It is this denial of the violence within colonialism that Sembene reacts against in both of these films. They act as counter-narratives to the dominant narratives of imperialism that exclude

---

[13] Ibid., pp. 19–20.

[14] I borrow this expression from Mehdi Lallaoui. During a talk on his film *Les Massacres de Sétif: le 8 mai 1945* at the ASCALF conference in London, in November 1996, he described the film as part of a '*combat pour la mémoire de la colonisation*' ['a struggle for the memory of colonisation']. The official French files concerning the massacres that followed the nationalist demonstrations in Sétif and other parts of Algeria in May 1945 were kept from Lallaoui as the French, more than 50 years after the event, still attempt to control how this period should be remembered. In a very real act of postcolonial defiance, Lallaoui broke into the relevant government office in order to consult the documents in question. An account of Lallaoui's talk is to be found in the *ASCALF Bulletin*, 14, (Spring/Summer 1997), p. 48.

[15] For the best accounts of the incidents at Thiaroye, see Myron J. Echenberg's 'Tragedy at Thiaroye: The Senegalese Soldiers' Uprising of 1944', in Peter C. W. Gutkind et al., *African Labor History* (Beverly Hills and London: Sage, 1978), pp. 109–28. See also his *Colonial Conscripts: The 'Tirailleurs sénégalais' in French West Africa, 1857–1960* (Portsmouth, NH; London: James Currey, 1991), pp. 101–4. An interesting account of the various artistic responses to the events at Thiaroye is to be found in Roger Little and Nicola Macdonald, 'The Thiaroye Massacre in Word and Image', *ASCALF Bulletin*, 8 (Spring/Summer 1994), pp. 18–37.

6.1 The *tirailleurs sénégalais* bury their dead after the massacre at Thiaroye
Camp de Thiaroye, Filmi Doomireew – Dakar, Senegal (all rights reserved)

the suffering and resistance of the colonised. Sembene sees this process as a fundamental element in forging truly independent nations in Africa. It has nothing to do with making the West feel guilty about its actions but everything to do with Africa writing itself into a history from which the West had previously attempted to exclude it:

> *Pour l'Afrique, c'est la première fois que nous présentons notre histoire. Et quand je présentais ce film [Camp de Thiaroye] pour la première fois à Dakar, l'Ambassadeur de France a quitté la salle. Cependant, nous ne le faisions ni par haine ni par esprit de vengeance. Mais c'est pour l'histoire de tous les peuples du monde. C'est un témoignage de notre passé dans l'histoire [...].*
>
> *On ne fait pas une histoire pour se venger, mais pour s'enraciner. Voilà pourquoi nous avons fait ce film pour le monde entier et non pour une race; c'est pour que vous sachiez que les noirs ont participé à la guerre, et que nous n'avons pas fini avec notre histoire qui est aussi la vôtre.*[16]

For us Africans this is the first time that we have been able to present our own history. When I showed this film [*Camp de Thiaroye*] for the first time, in Dakar, the French Ambassador walked out of the cinema. But we didn't make this film out of a spirit of hatred or vengeance. We made it for the sake of the history of mankind. It bears witness to our past in the history of mankind [...].

You don't tell a story for revenge but rather to understand your place in the world. That is why we made this film for the whole world and not just for our own race. We made it so that would know that blacks took part in the war, and that we have not yet finished with our history, which is also your history.

For Sembene, recording the African experience of empire is essential to the better understanding of the relationship between the coloniser and the colonised. *Emitaï* and *Camp de Thiaroye* are therefore as much about informing the West of the violent nature of colonialism as they are about promoting an African sense of history and identity. Both films also form something of a personal form of recollection as Sembene himself served as a *tirailleur* during the World War Two, and he spent many of his formative years in Casamance.

In keeping with the processes at work in Sembene's other films, both *Camp de Thiaroye* and *Emitaï* are visually structured around a number of rituals, concerning those of the military and, in the case of *Emitaï*, the fetishist practices of the Diola. This process is continued in the film, *Ceddo* (1976) (which will be examined later in this chapter), where Sembene opposes the rituals of the *ceddo* with those of the Muslims. It was argued in Chapter Three that Sembene's films of the 1970s rank as his most experimental and symbolic but, as we shall see below, the realism of his later work, including *Camp de Thiaroye*, is nonetheless punctuated by scenes that work in an explicitly non-realistic register. The examination of rituals and cultural signs has remained at the heart of Sembene's cinematic work.

In dealing with incidents from World War Two, Sembene engages with the enduring French myth that any excesses committed in the period between the fall of France in June 1940 and the rallying of French West Africa to the cause of the Allied forces late in 1942 were the result of the actions of a few rightwing fanatics who had been handed power by the Vichy regime. Increasing

---

[16] Samba Gadjigo et al., eds, *Ousmane Sembène: Dialogues with Critics and Writers* (Amherst: University of Massachusetts Press, 1993), pp. 82–3.

research into this troubled period in French history has cast serious doubts on this clear-cut distinction between those who were pro-Vichy and those who resisted the fascist regime. No less a figure than François Mitterrand, who appeared to have impeccable wartime credentials in the French resistance, has recently been shown to have been very close to the Vichy regime until mid-1943. In French Africa, the situation was equally ambiguous. French Equatorial Africa, under the leadership of Félix Eboué, rallied to the Allied cause, while the Governor-General of French West Africa, Boisson, remained loyal to Vichy, only to endorse de Gaulle's leadership upon the Allied landing in North Africa in November, 1942.[17] For Africans, very little changed during the Vichy period. Inhabitants of the *quatre communes* in Senegal lost their citizenship and voting rights, and the relatively liberal union laws, introduced by the Popular Front government of the mid-1930s, were repealed, but that was the major extent of the changes. In fact, Vichy could almost be seen in a more favourable light as, at least, conscripts were no longer being sent to Europe to die in a foreign war. On the outbreak of World War Two, the French had brought over 80,000 African troops to Europe and had mobilised another 90,000. Under de Gaulle's regime, over 100,000 African soldiers left for the various Allied fronts between 1943 and 1945.[18] Would young African conscripts have seen the right to fight for the freedom of France as an improvement in their way of life?

By blurring the distinction between Free France and the Vichy regime, Sembene deliberately seeks to show the continuity in colonial practice. He argues that, for the colonised, the political differences between the Vichy regime and that of de Gaulle hold no meaning. In Africa, the colonised remains a social and political inferior, under the yoke of French domination no matter which government is in charge. Speaking of those who were killed at Thiaroye, Sembene presents their resistance as the first tentative steps of the independence movement in the face of European domination:

> *Ces hommes ont été, si vous voulez, les premiers levains du mouvement de la lutte pour l'indépendance. Ils venaient d'être libérés en août 1944, et puis on les a tués en décembre 1944, en plein règne du Général de Gaulle. Et pour nous donc, que ce soit de Gaulle, Mitterrand, ou Pétain, c'est la même chose.*[19]

If you like, these men were the first to set in train the independence movement. They had just been liberated in August 1944 and then they were killed in December 1944. This was when de Gaulle was in power, so for us, de Gaulle, Mitterrand, Pétain are all the same.

---

[17] For a discussion of this ill-documented period in West African history, see Echenberg, *Colonial Conscripts*, pp. 87–104. See also Michael Crowder, *West Africa under Colonial Rule* (London: Hutchinson, 1968), pp. 487–90.

[18] Although Africans were no longer sent to Europe under the Vichy regime, the size of the standing army in French West Africa was doubled from 50,000 to 100,000 during this period, in order to protect the region from a possible Allied attack. See Echenberg, *Colonial Conscripts*, p. 88. In the sequence that opens *Emitai*, the *tirailleurs sénégalais* capture a number of young men who are conscripted into the army and sent off to the war in Europe. In fact, it is more than likely that such conscripts would have served in Africa.

[19] Gadjigo et al., *Dialogues with Critics*, p. 81.

In many ways, Sembene's charges against the French colonial regime resemble those levelled against Europe by Césaire in *Discourse on Colonialism*, where European crimes in Africa are compared to the actions of the Nazis during World War Two. The sole difference for Césaire is that the Nazis had the indelicacy to brutalise and pillage Europe rather than the *lesser* peoples of the Third World. For Césaire, Hitler represents the violence of colonialism brought to bear on Europe:

> Yes, it would be worthwhile to study clinically, in detail, the steps taken by Hitler and Hitlerism and to reveal to the very distinguished, very humanistic, very Christian bourgeois of the twentieth century that without his being aware of it, he has a Hitler inside him, that Hitler *inhabits* him, that Hitler is his *demon*, that if he rails against him, he is being inconsistent and that, at bottom, what he cannot forgive Hitler for is not crime in itself, the *crime against man*, it is not *the humiliation of man as such*, it is the crime against the white man, the humiliation of the white man, and the fact that he applied to Europe colonialist procedures which until then had been reserved exclusively for the Arabs of Algeria, the coolies of India, and the blacks of Africa.[20]

Sembene had already touched on the continuity between the Vichy and the Free French regimes in *God's Bits of Wood*. Dejean, the head of the Dakar-Niger line, is an unreformed, paternalistic and racist coloniser. He cannot envisage talks with the strike leaders because he believes the relationship between himself and the workers to be that of master and servant, not employer and employee. Speaking of the strike-leader, Bakayoko, Dejean lets his true feelings show: 'Ah, that one! He's going to find out what I'm made of! He'll speak French, and so will they! I should have had him hanged in 1942! If only the directors had listened to me!' (*GBW*, p.180). Clearly nostalgic for the more openly repressive Vichy regime, Dejean carries his racial hatred with him into the post-war era. The regime has changed but the personnel and the attitudes are largely the same. This process is more explicitly examined in the character of the prison guard, Bernardini. A retired officer from the colonial army, Bernardini now works for the colonial police and is charged with guarding and, it would seem, breaking the will of the strikers within his camp. In the original French version, Bernardini makes a revealing statement when he has one of the strikers tortured for insubordination (a statement which is inexplicably omitted from the English translation): 'C'est un truc que j'ai appris des Fritz' (*Les Bouts de bois de Dieu*, p. 361) ['I learned this one from the Krauts']. Precisely how Bernardini came to learn torture techniques from the Germans is not revealed but the fact remains that a representative of the French regime is seen to employ the practices of an army whose actions they themselves had demonised. As Césaire had argued in *Discourse on Colonialism*, Nazi torture techniques were vilified not so much because of their inherent brutality but because they were used upon Europeans. In a striking illustration of this view, the sadistic Bernardini sees them as fitting punishment for troublesome blacks.

As Sembene has explained in interviews, the exact date at which the events in *Emitaï* take place is deliberately left unclear so as to display the continuity in French colonial practice:

[20] Césaire, *Discourse on Colonialism*, p. 14 (italics in original).

160

Emitaï, Ceddo & Camp de Thiaroye

Je n'ai pas voulu indiquer dans ce film la date exacte à laquelle les événements se déroulent. C'est aux alentours de 1942-43-44. On ne sait pas si c'est au moment de la prise du pouvoir par de Gaulle au Sénégal ou en France. Ce que j'ai voulu suggérer c'est que pour nous .Africains il n'y a pas eu de différence entre les deux régimes. Nous étions toujours des colonisés. Les méthodes, certes, ont quelque peu changé mais l'objectif était toujours de maintenir l'Empire Français. On l'a bien vu après la libération de la France: c'est dans le sang qu'ont été étouffés les revendications africaines à Thiaroye au Sénégal, à Grand-Bassam en Côte d'Ivoire, à Sétif et Guelma en .Algérie, à Madagascar, pour ne rien dire d'Indochine.[21]

I didn't want to show the exact date at which the events in the film take place. It's somewhere between 1942 and 1944. We don't know if it's at the time when de Gaulle takes power in Senegal or in France. The point of this was to show that for us Africans there was no difference between the two regimes. We were still colonised. The methods changed slightly but the goal was still to maintain the French Empire. This was clearly seen after the liberation of France. African demands were drowned in blood at Thiaroye in Senegal, at Grand-Bassam in the Ivory Coast, at Setif and Guelma in Algeria, in Madagascar, not to mention Indo-China.

It is interesting to note that Sembene here explicitly links atrocities committed under Vichy with those committed under the Free French regime. The same link is, in fact, made in *Camp de Thiaroye* which, in a self-referential moment, touches on the massacres that had taken place in Casamance under Vichy. Sergeant-Major Diatta, the civilised and urbane Senegalese NCO, who seems the very image of the assimilated African, is appalled to learn, on his return to Senegal from a German POW camp, that his parents in Casamance have been killed during a French operation to requisition rice from the village of Effok. Having fought and suffered imprisonment on behalf of France, Diatta returns home to discover that, despite his actions, he remains one of the colonised (this issue will be examined further below). This discovery leads him, in Césaire-like fashion, to equate the massacre at Effok with the German atrocities at Oradour-sur-Glane in France, an equation which even the liberal French officer, Captain Raymond, cannot bring himself to accept.

In one of the most ironic scenes in *Emitaï*, we see Sembene, playing a *tirailleur sénégalais*, comment on the replacement of a photograph of Pétain with one of de Gaulle. This event takes place at a crucial moment towards the end of the film. The villagers have been given one last chance by the army to reveal the location of the rice that has been hidden by the women. Suddenly, a messenger arrives with the news that de Gaulle has replaced Pétain as head of the French state. Thus, the photograph of Pétain, which had stood framed behind the French commander when he sent the young conscripts off to war, is replaced by the photograph of de Gaulle. The *tirailleurs*, who had earlier led the conscripts away to the strains of *Maréchal, nous voilà*, are perplexed at this sudden change in authority. This confusion is given voice through Sembene's ironic comment about '*un chef à deux étoiles*' ['a one-star commander'] replacing '*un chef à sept étoiles*' ['a seven-star commander'].[22] Literally, Sembene presents

---

[21] Guy Hennebelle, 'Ousmane Sembène: "En Afrique noire nous sommes gouvernés par des enfants mongoliens du colonialisme"', *Les Lettres françaises*, 6–12 October 1971, p. 16.

[22] Playing his role in a wonderfully obtuse fashion, Sembene's indignant *tirailleur* asks the African NCO to explain this new development. As a veteran of the colonial army, the *tirailleur* is

the change in regime from Vichy to Free France as purely cosmetic, the replacement of one remote image by another. For Africans, the reality of French domination remains the same and this is brought home to the spectator as the troops open fire on the villagers in the final scene of the film. However, because of French pressure on the Senegalese authorities to have this scene cut, we do not actually see the soldiers shooting down the villagers. Instead, we simply hear the shots fired as the screen goes blank. However, the effect remains the same: French rule in Africa, whether that of Pétain or de Gaulle, is governed by a latent violence that eventually rises to the surface.

In *Camp de Thiaroye*, the brutality of the Free French regime is exposed in a rather less ironic fashion than in *Emitaï*. The returning African soldiers are not only met with the blatant racial prejudice of the white colonial officers but are visually presented as being once again imprisoned in the camp at Thiaroye. The soldiers have only recently been liberated from prison camps such as Buchenwald, and Sembene deliberately chooses to show them entering yet another concentration camp. The very first image we see of Thiaroye is that of one of the watchtowers shot from a medium distance. After the heroic opening scenes of the *tirailleurs'* arrival in Dakar, we are given a visual hint of the fate that awaits them. This menace increases as we see the men enter the camp. Shot from a high angle, as though from one of the watchtowers (two of which are now visible), we are given a sense of the men being watched over, as though the sentries in the watchtowers are there to keep them in, rather than keep enemies out (which indeed they are, although, as we later discover, their guns are not even loaded).

The principal character through whom Sembene evokes the spectre of the German prison camps is Pays. He has suffered deep mental scars from his experiences in Buchenwald and, symbolically, has been left mute by this trauma (the figure of the mad *tirailleur* was already examined in Chapter Two). He is literally unable to voice his pain. In keeping with the process at work in many of Sembene's films and novels, we are once again faced with the problematisation of the notion of silence. Pays' silence is emblematic of the silence surrounding the story of the massacre that took place at Thiaroye. Denied by the French and deliberately overlooked by the Senegalese authorities, keen not to offend their former colonial masters, the massacre at Thiaroye becomes an important symbol in the fight for the memory of colonisation. Sembene has described his film almost as an act of 'resurrection' for those who died at Thiaroye:

> [...] ces hommes ne mourront plus maintenant, grâce au cinéma. Les Français les ont tués, mais le cimetière existe encore à Dakar. Nous l'entretenons toujours, mais mon gouvernement n'en dit rien. Il n'existe sur aucun papier officiel. On ne vient pas fleurir les tombes. Jusqu'à ce film, c'étaient des tombes anonymes. Maintenant, elles ne sont plus anonymes. Quand nous recevons des amis, nous leur disons, '*Allons visiter le cimetière de Thiaroye*', et ils vont voir le cimetière. Il y a des tombes et des croix. Il n'y a ni noms, ni matricules. Mais c'est la mémoire de l'histoire. Et cela nous le gardons.[23]

[22] (cont.) imbued with a sense of military hierarchy and he refuses to accept the NCO's explanation. He claims that the replacement of Pétain by de Gaulle is the equivalent of the NCO taking orders from a simple *tirailleur* such as himself.

[23] Gadjigo et al., *Dialogues with Critics*, p. 83.

[...] thanks to the film, these men are no longer dead. The French killed them but their cemetery still exists in Dakar. We still take care of it but my government never mentions it. It does not appear on any offical document. No one comes to lay flowers on their graves. Before this film, these were simply anonymous graves but that has changed now. Now when we have friends visiting, we say, 'Let's go to the cemetery in Thiaroye', and they come with us to see the cemetery. There are graves and crosses but no names or identity numbers. But we are keeping alive the memory of their history.

The cinema thus acts as an intervention into both the political and the historical sphere, giving voice to a story that had ended in the silence of brutal repression.

One of the key scenes for our understanding of the fate that is to befall the *tirailleurs* is when Pays first discovers the barbed-wire fence enclosing the camp, which had previously been invisible because of the blinding-white light created by the sun on the sand of the *niaye*. As the men settle into their new quarters, we see a shot of Pays, filmed from behind, approaching the camp boundary, giving us our first glimpse of the barbed-wire. The camera then shifts to a low angle outside the fence looking up at Pays framed against the barbed-wire. Increasingly, the image of a prisoner is being presented to us. The camera moves continuously closer to Pays, following his gaze as he turns to look at the four watchtowers at each corner of the camp. These subjective shots convey the sense of unease felt by Pays. On the soundtrack, throughout the scene, we hear a haunting blues played on the harmonica (accompanied occasionally by the trumpet). The harmonica is the archetypal soldier's instrument (the soldier, Congo, plays the harmonica in several scenes, ironically playing *Lili Marlena*, renowned as the favourite song of both the French and German armies in World War One[24]) – this harmonica tune becomes a refrain as the film progresses, punctuating moments of tension and conflict. The camera finally presents a shot of Pays running his hand along the barbed-wire, moving in for a close-up of the hand itself as it gently touches the barbs. The sense of menace has increased with the spectator expecting Pays to cut his fingers as his hand tenses open and closed on the fence. The Corporal, who appears to be Pays' closest friend in the film, joins him by the fence. He picks up a handful of soil which he pours over Pays' hand. Then, taking Pays' hand in his own, he comforts him like a child, telling him that at long last he is home and that the horrors of Buchenwald are behind him. Pays seems calmed and reassured but, despite the Corporal's kind words, the fate that awaits them both is intimated in the shot of the two men framed against the barbed-wire as they return towards the barracks. They are both prisoners of the colonial system.

Perhaps the most interesting way in which Sembene presents the *tirailleur*'s resistance to colonial domination is through the use of imagery that links the *tirailleurs* to the German army. In their revolt against the French, the *tirailleurs* become transformed into their colonial master's enemy (as was mentioned earlier, the double irony being that it is the *tirailleurs* who fought the Germans

---

[24] The song, *Lili Marlena*, is used in Stanley Kubrick's anti-war film, *Paths of Glory* (1957), to illustrate the ties between the ordinary German and French soldiers who are shown to be callously mistreated by their officers.

in Europe while the colonial officers sat out the war). Pays' friend, the Corporal, also lapses into German when he is annoyed. He berates the chef because of the quality of the food and he insults a driver who almost runs over the soldiers. However, the link to the German army is achieved mainly through the visual motif of Pays' SS helmet. As the film progresses, the helmet becomes a sign of resistance. Pays refuses to let the two French soldiers who search the camp take it from him and he wears it when he is left to guard the General.

The symbolism of the helmet is demonstrated in the scene that immediately follows Pays' discovery of the fence. As two of the *tirailleurs* go towards the fence to hang their wet clothes out to dry, they find their path blocked by Pays, who is now wearing an SS helmet and a great-coat. For Pays, fences evoke the pain and suffering of the German concentration camps. The camera moves to a profile shot of Pays with the imposing watchtower in the background. Day turns to night as Pays turns to look at the watchtower and we fade into black and white images from World War Two. A German soldier looks through a pair of binoculars and this is followed by three still shots of dead prisoners hanging from or lying behind barbed-wire fences. On the soundtrack, we hear the rattle of machine-gun fire. Pays, who has suffered so much at the hands of the Nazis, seems to have developed a sixth sense as he anticipates the bloody end that awaits the *tirailleurs*. However, he cannot articulate his worries and his fellow soldiers take his warnings to be the ramblings of a madman. In a camp where many of the soldiers are known by the name of their country of origin (Niger, Côte d'Ivoire, Congo, Gabon, etc.), Pays appears to represent the suffering of Africa as a whole, a suffering that cannot be expressed in words but which sows the seeds of the *tirailleurs'* rebellion that is to bring about such swift and brutal revenge from the French military. Partly dressed in German uniform, Pays effectively 'dons' the mantle of opposition to French rule in Africa.

As was mentioned above, Sembene sees the events at Thiaroye as an important moment in the nationalist *prise de conscience* in Africa. The soldiers' revolt takes on such significance precisely because the *tirailleurs sénégalais* were seen as an integral part of the colonial regime. Often detested figures to their fellow Africans, the *tirailleurs* had loyally served the French cause in the conquest of Africa at the end of the nineteenth century and subsequently, in both world wars.[25] In many ways, they could be considered the model of assimilation. Therefore, Sembene takes great care to capture the pride that the soldiers take in their role as war veterans who have helped to liberate the 'mother country'. Throughout the film, the *tirailleurs* are deliberately presented to us as genuinely well-disciplined troops. The film is littered with scenes of the men drilling before their commanders. Indeed, as they march from the docks to Thiaroye, some of the local soldiers who see them pass comment enviously on their discipline and proud demeanour. Despite the sense of impending doom that pervades the film, Sembene never seeks to portray the *tirailleurs* merely as

---

[25] After the conquest had been completed, the colonial army was increasingly made up of African recruits. As we shall see below, the villagers in *Emitaï* are shot by *tirailleurs*. For a comprehensive history of the *tirailleurs sénégalais*, see Echenberg, *Colonial Conscripts*.

victims. They are experienced and disciplined soldiers who want to receive the same recognition as their French counterparts. In fact, we see the men involved in activities we might expect to see in any film about the army: the men talk of their wives, of their plans for the future, they go to visit prostitutes, they play football, they grow excited when they receive letters from home. Sergeant-Major Diatta is portrayed as the perfect NCO, fair and just with his men, and possessing a brilliant and cultured mind (perhaps too cultured: as Michel Ciment argues, Sembene rather overdoes his portrait of Diatta, showing scenes of him listening to Charlie Parker and Albinoni records, items which one would not necessarily expect to be in the possession of a soldier recently released from a German POW camp[26]).

However, the fact remains that the men are not treated by their white officers with the respect they feel they deserve (with the exception of the liberal Captain Raymond). They may have participated in the liberation of France but, upon their return to the empire, they find that, as far as the colonial army is concerned, their status is still that of subjects. This reduction in the men's status is brilliantly conveyed by Sembene when the men are forced to part with their American uniforms. Such was the state of their kit that they had been given American uniforms by the US army in which to return home. These uniforms become a sort of status symbol for the men, a badge that marks them out as veterans of the war in Europe. They also remove the men's colonised status, at least in appearance, and the men can imagine themselves as Americans. As Diatta is to discover when he visits the brothel in his American uniform, on the coloniser's scale an African-American is rated far higher than an African. Entering the brothel in his American uniform, he is greeted with the words, 'Hello Joe, you buy me a whiskey?' However, when the owner discovers his true origins, he is sent on his way, accompanied by cries of *'pas de bougnoules ici!'* ['no niggers allowed in here!']

The colonial army disapproves of its *indigènes* getting above their station and, although the *tirailleurs* are due to be demobilised within days, they are forced to replace their American uniforms with the distinctive red fez and white shorts of the standard *tirailleur*'s uniform. As with Pays' SS helmet, the use of costume in this scene is given a tremendous symbolic importance. Both literally and symbolically, the men are being obliged to don their former, servile identity. The camera lingers on the piles of boots and trousers which the soldiers cast upon the ground. As Pays queues to receive his uniform, the haunting harmonica tune returns. He turns to look at the watchtower and after a subjective shot of the tower, the image fades in a slow dissolve. The men have now regained the physical appearance that marks them out as inferiors. In the next scene, the camera follows the men back to their quarters where they sit and look at the floor disconsolately, unable to put into words their

---

[26] Michel Ciment, '*Le Camp de Thiaroye*, de Sembene Ousmane et Thierno Faty Sow', *Positif*, 333 (November 1988), p. 62. Ciment is very dismissive of the film which he finds heavy-handed in its criticisms of colonialism. While I would agree that the film lacks the creativity of earlier works such as *Emitaï* and *Ceddo*, it is not the dreary, badly filmed polemic which Ciment describes.

discontent. Their confusion grows as they verbally attack one another for being so miserable over a simple uniform until one of the men puts his finger on the problem: they feel ashamed.

The *tirailleurs sénégalais* may have been France's erstwhile partners in the conquest of its African empire, but they were nonetheless victims of French colonialism in their own right. The lesson that the soldiers learn in *Camp de Thiaroye* is that, no matter how much they do on behalf of their imperial masters, they can never escape their inferior status within the colonial system, and this sows the seeds of revolt. As Sembene argues, the *tirailleurs'* experiences in World War Two finally opened their eyes to the lie of equality which the colonial army had sold to them:

> *Mais ces soldats noirs ont été envoyés au front, pour participer à la libération de l'Europe. Pendant leur séjour au front ils ont fréquenté d'autres Européens, ils ont vu des familles, de lâches ou de braves Européens. Et lorsqu'ils sont retournés chez eux, ils n'étaient plus les mêmes. Ils ne pouvaient plus accepter ce qu'ils avaient accepté avant de partir. Et ils n'avient plus de respect pour ces officiers qui n'avaient pas participé à la guerre. Voilà tout le malentendu.*[27]

But these black soldiers were sent to the front to take part in the liberation of Europe. During their time at the front, they met other Europeans. They met families, they met cowardly and brave Europeans. And when they returned home, they were no longer the same. They could no longer accept what they had accepted before going to war. And they had lost all respect for those officers who had not taken part in the war. This is how the rupture began.

When they are offered only half the normal rate for their money, the French officers claiming that they may have stolen the money from corpses on the battlefield, the *tirailleurs* are incensed. Their discipline and obedience to their commanders breaks down as they lose faith in the colonial regime. When Sergeant-Major Diatta tries to argue their case, citing the many battles in which they had fought, the bigoted Labrousse merely writes the word *communiste* on a piece of paper that he hands to his fellow officers. The colonial officers are unable and unwilling to communicate with their African troops on equal terms. When the *tirailleurs* have taken the General hostage, he secures his freedom by lying to the men, promising that they will be paid in full, giving them his word as an officer: '*Vous avez ma parole d'officier-général.*' ['You have my word as a general']. His words mean nothing, just as Labrousse refuses to listen to the meaning of Diatta's words. There can be no dialogue in such a situation, only revolt. When Captain Raymond tries to talk 'sense' to Diatta, in order to have the General released, Diatta replies angrily: '*Et comment dois-je parler? Ou plutôt je ne dois pas parler. Je dois me taire, c'est ça? Et être complice d'une injustice?*' ['And how should I speak? Or rather I shouldn't speak. I should just keep my mouth shut, isn't that it, and silently comply with the injustice that's taking place?'][28] The *tirailleurs* had previously fought France's enemies but

[27] Gadjigo et al., *Dialogues with Critics*, p. 81.
[28] In the course of his speech, Diatta mentions the case of Captain Charles N'Tchoréré. When his battalion was captured, N'Tchoréré was ordered by his German captors to stand with the African rank and file soldiers. When he insisted on being treated as an officer, Captain N'Tchoréré was shot dead by the Germans. In the film, Diatta claims that the incident took

'maintenant nous nous combattons pour l'Afrique' ['now we are fighting for Africa']. Their revolt will now be voiced.

Camp de Thiaroye tells a tale of resistance of those Africans who were most closely linked with imperial power in Africa. As was mentioned above, the story of the massacre at Thiaroye was one deliberately occulted by both the Senegalese and the French authorities. However, after the release of Sembene's film and the very public debate that followed, it seems that the Fédération des Anciens Combattants was able to press its claims to have the cause of those killed at Thiaroye officially recognised by the state. On 1 December 1993, the anniversary of the massacre was officially proclaimed *journée nationale des anciens combattants*. Subsequently, in 1994, on the fiftieth anniversary of the 'incident', there was a procession from the Office des Anciens Combattants to the Place de l'Indépendance in Dakar for a wreath-laying ceremony at the monument to the Senegalese soldiers who died in both world wars. This was followed by a march to the cemetery in Thiaroye. However, the government's recognition of the 'incident' at Thiaroye did not extend as far as having either the Prime Minister, Habib Thiam, or the President, Abdou Diouf, attend the ceremony (the government was represented by the Ministre des Forces Armées, Madieng Khary Dieng). This arm's-length approach to the ceremony was reflected in the coverage of the occasion in the government newspaper, *Le Soleil*, which placed the story on an inside page, and, in a very sober report, gave the bare details of what had happened in Thiaroye fifty years earlier, obstinately refusing to cast any blame on the French military.[29] The opposition daily *Sud Quotidien* had no such qualms about explaining what it saw as the true significance of the events at Thiaroye, giving the story a front page headline and also dedicating an entire inside page to it. In fact, the headline could almost have been written by Sembene, so close is it to the thinking behind *Camp de Thiaroye*: 'Il y a 50 ans, "Thiaroye 44": une histoire à réhabiliter' ['50 years ago, "Thiaroye 44": a history in need of rehabilitation'].[30] Indeed, the 'message' that the journalist takes from the massacre is in keeping with the argument of Sembene's film:

> *Aujourd'hui encore, tous les peuples africains se reconnaissent à travers cette tragédie. Chacun de nous garde en lui le sentiment profond et vivace d'avoir une partie de soi dans les ruines du Camp de Thiaroye de même que dans le cimetière des soldats indigènes coloniaux de Thiaroye.*[31]

All Africans continue to see their own history in this tragedy. Each of us has the deep and painful feeling of having a part of us in the ruins of the camp at Thiaroye, as well as in the native soldiers' cemetery in Thiaroye.

Sembene's *Camp de Thiaroye* thus serves as an example of the power of film, a popular art form, to encourage debate and to push the postcolonial world to

---

[28] (cont.) place at Buchenwald. In fact, the historical incident took place at Airaines in France. See Echenberg, *Colonial Conscripts*, pp. 67–8.

[29] Djib Diedhiou, 'A nos martyres de Thiaroye', *Le Soleil* [Dakar], 1 December 1994, p. 3. There was a brief follow-up article in the next day's issue, giving an account of the ceremonies which took place on 1 December. See I. Mbodj, 'Simplicité et Solennité', *Le Soleil* [Dakar], 2 December 1994, p. 2.

[30] Samba Diop, 'Il y a 50 ans, "Thiaroye 44": une histoire à réhabiliter', *Sud Quotidien*, 1 December 1994, p. 1.

[31] Ibid., p. 6.

examine its history, to understand the reality of colonialism (it also serves as a rare example of African unity, the film being a Senegalese-Algerian-Tunisian co-production).

■ ■ ■

If *Camp de Thiaroye* tells the story of colonial repression of those who saw themselves as part of the colonial regime, then *Emitaï* is the story of colonial repression of a people, the Diola of Casamance, who are unable to come to terms with the violent situation with which the empire presents them. Whereas *Camp de Thiaroye* paints the colonial army as the villains of the piece, *Emitaï* goes much further in its exploration of the nature of the relationship between the coloniser and the colonised. Faced with the demands of the French military and its threat of the use of force, the menfolk of the Diola retreat into an extreme fatalism, continually turning to their many gods for answers that are not forthcoming. This does not mean that Sembene is dismissive of the Diola's culture and beliefs. On the contrary, the film depicts many of their rituals in loving detail. Despite his admission that certain scenes are his own reconstitution of the Diola's rituals, Sembene is keen to explain that his intention was to depict the richness and the original nature of Diola culture:

> *J'ai fait très attention de ne pas verser dans l'exotisme et le folklore. J'ai voulu suggérer que ces pratiques faisaient partie d'une culture. Je suis sûr que même des Africains ne comprendront pas ce film très enraciné dans la culture diola.*[32]

> I was very careful not to veer into exoticism and folklore. I wanted to suggest that these practices were part of a culture. I'm sure that even some Africans won't understand this film, which is deeply rooted in Diola culture.

The film bears ample witness to this as Sembene devotes several long scenes to the portrayal of Diola culture: their sacrifices to their gods, their funeral rituals, their spirituality. The gods themselves are given a 'material' presence in the film as the village chief Djiméko debates the fate of the village with them.

However, despite his respect for the Diola, Sembene sees their faith in their gods and the fatalistic approach to life that is inherent in this, as one of the principal causes of their defeat at the hands of the French (and of European domination in Africa, in general). This more complex attitude towards colonialism is sharply analysed by Sembene in the following terms:

> *Bien que respectant tous les croyants, je suis personnellement l'adversaire de toutes les religions. Ce sont des opiums. C'est particulièrement vrai au Sénégal. A l'époque de la résistance passive à la colonisation, les religions ont pu, parfois, entretenir la flamme de la résistance populaire mais dans mon film les fétiches incitent plutôt à la résignation. Je suis contre qui brosse un tableau idyllique de l'Afrique avant l'arrivée des Blancs. Il est vrai que ceux-ci ont, d'un côté aggravé considérablement la situation. A l'époque coloniale, il était de bonne guerre d'imputer tous nos maux au colonialisme car la contradiction fondamentale était entre colonialistes et colonisés. Aujourd'hui elle est entre le peuple et la bourgeoisie locale épaulée par le néo-colonialisme. Le sens de mon film, c'est qu'il appartient aux hommes de décider de leur destin, pas aux dieux. Par*

---

[32] Hennebelle, 'Ousmane Sembène: "En Afrique noire nous sommes gouvernés"', p. 16.

ailleurs, Emitaï est aussi, je le pense, un film contre la Négritude qui est devenue une idéologie mystificatrice.[33]

Although I respect all those who believe, I am personally against all religions. They are opiums and this is particularly true in Senegal. During the era of passive resistance to colonisation, religion was sometimes able to keep the flame of popular resistance alive, but, in my film, religion leads to a sense of resignation. I am against those who seek to paint an idealised picture of Africa before the arrival of the white man. It's true that the white man did make the situation much worse. In the colonial era, it became common to attribute all our ills to colonialism because the basic opposition in society was between colonisers and colonised. Today, the opposition is between the people and the local bourgeoisie, which is kept in place by the politics of neo-colonialism. My film argues that it is the duty of men, and not the gods, to create their own destiny. What's more, *Emitaï* is also a film opposed to Negritude, which has become a mystifying ideology.

Far from the dogmatic Marxist tag with which he is often labelled, Sembene shows himself to be much more open-minded when it comes to issues of religion and culture than this vision of his work allows. He may follow the Marxist line that religion is the opium of the people but this does not mean that he simply denigrates religions and their adepts. Rather, he examines the manner in which religion prevents men from creating their own destinies. His aim is to explain the social reasons behind colonialism and he refuses to content himself with an analysis that lays all the blame at the door of Europe. As in his story 'Tribal Scars or The Voltaique', where he discusses the role played by Africans in the slave trade, Sembene seeks to discuss the problems within African society which allowed European states to create their African empires. Explicitly linking the polarisation between Blacks and Whites, which constitutes the main thread in most critiques of empire, with the ideology of Negritude, Sembene declares that he will examine colonialism from a social and historical point of view, not a mystic and mystifying one. If one fails to examine the compromises and failures of African societies in the face of European domination, it is impossible to understand one of the questions at the heart of *Emitaï*: how can one group of Africans shoot down another for refusing to provide food for a foreign army fighting a war thousands of miles away? The simple answer is that Africa could not present a unified front against colonialism because of internal problems within African societies.[34]

However, Sembene does not paint a completely passive picture of the Diola. The village chief Djiméko has begun to lose faith in the gods and he leads the young men out to do battle with the French. However, they are quickly defeated and he is fatally wounded. When he is brought back to the giant, gnarled tree that is the home of the gods, Djiméko launches a verbal attack on the deities. They claim that he must die because he had refused to make the necessary sacrifices before going into battle, but Djiméko, defiant to

[33] Ibid.

[34] For an examination of the ambiguities within Africa which are revealed by *Emitaï*, see I. R., '*Emitaï* – Un film de Sembène Ousmane', *Le Monde Diplomatique*, 24, 279 (June 1977), p. 23.

the last, argues that his death may indeed be imminent but so too is that of the gods. However, Djiméko's spirit of resistance finds no echo amongst the other elders of the village, who still cling to their belief in the gods.

In contrast to the fatalism of the men, Sembene presents the women of the village as a force of resistance against the coloniser. As was argued in the previous chapter, in many of Sembene's films and novels, he seeks to radicalise the role of women by giving a political dimension to their traditional roles as mothers and providers. Thus, as the women seek to protect their families, they come into direct conflict with the colonial army.[35] As is shown in a number of long scenes in the first half of the film, it is the women who have put most work into producing the rice harvest, and they are unwilling to hand over the food that will feed their families throughout the long hot months ahead. The women's defiance also becomes a challenge to the authority of the men of the village, who dare not stand against the French but who do not want to lose face before their women. Sembene deliberately contrasts scenes of the men's fatalism with the resistance of the women: while the men consult their silent gods (who appear to have died just as Djiméko had predicted), the women defy the colonial authorities, preferring to suffer under the baking heat of the African sun rather than reveal where they have hidden the rice.

This contrast is perhaps best captured in the sequence in which the men set out to bury Djiméko. Sembene cuts from the scenes of the men singing their farewell to their dead chief to images of the women singing in solidarity with one another as they continue to thwart the French commander. The formal, ceremonial aspect of the funeral ritual is contrasted with the new ritual of resistance being forged by the women. When the men finally concede defeat and deliver the rice to the French, we see a complete inversion of male and female roles. It is the men who carry the rice while the women perform the burial ritual of the young boy who has been shot dead by the soldiers: carrying the spears abandoned by the men, the women effectively take their place as warriors. Perhaps shamed by the sound of the women singing the funeral songs they had previously sung, the men refuse to carry the rice any further in a final act of resistance, which is to result in their deaths.

It should not be forgotten that, at the time *Emitaï* was made, several Portuguese colonies were in the grip of ferocious anti-colonial struggles. It would seem that, at least in part, Sembene decided to locate his tale of colonialism in Casamance, amongst the Diola, as this ethnic group was also to be found in the neighbouring Portuguese colony of Guinea-Bissau, which had been engaged in an anti-colonial struggle since 1963. Sembene thus saw his film as an intervention in Senegalese colonial history but also as an encouragement to the rebels who were still fighting to liberate the last remains of the great European empires in Africa. Indeed, some of Amilcar Cabral's soldiers served as extras in *Emitaï*:

[35] The women's resistance to the colonial authorities is captured in a brief scene in which a little girl grabs at a *tirailleur*'s gun. The soldier takes a step backward but is followed by the child, forcing him to retreat further still. The women do not win their 'battle' with the colonial army but they, at least, succeed in delaying their defeat.

6.2 The women take on the role of the men as warriors
Emitai, Filmi Doomireew – Dakar, Senegal (all rights reserved)

Dis-membering Empire, Re-membering Resistance

Lors du tournage, des figurants venaient de Guinée-Bissao et les combattants et les maquisards d'alors nous ont beaucoup aidés. Lors de la première du film en Casamance, le président Cabral était venu voir le film avec ses combattants; à la sortie, tous sont venus nous dire qu'on avait fait un film pour eux et non pour les autres parce que c'était la même lutte.[36]

During the filming, extras came from Guinea-Bissau, and the rebels were a great help to us. At the film's premiere in Casamance, President Cabral came to see the film with his soldiers. Coming out of the cinema, they all came to tell us that they felt the film had been made for them because theirs was the same struggle.

Sembene uses his film to support Cabral's cause in Guinea-Bissau to rid Africa of the last vestiges of colonialism (similarly, in the story, 'Chaiba the Algerian', in *Tribal Scars*, Sembene tells the story of an Algerian murdered by the French police, in order to voice his support for the Algerian cause in their brutal war of independence with the French). Moreover, Cabral was a Marxist, who shared Sembene's vision of the nationalist struggle against colonialism as the first step on the road to a social revolution within African society itself (Cabral makes a cameo appearance on a poster in Rama's room in *Xala*). As Sembene shows by highlighting the dynamic role of female resistance to the French, the fight against colonialism opens the lid on a whole range of other social tensions and grievances that the simple overthrow of the empire cannot resolve.

■ ■ ■

Sembene's film *Ceddo* casts its investigation of the process of colonialism much wider than either *Emitaï* or *Camp de Thiaroye*. In fact, the film has been described by many commentators as the most ambitious African film ever made, as well as one of the most creative. *Ceddo* is an historical film that deliberately telescopes events from the seventeenth to the nineteenth century in West African history into the life of one small village at an unspecified moment in time. The film places a traditional African monarch side by side with a Christian missionary, a slave trader, and an ambitious imam. Out of this clash of different and competing cultures, Sembene produces a stinging critique of the role of Islam within African society. In fact, Islam is presented as just as much a colonising force within black Africa as was Europe. This was a rather controversial conclusion to arrive at in a country such as Senegal, which was then approximately 80 per cent Muslim (this figure has since risen to over 90 per cent). It has been argued by many critics that it was the 'offensive' nature of the arguments within the film that caused it to be banned by the Senegalese government. However, there seems no reason not to believe the official reason given by the government that the film was banned because the word *ceddo* was spelt not only wrongly, but in direct contradiction of statute 75-1026, governing the spelling of Wolof.[37] Sembene did not agree with the government's

[36] Nourredine Ghali, 'Ousmane Sembene. "Le cinéaste, de nos jours, peut remplacer le conteur traditionnel"', *Cinéma*, 208 (April 1976), p. 84.

[37] In a personal interview with Sembene at his office in Filmi Doomireew in Dakar on 30 November, 1995 (see Appendix), he confirmed to me that this was the real reason that the film

linguistic legislation and refused to spell his *ceddo* with one 'd'. This may seem a trivial point but it most definitely was not trivial to Sembene who, in the early 1970s, had poured a lot of money into a Wolof-language newspaper *Kaddu*, which promoted the use of Wolof, and respected the orthography of the linguist, Pathé Diagne (see Chapter Four). For Sembene, the question of the spelling of *ceddo* became a vital cultural matter:

> *Ça va loin! Car il s'agit de la culture africaine et de la langue wolof. Actuellement, au Sénégal, on s'efforce de nous incorporer dans la francophonie. Pourquoi être devenu indépendant si c'est pour être déraciné à l'intérieur même de sa propre culture? Le wolof est parlé par 80% de la population sénégalaise; il pourrait donc devenir langue nationale. Il s'agit de lutter pour notre nationalisme culturel. Nous avons créé des journaux en wolof, nous avons travaillé pendant des années à la codification de la langue! Devant l'ampleur de ce mouvement, le président Senghor a pris ce décret pour codifier d'une autre façon une langue qui n'est pas la sienne et qu'il ne parle pas!* [38]

This is a crucial issue! It's about African culture and the Wolof language. At the moment, efforts are being made to incorporate Senegal within 'la francophonie'. Why achieve independence if it's only to remain alienated from your own culture? Wolof is spoken by 80 per cent of the Senegalese population and could easily become a national language. We must fight for our national culture. We have created Wolof-language newspapers and we have worked for years to codify the language! Despite this vast cultural movement, President Senghor issued this decree, codifying in a completely different way a language that is not his and that he does not even speak!

In a film in which the resistance of African culture to foreign domination is a central issue, it is hardly surprising that the outspoken Sembene chose to stand his ground against Senghor, whom he saw as the original *aliéné culturel*, on such a sensitive question. The ban on the film was eventually lifted in 1984 and it went on general release in Senegal later that same year. [39]

The basic argument of *Ceddo* is that Islam destroyed the traditional African way of life, replacing the fetishist rituals and practices it found with its own Islamic rites. Opposing this disruption to the status quo, Sembene places the *ceddo* as defenders of black African culture. Both Sembene's vision of Islam and his view of the *ceddo* have been challenged by scholars and critics so it would seem appropriate to examine the standard representations of both in order to understand where Sembene departs from these interpretations of the African past.

As was argued in Chapter One, there exists a strong Islamicist tradition

---

[37] (cont.) had been banned. As for the susceptibilities of the fundamentalists, Sembene argued that such figures were non-existent in the period prior to the overthrow of the Shah of Iran by the Ayatollah Khomeini in 1979. Interestingly, Sembene claimed that the Shah had asked him for a copy of the film before the Islamic Revolution in order to help check the rise of Islam. Not wanting to deal with a figure so highly implicated in neo-colonial politics, Sembene refused. He then claims that he offered the film to Iran after the Islamic Revolution but, needless to say, they declined the offer. The story may be apocryphal but it certainly illustrates Sembene's distinctly secular resistance to the forces of colonialism and neo-colonialism.

[38] Farida Ayari et al., 'J.A. fait parler Sembène Ousmane: "La Culture est le levain de la politique mais l'intégrisme c'est le fascisme"', *Jeune Afrique*, 19 September 1979, p. 72.

[39] For a discussion of the critical and public reaction to *Ceddo* within Senegal, see Buuba Babacar Diop, 'Malaise autour de *Ceddo*', *Revue africaine de communication*, 7 (September–October 1984), pp. 45–52.

within Senegal which, with varying degrees of subtlety, attempts to describe Islam as an indigenous religion within black Africa, or at least as an inevitable outcome of the country's history. Amar Samb is quite categoric in his dismissal of those who would assimilate Islam with European colonialism:

> *Les esprits bien pensants qui assimilent l'Islam à un impérialisme colonisateur et exploiteur commettent un grave anachronisme. Ce n'est pas l'Islam qui a décidé en 1885 le partage brutal de l'Afrique en vue non seulement de piller ses richesses mais encore de détruire et de nier sa personnalité authentique et spécifique. La civilisation arabo-musulmane, loin de spolier notre continent de ce qu'il a de plus intime et de plus représentatif, a au contraire permis aux .Africains de lui apporter leur contribution à son enrichissement, à son épanouissement et à sa diffusion, et ce, avant l'apogée même de cette civilisation à l'élaboration de laquelle ont participé des peuples, des races, voire des continents.*[40]

The portrayal by these right-thinking people of Islam as a colonising and exploita-tive imperialism is completely anachronistic. It was not Islam that decided in 1885 upon the brutal scramble for Africa, which was designed not only to pillage the continent but also to destroy and to deny its authentic and specific personality. Far from plundering our continent of its most intimate and most representative elements, Muslim-Arab civilisation has, on the contrary, allowed Africans to contribute to the enrichment, the flowering and the spread of that civilisation. This was achieved at a period before Muslim-Arab civilisation, created by the hands of many peoples, races, continents, had even reached its peak.

In this view, Europe raped and pillaged while Islam brought spirituality and culture. Samb's vision of Islam is admittedly one of the most polemical, but even more moderate scholars, such as Cheikh Tidiane Sy (not to be confused with the head of the Tidiane brotherhood, who shares the same name), leave no doubt as to what they see as the inevitability of Islam's rise within black Africa. Examining the spread of Islam in the Wolof community, Sy plays down the role of Islamic colonisation and the destruction of the traditional social structure by the French, and declares that the spread of Islam is prin-cipally the result of factors within the Wolof community:

> *Tout d'abord il faut souligner que l'Islam représentait pour les Wolof un monothéisme révélé à caractère universaliste sans commune mesure avec le culte traditionnel. Cette supériorité donc de l'Islam les amenait à proclamer l'égalité des hommes devant Dieu.*[41]

First of all, we must underline the fact that Islam was regarded by the Wolof as a universal monotheism that was far superior to traditional cults. This evident superiority of Islam led them to proclaim the equality of all men before God.

In this vision, the Wolof would appear to have spent the preceding centuries simply waiting for Islam to come along to relieve them from their social injustices and their multitude of false gods.

The historian David Robinson has argued that the problem with many of the histories of Islam in West Africa is that they were written by Muslim scholars who believed wholly in Islam's mission to preach to 'the heathen'.[42]

---

[40] Amar Samb, 'L'Islam et l'histoire du Sénégal', *Bulletin de l'IFAN*, series B, 33, 3 (1971), pp. 461–2.

[41] Cheikh Tidiane Sy, 'Ahmadu Bamba et l'Islamisation des Wolof', *Bulletin de l'IFAN*, series B, 32, 2 (1970), p. 432.

[42] David Robinson, 'An Approach to Islam in West African History', in Kenneth W. Harrow, ed.,

These scholarly accounts are the ones most often cited by contemporary Islamic scholars. In a rather more factual account of the spread of Islam among the Wolof, Vincent Monteil argues that:

> *En dehors du Fouta, où les Toucouleurs ont commencé à être convertis dès le XIe siècle, et que les Almâmi avaient constitué en Etat musulman en 1776, l'ensemble des Wolof du Sénégal ne semble bien s'être islamisé, en masse, que vers la fin du XIXe siècle.*[43]

> Outside of Fouta, where the Toucouleurs had begun to convert as early as the 11th century, and where the Almami had established a Muslim state in 1776, the Wolof in Senegal do not appear to have rallied to Islam, on a large scale, until the end of the 19th century.

Islam may have become the dominant religion within the state but it was not an inevitable process. Rather, Islam was the winner in a clash of values between itself and those of the *ceddo* (this term is used for convenience – I will come to the complications surrounding the term, *ceddo*, below). Rebutting the arguments of Assane Sylla, who sees an Islamic morality in Wolof myths and tales, Lilyan Kesteloot and Bassirou Dieng argue that a distinctive *ceddo* morality is discernible in certain Wolof stories: '*tous les récits qui mettent en scène la royauté et la noblesse prônent* le système de valeur tieddo [ceddo] *qui n'a pas grande chose à voir avec la morale moderne*' ['all of the stories that deal with royalty and the nobility preach the *ceddo system of values*, which is completely different from modern morality'].[44] For centuries, Islam was the religion of an elite few but from the seventeenth century onwards, as West African society grew more and more unstable under the influence of the slave trade, Islam gradually became a force of resistance against the abuses of the traditional monarchical system. Sembene recognises this revolutionary aspect in the spread of Islam but he also sees other more sinister forces at work:

> [...] a wind of revolt was blowing under the banner of Islam. An internal revolt. People stood up against the traditional chiefdoms, accomplices or agents for European slave-traders. And yet, the Arab religious leaders had only two goals: to dominate through their religion, and to re-establish to their own benefit the Saharan trade which had been disrupted by the intervention of Europeans. The spiritual heirs of Islam brought a new life style which upset the very basis of society. In the name of Islam, the 'objects of pagan cult' were destroyed. People began changing names. Islam modelled itself on the ancient social organization. But it was implacably opposed to every traditional religious practice. (*MC*, pp. 4–5; I have made a few changes to the original translation, which is quite poor in places)

Islam may have seemed a better, more egalitarian option to some Africans at a specific point in their history, but that does not prevent it, in Sembene's

---

[42] (cont.) *Faces of Islam in African Literature* (London: James Currey; Portsmouth, NH: Heinemann, 1991), pp. 107–29. The influence of Islamicist discourse can be seen in many nineteenth-century descriptions of the *ceddo* as drunks and thieves. See Abbé David Boilat, *Esquisses sénégalaises* (1853; Paris: Karthala, 1984), pp. 308–9, and Yoro Dyâo and R. Rousseau, 'Le Sénégal d'autrefois. Etude sur le Oualo', *Bulletin du comité d'études historiques et scientifiques de l'A.O.F.*, 12 (1929), pp. 169–70, 206.

[43] Vincent Monteil, *L'Islam noir* (1964; Paris: Seuil, 1971), p. 107.

[44] Lilyan Kesteloot and Bassirou Dieng, *Du Tieddo au talibé: Contes et mythes wolof II* (Paris: Présence Africaine, 1989), p. 8 (emphasis in original).

view, from constituting a form of colonial domination. Indeed, many of the Islamic leaders who had promised to put an end to slavery within a certain community did not refrain from continuing the slave trade when it meant selling 'heathens' into slavery, or using them to help with the fast-expanding peanut production, which was becoming focused in the hands of Muslim leaders at the end of the nineteenth century.[45] It is the manner in which Islam destroyed the fetishist practices that had preceded it, and the occulting of real, temporal power behind religious arguments, with which Sembene disagrees. These processes form the heart of Sembene's reflection on the nature of Islam's rise in *Ceddo*.

The social group of the *ceddo*, which Sembene opposes to the preachers of Islam, was originally made up of slaves who were used as a warrior elite within Wolof society. This group, known alternatively as *jaami-buur* (literally, slaves to the monarchy), soon became a powerful social force in their own right. During the slave trade, the Wolof monarchy lost its role as arbiter of social disputes and, increasingly, the monarchy (the *garmi*) and the *ceddo* became a disruptive force within Wolof society. Neighbouring states were constantly raided in the search for slaves and other booty, and when all else failed they began to raid their own people. Thus, the era of the slave trade saw the rise of the *garmi* and the *ceddo* through the exploitation of the Wolof peasant (or *baadoolo*), the principal victim of these raids.[46] Therefore, the Wolof peasant grew increasingly distrustful of the traditional system of monarchical power as pillage seemed to become official state policy. This sowed the seeds of the revolt, which would eventually lead to the mass conversions to Islam when the traditional monarchical system was finally destroyed by French colonialism in the late nineteenth century.[47]

Why, therefore, does Sembene paint the *ceddo* as popular resistance figures? The answer would seem to lie in the fact that, despite their brutal treatment of fellow Africans, the *ceddo* were the fiercest opponents to the Islamisation of their country and they remained strongly attached to their fetishist practices. It would thus seem that Sembene seeks to create an amalgam between the oppositional character of the *ceddo* and the figure of the lowly *baadoolo*. As Buuba Babacar Diop has put it: '*Sembène a opté pour un* Ceddo baadoolo' ['Sembene chose a Ceddo baadoolo'].[48] This tampering with history has caught out more than one Western critic who has chosen to taken Sembene's reading of Wolof history at

---

[45] Martin A. Klein examines the relationship of Muslim leaders to slavery in his article, 'Servitude among the Wolof and the Sereer of Senegambia', in *Slavery in Africa: Historical and Anthropological Perspectives*, ed. by Suzanne Miers and Igor Kopytoff (Madison, WI: University of Wisconsin Press, 1977), pp. 343, 350–2. See also Boubacar Barry, *Le Royaume du Waalo, 1659–1859: le Sénégal avant la conquête* (Paris: Maspéro, 1972), pp. 142–7, 215–18. For a clear and concise history of the spread of the Islamic faith within Wolof territory, see Abdoulaye-Bara Diop, *La Société wolof: tradition et changement, les systèmes d'inégalité et de domination* (Paris: Karthala, 1985), pp. 215–62.

[46] Diop, *La Société wolof*, pp. 133–52.

[47] The best account of this turbulent period in Wolof society is Mamadou Diouf's *Le Kajoor au XIXe siècle: Pouvoir ceddo et conquête coloniale* (Paris: Karthala, 1990). See also Martin A. Klein, 'Servitude among the Wolof and Sereer of Senegambia', pp. 335–63.

[48] Buuba Babacar Diop, 'Malaise autour de *Ceddo*', p. 48.

face value. Roger Maria argues that: *'ceux qui étaient désignés par ce nom* [ceddo] *étaient dès le dix-septième siècle – et le film est très explicite sur ce point – les tenants de ce qu'on peut appeler la résistance populaire'* ['as early as the seventeenth century, those who were designated by this name [*ceddo*] – and the film is quite explicit on this point – constituted the forces of popular resistance'].[49] An anonymous critic, who styles himself, 'un patriote sénégalais', discerns much better the ambiguity of Sembene's choice of the *ceddo* as popular resistance heroes. Warning against a tendency within Senegalese Islam itself to cast all 'heathens' as *ceddo*, he argues that *'l'élargissement du terme* ceddo *qui a désigné par la suite* non-musulmans *ne doit pas introduire la confusion* ceddo = *masses populaires'* ['the opening up of the term *ceddo*, which came to mean *non-Muslim*, should not lead us wrongly to believe that *ceddo* refers to the masses'].[50] This particular Senegalese patriot obviously disapproves of Sembene's tampering with historical 'fact'.

No less a figure than the respected Senegalese historian Mamadou Diouf, himself the author of a study of the *ceddo* in the nineteenth century, has defended Sembene's version of Senegalese history as a challenge to the historian to question the manner in which Islamicists are currently attempting to rewrite the history of the region, placing Islam at the heart of a struggle against both injustice and foreign invasion (Diouf makes particular reference to the Islamic appropriation of the figure of Lat Dior). Having addressed the 'telescoping' of history that occurs in the film, Diouf seeks to explain rather than disqualify this process:

> *Ces rétablissements de la 'vérité historique' ne peuvent rien changer à la force et à la vérité du film qui s'est construit sur les ruines de l'histoire nationaliste et des trajectoires politiques centrées sur un clientélisme contrôlé de manière autoritaire par le groupe dirigeant, ses patrons impérialistes et ses alliés, les marabouts confrériques de l'arachide et autres détenteurs de légitimités historico-ethniques. En procédant par inversion, Sembène lance un véritable défi aux historiens, ceux-là même qu'il affuble du titre déshonorant de 'chronophage', reléguant ainsi l'activité historienne à celle de croque-mort, l'associant ainsi à la mort et au refus de l'implication dans les luttes du présent, dans la vie et ses passions et conflits. En bref, l'entreprise humaine où l'histoire est un enjeu.*[51]

These appeals to 'historical truth' do not take away from the force and the truth of the film, which is constructed upon the ruins of nationalist history and a political system based on clientelism. This system is controlled in authoritarian fashion by the ruling party, its imperialist bosses and its allies, the marabouts, who lead the Islamic brotherhoods and control the country's groundnut production. This ruling class legitimises its dominant position through a number of ethno-historical narratives. Sembene argues that, rather than making the past come to life, many historians are mere undertakers who consign the past to the history books and refuse to

---

[49] Roger Maria, '*Ceddo*', *Raison Présente*, 52 (October–December 1979), p. 125.

[50] Un patriote sénégalais S KH SY, '*Ceddo* ou le poids des mystifications en Afrique', *Peuples noirs/Peuples africains*, 2, 12 (November–December 1979), p. 41. One of the most comprehensive critiques of *Ceddo*'s tampering with history is to be found in Jean Copans, 'Entre l'Histoire et les mythes', *L'Afrique littéraire*, 76 (1985), pp. 57–9.

[51] Mamadou Diouf, 'Histoires et actualités dans *Ceddo* d'Ousmane Sembene et *Hyènes* de Djibril Diop Mambety', in Sada Niang, ed., *Littérature et cinéma en Afrique francophone: Ousmane Sembène et Assia Djebar* (Paris: L'Harmattan, 1996), pp. 25–6. For a discussion of the renaissance of Islam in Senegal in the wake of the Iranian revolution of 1979, see Momar Coumba Diop and Mamadou Diouf, *Le Sénégal sous Abdou Diouf* (Paris: Karthala, 1990), pp. 69–81.

become involved in contemporary debates. He presents historians, whom he refers to disparagingly as 'chronophage', with a challenge to engage with the present in their work.

For Diouf, *Ceddo* constitutes an intervention in contemporary Senegalese politics, challenging Islamic versions of history, and putting forward his more pluralist vision of Senegalese history (particularly in his empowerment of women through the character of the Princess Dior).

Sembene himself openly recognises the arbitrary nature of his historical depiction of the *ceddo* but he argues that he is doing this for his own political reasons: *'Je reconnais que ce n'est peut-être pas historique mais c'est ma version!'* ['I admit that the film is not historical but it's *my* version.'][52] In this light, the *ceddo* become yet another example of Sembene's creation of a radical African history which stresses African resistance to domination. The cause of the *ceddo*, who would not give up their culture, and that of the *baadoolo*, who were exploited by their political masters, are linked by Sembene, for whom the term *ceddo* appears to constitute a model of resistance to oppression. Sembene explains his conception of the *ceddo* in the following terms:

> *Le ceddo est un homme de refus. C'est ce refus qui est demeuré à travers les siècles, et qui a donné au mot sa signification. Chez les Ouolofs, les Serères, les Pulars, être ceddo, c'est avoir l'esprit caustique, être jaloux de sa liberté absolue. Etre ceddo, c'est aussi être guerrier: parfois combattant pour des causes justes, parfois mercenaire. Le ceddo n'est ni une ethnie, ni une religion, c'est une manière d'être avec des règles.*[53]

The *ceddo* is a man who refuses to bow. It is this idea of refusal which has been retained down through the centuries and which gives the word its meaning. For the Wolof, the Serer, the Pular, to be a *ceddo* is to maintain a caustic spirit, to be jealous of one's liberty. To be a *ceddo* is also to be a warrior, sometimes fighting for just causes, sometimes as a mercenary. The *ceddo* are neither an ethnic group nor a religion. It's a way of life, with its own rules.

This term of *homme de refus* aptly describes Sembene's oppositional attitude towards all that he perceives as unjust and, indeed, is a term that could be equally applied to figures we have examined earlier in this thesis: the *griot* in *White Genesis*, the blind beggar in *Xala*, the radical female intellectuals Rama in *Xala* and Tioumbé in *L'Harmattan* (in their case, they are *femmes de refus*). Sembene thus uses the *ceddo* as a symbol of defiance and resistance to all forms of domination.[54]

---

[52] Personal interview with the artist at Filmi Doomirew, 30 November 1995 (see Appendix).

[53] Guy Hennebelle, 'Sembène parle de ses films', *L'Afrique littéraire*, 76 (1985), p. 29. Sembene expresses similar views in an interview with Françoise Pfaff, 'Entretien avec Ousmane Sembène: à propos de *Ceddo*', *Positif*, 235 (October 1980), pp. 54–7.

[54] Perhaps the greatest of Sembene's *hommes de refus* is the legendary African warrior Samory Touré, a film of whose life Sembene has been striving to make for at least twenty-five years. Sembene describes Samory's resistance to the French, which lasted from 1882 to 1899:

> *Samory fait partie intégrale de notre histoire. Il n'était pas né de famille royale, mais il a fait des choses qui font dire qu'en Afrique il y a des hommes. Actuellement dans les cours d'histoire, Samory occupe une toute petite place à côté des Galliéni et autres Faidherbe! Même le colonialisme n'a pu effacer son nom en le présentant comme un barbare et une brute sanguinaire.*

> Samory is an integral part of our history. He wasn't of noble birth but his acts proved that there are noble men in Africa. At the moment, Samory is neglected in history classes, given a

Ceddo is a film that presents the struggle for power between different social groups and it represents this struggle as a battle between both opposing discourses and rituals. As with *Emitaï*, the rituals of both the fetishist monarchy and the Islamic preachers are captured by Sembene in painstaking detail. This attention to ritual has led some critics to describe *Ceddo* as Sembene's most *African* film:

> *Sembene Ousmane faisait du cinéma 'à l'occidentale' sur son pays. Avec* Ceddo, *il plonge des racines dans ce pays, son passé, sa culture. Un patrimoine, des rituels, un cérémonial, une tradition s'articulant en une vision naturellement théâtrale, à la fois ethnographique et symbolique, qui n'est pas sans affinités avec le cinéma nôvo brésilien. Un rythme lent, répétitif, insistant, la caractérise, tout à l'opposé des fulgurances du tropicalisme. Et dans ce passé, volontairement mal délimité, Sembene retrouve les sources des aliénations du présent, de la corruption de la bourgeoisie actuelle, des complicités religieuses, des contradictions politiques.*[55]

Sembene Ousmane used to make Western-style films *about* his country. In *Ceddo*, he is rooted *in* his country, his past, his culture. A heritage, a whole set of rituals and ceremonies, a tradition that is expressed through a naturally theatrical vision that is both ethnographic and symbolic, and which bears some traces of the Brazilian *cinema nôvo*. The film is characterised by a slow, repetitive, insistent rhythm that is far removed from the dizzying rhythms of standard 'tropical' depictions of Africa. And within this deliberately unspecified past, Sembene finds the source of today's ills: alienation, the corruption of the bourgeoisie and its religious allies, the contradictions of politics.

I would endorse the opinion that Sembene's cinema engages in a far more complex examination of his themes than the standard label of social realist allows, problematising the structure of his films in a provocative manner. However, I have serious reservations about the argument that suggests that *Ceddo* is more *authentically* African than *Xala* or *Le Mandat/Mandabi*. Is an African film more authentic because it is set in the African past and depicts the rituals and ceremonies of a rural community? As was argued in Chapter Three, Sembene is just as interested in exploring the rituals of urban society as those of rural society. The fact that *Le Mandat* and *Xala* deal with the modern African city cannot be used as proof that they are films *à l'européenne*. It is clear that, from *Le Mandat* onwards, Sembene develops a style that could be argued convincingly to be distinctively African but I do not think that it is helpful or, indeed, accurate to claim that a film is more *authentically African* simply because it deals with the rituals of a rural milieu. It is the attention to ritual and ceremony in itself which appears to be the distinguishing feature of Sembene's films from the late 1960s onwards. Sembene himself affirms his profound interest in ritual:

> *Le rituel est très important. En Europe c'est pratiquemment perdu. Chaque peuple a besoin de ses rituels [...]. Mon peuple se reconnaît dans le rituel. Les Européens ont du mal à le comprendre. Quand on perd ses rites on perd une partie de son âme.*[56]

---

[54] (cont.) minor role after the likes of Galliéni and Faidherbe! Even the colonial period couldn't get rid of him, although he was presented as a barbarous, bloodthirsty beast.

François Prelle, 'Ousmane Sembene à bâtons rompus', *Bingo*, 222 (July 1971), p. 57.

[55] Barthélemy Amenguel, '*Ceddo* de Sembene Ousmane', *Positif*, 195–96 (July–August 1977), p. 83 (emphasis in original).

[56] Personal interview, Filmi Doomireew, Dakar, 30 November 1995 (see Appendix).

Ritual is very important. In Europe, it's virtually been lost. Every people needs its own rituals [...]. My people finds its identity in its rituals but Europeans find this hard to understand. When you lose these rituals, you lose a part of your soul.

At the beginning of the film, it is the rites and ceremonies of the traditional monarchy that occupy centre stage. Many of the opening scenes are shot from the point of view of the people (the *ceddo*, in Sembene's sense of the term), who are standing before the king. Within the shot, the king and his entourage occupy the centre of the screen. However, the monarchy's dominant position appears to be far from secure and is threatened on several fronts. Some of the *ceddo* who have become wary of the steadily growing influence of Islam on the monarchy have taken the king's daughter Princess Dior hostage. Their spokesman, Diogomaye, plants the *samp* (the staff which acts as their symbol) before the king in an act of defiance that marks the *ceddo*'s refusal to convert to Islam (the figure at the top of the *samp* is female, a fact that will prove highly symbolic in light of the Princess's murder of the imam). Marginalised and excluded by their adherence to their values and their religion, the *ceddo* are forced into revolt.

The main threat to the monarchy comes from the representatives of Islam. Throughout this opening sequence, we can observe the imam and his disciples, who are seated to the left of the king and his entourage. This group is seen to have its own set of rituals, as they work their beads and recite their prayers. Gradually, as the film progresses, the imam's challenge to the monarchy grows. Apart from his obvious lack of respect for the king (he persistently refers to him by his name, Demba Waar, rather than by his title), the imam also seeks to transform one of the basic principles of the traditional monarchical system. Declaring that the matrilineal system of succession has been replaced by patrilineal succession, the imam is seen not only to attack the 'traditional' values of the monarchy, but also to relegate women to a lesser rank in society.

The imam's challenge to the monarchy is represented visually as he moves closer to the source of power that is the monarch's throne. This movement towards the source of power gradually progresses until the king dies, off camera, and the imam literally takes his place at the centre of the screen. Launching a *jihad* (the exact word used by him), the imam forces the *ceddo* into submission, murdering those who refuse to convert to Islam. This coup d'état marks the end of the entire traditional way of life: the imam has the pagan fetishes destroyed and, in a long and beautifully filmed scene, the *ceddo* are given Muslim names and have their heads shaved. Islam has taken over the state and the change in regime is marked even in the physical appearance of the people. Of the two Europeans who exist on the fringes of the society, it is the missionary whom the imam has killed, ruling out the spiritual competition from Christianity: the missionary's dream of a vibrant African Church is put on hold (in this dream, he imagines the main protagonists of the film attending and serving at a mass, while, in reality, his own church lies empty). However, the imam is willing to deal with the slave trader, from whom he buys the firearms necessary to take control of the village. Islam may have replaced the traditional monarchy but this will not put an end to the slave trade. The brutal rituals of the slave trader who stamps his slaves with the *fleur de lys*, and who buys goods for mere trinkets, will remain in place. In fact, the presence of the slave trader anticipates a later crisis in African society: the advent of European colonisation at the end of the nineteenth century. However, the Europeans are deliberately cast as marginal figures within the story. It should be noted that neither the missionary nor the slave trader speaks throughout the course of the film: in an inversion of the stereotype of the silent native of colonial cinema, it is the Europeans who are forced to play the role of extras in a story that is concerned with the history of Africa.

Another set of rituals exists outside the site of the village where the main events of the film take place. Within this space, the values of the *ceddo* are shown to reign supreme. The *ceddo* who guards Princess Dior exhibits many of these qualities: in defeating the warriors sent by the king to free his daughter, he displays the *ceddo*'s skill in warfare: *xeex*. Also, by his respectful but firm attitude towards the princess, he displays the values of *teranga* (generosity) and *jom* (pride/honour).[57] However, the *ceddo* is finally defeated by two men sent by the imam (who has no time for the question of honour involved in single combat) and it seems as though the last resistance of the *ceddo* has been overcome. Despite this defeat, the values of the *ceddo* are not dead as is shown by Princess Dior who, on her return to the village, shoots the imam (her act could be read as the revenge of the *samp*, which the imam burns before his coup d'état). Won over by the pride and honour of her *ceddo* captor, she rallies to his cause, and the film ends with her act of defiance. The *ceddo* who had been increasingly pushed to the margins of society in the film are shown by this scene to remain a force within Wolof society, and their values will not be so easily excluded by Islam. The Princess's actions, far from being an isolated act, must be seen symbolically in the light of the destitution of an entire people that we have witnessed in the rest of the film. The critic Serge Daney has described the film as combining two stories, the first being that of the people, and the second being that of the Princess:

> *Sembene [...] enlace les deux récits sans jamais les confondre, maintient la distance entre le récit de la résistance et la fiction de la révolte, entre le peuple et ses héros, entre le collectif et l'individuel, entre l'archéologie et la convention. En bon marxiste, il fait dépendre la prise de conscience individuelle de la résistance collective. Bref, la princesse n'est pas Zorro.*[58]

Sembene interweaves two stories without ever confusing them. He maintains a clear distance between the tale of resistance and the fiction of the revolt, between the people and their heroes, between the group and the individual, between archeology [of the people's history] and convention. As a good Marxist, Sembene depicts the awakening of the individual's conscience as an element of popular resistance. In other words, the princess is not Zorro.

The death of the imam cannot be seen as paving the way for the restoration of the traditional monarchy. Princess Dior does not take her father's place on the throne: instead, the film closes with a freeze-frame of her walking away from

---

[57] For a brief discussion of the Islamic and *ceddo* value systems, see Kesteloot and Dieng, *Du Tieddo au talibé*, pp. 5–15.

[58] Serge Dancy, '*Ceddo* (O. Sembene)', *Cahiers du Cinéma*, 304 (October 1979), p. 53.

the scene of the murder. The spectator is simply left to ponder on the questions that the film has raised about religion, power and the role of women.

Although the film is chiefly interested in exploring ritual, one of the main rituals examined in the film is primarily verbal. When the king addresses his people, he speaks through the *gewel* (a term largely synonymous with *griot*) Jaraaf because as monarch he cannot speak directly to his inferiors. This tradition is known as *jottali* – an indirect, formal type of communication that results in a very elaborate, ceremonial language. All public discourse passes through Jaraaf who elaborately reports both the language of the king and his interlocutor. The use of this device is a deliberate ploy by Sembene in his depiction of the clash between Islam and the *ceddo*. Mbye Boubacar Cham discusses the use of *jottali* in the following terms:

> Hence the consistently lofty and elaborate language in *Ceddo*, a language that is highly stylised and heavily laden with a wide variety of Wolof proverbs, praises (*tagg*), metaphors, and poetic devices, all of which combine to heighten dramatic tension, underscore contradictions, betray ulterior motives, and, most of all, expressively spell out the determination of and the nature of the clash between the two main conflicting forces in the society – forces of religious and political domination and the forces of resistance against domination.[59]

Jaraaf is not impartial: he lets his opinions be known in his addresses and it is clear that he is opposed to the *ceddo*. However, despite this antipathy towards the *ceddo*, he finds himself removed from his position after the imam's coup d'état (the imam also dismisses the other nobles who had helped him gain power). The tradition of *jottali* is maintained but the imam places one of his own disciples in the post. From this point onwards, all messages given by the *gewel* have a religious bearing.

As we saw in *White Genesis*, control of public discourse becomes a vital element in winning and maintaining power. The imam's coup d'état not only marks the introduction of a theocratic regime, it also marks the passage from an oral society to a society based on the rules and regulations of a single book: the Koran. This sacred text is seen throughout the film placed on the ground before the imam and it beomes the source of all the messages relayed by the new *gewel*. Serge Daney has stressed the importance of this shift within the film. While recognising the importance of ritual, he argues that the film is primarily concerned with uncovering a lost African discourse:

> *Récit d'un putsch avec intrusion du religieux dans le politique, passage d'un type de pouvoir à un autre, théocratique,* Ceddo *est aussi l'histoire d'un droit qui se perd: le droit de* parler. *Un droit mais aussi un devoir, un devoir mais aussi un plaisir, un jeu. Si l'imam gagne, ce n'est pas parce qu'il y a beaucoup de bonnes raisons socio-économiques à l'islamisation de la région, c'est parce qu'il introduit un élément au contact duquel les structures du pouvoir africain traditionnel vont imploser – et cet élément, c'est un livre, un livre qu'on récite. Entre le début et la fin du film, c'est le statut de la parole qui a changé. Au début, il est clair que nous sommes dans un monde où l'on* ne ment pas, *où toute parole, n'ayant d'autre garant que celui qui la profère, est 'd'honneur'. C'est comme si, lorsqu'il filmait ce peuple qui va être réduit au silence, Sembene tenait d'abord à*

[59] Mbye Boubacar Cham, 'Ousmane Sembene and the Aesthetics of African Oral Traditions', *Africana Journal*, 13, 1–4 (1982), p. 36.

182

lui restituer son bien le plus précieux: sa parole. Calcul tout ce qu'il y a de plus politique.[60]

Ceddo tells the tale of a putsch in which religion enters the political arena and brings about a change to a theocratic regime. *Ceddo* is also the story of a right which is being lost: the right to *speak*. A right that is also an obligation. An obligation that is also a source of pleasure, a game. The imam does not win because there are a lot of sound socio-economic reasons for the Islamisation of the region, but rather because he introduces a new element into society, which will bring about the implosion of traditional power structures – and this new element is a book, one that is *recited*. Between the start and the end of the film, it is the status of the spoken word that has changed. At the beginning, it is clear that we are in a world *where one does not lie*, where every word is guaranteed by the 'honour' of the person who proffers it. In filming this people who will be reduced to silence, it seems as though Sembene was interested in giving them back their most precious possession: their words. No gesture could be more political.

Effectively, Daney argues that Sembene seeks to depict the values held by an oral society. Rather than the tabula rasa, which Europe imagined in Africa before their discovery of the continent, or the pagan savagery described by many Islamic historians, traditional African society is presented as a valid and vibrant culture in its own right. It may not have been a perfect culture but it did not deserve the fate that was to befall it. One of the most important scenes in the film shows the *ceddo* hold a debate outside the village square where they discuss the threat to their way of life posed by the imam's increasing power over the monarch (Sembene himself plays one of the *ceddo* in this scene, so placing himself visually and verbally on the side of their cause[61]). After a long debate in which the values of their society are constantly evoked, they decide that they must make a stand against the power of Islam: it is this right to speak, to voice dissent, which will be lost once public discourse has become controlled by the dictates of the imam and his sacred book. Therefore, it is highly significant that the *ceddo* warrior's sole companion as he guards the princess is the *griot*, Seneen. It is he who will record the resistance of the *ceddo* and pass on this message of defiance to future generations (Sembene once again casts himself as a modern-day *griot* in telling his tale).

The film's concern with language and culture is also explored through an unusual use of music. The soundtrack was written by the renowned Cameroonian jazz musician Manu Dibango. The use of free jazz in a film about seventeenth-century Senegal has left some critics perplexed, wondering why a more traditional form of African music was not used (traditional African instruments, including the *balafon*, a type of xylophone, are in fact used at

---

[60] Daney, '*Ceddo* (O. Sembene)', pp. 51–2 (emphasis in original). As with anthropological literature, the cinematic representation of 'traditional' African societies has neglected the spoken word in favour of the depiction of rituals and dances. For an example of these archetypal images of Africa, see Pierre-L. Jordan, *Cinéma, Cinema, Kino* (Marseille: Musées de Marseille/ Images en Manœuvres Editions, 1992).

[61] It would appear that Sembene's decision to play one of the *ceddo* was also the result of more pragmatic considerations. He claims that it was necessary for him to have his head and beard shaved in the conversion scene in order to set an example for the villagers who were due to meet the same fate. See Pfaff, 'Entretien avec Ousmane Sembène', p. 156.

certain points in the film).[62] However, Sembene is deliberately seeking to evoke the black diaspora in the Americas by the use of this music in order to present another consequence of the downfall of the traditional African societies, when so many millions were brought from Africa into slavery. This sense of continuity between the suffering of the slaves and the downfall of the *ceddo* is most powerfully communicated in the scenes where we see the slaves being branded, while on the soundtrack we can hear a gospel tune (sung by the American group, the Godspells). Gospel music is closely associated with the black American community and the lyrics usually represent a spiritual resistance to the suffering of that community. These slaves will give birth to a black American culture, directly related to that of the *ceddo*, which will become centred around music and dance, which survived when so many other elements of *ceddo* culture were lost. Serge Daney has discussed the consequences of this '*tour de passe-passe entre le futur antérieur et le passé antérieur*' ['constant shifting from the future anterior to the past anterior'] within the film in the following terms:

Une chose est de percevoir dans la musique des opprimés l'expression et le reflet de cette oppression, une autre est d'arriver un jour à se poser la question: mais avant d'être condamnés à chanter leur condition, qu'est-ce qu'ils disaient? Et comment le disaient-ils? Le film de Sembene Ousmane hasarde une réponse, mais surtout permet de poser la question. Cela suffit à en faire un très grand film.[63]

It is one thing to perceive the music of the oppressed as an expression and a reflection of that oppression. It is quite another to ask oneself the question: before being condemned to sing their condition, what were they saying? And how did they say it? Sembene Ousmane's film hazards a response but more significantly it allows the question to be asked. That alone makes it a very great film.

Music is the major form of African culture that has survived the recent centuries of turbulence on the continent but what of all those elements which were lost: language, power, ritual, religion? These exist within music but that is no compensation for the loss of these vital cultural components. The power of Sembene's film is that he seeks to imagine that which was lost to Islam and Europe and, in so doing, he gives voice to a culture so often denied the very status of culture.

■ ■ ■

Emitaï and *Camp de Thiaroye* are both important films that seek to uncover the violence of French imperialism within Africa, while at the same time seeking to understand some of the failings of those African societies in their opposition to colonialism. However, *Ceddo* is a film which attempts to investigate the precise nature of the loss involved when one form of culture is oppressed and dominated by another. Sembene does not seek to demonise Islam, the main focus of his film, but rather to examine how the rise of an Islamic culture in black Africa dealt with the existing religious and cultural

---

[62] Un patriote sénégalais, '*Ceddo* ou le poids des mystifications en Afrique', pp. 37–46.
[63] Daney, '*Ceddo* (O. Sembene)', p. 53.

practices that it found in place. Islam is currently the dominant religion within Senegal and, as we have shown earlier, this situation lends itself to the argument that Islam *is* and therefore always *will be* the religion of the Senegalese state. Sembene counters such essentialist arguments that link the nation to any one religion, and historicises Islam's rise in Senegal. For Sembene, colonialism is a question of social and cultural domination and Islam, in this respect, is just as culpable as Europe. To paraphrase one of the key questions from Césaire's *Discourse on Colonialism* (quoted in Chapter One): is colonialism the best means of establishing a cultural dialogue? The response of both Sembene and Césaire is a resounding 'no'.

As was argued at the beginning of this chapter, Sembene sets about dismembering the discourse of empire (both Islamic and European), challenging its claims to authority. At the same time, he sets about re-membering resistance, seeking to intervene on behalf of those who are silenced or marginalised by the imperial discourse. If history is written by the winners, Sembene declares himself the champion of those who lose out in the process of social and cultural domination that is involved in any form of colonisation. He does not pretend to have unmediated contact with the pre-Islamic/pre-European African world, nor does he make himself the defender of 'traditional' African values (indeed, he problematises the very stereotype of such values). Instead, he uses his art to represent the resistance of Africans to all forms of domination. The cinema is perhaps a medium that lends itself to the act of 're-membering', as the spectator is obliged to recall events that occurred earlier in the story, not having the luxury of being able to flick back and forth across the pages of a book in the manner of the reader of a novel (this situation has been of course slightly altered by the advent of the home video recorder but the fact remains that most filmmakers outside the Hollywood system direct their films with a cinema audience in mind). The three films use visual motifs to capture a sense of what is being repressed by colonialism: the Diola prostrating themselves before their fetishes (*Emitaï*); the distinctive rituals of the *ceddo* and the traditional monarchy (*Ceddo*); and the image of Pays in his SS helmet, symbolising both the suffering and the resistance of an entire continent (*Camp de Thiaroye*). However, as Serge Daney argues in relation to *Ceddo*, Sembene is not merely interested in presenting images of what colonialism destroyed. He also seeks to uncover the voices of resistance to colonialism within these societies, allowing his characters to speak out against the injustices perpetrated in the name of empire. In these three films, Sembene creates an alternative history of colonialism to the one proposed by the discourse of empire, revealing the conflict and resistance that had effectively been erased from the coloniser's accounts. His art becomes an act of resistance in the struggle for the memory of colonialism.

7
Absence & Power

The Hollow Centre of the Neo-Colonial Order in
The Last of the Empire & Guelwaar

In the previous chapter, we examined the various processes by which Sembene challenges the coloniser's version of the empire, unearthing the violence and domination usually occulted by a legitimating discourse that seeks to sanitise the more unsavoury aspects of the colonial project. In each of the three films examined, Sembene deliberately focuses on hidden acts of colonial violence, which he interprets as being representative of the true nature of the colonial situation. However, the accession to independence by all of France's sub-Saharan African colonies between 1958 and 1960 and the liberation of the rest of the continent from British, Belgian, Portuguese and Spanish rule has not ended the West's domination of Africa. After the initial euphoria of the 1960s, the 1970s saw a realisation that living standards had not improved (if anything they had deteriorated) and that Africa, despite having freed itself from direct European political tutelage, had become increasingly dependent economically on the West. The exact nature of what has become known as the neo-colonial relationship between Africa and the West has been the subject of a widespread debate between historians, economists and sociologists (this debate will be addressed in greater detail below). However, what all sides will admit, is that there remains a general popular perception in Africa and, at least until the 1980s in certain intellectual circles in the West, that the real governments of African states are not to be found in places such as Dakar, Brazzaville and Abidjan but rather in Paris, Bonn and Washington.[1]

---

[1] For a brief account of the process of decolonisation, see David Birmingham, *The Decolonization of Africa* (London: University of London College Press, 1995) and Muriel Evelyn Chamberlain, *Decolonization: The Fall of the European Empires* (Oxford: Basil Blackwell, 1985). A more detailed analysis of the troubled issues concerning the transfer of power from Europe to Africa is to be found in Prosser Gifford and Wm. Roger Louis, eds, *Decolonization and African Independence: The Transfers of Power* (New Haven, CT, and London: Yale University Press, 1982).

Given the extent of the suspicions surrounding the nature of government in postcolonial Africa, it is hardly surprising that, in the two works by Sembene which focus most directly on the neo-colonial situation, the questions of absence and power are explicitly linked. In his 1981 novel, *The Last of the Empire*, we see a power vacuum develop as an autocratic head of state goes missing, leaving his unelected technocratic ministers to fight it out for his succession. All power within the state is seen to devolve from one man who is portrayed as ruling the country on behalf of the former colonial power in exactly the same manner as the governors-general of the colonial era. The novel thus describes the disappearance of both an individual and the source of all power in the state. The investigation of absence and power is worked out rather differently in Sembene's 1992 film *Guelwaar*. A dissident who speaks out against Africa's dependency on the West for financial handouts dies in murky circumstances, beaten to death by unnamed assailants (recalling the similar fate which was met by Oumar Faye, in *O Pays, mon beau peuple!*). On the day of the burial, the body is found to have gone missing. The film thus presents us not only with a search for the dissident's body but also with a search to unearth the radical discourse that had so threatened the nebulous forces of the neo-colonial regime that they had him killed.

It has been remarked by most critics that African writers have grown increasingly disillusioned after the optimism of the 1950s and 1960s. The relatively clear-cut issues of the nationalist struggle for independence were replaced by the seemingly intractable social questions facing the liberated continent. Hopes for a better future in an independent Africa soon gave way to an extreme pessimism with the manner in which events were unfolding. One-party states, military regimes, corruption, tribalism and an ever-spiralling debt gradually began to appear to be the fate awaiting all of Africa. The respected French critic Jacques Chevrier has noted that most writers responded to this situation with either extreme pessimism or by means of an escape through the imagination. This new generation of African writers is more concerned with formal experimentation, their multiple narratives acting as a reflection of a confused and polyphonic world. While remaining revolutionary in ideology, these writers do not address political questions in an explicit manner, seeking rather to effect a change in the way in which the reader imagines the world. As Chevrier has put it: '*A une écriture de la politique succède une politique de l'écriture*' ['Political writing has given way to a writing policy'].[2]

Sembene, however, has rejected the path chosen by the likes of Sony Labou Tansi and Williams Sassine in their phantasmagoric narratives of political despotism and crushed rebellions.[3] He remains resolutely committed to his Marxist ideals and his work has continued to address, in a more or less direct manner, the political and social questions facing modern Africa. It

[2] Jacques Chevrier, 'Roman africain: le temps du doute et des incertitudes', *Jeune Afrique*, 1 March 1989, p. 64.

[3] Sony Labou Tansi, *La Vie et demie* (Paris: Seuil, 1979). Williams Sassine, *Le Jeune homme de sable* (Paris: Présence Africaine, 1979).

would seem that neither the fall of the Soviet Union and its satellite states in Eastern Europe nor the failure of several attempts at constructing 'socialist' regimes in a number of African countries has dampened Sembene's enthusiasm for the Marxist cause. In this respect, *The Last of the Empire* and *Guelwaar* are of special interest to us as they actually seek to propose solutions to the problems facing postcolonial Africa. As has become clear in the course of our argument throughout this study, Sembene usually examines such issues through the prism of an individual consciousness that is seen to be representative of a more general condition. *The Last of the Empire* and *Guelwaar* are thus more explicitly political in their attack on the neo-colonial system than most of the texts we have previously examined (similarly, *God's Bits of Wood* and *L'Harmattan* are explicitly political considerations of the colonial era) but just how valid are Sembene's critiques of the neo-colonial order, and also how plausible is his vision of the means of escaping the current social and economic impasse in which Africa finds itself?

While both *The Last of the Empire* and *Guelwaar* deal with the politics of neo-colonialism, they are very different in terms of their analysis of the subject. *The Last of the Empire* is principally concerned with the means by which the former colonial power manages to maintain its dominant position within the former colonised state. Broadly sharing the approach of the *third worldist* school (although with some major differences, as we shall see below), which saw African independence as a complete sham, merely serving to camouflage the West's continuing rape of the African continent, Sembene describes a situation where the French are seen to control African politics through their political and military advisors to the government (we saw the same process at work in *Xala* when the French businessmen were removed from the Chamber of Commerce by the nationalists, only to return in an equally powerful but less prominent position). In *Guelwaar*, the focus has shifted from shady links with the former colonial power to an examination of the failure of African governments to offer a coherent programme of economic development to their people. In fact, their only policy appears to be to extract as much aid as possible from the West. The French are no longer seen to be a major force in the control of Senegalese affairs, but rather than this leading to a truly independent African political landscape we are presented with the vision of an Africa dependent on the charity of the West as a whole.

There are a number of reasons behind this shift in emphasis between the two works. Perhaps the most significant of these reasons has to do with the particular history of Senegal and, even more particularly, with the person of its poet-president Léopold Sédar Senghor. We will examine the nature of Senghor's thirty-year reign over Senegalese politics below (this period includes the 1950s, a decade during which Senghor and his party, the Bloc Démocratique Sénégalais, dominated pre-independence politics). However, before going any further, it is necessary to understand the arguments of the *third worldist* school that dominated most discussion of postcolonial politics from independence to the early 1980s. This school of thought was primarily driven by Marxist economists and historians and one can easily recognise many of its arguments in Sembene's writings, although, as I aim to prove, neither the *third worldists* nor Sembene were as schematic in their arguments as many recent critics of their ideas would lead us to believe.

The principal argument of the *third worldists* that African independence was a mere prelude to a different form of economic and political dependence upon the West was elaborated within years of the wave of African independences around 1960 (this 'dependency theory' of the *third worldists* had originally been applied to Latin America and was then directed towards former African and Asian colonies, a fact that many critics have raised in highlighting the tendency of *third worldism* to forget specifics and over-generalise). In one of the most famous *third worldist* texts, as early as 1962, René Dumont was to proclaim that there had been a *False Start in Africa*.[4] Over the next twenty years, works describing the means by which the West was continuing to subjugate Africa proliferated.[5] One of the best known and most influential *third worldist* texts was written by Tibor Mende who had been a highly placed UN official, and whose brief had been to establish the means of overcoming the economic problems facing underdeveloped countries. After he left this post at the end of 1971, Mende wrote a book with the highly significant title of *From Aid to Recolonization*, which set out his ideas on the relationship between the rich countries of the North and the underdeveloped countries of the South (this North-South paradigm has increasingly come to replace the former contrast between the West and the East):

> Out of a mass of economic, social, and technological changes a totally new system is emerging. It imposes new modes of social behaviour. It shapes its own set of new values. It begins to amount to a new culture. But, in the meantime, the Southern Hemisphere, by and large, has remained locked in its struggle to enter its first industrial revolution. This way, the psychocultural distance between the welfare units of the North Temperate Zone and of the materially backward countries of the Southern Hemisphere has been acquiring a new meaning. It is expressed less in calories or in per capita incomes than by an ever deeper grievance fed by the sense of humiliation caused by dependence and blocked horizons – a far more formidable barrier to communications than the mere material gap. This distance separating the familiar and the uncertain steadily broadens.[6]

The recurrent image in Mende's and other *third worldist* texts is of the underdeveloped world, helpless to protect itself against the predatory instincts of the developed world.

This tendency to stress the passiveness of the Third World in its relationship with the developed world has been criticised by many recent observers. In his *The State in Africa: the Politics of the Belly*, Jean-François Bayart has argued

---

[4] René Dumont, *False Start in Africa*, trans. by Phyllis Nauts Ott (London: Deutsch, 1966).
[5] Some of the key *third worldist* texts include another important work by René Dumont: *Pour l'Afrique, j'accuse: journal d'un agronome au Sahel en voie de destruction* (Paris: Presses Pocket, 1986). See also Samir Amin, *Accumulation on a World Scale: a critique of the Theory of Underdevelopment*, trans. by Brian Pearce (New York and London: Monthly Review Press, 1974) and his *L'Afrique de l'ouest bloquée* (Paris: Editions de Minuit, 1971); Immanuel Wallerstein, *The Capitalist World-Economy* (Cambridge: Cambridge University Press, 1979).
[6] Tibor Mende, *From Aid to Recolonization: Lessons of a Failure* (London: Harrap, 1973), pp. xiii–xiv.

that the *third worldist* school, by looking at African history and society uniquely in terms of their relationship with Europe, does not do justice to the true 'historicity' of African societies. For Bayart, the *third worldists* see no internal African political and social dynamics that exist independently of European influence.[7] Another argument (closely linked to the first), which is used to counter the *third worldists*, is that their Marxist interpretations of African society were wildly off the mark. *Third Worldism* was essentially a Marxist phenomenon that saw Fanon's *The Wretched of the Earth* as one of its founding texts. The messianic Marxist message of Fanon's impassioned outcry against colonialism became a *leitmotif* for virtually all *third worldist* writers. Accepting Fanon's analysis of the FLN's struggle against the French in Algeria as the beginning of a social revolution, *third worldist* writers continually evoked the image of a radical Third World peasantry and proletariat which were about to bring down the neo-colonial regimes that were effectively seen as ruling Africa on behalf of the Western powers.[8] It was already argued in Chapter Two that the revolutionary potential seen by many Marxists (including Sembene) in the African independence movements proved to be an illusion. Critics of the *third worldists* have interpreted these Marxist readings of African history as further proof of their lack of engagement with the dynamics of African society.

Despite the validity of many of the criticisms advanced against *third worldism*, I would agree with Axelle Kabou in arguing that completely to dismiss this work is to lose a vital framework within which to examine the very real means by which the West continues to dominate the Third World.[9] Even within the *third worldist* school itself, there was an awareness by the mid-1970s that its revolutionary analyses of the 1960s had been over-optimistic. The Marxist Gérard Chaliand, often associated with *third worldist* thinking, sought to demystify the notion of a revolutionary Third World in his book, *Revolution in the Third World: Myths and Prospects* (1976):

> The revolutionary potential of the Third World had been overestimated, and too much importance was assigned to the possible role of revolutionary ideology, without always evaluating just what sort of society the ideology was to be grafted onto and under what circumstances. The ideology spread by an active minority is of prime importance, but it is wrong to shrink from acknowledging the importance of the historical and cultural texture of a society, which conditions much of its behaviour and attitudes.[10]

Rejecting vulgar Marxist interpretations of African history, Chaliand calls for an approach that tries to adapt Marxist principles to African realities rather than fitting the reality to the ideology. The present study has consistently argued that such an approach has been advocated by Sembene throughout his

[7] Jean-François Bayart, *The State in Africa: the Politics of the Belly* (London: Longman, 1993).

[8] For a critical analysis of Fanon's messianic Marxism, see Gérard Chaliand's introduction to the recent Folio edition of *Les Damnés de la terre*. Gérard Chaliand, 'Frantz Fanon à l'épreuve du temps', in Fanon, *Les Damnés de la terre* (1961; Paris: Gallimard, Collection Folio, 1991), pp. 7–36.

[9] See Axelle Kabou, *Et si l'Afrique refusait le développement?* (Paris: L'Harmattan, 1991), pp. 46–54.

[10] Gérard Chaliand, *Revolution in the Third World: Myths and Prospects* (Hassocks, Sussex: The Harvester Press, 1977), pp. 185–6.

career. He believes that Marxism must earn its universal credentials by proving it can find solutions to African problems. This idea of an open, undogmatic Marxism is expressed by another Senegalese Marxist Amady Aly Dieng (who is listed in *The Last of the Empire* as a resistance figure to be rated alongside Fanon and Cabral as a guru for modern African youth[11]):

Le marxisme est une science inachevée; il demande à être enrichi à la lumière des données nouvelles de notre monde. Il exige une synthèse nouvelle, car l'histoire se déroule à une allure vertigineuse. Des événements de grande portée comme le développement extraordinaire des techniques et des sciences, des mouvements de libération nationale en Asie et en Afrique où les difficiles problèmes de la construction du socialisme posent des problèmes inédits auxquels le marxisme doit répondre. C'est à ce prix seulement qu'il fera la preuve de son caractère universel.[12]

Marxism is an incomplete science that needs to be reviewed in the light of developments within the modern world. It requires a new synthesis as history is unfolding at an alarming rate. We are witnessing hugely significant events such as the extraordinary developments in science and technology, the national liberation movements in Asia and Africa where the difficult problems facing the construction of socialism pose unheard of problems that Marxism must resolve. It is only once such a task of reassessment has been carried out that Marxism can prove its universal credentials.

There have been several attempts at founding socialist regimes in independent Africa. In *The Last of the Empire*, the names of a number of militant African leaders, who proclaimed socialist values, appear on several occasions as figures to inspire change in modern Africa: Kwame N'Krumah of Ghana, Sékou Touré of Guinea, Modibo Keïta of Mali, Julius Nyerere of Tanzania, are just some of the names mentioned. However, none of these heads of state was able to found viable socialist states.[13] Even Nyerere's Tanzania, which was for a long time held up as a shining example of African socialism, began to come under heavy criticism from observers towards the end of the 1970s, as it became clear that the notion of *ujamaa*, or village socialism, was far from the success that earlier reports had suggested. In one of the most influential and comprehensive accounts of Tanzanian socialism, Goran Hyden has argued that Nyerere's state proved itself as incapable as other African states in its attempts to 'capture' the peasantry, which remained a virtually autonomous force, existing largely outside the state sector.[14] This inability to 'capture' all the

---

[11] Ousmane Sembene, *The Last of the Empire*, trans. by Adrian Adams (London: Heinemann, 1983), p. 155. Further refernces to this novel (hereafter *LE*) will be given in the body of the text.

[12] Amady Aly Dieng, *Hegel, Marx, Engels et les problèmes de l'Afrique noire* (Dakar: Sankoré, 1978), p. 38.

[13] For a discussion of the regimes set in place by N'Krumah, Touré and Keïta, see Chaliand, *Revolution in the Third World*, pp. 111–17.

[14] See Goran Hyden, *Beyond Ujamaa in Tanzania: Underdevelopment and an Uncaptured Peasantry* (London: Heinemann, 1980). Hyden's analysis of African peasant societies is highly revealing and helps to examine more clearly the relationship between the capitalist economy and the peasant mode of production. He argues that his criticism of socialist failures in Tanzania is designed to pave the way for a socialism that will be capable of responding to the complexities of the African situation. While I do not wish to deny the significance of Hyden's findings, I believe that he romanticises the African peasantry to an alarming extent. In his introduction, he claims that in the West 'we have lost the sense of the ultimate meaning of life [...]. In the eyes

forces within society, to convince them of the necessity of a fundamental transformation in social relations, has proven to be beyond the means of socialist (and other) regimes in Africa.

Whatever about the failings of the attempts by figures such as Julius Nyerere and Modibo Keïta to establish socialist regimes, there have been many more African regimes that have proclaimed themselves 'socialist' without displaying any signs of left-wing leanings. For many of the regimes that took over the reins of power in the 1960s, a declaration of socialist aspirations was simply a means of defusing criticism of their lack of coherent social programmes. Gérard Chaliand has described this process in the following terms:

> The term *socialism* has been widely abused – especially where the notion of socialism had only recently penetrated countries where the demands, or at least the yearnings, for social justice were widespread. There, proclaiming their intention to create a more egalitarian society was simply one way for the new ruling team to gain popular support.[15]

Chaliand argues that the anti-imperialist nationalist movements that came to power upon African independence had been united only by their opposition to the empire. Internal social problems within African society were overlooked as Africans fought their common enemy. However, to the dismay of those on the left of the independence movement, it transpired that the nationalists had no intention of facing up to such social problems, and were keen to maintain the image of a unified, classless nation that had proved so powerful during the drive for independence. The most ironic aspect of many of these blatantly nationalist governments claiming themselves to be practising 'scientific socialism' or its variant, 'African socialism', is that the class struggle, the key principle of Marxist-Leninist philosophy, is totally absent from their thinking. As Communism reached Africa in the aftermath of World War Two, it was by that stage in its Stalinist mode, and most African 'socialists' appear to have interpreted socialism as the construction of an all-powerful state sector, with the domination of a single party, and especially of its leader, the father of the nation.

Senghor's Senegal was a prime example of a nationalist-led state that proclaimed itself to represent 'African socialism' (Senghor's political philosophy is contained in volumes 2 and 4 of his *Liberté* series of books[16]). We saw in Chapter One how the editor of *Dakar-Matin* (now *Le Soleil*), the newspaper of the ruling Parti Socialiste (then the Union Progressiste Sénégalaise), criticised Sembene's film *Le Mandat/Mandabi* for its negative approach in addressing

---

[14] (cont.) of people of pre-modern societies we are socially handicapped. We are not sensitive and responsive to the same full range of human values as they are' (p. 2). Such idealisation of pre-modern societies is as problematic as the Western ethnocentrism that he is so keen to denounce. For another view of the socialist experiment in Tanzania, see Andrew Coulson, ed., *African Socialism in Practice: The Tanzanian Experience* (Nottingham: Spokesman Books, 1979).

[15] Chaliand, *Revolution in the Third World*, pp. 101–2.

[16] See Senghor's *Liberté 2: Nation et voie africaine du socialisme*; *Liberté 4: Socialisme et planification* (Paris: Seuil, 1983). Volumes 1, 3 and 5 of Senghor's collected essays and speeches deal with cultural issues.

issues of social conflict. It was argued that the role of all decent Senegalese patriots, especially the artist, was to help in the arduous process of nation-building. Such a belief presents the nation as a single entity with a common set of goals and aspirations. The interests of the wealthy government official, the lowly peasant and the unemployed urban youth are all shown to be subsumed into the greater interests of the nation where all conflict miraculously disappears.

In May/June 1968, Senegal was paralysed by a wave of social protest led by university students and the trade unions, which had grown increasingly frustrated at the country's declining economic fortunes. Senegal had been a de facto one-party state for a number of years as opposition parties were either outlawed or integrated into the ruling party, so for many the 1968 riots were the result of an anger that could find no legitimate political outlet. The crisis was finally defused in mid-June and, on 14 June, Senghor addressed the nation in a speech which left no doubt about the nature of his regime:

> *Le problème le plus grave qui se pose aujourd'hui, à nous, est celui de notre indépendance nationale, dont le maintien, voire la consolidation conditionne la solution efficace de tous les problèmes. Or, cette indépendance est brutalement menacée. Les pillages et incendies du 31 mai, la fabrication de bombes à la nitroglycérine à la Faculté des Sciences, tout cela n'est pas 'sénégalais', tout cela est marqué du sceau de l'impérialisme étranger.*
>
> *[...] L'essentiel est que, devant les périls qui menacent la Nation, qui menacent notre indépendance, nous nous cherchions, nous dialoguions, nous aboutissions à un accord conciliant – dans l'établissement de la justice sociale, le maintien des libertés publiques, mais aussi de* l'autorité de *l'Etat. En un mot, nous devons poursuivre la Révolution que nous avons commencée en 1945-46. Nous devons agir au lieu d'être agis. Agir par nous-mêmes, pleinement Sénégalais, et pour nous-mêmes, Sénégalais, et non pour être agis par Sénégalais interposés et pour le nouvel impérialisme, étranger à l'Afrique. Je dis: Agir pour que Vive le Sénégal!* [17]

Today, the most serious problem facing us is that of our national independence, of which the safeguarding, not to say the consolidation, sets the conditions for a genuine solution to all our problems. At the moment, this independence is under a savage threat. The pillage and arson of 31 May, the construction of nitroglycerine bombs in the Science Faculty, that is not 'Senegalese'. Such behaviour is marked with the seal of foreign imperialism.

[...] In the face of all these dangers threatening the Nation, threatening our independence, it is essential that we look to each other, that we engage in a dialogue, that we come to an agreement that will reconcile our differences – in establishing social justice, in maintaining public freedom, but also in maintaining the *authority of the State*. Basically, we must continue the Revolution we began in 1945-46.

---

[17] *Dakar Matin* (14 June 1968). Quoted in Abdoulaye Bathily, *Mai 68 à Dakar ou la révolte universitaire et la démocratie* (Paris: Editions Chaka, 1992), pp. 99–100 (my emphasis). It is both ironic and highly significant that this speech does not figure in Senghor's collection of political speeches and essays from the period 1960–73. In fact, none of Senghor's speeches from that most troubled year in post-independence Senegalese history appear in the book. The sole references to the events of May/June 1968 are to be found in a speech to the students at the University of Dakar from September 1969 in which Senghor stresses the achievements of his government in the educational sector. See Léopold Sédar Senghor, *Liberté 4: Socialisme et planification*, pp. 386–96. As one might expect from a politician, Senghor seeks to present his reign as an almost totally positive and trouble-free time in his country's history.

We must be actors rather than victims. We must act by ourselves and for ourselves, in our full capacity as Senegalese. We must not be the victims of the actions of Senegalese acting on behalf of a new imperialism, foreign to Africa. I say: Let us Act so that Senegal Will Survive!

For Senghor, the nation stands above all other considerations. The rioting of the students is argued to be a profound attack on the very existence of that nation. To act in such a manner is to be literally 'unSenegalese', to place oneself outside the great family of the nation (one could equally ask the question of Senghor whether the government's decision to call out its troops as well as the French intervention force stationed just outside Dakar was a very *Senegalese* action). Senghor, therefore, comes to the conclusion that the students are acting under the influence of a foreign ideology which, although he does not name it directly, is clearly that of communism.[18] In effect, the students are accused of merely aping the student protests that had taken place in France in May 1968.

In contrast to the *foreign* revolution imported by the students, Senghor argues that the true Senegalese revolution is independence itself. He claims that the path followed by the founders of the state, from World War Two to 1968, is that of true independence from France (many of the student and trade union protests focused on the dominant role that France continued to play in the Senegalese administration and economy after almost a decade of independence). However, as many commentators have pointed out, Senghor was a very late convert to the whole notion of independence from France, as he had favoured a close-knit confederation of African states with France right up until the collapse of the Mali federation in 1960.[19] In fact, rather than constituting a break with France, Senegalese independence is remarkable primarily for the continuity between the colonial and postcolonial regimes. Boubacar Barry explicitly links this process to the person of Senghor himself:

> A tireless defender of blackness, Senghor also believed deeply in France's genius and its civilising mission in Africa. He believed in this model and in the ties of interdependence between the metropole and the colonies. It was through co-operation with France, broadened into the Euro-African framework, that Senegal should gradually free itself from the colonial past. Under this ensign he governed independent Senegal as the incarnation of the last French consul.[20]

This image of Senghor as an honorary French consul, ruling independent Senegal on behalf of the former colonial masters, is used by Sembene throughout *The Last of the Empire* (Sembene's claim in the author's foreword that the book is about the imaginary country of *Sunugal* only serves to highlight his satirical approach). One of the meanings of the novel's title refers

---

[18] Abdoulaye Bathily claims that the foreign ideologies against which Senghor was warning were those of communist China and the social protest movements of the United States. Senegalese relations with the Soviet Union were actually quite warm in the late 1960s. See Bathily, *Mai 68 à Dakar*, pp. 15–16.

[19] For an analysis of the process of decolonisation in Senegal, see Boubacar Barry, 'Neocolonialism and Dependence in Senegal, 1960–1980', in Gifford and Louis, *Decolonization and African Independence*, pp. 271–94.

[20] Ibid., p. 294.

specifically to the overthrow of the Senghor figure, Léon Mignane, from power (the other linked meaning, referring to the character of Cheikh Tidiane Sall will be discussed below). To rid Senegal of Senghor/Mignane is the first step in gaining a meaningful independence from France. This animosity towards Senghor is, no doubt, in part personal. *The Last of the Empire* was Sembene's first work since his film *Ceddo* had been banned by Senghor in an act which was merely the latest in a series of run-ins between the two men. The political and artistic differences between them had obviously caused a lot of resentment on Sembene's part (he was after all in the weaker position of the two and could not use his political weight to have Senghor's poetry banned, no matter what he may have thought of it).

In an interview from the late 1970s, Senghor revealed both his general distrust of cinema as an art form, and particularly of the political engagement of Sembene's films:

> *Nous avons de bons cinéastes, je le sais. Le plus connu est M. Ousmane Sembène, qui se proclame marxiste-léniniste. Démocrates, nous l'avons aidé. Nous souhaitons seulement que ses films soient moins superficiels, moins politiques, donc plus nègres, plus culturels – au sens de la profondeur. Encore une fois, nous avons aidé les jeunes cinéastes sénégalais. J'aimerais seulement qu'il y eût un cinéma fidèle aux valeurs de la Négritude.*[21]

> I know that we have good filmmakers. The best known is Mr Ousmane Sembène who claims to be a Marxist-Leninist. As democrats, we have helped him. However, we wish that his films were less superficial, less political, and therefore more black and more cultured – that is to say, deeper. What is more, we have helped out many young Senegalese filmmakers. I only wish there were a cinema that was faithful to the values of Negritude.

Senghor accuses cinema of lacking 'authenticity' as an African art form, and attacks Sembene for his polemical style. He firmly establishes himself on the moral and artistic high ground: as a true 'democrat', his government (although one is left to wonder if the 'nous' which Senghor utilises refers to the actions of his government or is intended as a royal 'nous/we') helps to finance Sembene's work but *they* (that is, the regal Senghor) would like these films (as well as those of other Senegalese filmmakers) to be less 'political' and more 'cultural', and being more 'cultural' for Senghor means adopting the values of Negritude. The ideological nature of his own work is overlooked (Negritude was after all the official state ideology of Senghor's Senegal) and is passed off as being an 'authentic' cultural expression of the African soul. Later in the same interview, Senghor answers criticisms of his censorship of Sembene's work in the following terms:

> *Nous exerçons une censure sévère parce qu'il faut respecter la vérité intellectuelle et morale. Sous prétexte d'être à gauche, on ne peut trahir la vérité. Sous le prétexte d'être 'révolutionnaire', on ne doit pas enseigner la haine. Voilà dans quel sens nous exerçons la censure.*
>
> *Dans tous les pays du monde, il y a la censure cinématographique. Surtout dans les pays communistes, on l'oublie un peu trop.*[22]

---

[21] Léopold Sédar Senghor, *La Poésie de l'action* (Paris: Stock, 1980), p. 231.
[22] Ibid., p. 232.

We apply a strict censorship because intellectual and moral truth must be respected. One cannot betray the truth under the pretext of being on the left. One cannot teach hatred under the pretext of being 'revolutionary'. It is in this context that we use censorship.

In every country in the world, there is film censorship, especially in Communist countries. We forget that a bit too readily.

In this vision, Senghorian Negritude becomes the guardian of the essential truths of African life, truths to which Sembene and his kind are unable to gain access because of their espousal of the foreign cause of Marxism: Sembene's work 'disrespects' the truth in its very essence because it refuses to acknowledge the truth of Negritude. However, at the same time, Senghor also admits the ideological nature of his government's policy on censorship, invoking the use of censorship by all regimes, particularly those in communist states. Essentially, he classes Sembene as an ideological and artistic enemy. Given the bitter nature of this political and artistic dispute between the two men, it is hardly surprising that the portrait of Senghor/Mignane in *The Last of the Empire* is highly vitriolic (as one would expect in a political satire), poking fun at the diminutive size of the President and his attempts to stave off the ravages of old age. In another bitter aside, Senghor/Mignane is said to have a blood group that is usually only found in Europe, leading the French ambassador to remark: 'Since when is there such a thing as an Aryan Negro?' (*LE*, p. 19). Perhaps the crowning insult is the fact that Senghor/Mignane's wife is discovered to be having an affair with one of his government ministers.

At the same time as he shows Senghor/Mignane's star to be on the wane, Sembene takes great pleasure in carrying out some self-publicity. Several characters quote lines from the poet, variously referred to as both Sembene and Sembleme (these lines would appear to have been written specially for the novel as they are not to be found in any of Sembene's works prior to *The Last of the Empire*). At one point, Cheikh Tidiane's corrupt son Dioulmé even declares that he and his fellow Senegalese businessmen have changed their title to 'economic operators' rather than 'businessmen' because of Sembene's satirical portrayal of African businessmen in *Xala* (*LE*, p. 143). It had been clear for several years prior to Senghor's decision to step down from the presidency that his grip on power was slipping so it would appear that Sembene intended to be the first writer to wish his old nemesis good riddance, arranging for the novel to be published shortly after Senghor's retirement on 31 December 1980.

However, Sembene's attack on Senghor's regime is more than a simple ragbag of personal slander and vague political criticisms.[23] He is deeply concerned

---

[23] The critic, Hal Wylie, has argued that Sembene is both too harsh and too vague in his criticisms of Senghor's regime: 'It is obvious that Sembène is angry with Senghor, but the charges against Mignane always remain rather vague, basically corruption and neo-colonialism. It is clear that he is not accused of torture, political assassination etc. Given this record, the author's bashing of Senghor/Mignane seems heavy-handed.' See Hal Wylie, 'The Political Science of Sembène and Fall: Senghor Revisited', in Régis Antoine, ed., *Carrefour des cultures* (Tübingen: Narr, 1993), p. 364. Wylie's defence of Senghor seems to rely solely on presenting the case that he was not as bad as other African leaders, therefore Sembene is unfair in singling him out for criticism. Not

with examining the nature of power in a one-party state, and also with the means by which a nationalist government defuses social conflict through the mystifying discourse of the nation. Dealing with the latter point first, it is clear that one of the main focuses of Sembene's attack is the entire notion of Negritude. For Sembene, Negritude is a nationalist discourse that aims to cast Africans, in this case, the Senegalese, in terms of race, before all other considerations, in particular those of class and gender. This allows the Senghor regime to appear radical while, in fact, remaining resolutely conservative. To put it in the words of Madjiguène, the liberated partner of the journalist Kad: 'The Léon Mignane style socialism trick always pays [...]. You signal left and turn right' (*LE*, p.137). Sembene ironically has Mignane's version of Negritude dubbed *Authenegrafricanitus*, and he has Cheikh Tidiane confront Mignane over the contradiction in proclaiming the virtues of an essentialist black nature while his own lifestyle is so obviously European. This contradiction or, to be more precise, hypocrisy, within Negritude has been analysed by René Depestre in his book, *Bonjour et adieu à la négritude*:

> *Loin d'armer leur conscience contre les violences du sous-développement, la négritude dissout* ses *nègres et ses négro-africains dans un essentialisme parfaitement inoffensif pour le système qui dépossède les hommes et les femmes de leur identité. Aujourd'hui les 'négrologues' de la négritude la présentent sous la forme d'une conception du monde qui, dans des sociétés américaines ou africaines, serait exclusive aux Noirs, indépendamment de la position qu'ils occupent dans la production, la propriété, la distribution des biens matériels et spirituels.*[24]

Far from arming their consciences against the violence of under-development, Negritude dissolves *its blacks and its black Africans* in an essentialism that holds no threat for the system which is dispossessing men and women of their very identities. Today, the 'negrologues' of Negritude present their ideology as a conception of the world that is exclusive to the blacks of Africa and America, independent of their place within the mode of production, property and the distribution of material and spiritual goods.

Throughout *The Last of the Empire*, Sembene presents Senghor/Mignane as a cunning, Machiavellian politician who is able to manipulate all around him. Such is the extent of his individual power over the nation that his disappearance

---

[23] (cont.) only is this negative defence of Senghor something of a case of damning with faint praise but the manner in which Wylie dismisses the charges of corruption and neo-colonialism seems to suggest that such abuses of power are simply to be accepted in African states. Wylie seems much more sympathetic towards Aminata Sow Fall's depiction of the African head of state in her *L'Ex-père de la nation* (Paris: L'Harmattan, 1987). Far more loosely based on Senghor's regime, Sow Fall presents the eponymous ex-President as an idealistic figure, manipulated by corrupt forces. Written in the first person, from the point of view of the fallen leader, now languishing in a prison cell, the novel is deeply sympathetic towards the motivations that had driven him throughout his career. See my article, 'Representing Senegal: Narratives and Counter-Narratives of the Nation in the Work of Ousmane Sembene and Aminata Sow Fall', *ASCALF Bulletin*, 18 (Spring/Summer 1999), pp. 18–27. See also Peter Hawkins, 'Marxist Intertext, Islamic Reinscription? Some Common Themes in the Novels of Sembène Ousmane and Aminata Sow Fall', in *African Francophone Writing: A Critical Introduction*, ed. by Laïla Ibnlfassi and Nicki Hitchcott (Oxford: Berg, 1996), pp. 163–9.

[24] René Depestre, *Bonjour et adieu à la négritude* (Paris: Robert Laffont, 1980), pp. 82–3 (italics in original).

precipitates the fall of the government. A sort of African Sun King, at the height of his power in the 1970s, Senghor could virtually claim 'l'Etat, c'est moi'. The personal nature of Senghor's government was recognised by both his friends and enemies alike. At the height of the social crisis precipitated by the events of May 1968, Senghor turned to the leaders of the powerful religious brotherhoods for support. El Hadj Falilou Mbacké, the Khalife-General of the Mouride brotherhood, gave Senghor the following glowing testimonial:

> *J'apporte au chef de l'Etat mon soutien le plus complet en toutes circonstances, je lui renouvelle mon amitié et mon indéfectible attachement. Soyez tous disciplinés. Que l'on sache surtout que comme toujours le dernier mot appartiendra à la légalité. Disciples mourides, mes instructions ont été toujours bénéfiques pour vous, et le seront toujours. Je conclus en vous affirmant que Dieu a protégé Léopold Sédar Senghor contre toutes menées subversives.*[25]

> I give the head of state my complete support in all circumstances. I want to publicly proclaim my friendship and my undying attachment to him. Retain your discipline. Remember that the law will hold sway at the end of the day. Mouride disciples, my instructions have always been, and always will be, beneficial to you. I would like to conclude by confirming to you that God has protected Léopold Sédar Senghor against the forces of subversion.

Although himself a Catholic, Senghor developed a good working relationship with Senegal's Islamic leaders and he was a personal friend of El Hadj Falilou Mbacké. For the Islamic brotherhoods, Senghor's hold on power acted as a guarantee that their major agricultural interests would continue to be subsidised by the government. Indeed, as befits such a clientilist system, Senghor was well known for receiving visits from representatives of the Islamic chiefs (amongst others) on virtually a daily basis (although that is not to suggest that he gave in to their every whim – as President he was, after all, the dominant partner in the relationship).[26]

A man who was very much opposed to Senghor was the Senegalese linguist and historian Pathé Diagne (it will be recalled that he worked on the short-lived Wolof language journal *Kaddu*, with Sembene). Shortly after the end of Senghor's reign, Diagne wrote a damning political obituary for the ex-president:

> *L.-S. Senghor a laissé l'image, au-dehors bien entendu, d'un intellectuel libéral. Il fut, au-dedans, un chef d'Etat surtout pointilleux quant au respect de l'homme et du capital français. Ceux-là, il n'y touchait pas. Pour le reste, il était un souverain à sa manière. Avec l'économie, la religion, la culture ou l'institution, il agissait à sa guise. Intellectuels, chefs religieux, hommes politiques s'étaient habitués à le servir. Ces vingt années de monocratie ne peuvent manquer de laisser des traces.*[27]

> To the outside world, L.-S. Senghor has left behind the image of a liberal intellectual. Within Senegal, he was a head of state who cared particularly about respect for the

---

[25] Published in *Dakar-Matin* (1 June 1968). Quoted in Bathily, *Mai 68 à Dakar*, p. 81.

[26] For an account of the role of the Islamic brotherhoods in Senegalese politics, see Donal Cruise O'Brien's seminal work, *The Mourides of Senegal: The Political and Economic Organization of an Islamic Brotherhood* (Oxford: Oxford University Press, 1971). A more recent study of the role of the brotherhoods is to be found in Leonardo A. Villalón, *Islamic Society and State Power in Senegal* (Cambridge: Cambridge University Press, 1995).

[27] Pathé Diagne, ed., *Quelle démocratie pour le Sénégal?* (Dakar: Sankoré, 1984), pp. 11–12.

individual and for French capital. These two areas were left in peace. As for everything else, he pleased himself in regal fashion. As regards the economy, religion, culture and the institutions of the state, he did with them as he pleased. Intellectuals, religious leaders, politicians all became used to serving him. His twenty years of monocracy will most definitely leave their mark.

Senghor's reign is thus characterised by an autocratic approach that many have described in monarchic terms. Indeed, in Jackson and Rosberg's well-known study *Personal Rule in Black Africa*, Senghor is classified as a *princely* ruler.[28]

This personalised rule became the focus of much debate when Senghor had the constitution changed in 1978 to allow him to name his successor, by ensuring that the sitting Prime Minister, to be chosen by the President, would replace the latter upon his retirement. This monarchical attitude towards power is reproduced in *The Last of the Empire*. Sembene begins the novel with the arrival of Mam Lat Soukabé, one of the pretenders to Senghor/Mignane's position. He arrives at a cabinet meeting to be greeted with the suspicions of his colleagues who believe that he may have had something to do with the disappearance of the Venerable One, as Léon Mignane is referred to by his respectful disciples in the cabinet. Apart from the Doyen, Cheikh Tidiane Sall, the cabinet is made up of technocrats who owe their positions entirely to the president. The narrator, whose sarcastic political and personal commentary punctuates the novel,[29] reveals the fears of the cabinet at the loss of their political and spiritual mentor:

> The Venerable One's absence distressed them all. Not one of them had stood for election. Few of them could rely on any degree of electoral support. Léon Mignane has recruited them, and entrusted each of them with a portfolio under his supervision. With the exception of Cheikh Tidiane Sall, not one of them had yet reached the age of fifty. When ousting his former associates of the 1940s, 1950s and 1960s, Léon Mignane had told Cheikh Tidiane: 'I'm going to call on the young. The second generation of Independence.' He alone had raised Daouda (whom he called David) to the Prime Minister's pedestal. By tapping the second generation and channelling it into his government, Léon Mignane had broadened and strengthened his power base. (*LE*, p. 11)

Senghor/Mignane is thus presented as a clinical political operator who is willing to use his 'friends' to ascend the ladder to power and who will just as soon kick the ladder out from underneath them if they try to follow him up.[30]

---

[28] Robert H. Jackson and Carl G. Rosberg, *Personal Rule in Black Africa: Prince, Autocrat, Prophet, Tyrant* (Berkeley, Los Angeles, London: University of California Press, 1982), pp. 89–97.

[29] Mary N. Layoun argues that the use of personal asides, proverbs, sayings, etc. in *The Last of the Empire* seeks to return the novel's narrative to the voices excluded from the palace politics witnessed in the story. Layoun, 'Fictional Formations and Deformations of National Culture', *South Atlantic Quarterly*, 87, 1 (Winter 1988), pp. 60–5.

[30] In an episode that clearly parallels Senghor's constitutional wrangle with the then head of government Mamadou Dia in December 1962, the narrator describes how Léon Mignane has his colleague Ahmet Ndour imprisoned for an attempted coup d'état. The facts surrounding the actual power struggle between Dia and Senghor remain unclear with Dia claiming that it was, in fact, Senghor who had carried out a coup. The net result was that Dia went to prison for over ten years. Dia's version of the events surrounding the affair can be found in his *Mémoires d'un militant du tiers monde* (Paris: Publisud, 1985), pp. 143–64.

Even his oldest ally the Doyen is seen to be expendable once he starts to disagree with the manner of Mignane's rule and the direction of his policies.

The shadow cast by the Venerable One over proceedings, despite his physical absence, is perhaps best illustrated in the image of his ornate 'throne', which sits empty at the end of the cabinet table throughout the scenes featuring the members of the cabinet. An imposing structure, with its carved figures, representing the myths and legends of various African countries, the throne exerts a particular fascination on Daouda, who as Prime Minister is set to be Léon Mignane's successor. A shy technocrat, Daouda is daunted at the prospect of taking power (his position as a lower-caste person does not help matters). Alone in the cabinet room, he looks at the throne, the most visible symbol of the Venerable One's power, in a state of extreme anxiety:

> Daouda was discovering the throne for the first time. He was fascinated, as if attracted by a supernatural power. Timidly he drew near. The hand-embroidered cushion of Kashmir silk charmed him. He held out his hand to touch the fabric. His heart beat twice as fast. A tide of warm blood flooded up his arm from his fingers. When his middle finger touched the cushion's seam, his blood flowed more quickly, piercingly chill. It seized his whole body. He withdrew his hand as if scorched, breathing heavily. He glanced fearfully at the walls, the folds of the curtains, the masks and statues. He was certain someone was spying on him. He turned around quickly. No one! But the feeling remained. (*LE*, p. 17)

Daouda is seen to perceive of Léon Mignane's power in supernatural terms. It is almost as though the throne is possessed with the spirit of the missing President, watching over Daouda and preventing him from sitting in his seat, an act which would see him, at least symbolically, take over from the Venerable One as head of state.[31]

However, the Venerable One's grip on his disciples is not as strong as it at first appears to be. Within two days of his disappearance, the question of his successor has split the cabinet into two camps, each backing one of the candidates, Daouda and Mam Lat Soukabé.[32] Long before the *dénouement* of the story, Daouda has sufficiently overcome his fears to sit upon the Venerable One's throne. The President had not realised the extent to which the example of his personal rule would rub off on his young protégés. The struggle between Daouda and Mam Lat Soukabé has no ideological basis and revolves purely around questions of caste and personality. Daouda is a technocrat who may make the system run more smoothly but he has no programme for

---

[31] This same sense of an absent presence is examined in one of the key texts on the construction of racial identity, Jean Genet's *Les Nègres*: see his *Œuvres Complètes*, 5 (Paris: Gallimard, 1979). Throughout the play, a sarcophagus draped in a sheet occupies the centre of the stage. Said to contain the body of a white man murdered by the *nègres*, the sarcophagus, in fact, turns out to be empty. It is a symbolic object on to which meaning is projected. The echoes of Genet's play are even stronger in *Guelwaar* in which an empty coffin is one of the central visual motifs. For a discussion of Genet's play, see J. P. Little, *Les Nègres* (London: Grant & Cutler, 1990).

[32] The rivalry between Daouda, the technocrat, and Mam Lat Soukabé, the populist, closely parallels the political tensions between Abdou Diouf and Babacar Ba throughout a large part of the 1970s. See Momar Coumba Diop and Mamadou Diouf, *Le Sénégal sous Abdou Diouf* (Paris: Karthala, 1990), p. 90.

government. Mam Lat Soukabé is merely an opportunist who is seeking to rise to power on the back of his aristocratic ancestry. Indeed, the ease with which the two men and the other members of the cabinet conceal the truth behind the disappearance of the President and the death of his chauffeur suggests that Léon Mignane's disciples are just as adept at manipulating public opinion as their political father had been. Rather than revealing the intrigue and palace politics at work at the top of the state, the death of the chauffeur Siin is transformed into a campaign against urban youth, which is blamed for the murder (this urban youth is given its chance to avenge the sullying of its character in the coup d'état that follows). The impression given to us of the state's political elite is of a class interested solely in securing its share of the neo-colonial cake. Sembene would argue that whichever of the two possible successors were to become President, power would still reside in the hands of Jean de Savognard, the French ambassador, and Adolphe, the adviser to the Venerable One, who loiters quietly in the background throughout the course of the novel.[33]

The one figure of dissent within the cabinet is the Doyen, Cheikh Tidiane Sall. A close friend and colleague of Léon Mignane since the colonial era, he has come to doubt the course of action adopted by the President since independence. Tired of politics, he is set to retire on the day that we learn of the President's disappearance. In a series of flashbacks, we are given a picture of the reasons behind the Doyen's disillusionment with Léon Mignane. He confronts the President over his decisions to recognise Israel officially and to participate in the creation of an African Intervention Force, seeing both of these policies as designed solely to please his Western allies. In keeping with the nature of the President's rule, one of the main arguments between the two men arises over the decision by the cabinet to buy a jet aeroplane for the President's seventieth birthday (in fact, he is older than this but vanity has caused him to hide his true age). Asked to give a speech at the birthday celebrations, the Doyen decides to speak out publicly against the mismanagement and corruption that he sees everywhere around him. Railing against 'the blindness of certain rulers' (*LE*, p. 41), he advocates the enfranchisement of the younger generation, which is seen to be almost totally devoid of any hope for the future. According to the Doyen, the problem is that the government is led by people whose allegiance is mainly to the former colonial power, which effectively perpetuates the politics of the colonial era, a situation that is reinforced by the role of French advisers at the highest levels of the state:

> Let us further acknowledge that colonialism no longer consists in occupying land, but in demeaning the minds, crushing the culture and distorting the growth of a society, and imposing an armada of obtuse advisers whose role within our new

---

[33] The character of Adolphe appears to be modelled on Jean Collin who as Minister for the Interior had already found himself the subject of Sembene's satire in *Xala* (see Chapter Four). Upon Abdou Diouf's succession to the presidency, Collin was given charge of the President's office, a position of great influence and power. For the opposition within Senegal, Collin was seen as the *éminence grise* behind both Senghor and Diouf. His dismissal from the President's office in 1990 was seen as a symbol of the decline in Senegal's dependence on France. See Diop and Diouf, *Le Sénégal sous Abdou Diouf*, pp. 101–14.

administration is not to help us, but to curb every daring reform, every enterprising spirit. (*LE*, p. 39)

The Doyen's rebellion against Léon Mignane is a result of a growing number of questions that he has begun to ask himself in the twilight of his career. He reflects on his life, which has seen him move from support for assimilation to the espousal of autonomy and, finally, independence. For most of his life, he had believed himself to be French but now, in his final years, he has broken the hold of his former colonial master. In an interesting *mise en abyme*, Sembene has the Doyen plan out his memoirs, which he is to write with the independent and oppositional journalist Kad. These memoirs are to be entitled *The Last of the Empire* and they will recount the Doyen's evolution and, in effect, that of twentieth-century Africa. The story within the story is also that of Africa's liberation from the former empire.

In many ways, the Doyen's career has been one of missed potential. Sembene depicts him as someone around whom a real opposition to neo-colonialism could have been formed but his devotion to his 'friend' Léon Mignane and his position within what had primarily been a one-party state have kept him on the side of power throughout his career. Even after his caustic 'birthday speech', the President decides to keep him within the government in order to give the impression that his is an open government where debate is always welcome. For Sembene, this is one of the tragedies of the one-party regime, as all shades of opinion are co-opted into the Party where they become silenced under the dictates of the party line. The extent to which opposition to the party line, which effectively means the presidential line, is allowed is clearly shown in the scene where the Doyen single-handedly takes on the rest of the cabinet over the decision to create an African Intervention Force. The Doyen wins the argument in the face of much personal abuse from the President's young disciples but his objections will be ignored when it comes to determining government policy. Rather than being encouraged, oppositional discourse is seen to be stifled and contained. However, this attack by the Doyen is the final straw for the President and he decides to isolate him gradually within the cabinet, as a prelude to removing him entirely:

> Had he not perhaps underestimated Cheikh Tidiane? It was time to to get rid of him. As was his wont, he would avoid openly opposing him. Especially now. He would proceed by stages, discredit him to make him unpopular, then isolate him. Whatever his age, a serpent secretes venom. The solitary exercise of power had made him more vulnerable. He had relied on the younger men to counter Cheikh Tidiane. But none of them had the fire, the zeal, the ability to deploy facts, needed to reduce him to silence. (*LE*, p. 98)

In Léon Mignane's government, there can be only one voice and that is his own. If you are not with him, you are against him. If you are against him, you find yourself marginalised and effectively silenced.

When the Doyen retires, it is highly symbolic that Sembene has him walk the short distance from his office in the Ministry of Justice to his home on the

Plateau. He has literally descended from high office to street level. He has left the rarefied atmosphere of the cabinet and its palatial intrigues and finds himself amongst the ordinary people and their day-to-day worries. He overhears a man telling his cousin about the death of his young wife and observes a leper scratching his worn and festering body against a wall to relieve the pain. This descent into everyday reality serves to highlight the separation between politics and the people, and also accelerates the Doyen's radicalisation.

The Doyen's *prise de conscience* is aided by his meeting with the journalist Kad. A maverick figure who has a reputation for honesty and integrity, Kad is linked to such illustrious African radicals as Lumumba, Cabral and Fanon, whom he is said to have interviewed during his career. Even his name is given a symbolic meaning, as the *kad* is a tree that has no leaves during the rainy season, therefore not allowing the chiefs to take shelter while the peasants work in the rain (*LE*, p. 129). Kad is presented to us as another source of oppositional discourse within the neo-colonial order. His meeting with the Doyen and the memoirs they intend to write are seen as a guide for the young generation in their fight against the neo-colonial regime.

However, despite their independent and oppositional credentials, both Kad and the Doyen are seen to support the military coup that topples Mignane's faltering regime. Both men seem to accept the claims of the Committee of High-Ranking Officers that they intend merely to clean up corruption before passing power over to a freely elected government. Alongside this military coup, we see a popular revolt led by the much-maligned urban youth (earlier blamed for the murder of the President's chauffeur). Portrayed by Sembene as a good-humoured movement, we see a group of youths symbolically tear down the statue of Faidherbe, who was responsible for the beginning of the systematic conquest of Senegal in the 1850s.

Neither Sembene's vision of the African military nor that of the urban youth rings particularly true in the light of recent African history. Despite the Doyen's confident claim that the only military coups to have turned into dictatorships were those of Idi Amin in Uganda and Bokassa in the Central African Republic, history would indicate otherwise. Mobutu Sese Seko swept to power in a military coup in Zaïre in 1965 and we have only recently witnessed the end of his bloody and corrupt reign.[34] Liberia, Sierra Leone and Somalia have for several years been in the grip of terrible civil wars because of the power struggle between various military commanders. The Congo only emerged from thirteen years of military rule in 1992 (the country was recently plunged into chaos upon the outbreak of violent confrontations between the army and the personal militia of the country's former military dictator), and Nigeria's latest return to democracy owed much to the sudden death in 1998 of General Abacha, the country's military leader. Although the Doyen's claim that people are more tolerant towards corrupt and brutal *civilian* regimes has more than a grain of truth to it, it is simply not the case that the African military, despite all its rhetoric, has acted in the name of justice and equality.

[34] See *Libération*, 19–20 April 1997, pp. 4–5.

In his book *Coups and Army Rule in Africa*, Samuel Decalo has argued that the African military has not shown itself to be any less corrupt than its civilian counterparts, and despite their claims to be acting as interim governments, the generals are usually fairly difficult to remove once they are ensconced in power.[35] Equally, the urban youth is not usually as peaceful or as disciplined as Sembene presents it in his novel. The events of May 1968 had been far from peaceful and, more recently, there were particularly violent riots in Senegal around the 1993 elections. In one incident at a rally held by the main opposition party, the PDS, five policemen were killed.[36]

The Last of the Empire is a novel that sums up Sembene's frustrations with Senghor's regime. He focuses his criticisms upon the autocratic nature of Senghor's rule and on his policy of continued dependence upon the French. However, there seems to be no coherent opposition to the regime, only fragmented pockets of resistance. It seems to be this lack of a true opposition that pushes Sembene to imagine the unlikely marriage of the military and the unemployed urban youth. This rebellion constitutes a real end to colonialism, which Sembene believes had merely changed its skin in the transfer of power from the French to the Senegalese authorities. Many of the statements made by the Doyen are explicitly nationalist in tone, calling for the nation's affairs to be run in the interest of the *Sunugalese*, and not those of the French (at one point, Mignane/Senghor is attacked for having a French wife). Before society can be transformed, the long-awaited overthrow of the French must finally be accomplished.

The reign of Abdou Diouf since 1981 has lessened Senegal's dependence upon France but has not managed to extricate the country from its economic difficulties. In contemporary Senegal, one is as likely to find German or American companies as French ones (when one finds companies at all). Economic domination has consequently come to be seen in terms of a general dependence upon the West as a whole, rather than as a cause of complaint against the French. The French political economist, Catherine Coquery-Vidrovitch, has assessed the role of the French in independent Africa in the following terms:

> French or not, domination of the South by the North would have expressed itself in more or less the same way and in the same channels, and it would have exploited the same collusion of national governments reflecting the interests of factions (rather than classes) which would probably have led to the same mistakes.[37]

Therefore, when Sembene came to make his film *Guelwaar* in 1992, his focus in attacking the neo-colonial regime had shifted to an attack on the dependency mentality in general and to the abrogation of political responsibility within the African political elite.

[35] Samuel Decalo, *Coups and Army Rule in Africa: Studies in Military Style* (New Haven, CT, and London: Yale University Press, 1976).

[36] For an account of this incident and other recent cases of social unrest in Senegal, see Ralph Uwechue, ed., *Africa Today* (London: Africa Books, 1996; third edition), pp. 1286–91.

[37] Catherine Coquery-Vidrovitch, 'The Transfer of Economic Power in French-Speaking West Africa', in Gifford and Louis, *Decolonization and African Independence*, p. 130.

■ ■ ■

Guelwaar is based on a true story but Sembene appears to have seen the original tale of religious tension as a good starting point for a tale that sets out to show people of different religions what they have in common.[38] The Muslims and the Christians become involved in a tense stand-off outside the cemetery but the fact of the matter is that there is literally no substance to the dispute. The whole affair is simply the result of an administrative error that has seen the body of Guelwaar, a Christian, buried in a Muslim grave. Indeed, there is a good record of religious tolerance in Senegal: Senghor was a Catholic, as was Senegal's first black deputy to the French parliament, Blaise Diagne.[39] In *Guelwaar*, it is the Deputy/Mayor who tries to push his Muslim constituents' claims in the dispute, even going so far as to assert that Islam is an indigenous religion, and seeking to portray the Christians as aliens. In a film where we meet very few figures of power (especially compared to the palace politics described in *The Last of the Empire*), the Deputy/Mayor's role is highly significant. His is a clientilist relationship with his constituents. In an embodiment of the process described by Guelwaar in his speech, the Deputy/Mayor tells the villagers to return home and await the food aid which he has obtained for them. This is neo-colonial politics at work on the ground: an African middleman passes on the aid he has received from the West and, in repayment, he is re-elected every four years. If he favours the Muslims that is because they represent the overwhelming majority of the population and thus dictate the outcome of elections, something which is a priority amongst the considerations of most politicians. Senegal is fortunate in its largely peaceful cohabitation between different religious and ethnic groups – one can readily find examples of other African states where politicians are more than willing to exploit such potentially explosive tensions.

Sembene does not take the Christian side in the argument in order to engage in a gratuitous attack on the Muslim community. While it is true that he ridicules the obstinate and belligerent Mor Ciss, he presents the village imam as a man of great honour and integrity. As a minority, the Christians are

---

[38] Sembene discusses the story that would become *Guelwaar* in 'Cinéma et littérature en Afrique noire: entretien avec Sembene Ousmane', in *Protée noir: essais sur la littérature francophone de l'Afrique noire et des Antilles*, ed. by Peter Hawkins and Annette Lavers (Paris: L'Harmattan, 1992), pp. 214–15. In this inteview, he argues that the story represents the failure of the state to create a role for itself other than that of referee between disputing social groups.

[39] For a discussion of religion in Senegal, including some interesting newspaper editorials voicing broad Islamic support for the Pope's 1992 visit to Senegal, see Makhtar Diouf, *Sénégal, les ethnies et la nation* (Paris: L'Harmattan, 1994), pp. 42–3. The separatist movement in Casamance, which has been waging sporadic war against the Senegalese government since the early 1980s, and which is primarily centred around the Diola ethnic group, has more to do with government neglect of this underdeveloped area of the country than with any real ethnic tensions. In 1989, a number of serious incidents involving the Mauritanian and Senegalese armies along the border of the two countries created a volatile situation in which tension between blacks and Moors erupted into violence in both countries. However, relations between the two communities have improved in the intervening period.

presented as having an outsider's perspective on Senegalese society and are therefore more critical of the status quo (there is a current of public opinion in Senegal that believes that Christians are more serious and better workers than Muslims because they have to try harder to succeed).[40] We should also be aware of a kind of Joycean impulse in Sembene's focusing on a minority social group. Joyce presents a Jew as the hero of his Irish epic, *Ulysses*,[41] and Sembene presents a Christian as the hero of his tale of Senegalese resistance to neo-colonialism: one can tell a lot about a nation by the manner in which it deals with its minorities, and such people are particularly vulnerable in weak neo-colonial regimes. In *Guelwaar*, Sembene seeks to empower his nation's Christian community, pushing them to the centre of the political stage. Effectively, the film constitutes an attempt to recover the deceased Guelwaar both physically and politically. A political dissident and a Catholic, Guelwaar presents a troubling figure in a socially conservative and predominantly Muslim society (it will be recalled that over 90 per cent of the Senegalese population are Muslims). The film thus raises vital questions concerning the respect for minority groups and the treatment of dissonant voices within Senegalese society.

Far from glorifying the Christian community, Sembene presents his Christian characters as people struggling to make ends meet in a harsh neo-colonial world. In many ways, Guelwaar's family constitutes a physical embodiment of the suffering body politic of the nation. The youngest son Aloys has been left crippled after an accident in his childhood, while his elder brother Barthélémy has abandoned Senegal, both physically and emotionally, taking up citizenship in France, the country where he has lived for many years. Therefore, it is left up to the daughter Sophie to provide for the family, which she does by becoming a prostitute in Dakar. This sacrifice of her 'honour' in her family's name becomes the *sine qua non* of their material existence. Sophie may not be the virtuous 'black woman' of Senghor's poetry but her actions are necessitated by the nation's poverty and she bravely and willingly shoulders her responsibility.[42] In their day-to-day lives, millions of Africans are forced to find the means of eking out a living without resorting to the begging that Sembene views as the sole economic policy of most African states.[43]

---

[40] In a number of interviews following the release of *Guelwaar*, Sembene has spoken of his respect for the Catholic church's attempts to 'Africanise' itself in the period since independence. He is particularly impressed by the courageous manner in which it has stood up to corrupt regimes in South Africa and Zaïre. He also sees the Senegalese Catholic church as less implicated in the failures of the country's regime because of its minority status. See Françoise Ploquin, 'Le remède de l'Afrique est en Afrique; entretien avec Ousmane Sembene', *Diagonales*, 25 (January 1993), p. 5; Sada Niang and Samba Gadjigo, 'Interview with Ousmane Sembene', *Research in African Literatures*, 26, 3 (Autumn 1995), pp. 175–6.

[41] James Joyce, *Ulysses*, ed. by Danis Rose (1922; London: Picador, 1997).

[42] An ever-increasing number of African women have been forced into prostitution as the economic situation has worsened. For an account of some of the problems facing African women in a city such as Dakar, see Jean-François Werner, *Marges, sexe et drogues à Dakar: enquête ethnographique* (Paris: Karthala/ORSTOM, 1994).

[43] Moussa Bathily takes a comic look at the relationship between Western 'aid' donors and African 'aid' recipients in his film *Petits Blancs au manioc et à la sauce gombo* (1982).

This examination of the body politic of the African state is perhaps best illustrated in relation to the character of Barthélémy, Guelwaar's eldest son. At first, he appears to be the classic example of the alienated African. He constantly gripes about his home country, and even goes so far as to refuse his Senegalese nationality. However, by the end of the film, he has been transformed and he proudly proclaims to the police chief, Gora: '*J'ai toujours été sénégalais*' ['I have always been Senegalese']. Although this treatment of the character of the alienated *émigré* may appear fairly schematic at first, this element of the story is, in fact, cleverly handled by Sembene. In an early scene, when Gora and Barthélémy arrive at the Muslim village to look for Guelwaar's body, there is a highly symbolic moment. The camera focuses on the upper branches of a baobab tree and, as it pans down the tree, we see Barthélémy urinating on its base. The baobab tree is the national symbol of Senegal and this action basically sums up what Barthélémy thinks of the country in the early stages of the film. However, by the end of the film, his self-imposed isolation from the country is at an end, as he joins in his people's struggle. He appears increasingly to be his father's son as he defends his sister's prostitution to Abbé Léon in the following terms: '*Il ne peut y avoir de vertu dans la misère et la pauvreté*' ['There can be no virtue when people live in misery and poverty.']. As an emigrant, Barthélémy has been forced out of the neo-colonial state due to economic necessity (as is the case for many Africans). The suggestion would appear to be that, once the yoke of dependency has been thrown off, these absent figures will be able to return home. As with *The Last of the Empire*, we can see the desire to create a national politics in which the whole nation participates. The hollow centre of the neo-colonial order must be filled with an inclusive, democratic politics.

The notions of absence and presence are highlighted from the very beginning of *Guelwaar*. We discover in the opening stages of the film that the eponymous hero of its title, Pierre Henri Thioune, known as Guelwaar, is dead. From the start of the film therefore, Guelwaar acts as an absent presence upon the events of the story. In a silent opening shot, we see Guelwaar's son, Aloys, limping down a dark, deserted street. The camera follows him into a house and, as he switches on the lamp, we see pictures of the Holy Spirit and the Pope, thus bringing out the religious theme that will play a vital role later in the film. After telling his mother and sister of Guelwaar's death, he opens the suitcase that he has carried home with him and takes out his father's wedding ring, which he hands to his mother. We see the mother Nogoye Marie, in close-up, staring at the ring and, as she doubles over in grief, the camera travels up to look at her wedding photograph on the wall. The image dissolves into a flashback of Guelwaar's and Nogoye Marie's wedding day. This process is followed throughout the film as Guelwaar's absence is countered by flashbacks presenting what he represented to his family and friends, and also his enemies.

In the early stages of the film, we see a procession of Guelwaar's friends and relations arriving at the family home to attend the ceremony. Sembene is keen to show as much respect as possible for their religion with Christian

7.1 Guelwaar with his wife Nogoye Marie
Guelwaar, Filmi Doomireew – Dakar, Senegal (all rights reserved)

hymns heard on the soundtrack throughout these scenes. However, one cannot hold a funeral without a corpse, so the mourners are left to reminisce about their dead companion and to speculate on what has happened to his body. This waiting is particularly hard on Nogoye Marie who is overcome with grief. In one of the most moving scenes in the film, the camera moves from a shot of the clock ticking on the wall, then moves across the room to Nogoye Marie who is kneeling beside Guelwaar's empty suit which is laid out upon the bed, in a grotesque and grimly comic parody of a real corpse. After her daughter Sophie has left the room, she addresses her absent husband. Her complaint is a mixture of anger at him for his domineering ways and also of frustration that he has gone, leaving her behind to cope by herself. However, she is also angry at his friends who live on while her husband has been murdered. They had nominated him to speak out at the aid rally but it is Guelwaar who must face the consequences. At the end of the film, Nogoye Marie taunts them with what she perceives as their cowardice.

It is interesting to note that, apart from the first flashback to Guelwaar's wedding and the men's recollection of the story of how Guelwaar had seduced the imam's wife in his youth, all the other flashbacks seek to portray the forceful, oppositional nature of Guelwaar's personality, leading up to the climactic speech at the aid rally. Sembene deliberately has two of these flashbacks appear as the memories of representatives of the Establishment. They are not simply the rose-tinted memories of family and friends. When Guelwaar's son Barthélémy goes to see the police chief Gora to report the disappearance of his father's body, this sparks off the memory of Gora's only previous meeting with Pierre Henri Thioune. In this flashback, Guelwaar comes across as an assertive and strong character who forces Gora's respect (throughout the scene, he speaks in Wolof, refusing to deal with the administration in French, the 'official' state language). He has come to report that hooligans have been harassing the women attending meetings in his home. He openly admits that the women discuss politics and defiantly asks Gora: 'Is there a law against discussing the awful situation in our country?' When Gora attempts to turn the tables on Guelwaar by asking if he knows anything of a recent incident in which three peasants had their arms broken, Guelwaar replies that Gora should instead ask why only their arms were broken. In a parting comment, he declares: 'We may be Christians but we won't turn the other cheek. Thank you for listening.' Throughout the scene he has spoken in Wolof but we learn that he can speak French as he has already written out his statement, which he hands over to Gora. The image of the Senegalese patriot is completed as Guelwaar leaves the station. The camera looks from behind as we see Guelwaar framed in the doorway with the Senegalese flag rising up above him (Sembene does not overplay the symbolism: this image lasts only a few seconds as Guelwaar departs with the children who had been waiting for him outside the station). It is as though he, and not the police, is the force of justice.

The flashbacks finally build up to Guelwaar's speech at the aid rally. As the Catholics wait outside the Muslim cemetery, Nogoye Marie feels as though her husband is calling out to her. She then remembers, in a flashback, a conversation she had with Guelwaar as he was leaving to speak at the rally. She is ashamed at her daughter's prostitution and she challenges her husband over this. However, Guelwaar replies that it is better to earn money than to accept charity from others. This declaration on the situation within Guelwaar's own home prepares the way for the subject of his speech at the rally where he widens this argument to include the whole nation, accusing the country of begging from others.

It is through the eyes of the army officer who arrives to oversee the dispute at the cemetery that we witness Guelwaar's speech. The crowd cheers and roars while drummers beat out a pulsating rhythm (we saw similar scenes in the nationalist ceremony at the beginning of *Xala*). The camera moves from the drummers to the crowd, then finally moves in a travelling shot towards Guelwaar standing on the podium waiting to speak. He raises his right hand and points his index finger into the air (an act which silences the crowd) and the camera moves in closer and closer as though drawn towards this finger pointing into the air. Then, he launches into his tirade against food aid:

> You point your finger to show someone the way. You all know that. But opening your five fingers to a passer-by, that's begging. Our leaders have gathered us here. You know why? Just to receive this aid. And now our leaders offer profuse thanks to all our distinguished benefactors in the name of us all, present and absent. And our leaders preen themselves and strut about as if this aid were the fruits of their labour. What a disgrace! And we silent people with no voice and no shame dance before this aid. What humiliation! [...] This aid affair has been going on for thirty years here and elsewhere. This aid they're distributing to us will kill us. It has killed all our dignity and pride. We are without shame. Nobody has any dignity left. I tell you, these countries sending us aid send it grudgingly. They laugh at us back in their homes. And our sons and daughters who live abroad among these people feel terribly humiliated. They can't look anyone in the eye for shame. It's true that here in our country we've had problems. We have our problems but we should be dealing with them ourselves. Not someone else! We, on our own![44]

Guelwaar deliberately opens his speech by using a concrete image, which appears in the form of a proverb. Addressing his people in Wolof, rather than the French favoured by the public officials in the film, he seeks to cast the problem of economic dependence on the West in terms to which his audience can easily relate. It is to this end that he quotes the Senegalese wise man, Kocc Barma (who was discussed above in Chapter Two):

> Our ancestor Kocc Barma said: 'If you want to kill a proud man, supply all his everyday needs and you'll make him a slave.' Yes, a slave! I said before that any pride we had left has been consumed by this aid [...]. Famine, drought and poverty – do you know why they happen? You want to know why? If a country is always taking aid from other people, that country, from generation to generation, will be able to say only: *'Jerejef! Jerejef! Jerejef! Jerejef!'* ['thank you' in Wolof].

---

[44] In the film, Guelwaar speaks in Wolof. I am here quoting from the English sub-titles. The version of this speech in the later novel is different in several respects. See Ousmane Sembene, *Guelwaar* (Paris: Présence Africaine, 1996), p. 140.

Guelwaar's aim is to shame his audience into a recognition of the manner in which they are leading their lives. Effectively, he tells them they are becoming a nation of beggars, and he appeals to their sense of pride to turn away from such policies. The main purpose of the film is to give voice to Guelwaar's message, which had so troubled the authorities that they had him killed. As the critic Vincent Vitrican has written of the film: '*il s'agit d'abord de recouvrer l'intégrité d'une parole, d'un acte politique*' ['it is chiefly concerned with recovering the integrity of one man's words and of a political act'].[45]

Many economic commentators have written on the nature of Western aid (or North/South aid). Tibor Mende pointed out in the early 1970s that a large proportion of 'aid' to the Third World was in fact tied to agreements concerning the purchase of goods from the donor country. Even the distribution of food aid is of more benefit to the West than the Third World as it costs rich countries more to keep their food surpluses in storage than it does to distribute them free in Africa, while such interventions harm the development of an indigenous system of food production in poor countries.[46] Gérard Chaliand is equally dismissive of the notion of a benevolent West, striving to aid Africa towards development:

> In the [final] analysis, aid serves the trade interests and still more the strategic and political designs of industrialised countries. In maintaining and spreading influence, aid is, after all, the cheapest thing at hand [...]. France directs its aid toward the franc zone. Such 'aid', whose free portion constantly drops, deepens the indebtedness of the poor countries and drives more and more of them to the point where they can see no prosepct ahead but that of chronic debt.[47]

Most 'aid' in the 1960s and 1970s was in fact given in the form of loans which, as Chaliand predicted, resulted in the amassing of huge debts in virtually all African countries. In the 1980s, aid to Africa dropped off as the continent ceased to be an important pawn in the Cold War politics of the United States and the Soviet Union. At the same time, the World Bank and the International Monetary Fund produced their structural adjustment programme, designed to rein in public sector expenditure in Africa, and to control the continent's spiralling debt. With the decline of *third worldist* economists and the victory of the United States in the Cold War, Africa was left with no allies in the West calling for aid to the Third World, as ultra-liberal economists such as Francis Fukuyama decreed that free-market capitalism was the final stage in the evolution of man.[48]

It is in such a seemingly hopeless state of African dependency upon the West that one must examine Sembene's argument in *Guelwaar*. Essentially, Sembene is trying to propose a means of combating the nebulous and elusive forces of contemporary neo-colonialism. No longer are the French and their African allies the source of all the continent's woes. Instead, we are presented with a situation where Africans allow themselves to be dominated by placing

[45] Vincent Vitrican, '*Guelwaar*', *Cabiers du Cinéma*, 474 (December 1993), p. 81.

[46] Mende, *From Aid to Recolonization*, pp. 35–55.

[47] Chaliand, *Revolution in the Third World*, p. 17.

[48] Francis Fukuyama, *The End of History and the Last Man* (London: Hamish Hamilton, 1992).

their future in the hands of others. This argument has been put forward by several African commentators in recent years. Perhaps the most impassioned and certainly the most polemical of these arguments has been proposed by Axelle Kabou in her provocatively titled book, *Et si l'Afrique refusait le développement?* [49]

The basic premise of Kabou's book is that Africa does not wish to become industrially and economically developed. She believes that Africa is trapped in a particularist culture, resolutely refusing to adopt what it sees as Western values. Although she recognises that Africa suffered greatly under slavery and colonialism, she argues that to retreat into a mythic African past, blaming the West and its civilisation for all their woes, is merely to retreat from the very pressing issues facing modern African society:

> [...] *le droit à la différence qui en lui-même est déjà loin d'être clair, sert en Afrique à autoriser les comportements les plus rétrogrades et les démarches les plus préjudiciables à la liberté et à la dignité des Africains. Il se manifeste par une sorte de détermination altière à n'être que soi et rien d'autre, et surtout à n'y voir aucun inconvénient, quand bien même le plus grand exploit en matière d'auto-réhabilitation ne consisterait qu'à diaboliser les idées nouvelles, à ériger la mendicité en principe de développement, et à liquider les gêneurs.* [50]

> [...] in Africa, the ambiguous notion of the right to be different serves to legitimise thoroughly regressive behaviour and permits moves that prejudice the liberty and the dignity of Africans. This manifests itself in a haughty determination to be oneself and nothing else. This 'auto-rehabilitation' is not seen to be in any way incovenient, even though this process involves demonising new ideas, elevating begging as the prime means of development, and wiping out all those who argue against such ideas.

This vision of begging as the only state policy on development, and of the silencing of all dissent could equally be applied to *Guelwaar*. Kabou argues that it is time for Africans to take control of their own lives. She claims that rather than blaming the West for cutting back on aid, Africa should be amazed that the West was willing to pay for so long:

> [...] *au lieu de simuler la surprise à chaque baisse des subsides, les Africains devraient d'abord se convaincre que la conduite de la destinée d'un continent ne se partage pas avec l'étranger. En d'autres termes, l'Afrique est responsable de son histoire, dans l'exacte mesure où les victimes des expansionnismes divers n'en sont pas moins condamnées à en payer les pots cassés. Pourquoi l'Afrique devrait-elle être une exception à cette règle historique?* [51]

> [...] instead of feigning surprise every time subsidies are reduced, Africans must come to realise that one does not pilot the course for a continent's future with foreign powers. In other words, Africa is responsible for its own history for the simple

---

[49] Sembene confirmed to me in an interview at Filmi Doomireew, Dakar on 30 November 1995, that he had read Kabou's book and that he agreed with its basic premise. He did not say if the book had any bearing on the writing of the script for *Guelwaar* (see Appendix). Another influential book which deals with the issue of African economic stagnation is Edem Kodjo's *Et demain l'Afrique* (Paris: Stock, 1986). Kabou makes numerous references to this work in her text.

[50] Kabou, *Et si l'Afrique refusait le développement?*, pp. 118–19.

[51] Ibid., p. 115.

reason that the victims of expansionist policies are the ones who must attempt to put things right. Why should Africa be an exception to this historical rule?

Both Sembene and Kabou seem to be describing a situation where dependency has become institutionalised. Africans have developed a dependency mentality because their politicians have set a structure in place which the conservatism of African society prevents from being challenged. This is how Kabou describes the social function of the 'myth' of African development:

> *Le mythe de la volonté africaine de développement paraît remplir trois fonctions essentielles: disculper d'avance la classe politique de tout soupçon d'incompétence en détournant les esprits vers un interminable complot international, car plus cela dure plus on a de raisons de rester au pouvoir; parquer indéfiniment les Africains dans des partis uniques censés canaliser efficacement les énergies vers des objectfis de développment singulièrement flous; engraisser une foultitude d'experts en perpétuelles missions et recherches dont l'utilité, jaugée à l'aune de l'aggravation du sous-développement, ne souffre aucune discussion.*[52]

The myth of Africa's desire to develop appears to fulfill three essential functions: exonerating the political class of any suspicion of incompetence by pointing towards an unending international plot, as the longer this plot exists the longer politicians must cling to power in order to fight it; condemning Africans to remain within single-party systems that are supposed to channel energy more efficiently towards hopelessly vague developmental objectives; greasing the palms of a multitude of experts on permanent research missions, whose usefulness is never questioned because the ever-worsening crisis of under-development creates more demand for their services.

Kabou sees the only way out of Africa's economic and social mess in the establishment of a veritable union between African states, which would enable them to compete with the industrial nations on some sort of equal basis. Sembene does not propose any such concrete alternative but his story does end with an act of resistance that puts Guelwaar's words on the rejection of aid into practice. As the Christians return home with the body of their former companion, they come across a truck delivering food aid to the village they have just left. The children who lead the procession, carrying a crucifix made from twisted pieces of old metal, stop the truck. They hand their crucifix back one by one until it is finally left in the hands of Abbé Léon. This seems to be a definite echo of Guelwaar's declaration to Gora that the fact that they are Christians does not mean that they will always turn the other cheek. The crucifix is left behind as they climb on to the truck and begin to empty the sacks of food out on to the ground. Abbé Léon and the elders complain but Nogoye Marie reminds them of the commitment they had made to Guelwaar. This signals the final flashback of the film as we once again see Guelwaar's speech at the aid rally. Half way through the speech, we return to the present as we see the procession pass over the food scattered on the ground, while Guelwaar's words continue to be heard on the soundtrack. The speech which had cost him his life is seen to have borne fruit. His radical voice has not been silenced. The absence brought about by death itself has been overcome. In a

[52] Ibid., p. 18.

213

caption that appears just before the closing credits, the film is called a '*légende africaine de l'Afrique du XXIe siècle*' ['African legend for the Africa of the 21st century']. The Christians' actions are presented as a possible way forward for Africa. In many ways, it is a symbolic enactment of Kabou's declaration that Africa must unite and reject dependency.

■ ■ ■

The Last of the Empire and *Guelwaar* constitute attempts to find a way out of Africa's current economic, political and social impasse. Dealing with different eras and differing conceptions of the neo-colonial enterprise in Africa, both works share a desire to see a profound change in the structure of power between the West and Africa, but readily point out that such a change can only be effected by a total transformation of the nature of African politics. Gone is the era when all the blame could be laid at the feet of the ogre of a scheming and predatory West. *The Last of the Empire* offers the perspective of an unholy alliance between the military and the urban unemployed but this approach is abandoned in *Guelwaar* where a less concrete but more hopeful vision of a reassertion of African pride and dignity is proposed.

In *Guelwaar*, Sembene argues that the future for Africa lies in assuming responsibility for its own economic survival. Although he is not as explicit as Axelle Kabou, Sembene appears to suggest that Africa must unite in order to prosper. Many economic commentators have reflected on the desirability of the creation of large economic federations in Africa that would especially benefit the smaller nations, which have inherited the least prosperous and most unworkable states from the colonial era (e.g. Burkina Faso, Gambia). The Senegalese philosopher, Souleymane Bachir Diagne, recognises the desirability of such a prospect but warns of the democratic culture required for the creation of any international body:

> *Le vœu de voir se constituer de grands ensembles qui dépassent la balkanisation en micro-Etats insiste souvent, et à juste titre, sur l'unité culturelle profonde des nations. Sans doute cette unité est-elle réelle, mais il y faut aussi, c'est l'évidence, des niveaux comparables de culture socio-politique: les unions qui font les grands ensembles ne se conçoivent, au bout du compte, qu'entre des Etats qui partagent une même culture démocratique et entre lesquels un accord établi a la force contraignante du droit. Elles ne sont pas pensables entre des autocraties où tout est à la merci des humeurs du Prince et de l'arbitraire d'un Etat qui n'est pas de droit.*[53]

The desire to witness the development of large groupings which go beyond the balkanisation of Africa into micro-states is often based, and rightly so, on a belief in the profound cultural unity of such nations. Without doubt, this unity is genuine but it goes without saying that one also needs a comparable socio-political culture: the unions that create large groupings only occur when one is dealing with states with the same democratic culture and when this agreement is backed up by the rule of law. No such union is possible when dealing with autocracies where everything

---

[53] Souleymane Bachir Diagne, 'A partir d'une évidence', in *La Culture du développement*, ed. by Souleymane Bachir Diagne (Dakar: CODESRIA, 1991), p. 3.

depends on the humour of the Prince and on the arbitrary structures of a state that does not obey the rule of law.

One need only think of the difficulties currently being experienced by the European Union in its moves towards economic and political union to recognise the problematic nature of the dissolution of national sovereignty. In an area of the world considered to have the most stable democracies, it has taken forty years to reach a stage where the nations involved are even set to consider the prospect of creating a single currency. In Africa, where democracy remains fragile and, in many cases, non-existent, such an international union would seem a rather remote prospect at the current time. Would an Omar Bongo (Gabon) or a Paul Biya (Cameroon) consider relinquishing some of their political control to an international body when they are unwilling to allow political competition within their own countries?

Within such a seemingly hopeless situation, Sembene has decided that it is his role as an artist to provide alternative visions to the ones provided by the state and the other dominant groups in his society. Although he remains convinced of the necessity of the implementation of a Marxism yet to prove its credentials in any African state, Sembene's films and novels are rarely as dogmatic as some of the artist's public pronouncements. His work deliberately sets out to fashion a discourse of resistance, to give voice to those stories that find no other public outlet in the relatively closed space of neo-colonial public discourse. Sembene's radical African heroes – from the wise man Kocc Barma to his radical Christian Pierre Henri Thioune; from the defiant and proud *ceddo* to his radical, feminist student Rama – offer images of resistance and the prospect of a better future.[54] It may be argued that such heroic images are utopian, but history has taught us that utopias often play an important part in the motor of history.[55]

In many ways, Sembene's attempts to re-think the relations between Africans mirrors Fanon's efforts to imagine a 'new man' in his work. Like Fanon, Sembene calls on his fellow Africans to turn their backs on the bourgeois humanist model of Europe, not in order to retreat into some essentialist black identity, but rather to create a new vision of humanity. The closing lines of *The Wretched of the Earth* seem particularly apt in relation to Sembene's work: 'For Europe, for ourselves and for humanity, comrades, we must turn over a new leaf, we must work out new concepts, and try to set afoot a new man.'[56] Many postmodernist/poststructuralist critics have criticised such attempts to forge counter-narratives of liberation and resistance as being derivative of the 'universalising' Western discourses of humanism and nationalism (Marxism is equally perceived as an 'alien', universalising discourse in Africa). However, I would agree with Neil Lazarus in arguing that it is a mistake 'to concede the

[54] In an example of his own oppositional and resistant nature, Sembene has struggled for over twenty years, so far in vain, to find the finance necessary to bring the story of his most cherished resistance figure, the nineteenth-century general and statesman Samory Touré, to the screen.
[55] Gérard Chaliand makes this same point in relation to the work of Frantz Fanon. See Chaliand, 'Frantz Fanon à l'épreuve du temps', p. 36.
[56] Fanon, *The Wretched of the Earth*, p. 255.

terrain of universality to these Eurocentric projections'.[57] Borrowing from the work of both Said and Lenin, Lazarus argues that the postcolonial writer/ intellectual has a fundamental role to play in imagining modes of resistance to the dominant ideologies of his/her society. In the context of the modern capitalist world system, which is in the process of creating a genuine global culture while at the same time reinforcing pre-existing structural inequalities,[58] this need to imagine alternatives is all the more pressing. In this light, Lazarus sees the conclusion of *The Wretched of the Earth* as providing a useful theoretical opening:

> Where postmodernist theory has reacted to the perceived indefensibility of bourgeois humanism and of colonial nationalism by abandoning the very idea of totality, a *genuinely* postcolonial strategy might be to move explicitly, as Fanon already did in concluding *The Wretched of the Earth*, to proclaim a 'new' humanism, predicated upon a formal repudiation of the degraded European form, and borne embryonically in the national liberation movement.[59]

Sembene's films and novels combine Marxism with a concern for issues of gender and culture in order to explore alternative visions of Africa. Although undoubtedly derivative of Western discourses, Sembene would argue that the notions of 'oppression' and 'resistance' are universal phenomena, even if they are to be found in a multitude of guises, depending upon the social context. By representing the resistance to oppression within his society, Sembene seeks to preserve his dream of an egalitarian, Marxist future. This is the utopian vision which he hopes will inspire his fellow Africans to create a more just society. Only history can determine the ability of this dream to survive and perhaps one day to become a reality.

[57] Neil Lazarus, 'Disavowing Decolonization: Fanon and the Problematic of Representation in Current Theories of Colonial Discourse', *Research in African Literatures*, 24, 4 (1993), p. 93.

[58] Neil Smith examines this process in *Uneven Development: Nature, Capital and the Production of Space* (1984; Oxford and Cambridge, MA: Basil Blackwell, 1990).

[59] Lazarus, 'Disavowing Decolonization', p. 93 (stress in original).

Conclusion

The concern with form and structure that is to be found in Sembene's tales of Senegalese resistance has been examined throughout this study. The aim of such an approach is not to bestow Sembene with the mythical values of the Great Writer (I am in no way seeking to return to a Leavis-style equation between great writing and moral values) but rather to allow his work to be examined in its full complexity. By analysing Sembene's textual as well as social challenge to the hegemonic discourses of his society, the standard account of his work as well-meaning but rather naive and monolithic in its Marxism can be seen to be both misleadingly partial and, in certain cases, ideologically motivated.

For the purposes of presenting this argument, shorter texts such as *Tribal Scars* and *White Genesis*, which have up until now received very little attention from critics compared to the novels *O Pays, mon beau peuple!*, *L'Harmattan* and, most notably, *God's Bits of Wood*, have been positioned at the centre of Sembene's œuvre. I am not suggesting that these epic novels are inferior to the shorter texts. As was argued in Chapter One, *God's Bits of Wood* remains one of the key texts of African literature. However, I feel that the tendency to concentrate upon the epic novels has helped to create a false picture of Sembene's work. Since the publication of *L'Harmattan* in 1963 (a novel that Sembene began writing prior to his return to Africa in 1960), Sembene has tended to write shorter, more elliptic and ironic works with the novella becoming his standard form. Indeed, some of his early novels, including *L'Harmattan*, are highly fragmented texts, despite their overall epic tone. Even in *God's Bits of Wood*, his most universally acclaimed novel, none of the book's twenty sections is over thirty pages long (equally, the four hundred pages of his most recent 'epic' novel, *The Last of the Empire*, is divided into no less than forty-six chapters). This fragmentation of the text, the use of short, often self-contained scenes, has passed virtually unnoticed by most critics of these

217

works, anxious to have Sembene conform to a standard Zola or Malraux-inspired version of the naturalist/social-realist novel. Similarly, the multiplicity of narrative voices in these novels (still informed by the writer's consciousness, however), which results from his decision to eschew the character of the individual male hero (with the exception of his first two novels, *Black Docker* and *O Pays, mon beau peuple!*), has not led critics to investigate the structure of these works in any great detail.[1] A radical reinterpretation of Sembene's early novels will thus be a vital step in the reassessment of his work which this study hopes to inspire.

The re-centring of the focus on Sembene's literature, which has been carried out in this study, has deliberately been centred around the short stories in *Tribal Scars* and the novella *White Genesis* for a number of reasons. Chief amongst these is the manner in which both works problematise the whole notion of storytelling. Secondly, both of these texts constitute a reflection upon art and society that appears to have preoccupied Sembene in the early years of Senegalese independence. Upon his return to Africa, after twelve years of exile in Europe, Sembene was able to see for himself the extent of the problems facing the newly liberated nations across the entire continent. The Fanonian, messianic belief in an imminent revolution to be born of the African independence movements, which had been clearly visible in both *O Pays, mon beau peuple!* and *God's Bits of Wood*, was replaced by a more disillusioned and ironic but also more imaginative and more comprehensive understanding of the dynamics of his society. This questioning of his art and his beliefs would also lead him to take up a cinematic career in which the problematisation of storytelling would be as prevalent as in his literature.

It was argued in the first chapter that Sembene's work is highly concerned with the notion of representation. In both his films and his literature, he constantly seeks to challenge the dominant discourses of his society. The legitimising power of such discourses is especially powerful in the emergent nations of the Third World where the play of nationalist forces and the attempts to establish the authority of the state are often of vital cultural and political importance. This examination of the dominant discourses of Senegalese society was seen to be a major thematic and structural concern in *Tribal Scars*. Sembene uses the *architecture secrète* of the collection to challenge the authority of certain hegemonic discourses within his society. At least within the imagined Senegal of his fiction, Sembene opens up the field of public discourse by giving voice to marginalised groups within society that are neglected or misrepresented (in Sembene's view) by the dominant nationalist, Islamic and racial or eurocentric discourses. Playing on the notion of silence, Sembene presents us with characters either unable or unwilling to speak out against the injustice that is seen to reign all around them. The stories thus become a pointed attempt to carve out a space for a discourse of resistance around which to crystallise the scattered and fragmented acts of rebellion recorded within the collection.

Only four of these stories were examined but the same arguments could be

---

[1] Roger Chemain's analysis of *God's Bits of Wood* is a noteworthy exception. See Roger Chemain, *L'Imaginaire dans le roman africain* (Paris: L'Harmattan, 1986), pp. 161–4.

made concerning all the other stories in the collection (indeed, several stories including 'Chaiba the Algerian' and 'Her Three Days' were mentioned in later chapters on colonialism and the representation of women, respectively). The agonised silence of the shop steward Malic and his fellow workers in 'A Matter of Conscience' is a prime example. Sembene had shown his faith in the trade union movement in *God's Bits of Wood* but through his portrait of the extravagant, womanising and hypocritical Ibra in 'A Matter of Conscience', he argues that the union leaders of independent Senegal have let their people down and are simply taking the place of their old colonial masters. Betrayed by leaders such as Ibra, Malic and the other workers lack the courage to defend their interests but, at least, there is a realisation (one of the *prises de conscience* referred to in the story's French title) at the end of the story that their leaders are no longer working in their interest. As one of the workers says: 'Those types have nothing in common with us. They're black outside – but inside they're just like the colonialists' (*TS*, p. 33). The irony is evident and shows that, even if the workers do not dare to stand up to their leaders, they are resistant to the path that they are taking. The workers know their leaders' game and Sembene, through voicing their half-spoken concerns, hints that these leaders may not be allowed to get away with their corrupt ways forever.

The remaining stories in *Tribal Scars* thus deserve to receive the critical attention afforded to 'In the Face of History' and 'Tribal Scars or The Voltaique' but which the scope of the present study did not allow me to undertake. It should not be imagined that certain of Sembene's works were omitted because they were of lesser significance than those examined. The sheer scale of Sembene's œuvre, which currently stands at ten books and an equal number of films, was always going to entail a selective approach. The short films *Borom Sarret* and *Taaw*, together with the novella *Niiwam*, could easily have been more closely examined in Chapter Three in which the representation of the African city is examined. Equally, the character of Digbé from *L'Harmattan* could have played a more prominent role in the discussion of fetishism in Chapter Four. The aim of this study was not to give a comprehensive survey of Sembene's entire œuvre but rather to carry out the groundwork for a new approach to his work that can be complemented by further research.

The other key text examined was *White Genesis*. The problematisation of the role of the storyteller in this novella opens up a debate that has long been avoided in African literature. The parallels drawn between the traditional *griot* and the modern African writer have, on the part of writers and critics, remained deliberately vague in their assumptions concerning both oral literature and modern African writing. In many respects, such comparisons have come to act as a shorthand which replaces any genuine reflection on the role of literature in modern Africa. Unlike the vast majority of African writers, Sembene does not belong to an educated elite. Having received little formal education, he became interested in literature while working as a trade union spokesman for African workers in France with the Communist trade union, the CGT. He therefore escaped from the two conceptions of the writer that have dominated amongst the African elite: the Romantic vision of the artist, and the nostalgic vision of the *griot*. The contradictory nature of a situation whereby a Western-educated elite wrote about the concerns of their class while claiming direct descent from the *griot*, viewed as the guardian of a uniquely African form of knowledge, was not lost on Sembene. As a committed Marxist, he associates himself with a vision of the *griot* as the noble guardian of truth and justice. Such a vision is deliberately partial but it serves to clarify Sembene's artistic and political project. His writing claims its descent from the oppositional role allotted to the *griot*. For Sembene, those who glibly praise the traditional values of African society, which they believe the *griot* to embody, while themselves writing for Western or Western-educated audiences, are to be denounced as hypocrites.

The problematisation of the role of the writer takes on an extra dimension in the African context. Despite his attempts to address the problems of the masses in his work, the fact remains for Sembene that the vast majority of Africans are illiterate, and are therefore unable to read his work. Consequently, alongside the contemplation within his literature on the role of the writer and storytelling, he carried out an even more concrete reflection on the subject through his decision to establish himself as a filmmaker in an attempt to reach a wider public. His cinematic work has proven to be equally engaged with the questions of discourse and representation. In his film *Ceddo*, this problematisation of the role of the *griot* and, more widely, of the control of public discourse can clearly be seen to be at work. One of the first steps taken by the imam on his accession to the throne is to replace Jaraaf, the *gewel*, with one of his own followers. The *gewel* acts as a mediator between the monarch and his subjects, therefore it is vital for the imam to have one of his supporters controlling the nature of public discourse. The discourse of the traditional monarchy will be replaced by a specifically Islamic discourse.

The analysis of *Le Mandat/Mandabi* allowed a closer examination of the question of representation in relation to Sembene's cinema. The critical debate that surrounded the film constantly harked back to the issue of its 'authenticity' as an African film: was it a 'true' representative of African cinema, and, consequently, did it 'truly' depict life in Africa? Central to this debate was the issue of the film's representation of the urban streetscape of Dakar. Opinion was polarised between those who saw Africa as quintessentially rural and those, mainly on the left, who saw the depiction of the urban space as a fundamental criterion for the emergence of an African cinema. Sembene's view of the city and country is far more complex than these opinions allow. In his view, the poor neighbourhoods of Dakar, and particularly the poor people who lived in them, were a reality which no-one had dared to represent on screen prior to him. Therefore, in *Le Mandat/Mandabi*, Sembene seeks literally to *represent* the urban poor, to show the world the conditions of their existence. In this way, the act of filmmaking itself becomes an act of resistance.

The example of Sembene's film *Xala* provided a particularly useful case study in the examination of the possibilities for the creation of a popular, radical African cinema. A hugely successful film within Senegal and West Africa in general, *Xala* served notice that African cinema may not always remain trapped inside its present enclaves of the French Cultural Centres within Africa, and the various film festivals on the continent and in Europe. While it is regrettable that the success of *Xala* did not create the breakthrough in terms of the distribution and production of African films which was hoped for at the time, it is difficult not to agree with Pierre Haffner's assessment that the very existence of an African cinema, considering the continent's current economic predicament, is a remarkable achievement in itself. Such an achievement may count for little if the films in question are not seen by an African audience, but the creation of a large body of African films may, in the future, provide a useful back catalogue for an enlightened generation of African cinema and television programmers.

Sembene has gone further than most filmmakers in his attempts to reach a wide, popular audience. Despite his advanced years, he still tours the Senegalese countryside (although less than in the past) showing his films in local halls and schools, and organising debates with the villagers after the projections. Sembene claims that the villagers display a sharper aesthetic and social understanding of his films than most critics (although it must be said that Sembene does not have a very high opinion of critics, in general). It would be very useful for a study of these educational film tours to be undertaken before it is too late (Sembene is now a septuagenarian). As far as I am aware, no other critic has followed up on Pierre Haffner's fascinating study of African audience response to films in his *Essai sur les fondements du cinéma africain*. A study of audience reactions to Sembene's films would indeed act as a useful counterbalance to Haffner's account of the reactions to foreign films (mainly Kung-Fu movies and Bollywood melodramas). It would be of great benefit to the critic to understand the status enjoyed by Sembene's highly political cinematic texts with a popular African audience. Are they dismissed as fantasies? Do they lead to a questioning of the issues raised? Do they help to create a new space for public discourse with which to challenge the dominant discourses of the state and Islam?

It would be naive to overstate the influence that works of fiction can have in fashioning social consciousness and, even if one accepts such an influence, it is impossible to quantify the phenomenon. Sembene himself recognises the political limitations of his work:

> *Je considère le cinéma comme un moyen d'action politique. Mais je suis contre le 'cinéma de pancartes'. Je sais bien que je ne changerai pas la réalité sénégalaise avec un seul film. Mais je crois qu'un groupe de cinéastes peut contribuer à développer des prises de conscience.*[2]

I see cinema as a form of political action. But I'm against 'slogan cinema'. I know that I won't change Senegalese society with one film. But I believe that a group of filmmakers can help to develop a political consciousness.

However, the influence of cinema can sometimes be directly felt. Within five years of the release of the film *Camp de Thiaroye*, the Senegalese government had declared that 1 December, the anniversary of the massacre at Thiaroye,

---

[2] Guy Hennebelle, 'Ousmane Sembène. "En Afrique noire nous sommes gouvernés par des enfants mongoliens du colonialisme"', *Les Lettres françaises*, 6–12 October 1971, p. 16.

should be a day of commemoration for the Senegalese who died in both world wars. Sembene's film did not achieve this by itself but the film appears to have given a determining final thrust to the demands of the Senegalese veterans' associations to have the massacre commemorated. The success of *Camp de Thiaroye* as a film serves as an example that cinema can directly influence the political sphere, although it cannot do so on its own (the existence of an organised veterans' lobby provided the necessary action to have their demands met). The commercial success of *Xala*, and, more recently, the relative success of *Guelwaar* during its short release in Dakar,[3] begs the question as to whether these films influence the manner in which the cinema-going public perceives the post-independence regime. Whatever the impossibility of quantifying this phenomenon, the fact remains that Sembene's films open up an oppositional discourse that voices resistance to those in authority. Films continue to exist both physically and in people's minds long after their release. While in Dakar in 1995, I came across a number of video copies of *Guelwaar* available on the city's markets. As such copies are, inevitably, illegal pirate copies, one cannot record the number of people who see them. Research remains to be carried out to determine just how conscious Africans are of a radical African cinema.

The manner in which Sembene challenges standard representations of his society in both his films and his books has been the main focus of this study. It is notoriously difficult for the Western critic to fully address the complexities of African societies, which often appear exotic and impenetrable to the Western eye. However, this does not mean that the Western critic's work should be immediately dismissed because of a perceived eurocentrism. I would agree with Roger Little in declaring that being an outsider in relation to African society is merely an inescapable fact:

> *Sortir de notre peau blanche et partant de notre culture est fatalement exclu. Comme le rappelle Todorov dans* Nous et les autres, *'on n'en a jamais tout à fait fini avec l'ethnocentrisme'. Si, plus loin dans le même ouvrage, il opine que 'pour éprouver l'autre, on n'a pas besoin de cesser d'être soi', nous pensons qu'au contraire on ne saurait cesser d'être soi, si oublieux, voire si généreux que l'on puisse être.*[4]

Stepping outside of our white skin and leaving behind our cultural baggage is simply impossible. As Todorov reminds us in *Nous et les autres*, 'one never escapes completely from ethnocentrism'. Later in the same work, Todorov offers the opinion that in order 'to experience the other, one does not have to cease being oneself'. On the contrary, I would argue that one can never cease being oneself, no matter how self-effacing or generous one attempts to be.

The inescapable eurocentrism of a Western critic must be taken into account when appraising his/her work but should, in no way, be used to disqualify such work. The assumption on the part of a Christopher L. Miller that there is

---

[3] *Guelwaar* was shown at the *Foire* in Dakar throughout December 1993. The film was quite successful, but the exclusive nature of the cinema, with prices ranging from 2,000 to 5,000 CFA, meant that it could not hope to attract a 'popular' audience. For details of the film's release and other information on recent developments within Senegalese cinema, see Elizabeth Mermin, 'A Window on Whose Reality? The Emerging Industry of Senegalese Cinema', *Research in African Literatures*, 26, 3 (Autumn 1995), pp. 120–33.

[4] Roger Little, *Nègres Blancs: Représentations de l'autre autre* (Paris: L'Harmattan, 1995), p. 12.

an *authentic* African point of view to which the Western critic should vainly aspire is vitally flawed. While one cannot but accept that an African critic may very well have a different set of assumptions from the Western critic, there is absolutely no means of establishing the existence of a single, unified African view on African issues. Will a Muslim from Dakar see eye to eye with one of the many recent converts to the Protestant Evangelical churches in Kenya? What would either of these two have in common with a pygmy from the jungles of Equatorial Africa? To echo the words of the Congolese philosopher Charles Z. Bowao quoted earlier, African ethnocentrism is no more objective in status than European ethnocentrism. In the light of such a situation, critics must simply attempt to master the material at their disposal to the best of their abilities.

This desire to explore the intermingling and sometimes open combat between various discourses within Senegalese society has led me to use quite a large body of material, which will possibly be unknown to many Western readers (not to mention those Africans unfamiliar with West African history – far too often the simple fact of the vastness of Africa as a continent is ignored by both Western and African critics). Some critics may disapprove of the lack of theoretical references but these have deliberately been kept to a minimum in order to give more space to this African material. My explicit debts to such critics as Aijaz Ahmad, Neil Lazarus and Mamadou Diouf have largely been confined to the first two chapters where I set out my theoretical framework.

Two of the most telling ironies of postcolonial studies are that a highly developed theory has evolved, primarily within the last decade or so, while many of the main postcolonial texts remain difficult to obtain (the situation with films is even worse), and secondly, that this theory has a tendency to make generalisations about areas of the world with vastly different histories.[5] It is because of this conscious desire to address some of the specific issues facing Senegalese society (and, also, to a certain extent, Africa, in general) that I have examined texts by Assane Sylla, Amar Samb and Souleymane Bachir Diagne, amongst others. As is clear from the very title of Mamadou Diouf's essay 'Représentations historiques et légitimités politiques au Sénégal (1960-1987)', which has been examined at length at various points in this study, there has been a tremendous struggle between competing social discourses for authority in the arena of historical representation within independent Senegal, a struggle that can be quite bewildering for the uninitiated.

One of the most complex subjects analysed in this study has been that of fetishism. The widespread belief in supernatural practices that one finds in African countries presents a problem for the largely secular and rational Western critic, not inclined to accept the reality or efficacy of such practices. However, the question of the truth behind such beliefs is largely secondary to the simple fact that many Africans simply *do* believe in them. As a Marxist, Sembene would not be sympathetic to belief in the supernatural, but he is keenly aware

[5] Witness the manner in which many Third World critics rounded on Fredric Jameson for his generalisations about Third World literature in his controversial essay, 'Third-World Literature in the Era of Multi-National Capitalism', *Social Text*, 15 (1986), pp. 65–88.

of the role which it plays in the daily lives of the characters whom he describes in his books and his films.[6] In the chapter on *Xala*, I relied heavily on a number of psychological studies carried out in the Dakar area around the time at which the film was made. To apply a Western psychoanalytical framework to an African situation in which the structure of the family is so different from that of its Western counterpart would, to my mind, have been an unacceptable imposition. Instead, it was decided to examine the different representations of fetishism. Between the dismissive discourse of the West (begun by Hegel almost two hundred years ago) and the distinctly traditionalist discourse of those who actively believe in fetishist practices, it was found that the psychological studies examined provide a more complex vision of a rapidly evolving society where the supernatural still retains a power which can resurface at short notice. By allying them with the cause of the dispossessed within Senegalese society, Sembene invests fetishist practices with a social consciousness denied to them by all of these other discourses. His intervention is made at the level of representation, the manner in which the supernatural is perceived within society, and it is at this level that I believe one can most profitably examine the film in the absence of a fully developed, coherent psychoanalytical theory adapted to the realities of African societies. Essentially, fetishism functions as a shaping contribution to the overall economy of the film.

A similar problem with the use of Western psychoanalytical theory is to be found in relation to the role of women within African literature and cinema. As was argued in Chapter Five, there is an ongoing debate between feminist critics which has seen those from the Third World accuse their Western counterparts of making extremely general assumptions about the role of women within Third World countries. Rather than the largely psychoanalytical approach of Western critics, these Third World critics have proposed an approach in which the issues of gender, class and race are combined. Once again, I have chosen to steer clear of a psychoanalytical approach fraught with such methodological difficulties and have instead concentrated on the manner in which Sembene challenges the standard representations of women to be found in African literature and cinema, and also those proposed by the discourses of Negritude and Islam.

The examination of the representation of empire and that of neo-colonialism in the final two chapters of this study forms the centre of my reflection upon Sembene's oppositional discourse. In this respect, *Ceddo* appears as the key text in Sembene's entire œuvre. A film that actively seeks to reinterpret the past in order to challenge the nationalist and Islamic discourses of contemporary Senegal, it acts as an examination of the processes involved in cultural and

---

[6] The term 'magic realism' (originally applied to South American writers such as Gabriel Garcia Márquez and Maria Vargos Llosa) has been applied to many postcolonial texts in which reality and the supernatural are shown to be rather fluid concepts. One of the major postcolonial practitioners of this form of writing is the Anglo-Indian writer, Salman Rushdie. See especially his *Midnight's Children* (1981; London: Vintage, 1995). A major exponent of this form of writing in Francophone Africa was the Congolese writer Sony Labou Tansi who died in 1995. See his novels, *La Vie et demie*, and *The Seven Solitudes of Lorsa Lopez*, trans. by Clive Wake (London: Heinemann, 1995).

social domination. In Sembene's view, Islamic leaders appropriated the forms of traditional monarchical power after the fall of the Senegalese monarchies at the end of the nineteenth century. Effectively, this led to an 'islamisation' of Senegalese history. Therefore, Sembene's intervention in Senegalese history seeks to redress the balance and to reveal the historical processes that have become occulted by the powerful myth of the Islamic nation of Senegal. Sembene equally challenges French imperial discourse in *Emitaï* and *Camp de Thiaroye*. The processes at work in the neo-colonial order are revealed in *The Last of the Empire* and *Guelwaar*.

However, Sembene's version of Senegalese history is not an objective history either. He deliberately combines the notion of popular resistance to foreign domination with that of the *ceddo*'s stubborn defence of their animist ways in the face of Islam. These historical falsifications have not been hidden in this study, but rather I have tried to examine Sembene's purpose in creating these counter-narratives of Senegalese history. One may justifiably object that Sembene's historical narratives are as ideologically compromised as those which he sets out to criticise, but Sembene does not seek to present his stories as the 'objective' truth. His narratives are precisely designed to be ideological, to espouse his Marxist viewpoint. While one cannot deny the reality of objective historical facts, the situation becomes far more unclear when we are presented with even the most simple historical narrative. Professional historians may argue over the small print and the fine details, but the broader picture of history in Africa (as elsewhere) is made in the public sphere. Sembene, therefore, creates a history of resistance, using both historical and fictional situations. His aim is to voice the resistance to domination that would otherwise have no public outlet, speaking out on behalf of those who are marginalised and oppressed, yet still defiant, within his society. He constantly seeks to imagine alternatives, both in terms of the form and the media which he uses, and also in terms of the pluralist social vision which he expresses. In keeping with Salman Rushdie's ideas on the power of fiction to challenge the authority of dominant narratives, Sembene 'redescribes' Africa in his own manner. Sembene's Africa may not be *authentic*, but it reflects his Marxist vision of an Africa that refuses to submit.

The danger for a radical artist such as Sembene is that he will allow himself to be 'appropriated' by the regime in power, which will attempt to defuse his radical message by claiming that the very existence of his oppositional work proves the justice and equity of their rule. In a 1971 interview, Sembene spoke of the problematic status of his artistic discourse in the single-party regime of Senghor's Senegal:

> *Je me rends parfaitement compte que je sers pour le moment d'alibi à Senghor qui peut laisser entendre à l'étranger: 'Voyez comme je suis libéral: je laisse Sembène faire des films de contestation'. C'est une contradiction que j'essaie d'utiliser au mieux.*[1]

I understand completely that I serve as an alibi for Senghor because he can say to the outside world: 'See how liberal I am: I let Sembene make oppositional films.' I'm in a contradictory position but I try to make the best of it.

---

[1] Guy Hennebelle, 'Ousmane Sembène. "En Afrique, nous sommes gouvernés"', p. 16.

Effectively, Sembene argues that he is obliged to work within the contradictions of his society. In many other African countries, his work would have been banned and he would most likely have spent a large part of the last thirty years in prison. However, he has refused to allow the 'liberal' arts policies of Senghor and Diouf to temper his antipathy towards their regimes. The risk of having his work 'co-opted' by the government is simply a risk he must run.

The ambiguity of Sembene's position is encapsulated in an incident from 1993 when he was awarded the *Grand Prix du Président de la République pour les arts et lettres* for his lifetime's work. As is usually the case with such awards, the Senegalese president Abdou Diouf had no part in the decision of the jury, and, judging from the newspaper reports, he was very uneasy at the awards ceremony in the national theatre. Faced with one of his government's most ardent critics in Sembene, Diouf's speech was deliberately ambiguous, and involuntarily comic: *'autodidacte, vous avez atteint, grâce à un travail opiniâtre, les cimes de la notoriété'* ['a self-educated man, you have gained notoriety through your outspoken work'].[8] The general unease appears to have been shared by Sembene, and the final line from the report on the awards ceremony displays his attitude towards such attempts to 'appropriate' his work: *'Sembene après un bref entretien avec le chef de l'Etat n'a pas attendu la fin de la cérémonie pour disparaître subrepticement'* ['After a brief discussion with the head of state, Sembene slipped quietly out of the building before the end of the ceremony'].[9] Although agreeing to attend the ceremony, Sembene nonetheless keeps his distance from the Diouf regime, refusing to become an 'official', 'state' artist. He has often spoken of this desire to maintain his artistic independence:

> *[...] je ne veux pas de poste politique; je ne veux même pas de poste bénévole, car chez nous, avec les postes bénévoles, le chef d'Etat alloue une certaine somme à des artistes pour qu'ils écrivent, et finalement ces artistes n'écrivent pas! Si je voulais un tel poste, je serais obligé de prendre mes licences avec les partis en compétition, et je ne veux pas qu'ils m'utilisent! Cependant, si j'ai un mauvais président, j'en suis responsable et ce qui me donne le droit de le juger c'est justement que je me sens responsable et concerné.[10]*

> [...] I don't want to be a political appointee; I don't even want a 'voluntary post' because, in our country, what happens is that the head of state allocates a certain amount of money to allow such artists to write, and none of them end up writing anything! If I wanted a job like that I'd work with the various political parties but I don't want to be used by them! However, if there's a bad President in the country, what allows me to judge him is that I am responsible only to myself and I can express my own concerns.

Sembene may rely on the benevolence of the government to carry out his artistic enterprise, but his work will continue to imagine alternatives to 'official' versions of the truth. Appearing on a stage with the president does not mean that he is willing to share a platform with those in power: Sembene voices the resistance of those on the margins of his society.

---

[8] Alassane Cissé, 'La Fête de l'esprit', *Sud Quotidien*, 18 November 1993, p. 2.

[9] Ibid.

[10] Pierre Haffner, 'Eléments pour un autoportrait magnétique', *L'Afrique littéraire*, 76 (1985), p. 23. The article is made up of a series of quotes from interviews given by Sembene during a visit to Zaïre in November 1977.

Appendix

Interview with Sembene at Filmi Doomireew, Dakar
30 November 1995*

David Murphy: *Votre premier livre,* Le Docker noir, *parle de la communauté africaine à Marseille pendant les années cinquante. L'écrivain jamaïquain, Claude McKay, traite lui aussi des problèmes de la communauté noire à Marseille à une autre période, celle des années vingt, dans son livre,* Banjo. *L'aviez-vous lu avant d'écrire* Le Docker noir*?*
Your first novel, *Black Docker*, deals with the African community in Marseilles during the 1950s. The Jamaican writer, Claude McKay, also deals with the black community in Marseilles during an earlier period, the 1920s, in his novel, *Banjo*. Had you read this book before writing *Black Docker*?

Sembene: *Non, je ne l'avais pas lu. Je ne l'ai toujours pas lu d'ailleurs. Je ne crois pas que le livre était disponible à l'époque coloniale. Je sais qu'il y a des gens qui ont écrit des comparaisons sur les deux livres mais moi je ne l'ai jamais lu.*
No, I hadn't read it. I still haven't read it either. I don't think it was available during the colonial period. I know people have written comparisons of the two books but I myself haven't read it.

D. Murphy: *Est-ce que vous vous identifiez plus au travail des écrivains noirs des Etats-Unis comme Richard Wright, James Baldwin, Ralph Ellison, qu'au travail de certains écrivains africains de l'époque coloniale qui parlaient d'une Afrique mythique, d'une Afrique du passé?*
During this period, did you identify more with the work of black writers from the United States like Richard Wright, James Baldwin, Ralph Ellison, than with

---

* Due to technical problems, the sound on the recording of this interview was inaudible. I was therefore obliged to reconstitute the interview from my notes. Although the words attributed to Sembene may not always be the exact words he used, every effort has been made to capture the tone and especially the content of his answers. However, all quotes in French from the original interview cited in the main body of the text do use Sembene's exact words.

the works of African writers who wrote about a mythical Africa of the past?

Sembene: *Mais moi, je* suis *Africain. Pourquoi je dois aller chercher quelque chose aux Etats-Unis? Je ne suis pas obligé de chercher une identité. Je suis Africain. Pour moi, l'Afrique est le centre du monde. Les Etats-Unis, l'Europe, c'est la périphérie pour moi. Je suis né en Afrique, je ne suis pas né dans les ghettos des grandes villes américaines comme les noirs du diaspora.*

But I *am* African. Why would I go looking for something in the United States? I don't have to search for an identity. I'm an African. For me, Africa is the centre of the world. The United States and Europe are on the periphery of my world. I was born in Africa not in the ghettos of a big American city like the blacks of the diaspora.

D. Murphy: *Si je pose la question c'est parce que vous avez souvent dit que vous vouliez créer une autre image de l'Afrique que celle des écrivains de la Négritude. Mais l'action de votre premier livre se déroule en France, dans une communauté raciale mixte et traite des problèmes entre blancs et noirs, sujet dont on parlait souvent chez les écrivains américains. Je me demandais simplement si ces écrivains vous ont influencé.*

The reason why I asked the question is that you have often said that you wanted to create a different image of Africa from the one put forward by Negritude writers. But the story of your first novel is set in France, in a racially mixed community, and it deals with problems between blacks and whites. This is a subject that black American writers often deal with. I was simply wondering if these writers had influenced you.

Sembene: *Vous savez, je ne me pose pas ce genre de question. Ça, c'est votre travail. Bien sûr, d'autres écrivains africains n'avaient pas la même conception de l'Afrique que moi. Ils parlaient du côté mythique, un peu naïf. Mais moi, j'écris et c'est tout. J'ai pas besoin des autres. Je suis le centre du monde.*

You know, I never think about things like that. That's your job. Of course, there were other writers who didn't have the same conception of Africa as me. They spoke a bit naïvely about the mythical side of things. But I just write and that's all there is to it. I don't think about other writers. I'm the centre of my world.

D. Murphy: *Dans* Le Docker noir, *Diaw Falla n'arrive pas à justifier sa voix en tant qu'écrivain africain et autodidacte. Est-ce que ce roman, avec sa mise en abyme d'un écrivain africain écrivant son premier livre, était une tentative d'adresser des problèmes auxquels vous vous trouviez confrontés au début de votre carrière littéraire?*

In *Black Docker*, Diaw Falla is unable to legitimate his position as a self-educated, African writer. Is the novel, with its *mise en abyme* of an African writing his first novel, an attempt to address the problems you faced at the outset of your literary career?

Sembene: *Vous savez, il n'y a pas de races: le jaune, le noir, le blanc, ca n'existe pas. Pendant les années cinquante, j'ai essayé de combattre le régime colonial. A ce moment-là, on* *ne croyait pas qu'un Africain pouvait être scientifique. Les Français ne permettaient pas aux Africains de devenir physiciens, etc. A l'époque, on voulait proclamer notre droit.*

You know, there are no races: yellow, black, white, none of them exists. During the 1950s, I tried to fight against the colonial regime. At the time, nobody believed that an African could master science. The French wouldn't allow Africans to become physicists, etc. At the time, we wanted to claim our human rights.

D. Murphy: *On parle de vous surtout comme écrivain engagé mais on voit que dès le début de votre carrière, avec cette mise en abyme dans* Le Docker noir, *il y a déjà une réflexion sur la forme. Est-ce que cela vous gêne en tant qu'artiste que la critique porte souvent sur les thèmes de vos livres sans vraiment examiner la structure et l'aspect esthétique, qui sont pourtant les voies par lesquelles un artiste transmet son message?*

You are often referred to as a committed writer but we can see that from the start of your career, with the *mise en abyme* in *Black Docker*, you were already concerned with the form of your work. Does it bother you as an artist that criticism often deals with the themes of your books without looking at the structure or the aesthetic aspect, which are the means by which an artist transmits his message?

Sembene: *Mais ça, c'est leur problème. Ça ne m'intéresse pas. Quand j'écris un livre c'est fini. Je ne veux pas passer mon temps à réflechir sur les raisons pour lesquelles j'ai fait ceci ou cela.*

But that's their problem. I'm not interested in all that. When I write a book, it's finished for me. I don't want to spend my time thinking about why I did this or that.

D. Murphy: *Dans vos deux premiers livres,* Le Docker noir *et* O Pays, mon beau peuple!, *on a l'impression que les femmes sont plus passives que celles qu'on trouve dans le reste de votre œuvre. Est-ce que vous trouviez difficile d'écrire des rôles pour des femmes à cette époque?*

In your first two books, *Black Docker* and *O Pays, mon beau peuple!*, the female characters seem to be a lot more passive than the ones we find in your later works. Did you find it difficult to write female roles at first?

Sembene: *C'est à cause de questions comme celle-là que je n'aime pas donner des interviews. Vous les universitaires, vous êtes ce que j'appelle des 'chronophages'. Vous comprenez? 'A quel moment vous avez fait ceci ou cela?' Vous êtes tous des disciples de Freud en plus. Je ne me pose pas de telles questions.*

It's because of questions like that that I don't like giving interviews. You academics are what I call 'chronophages'. Do you know what I mean by that? 'When did you do this or that?' What's more, you're all disciples of Freud as well. I don't ask myself questions like that.

D. Murphy: *L'image que vous donnez de la femme dans votre société est assez complexe. Les femmes dans votre œuvre sont souvent conscientes de leur position inférieure mais leur* *éducation leur a appris la soumission, et la rivalité entre les femmes empêche une solidarité entre elles. Comment voyez-vous l'évolution de la femme ici au Sénégal?*

The image you present of women in your society is fairly complex. The women in your work are often aware of their inferior position but their education has taught them to be submissive, and the rivalry between women prevents solidarity from developing. How do you see the evolution of women's role in society here in Senegal?

Sembene: *Mais la femme africaine est plus libre que la femme européenne! Vous posez cette question parce que les Européens pensent que la femme africaine est soumise. En Afrique, la femme et l'homme détiennent deux pouvoirs séparés dans des domaines bien délimités.*

But the African woman has more freedom than the European woman! You ask the question because Europeans think that the African woman is oppressed. In Africa, women and men have separate powers in strictly defined areas.

D. Murphy: *C'est peut-être vrai que la femme africaine est plus libre qu'on ne le pense en Europe. Mais dans* Taaw, *par exemple, on voit Yaye Dabo qui répudie son mari et qui est choquée par son propre comportement. Cela va contre son éducation.*

It might be true that the African woman has more freedom than it is thought in Europe. But for example, in *Taaw*, we see Yaye Dabo repudiate her husband and she is shocked by her own behaviour. It goes against her education.

Sembene: *Ecoutez, il y a la mère. Elle ressent certaines choses. Pour elle, ses enfants passent avant tout. Elle veut qu'ils réussissent. Dans votre pays, on s'est entretué pendant trente ans. Pensez à toutes les femmes qui sont veuves ou qui ont perdu des enfants. Une mère est une mère dans n'importe quel pays du monde, vous voyez?*

Listen, the mother exists. She feels certain things. Her children are more important to her than anything else. She wants them to succeed. In your country [Ireland], people have been killing each other for thirty years. Think of all those widows or those women who have lost children. You see, mothers are the same in every part of the world.

D. Murphy: *Pendant les années cinquante, vous avez habité en France. A quel moment êtes-vous retournés en Afrique?*

During the 1950s, you lived in France. When exactly did you return to Africa?

Sembene: *Je suis retourné après l'indépendance.*

I returned after independence.

D. Murphy: *Est-ce que* Voltaïque *et* L'Harmattan *ont été écrits en Afrique? Et dans quel ordre?*

Were *Tribal Scars* and *L'Harmattan* written in Africa? And in which order did you write them?

Interview with Sembene

Sembene: *Je ne sais plus en quelle année on les a publiés.*
I can't remember which year they were published.

D. Murphy: *1962 et 1963.*
1962 and 1963.

Sembene: *Oui, je les ai écrits après mon retour en Afrique.*
Yes, I wrote them after my return to Africa.

D. Murphy: *Est-ce que vous avez écrit* Voltaïque *en tant que recueil avec une structure bien définie? Ou est-ce que vous avez simplement rassemblé des nouvelles que vous aviez écrites au cours d'une certaine période, ou que vous aviez fait publier dans des revues peut-être?*
Did you write *Tribal Scars* as a collection with a specific structure? Or did you just group together stories that you had written over a certain period, or that might have been published in journals perhaps?

Sembene: *Moi, j'écris toujours. Je suis toujours en train d'écrire quelque chose. Même maintenant, j'ai des nouvelles chez moi que je n'ai pas publiées.*
I'm always writing. I'm always in the middle of writing something. Even now, I have stories at home that I haven't published.

D. Murphy: *Mais était-ce un choix conscient de placer la première et la dernière histoire là où elles sont. 'Devant l'histoire' avertit le lecteur tout de suite de la question de la forme en se référant aux deux significations du terme 'histoire'. Puis, 'Le Voltaïque' nous donne toutes ces différentes versions de l'histoire des balafres, et, à la fin, le narrateur demande au lecteur ce qu'il en pense.*
But were the choices for first and last story deliberate? 'In the Face of History' sets the reader thinking about questions of form straight away by referring to the two meanings of 'histoire'. Then, 'Tribal Scars or The Voltaique' gives us all those different versions of the history of scarification, and at the end, the narrator asks the reader for his opinion.

Sembene: *L'histoire des balafres était quelque chose sur laquelle j'avais fait beaucoup de recherches au moment où j'écrivais un livre sur l'esclavage que je n'ai jamais publié. J'ai constaté que les esclaves qui arrivaient aux Antilles ne portaient pas de marques sur leur visage. Les esclaves ne devaient pas porter de cicatrices. Alors, j'ai parlé avec beaucoup de gens et j'ai découvert que ce phénomène se limitait à l'Afrique littorale. Au début, les gens portaient des balafres pour ne pas devenir des esclaves. Mais on ne veut pas me croire. On donne des explications mythiques et symboliques.*
The history of scarification was a subject that I had researched heavily when I was working on a book about slavery that was never published. I noticed that the slaves that made it to the Caribbean had no marks on their faces. The slaves had no scars. So, I talked with a lot of people and I discovered that the whole phenomenon [of scarification] was limited to the coastal regions of Africa. In the beginning, people scarred their faces to avoid becoming slaves.

But people don't want to believe me. They give mythical and symbolic explanations.

D. Murphy: *L'école de la Négritude se voulait la voix de la tradition. Est-ce que* Voltaïque *est en quelque sorte une tentative d'approprier la tradition pour vos propres fins?* The Negritude school saw itself as the voice of tradition. Was *Tribal Scars* an attempt to appropriate tradition for your own ends?

Sembene: *Je dirais que c'est plus qu'une tentative. Je le fais.* It's more than just an attempt. I do appropriate it.

D. Murphy: *Vous vouliez placer l'Afrique dans l'histoire plutôt que dans le domaine mythique de la tradition?* You wanted to situate Africa within history rather than in the mythical world of tradition?

Sembene: *Mais l'Afrique a toujours existé dans l'histoire. Pour moi, elle est le centre du monde!* But Africa has always existed within history. For me, Africa is the centre of the world!

D. Murphy: *Oui, mais ce que je voulais dire, c'est que vous vouliez expliquer les traditions africaines d'une façon plus concrète: échapper à cette Afrique mythique, montrer aux gens que l'Afrique était le centre du monde si vous voulez! Expliquer aux Africains comment ils sont arrivés à ce point de leur histoire.* Yes, but what I mean is that you wanted to explain African traditions in a more concrete way: to escape from the mythical Africa, to show people that Africa is at the centre of the world, if you like! To explain to Africans how they reached this point in their history.

Sembene: *Oui, il fallait montrer aux gens qu'ils avaient une part de responsabilité dans leur histoire. Que l'esclavage existait chez nous, que des Africains ont aidé à asservir d'autres Africains. Il faut assumer notre histoire.* Yes, it was necessary to show people that they had to share responsibility for their own history. To show them that slavery existed here and that Africans helped to enslave other Africans. We must assume responsibility for our history.

D. Murphy: *Depuis* Voltaïque, *vous avez écrit principalement des nouvelles. Alors la nouvelle est un genre où on esquisse, où on ne dit pas tout, et qui porte souvent un regard ironique et désabusé sur son sujet. Cela contraste fortement avec le côté épique de romans comme* O Pays, mon beau peuple! *et* Les Bouts de bois de Dieu. *Est-ce une réflexion du passage de l'optimisme d'avant l'indépendance au pessimisme et à la déception de l'après-indépendance?* Since *Tribal Scars*, you've mainly written shorter works, short stories and especially novellas. The novella is a genre in which the story is sketched, where not everything is said, and which often casts an ironic and disillusioned eye on its subject. There's quite a contrast here with the epic elements of novels such as *O Pays, mon beau peuple!* and *God's Bits of Wood*. Is this a reflection of the move from the optimism of independence to the pessimism and disappointment of post-independence?

Sembene: *Mais pourquoi la nouvelle est ironique et désabusée? C'est vous qui dites que la nouvelle est comme ça. Moi, j'écris, c'est tout.*
But who says the novella is ironic and disillusioned? That's what you say. I just write and that's it.

D. Murphy: *Oui, mais vous acceptez quand-même que dans vos premiers romans, surtout* Les Bouts de bois de Dieu, *il y a un côté épique qu'on ne trouve pas dans vos œuvres plus récentes?*
Yes, but you must accept that your first novels, and *God's Bits of Wood* in particular, have an epic side that we don't find in your later work.

Sembene: *Moi, j'écris. Je fais des films. Je ne me pose pas ces questions-là. Ça, c'est le travail de la critique.*
I write. I make films. I don't think about questions like that. That's the critic's job.

D. Murphy: *Dans votre œuvre littéraire et cinématographique vous semblez souvent structurer l'histoire autour de la notion de silence. Par exemple, 'La Noire de' et* Guelwaar *donnent une voix à des personnages qui sont morts. Les morts ne peuvent pas parler mais l'artiste peut le faire à leur place. Je pense aussi à Pays dans* Camp de Thiaroye *qui ne peut pas exprimer sa peine, ou Thierno dans* Niiwam *qui est obligé de garder le silence, de garder son terrible secret. Comment expliquez-vous ce paradoxe du silence et de la parole dans votre démarche artistique?*
You often seem to structure your films and fiction around the notion of silence. For example, 'The Promised Land' and *Guelwaar* give a voice to two dead characters. The dead cannot speak but the artist can speak for them. I'm thinking also about Pays in *Camp de Thiaroye* who cannot express his suffering, or Thierno in *Niiwam* who has to keep quiet in order to keep his terrible secret. How do you explain this paradox of silence and language in your art?

Sembene: *Le langage est comme ça. Parfois on n'a pas besoin de parler pour exprimer quelque chose.*
Language is like that. Sometimes you don't need to speak to explain something.

D. Murphy: *Mais la parole semble être liée à l'idée du pouvoir dans votre œuvre.*
But language seems to be linked to power in your work.

Sembene: *On n'a pas besoin de parler pour avoir le pouvoir. Le pouvoir existe. J'essaie de représenter la vie telle que je la vois.*

You don't need to speak to hold power. Power exists. I try to present the world as I see it.

D. Murphy: *Vous allez peut-être dire que j'essaie de vous flatter mais je trouve qu'il y a une réflexion dans votre œuvre sur la question de la forme que la critique néglige. On parle tout le temps de votre engagement mais vous n'écrivez pas de tracts politiques. Vous avez dit vous-même dans d'autres interviews que vous ne faites pas une 'littérature de pancartes'.*
You might think that I'm trying to flatter you but I think that your work contains a serious reflection on questions of form, a reflection that is neglected by the critics. Critics constantly write about your commitment but you don't write political pamphlets. You've said yourself in interviews that you don't write a 'slogan literature'.

Sembène: *Vous savez, le critique africain parle constamment de l'engagement même sans savoir ce que veut dire l'engagement. Tous les critiques africains veulent faire la révolution par procuration. Vous connaissez Maguèye Kassé à l'université [de Dakar]? Deux fois il y a eu des séminaires sur mon travail à l'université et on n'a pas arrêté de parler de l'engagement. C'est un côté où peut-être l'Européen pourrait apporter quelque chose, un regard sur la forme. Ici on n'arrive pas à le faire. Je ne fais pas une littérature du 1er mai. La critique en Europe est en avance dans ce sens-là. Oui, je suis artiste. En tant qu'artiste, tout ce qui m'intéresse c'est de rester au plus près de mon peuple.*
You know, African critics constantly speak about commitment without even knowing what it means. African critics all want to carry out the revolution by proxy. Do you know Maguèye Kassé from the university [of Dakar]? He's held two conferences on my work in the university and they never stopped talking about commitment. Maybe the European critic could be useful in introducing a deeper reflection on the question of form. You just don't get that here. I don't write a literature of political slogans. European criticism is more developed in this area. Yes, I'm an artist, and as an artist, what interests me is to remain as close to my people as possible.

D. Murphy: *Dans la préface de* Véhi-Ciosane, *le narrateur dit qu'on lui a demandé de ne pas raconter cette histoire d'inceste. Est-ce que c'est le but de votre œuvre de créer un discours autour de sujets comme la religion, la politique, la tradition, des sujets qui semble-t-il sont trop souvent passés sous silence?*
In the preface to *White Genesis*, the narrator claims that he was asked not to recount this story of incest. Is it the aim of your work to create a discourse around subjects like religion, politics, tradition, subjects that often seem to pass uncontested?

Sembène: *Ces choses font partie de la vie. Il faut en parler. J'ai fait un film de* Véhi-Ciosane *que j'ai censuré moi-même. Le film dure vingt-deux minutes. On a fait une projection et la discussion après a duré trois heures. On a dénoncé l'inceste qui est une chose dont on n'aime pas parler dans n'importe quelle société. Il faut que les gens parlent.*
These things are all part of life. We need to talk about them. I made a film of *White Genesis* but I ended up censoring it myself. The film lasts 22 minutes. We

showed it to the public and the debate lasted three hours. The film denounces incest, a subject that people don't like to talk about in any country. But people must keep talking to each other.

D. Murphy: *En Afrique, la tradition est souvent citée pour défendre certaines valeurs conservatrices. Mais dans votre œuvre, vous essayez de dégager un sens plus positif des traditions, quelque chose qui peut servir aux gens dans l'Afrique actuelle. Est-ce que vous essayez de contrer les arguments des traditionalistes en présentant des personnages traditionnels comme le* griot, *le sage Kocc Barma, le guerrier* ceddo, *comme des 'hommes de refus'?*
In Africa, tradition is often quoted to defend certain conservative values. But in your work, you try to open up traditions to more positive readings that are useful in contemporary Africa. Are you attempting to go against the arguments of traditionalists when you present traditional characters such as the *griot*, the wise man Kocc Barma, the *ceddo* warrior, as 'oppositional figures'?

Sembene: *Oui. Vous voyez, il y a de bonnes et de mauvaises choses dans la tradition. Je ne suis pas un expert sur Kocc Barma ni sur son époque mais si je ne me trompe pas, c'était l'époque de l'esclavage. Vous voyez?*
Yes. You see, there are good and bad elements in tradition. I'm no expert on Kocc Barma or his era but, if I'm not wrong, it was the era of the slave trade. Do you see what I mean?

D. Murphy: *Vous essayez de souligner ce qui est pratique pour l'Afrique moderne dans la tradition? Vous donnez une version alternative des traditions africaines?*
You're trying to point out elements of tradition that are practical within modern Africa? You're giving an alternative version of African traditions?

Sembene: *C'est ça. J'ai fait la même chose pour* Ceddo. *Je reconnais que ce n'est peut-être pas historique mais c'est* ma *version. Vous savez, les Wolof sont l'ethnie la plus bâtarde au Sénégal. Ils regardent vers l'Occident ou vers la Mecque. Ils ne s'intéressent pas à l'Afrique.*
Exactly. I did the same thing in *Ceddo*. I admit that the film is not historical but it's *my* version. You know, the Wolof are the most bastardised ethnic group in Senegal. They're always looking towards the West or Mecca. They're not interested in Africa.

D. Murphy: *Est-ce que vous percevez Samory Touré, qui vous préoccupe tant, lui aussi comme un 'homme de refus'?*
Do you consider Samory Touré, with whom you have been preoccupied for so long now, as an oppositional figure?

Sembene: *Ce n'est pas mon interprétation. Ce sont les faits. J'étais intrigué par ce personnage qui a combattu les Français pendant dix-huit ans sans quitter l'Afrique occidentale. Je voulais connaître ses méthodes, sa motivation. Je cherche à savoir pourquoi certains peuples ont résisté plus longtemps que d'autres. Les Wolof ont résisté un certain temps puis ils ont cédé.*

That's not just my interpretation. They're facts. I was intrigued by this character who had fought the French for 18 years without ever leaving West Africa. I wanted to find out about his methods, his motivation. I'm trying to find out why certain people resisted longer than others. The Wolof resisted for a while and then surrendered.

D. Murphy: *Le film va se faire?*
Will the film [about Samory] ever be made?

Sembene: *C'est un rêve. Il faut rêver.*
It's a dream. You have to dream.

D. Murphy: *La question des langues africaines, dans votre cas le wolof, a toujours joué un rôle dans votre œuvre. Pourquoi n'avez-vous pas continué à écrire en wolof après la publication de* Ceddo? *
The question of African languages, and in your case Wolof, has always played an important role in your work. Why didn't you continue to write in Wolof after the publication of *Ceddo*?

Sembene: *La question des langues est toujours une affaire politique. Avant tout, les Africains sont pragmatiques. Un Wolof va se dire 'il faut que j'apprenne le français pour trouver un travail'. C'est comme ça que ça se passe. C'est la question économique qui compte avant tout. Pourquoi écrire en wolof si on va interdire le livre? Senghor était analphabète dans sa propre langue. Le mot 'ceddo' vient du pulaar et il y a gémination. On avait des linguistes africains avec nous au journal* Kaddu *et Senghor avait un linguiste autrichien comme conseiller. Nous avons raison. Pourquoi écouter un Européen? Ça concernait les Africains, ça vient du pulaar.*
The language question is primarily a political matter. Above all, Africans are pragmatic. A Wolof says to himself 'I have to learn French to get a job'. That's how it works. It's economic factors that determine these things. Why write in Wolof if the book will be banned? Senghor was illiterate in his own language. The word 'ceddo' comes from pulaar and there is gemination [i.e. a double 'd', not a single 'd' as Senghor argued – see Chapter Six]. There were African linguists working with us on the newspaper *Kaddu* and Senghor had an Austrian linguist as his adviser. We were right. Why listen to a European? This was an African matter, the word comes from pulaar.

D. Murphy: *Mais la censure de* Ceddo *n'était pas simplement une question linguistique quand-même? Il y avait aussi votre interprétation plutôt controversée de l'histoire sénégalaise, non?*
But the censorship of *Ceddo* wasn't simply to do with linguistics, was it? Was it not also linked to your controversial interpretation of Senegalese history?

---

* A novel version of *Ceddo* was written by Sembene and it appears in certain bibilographies of his work. However, I have been unable to ascertain if the novel was ever published. Therefore, I have chosen not to include it in my bibliography.

Interview with Sembene

Sembene: *Pas vraiment. Le film est sorti avant la naissance du mouvement intégriste. C'était avant la révolution islamique en Iran. Vous savez, le Shah d'Iran voulait une copie du film et j'ai refusé. Puis, quand Khomeini a pris le pouvoir je leur ai offert une copie gratuite et on m'a refusé! C'est ça l'histoire.*

Not really. The film was released before the birth of the fundamentalist movement. It was before the Islamic revolution in Iran. You know, the Shah of Iran wanted a copy of the film and I turned him down. Then, when Khomeini took over, I offered them a copy and they turned me down! That's history for you.

D. Murphy: *Qu'est-ce qui est arrivé au journal, Kaddu, dont vous avez parlé tout à l'heure?*

What happened to the newspaper, *Kaddu*, that you mentioned earlier?

Sembene: *On perdait de l'argent. Moi, je donnais beaucoup d'argent pour permettre au journal de survivre mais ça ne pouvait pas continuer indéfiniment.*

We were losing money. I put in a lot of my money to allow the newspaper to survive but it couldn't go on forever.

D. Murphy: *Est-ce que vous pensez que cette question des langues est toujours une question importante?*

Do you think that the language question is still important?

Sembene: *Vous savez, l'Afrique francophone est la partie de l'Afrique qui était la plus colonisée. La plupart des administrateurs africains ont reçu leur éducation dans les écoles de l'administration coloniale. S'il n'y avait pas eu l'indépendance, c'était des gens qui allaient devenir garde-cercle ou quelque chose comme ça. Ici au Sénégal, nous avons une semaine des langues nationales. Ça me fait penser à ma jeunesse pendant l'époque coloniale quand il y avait des semaines coloniales. Toute l'année on apprenait l'histoire et la culture françaises et puis on avait une semaine de culture locale. C'est la même chose maintenant.*

You know, Francophone Africa was the most colonised part of Africa. Most of the African civil servants were educated in schools set up to train people for the colonial service. If we hadn't gained independence, these people would have become colonial officials. Here in Senegal, we have a national languages week. That reminds me of my childhood during the colonial era when there was a colonial week. Throughout the year, we learned about French history and culture, and then we had one week of local culture. It's the same thing nowadays.

D. Murphy: *En principe, le cinéma devrait vous permettre d'atteindre le public auquel vous ne pouvez pas parler à travers vos livres, mais malheureusement on voit rarement les films africains en Afrique. Qu'est-ce qu'on pourrait faire pour améliorer la situation?*

In principle, cinema should allow you to reach a wider public, the people you can't reach through your books, but unfortunately one rarely sees African films in Africa. How can the situation be improved?

Sembene: *Il n'y a pas de politique culturelle en Afrique. Les hommes politiques pensent*

237

qu'il suffit de manger et puis de chier et tout va bien! J'ai entendu à la radio l'autre jour que la Banque Mondiale/FMI a dit qu'il fallait peut-être développer la culture en Afrique parce que ça pourrait aider l'économie! Quand j'étais dans votre pays, j'ai commencé par lire des écrivains du théâtre. Comment s'appelle le type? Enfin, bon. De toute façon, vous vous entretuez en Irlande depuis vingt-cinq ans mais vous êtes fiers d'un écrivain comme Joyce. La culture est quelque chose qui unit un peuple. Le problème avec le cinéma, c'est que c'est une industrie. C'est contrôlé par les Américains. Je fais des films à réflexion. Il faut faire réfléchir le public. Pas tout le temps, mais [...]

There is no cultural policy in Africa. Politicians think it's enough to eat and shit and everything's alright! On the radio the other day, I heard that the World Bank/IMF said that it might be a good idea to develop culture in Africa as that might help the economy! When I was in your country, I began by reading Irish plays. What's that guy's name? Oh well. Anyway, you've been killing each other in Ireland for 25 years but you're proud of a writer like Joyce. Culture is something that unites a people. The problem with cinema is that it's an industry. It's controlled by the Americans. I make films designed to make you think. You have to make the public think. Not all the time, but [...]

D. Murphy: *Est-ce vrai que, dans le passé, vous alliez dans de petits villages de la brousse pour montrer vos films?*

Is it true that, in the past, you used to go into small villages in the bush to screen your films?

Sembene: *Je le fais encore. Les autres ont montré des films les 25, 26, et 27 [novembre 1995] pendant que j'étais au Cameroun. On les montre gratuit dans les villages. On demande 200 CFA dans les lycées pour amortir les frais. C'est important pour moi de voir comment les gens 'lisent' mes films. C'est dommage qu'on ne va pas en brousse bientôt. Il faut voir comment les gens réagissent devant les films. C'est tout autre chose qu'en Europe. Il me faut ce contact avec mon peuple. Dans d'autres pays africains, je serais déjà en prison mais ici le peuple m'aime trop. Une fois, je suis rentré dans la voiture d'un blanc. C'était de ma faute mais les gens ne voulaient pas entendre raison. J'ai dû aller voir le blanc après pour lui payer les frais. Le peuple va trop loin parfois. Je ne travaille que pour mon peuple.*

I still do. The others [his staff at Filmi Doomireew] showed some films on 25, 26 and 27 [November 1995] while I was in Cameroon. We show them free in the villages. We ask for 200 CFA in the schools so that we can break even. It's important for me to see how people 'read' my films. It's a pity we're not going into the bush again soon. You should see how people react to films. In other African countries, I'd already be in prison by now but here the people love me too much. Once I crashed into a car driven by a white man. It was my fault but the people didn't want to know. I had to go and see the white man afterwards to pay for the damage. The people go too far sometimes. I only work for my people.

D. Murphy: *Le rituel joue un rôle capital dans votre œuvre cinématographique: on voit les rites du fétichisme et de la consommation dans Xala. Est-ce un principe organisateur de votre cinéma?*

Ritual plays a vital role in your cinematic work: we see the rituals of fetishism and consumerism in *Xala*. Is this one of the organising principles of your cinema?

Sembene: *Oui, le rituel est très important. En Europe, c'est pratiquement perdu. Chaque peuple a besoin de ses rituels.*

Yes, ritual is very important. In Europe, it's practically disappeared. Each people needs its own rituals.

D. Murphy: *Vous avez souvent dit que le cinéma était l'art moderne qui se rapprochait le plus de l'art du griot, avec son mélange du geste, du rituel, et de la parole.*

You've often said that cinema is the modern art form that is closest to the art of the *griot*, with its mixture of gesture, ritual and words.

Sembene: *Oui, mon peuple se reconnaît dans le rituel. Les Européens ont du mal à le comprendre. Quand on perd ses rites, on perd une partie de son âme.*

Yes, my people recognise themselves through rituals. Europeans find this hard to understand. When you lose your own rituals, you lose a part of your soul.

D. Murphy: *Votre dernier film,* Guelwaar, *dénonce l'institutionalisation de la mentalité de dépendance en Afrique. Et cela, une dizaine d'années après avoir dénoncé la dépendance sur l'ancien colonisateur dans* Le Dernier de l'empire. *Alors que pensez-vous de la situation actuelle en Afrique?*

Your most recent film, *Guelwaar*, denounces the institutionalisation of a dependence mindset in Africa. And that was 12 years after you had denounced dependence on the former coloniser in *The Last of the Empire*. So, what do you think of the current situation in Africa?

Sembene: *C'est pire! Mais je suis toujours optimiste. Il faut être optimiste.*

It's worse! But I'm still optimistic. You have to be optimistic.

D. Murphy: *Que pensez-vous de la thèse avancée par Axelle Kabou: que l'Afrique 'refuse le développement'?*

What do you think of Axelle Kabou's argument: that Africa is 'refusing development'?

Sembene: *Elle a raison. Beaucoup de gens l'ont critiquée mais moi je la défends partout. Je ne la connais pas et je ne cherche pas à la connaître. Mais elle a dit quelque chose qu'il fallait dire et je la respecte pour cela.*

She's right. A lot of people have criticised her but I've always defended her. I don't know her and I don't want to meet her. But she said something that had to be said and I respect her for that.

D. Murphy: *Alors les Africains refusent le développement?*

So Africans are refusing development?

Sembene: *Attention! Ce sont les hommes politiques qui refusent le développement.*
Careful! It's the politicians who are refusing deveopment.

D. Murphy: *Axelle Kabou pense que l'absence d'une véritable unité africaine est une des causes majeures de l'état actuel du continent. Etes-vous d'accord?*
Axelle Kabou thinks that the absence of a genuine African unity is one of the major causes of the current state of the continent. Do you agree?

Sembene: *Je crois qu'il faut d'abord commencer par des unions régionales. C'est une étape nécessaire dans le développement de l'Afrique.*
I think we should start by creating regional structures. It's a necessary step in the development of Africa.

D. Murphy *La chute des régimes communistes de l'ancienne URSS et en Europe orientale et centrale a mis fin à l'enjeu politique qui opposait l'Est à l'Ouest. Quelles sont vos réflexions sur la situation actuelle dans le monde?*
The fall of the communist regimes of the former USSR and of Eastern and Central Europe has put an end to the stand-off between East and West. What do you think about the current state of the world?

Sembene: *Le libéralisme ne remplacera jamais le communisme. L'Afrique a besoin du communisme. Le capitalisme ne marche pas, regardez les Etats-Unis. C'est le pays le plus individualiste du monde. En Europe, vous pensez qu'il suffit d'avoir de l'argent dans votre compte en banque et tout va bien. Le communisme est le seul système qui peut aider l'Afrique. L'Union Soviétique a formé des mécaniciens, des artisans, dont l'Afrique avait besoin: son déclin est une perte pour l'Afrique. Le communisme, c'est le seul espoir de l'Afrique.*
Liberalism will never replace communism. Africa needs communism. Capitalism doesn't work, just look at the United States. It's the most individualistic country in the world. In Europe, you think it's enough to be wealthy and everything's alright. Communism is the only system that can help Africa. The Soviet Union trained mechanics and artisans that Africa needed: its demise is a loss for Africa. Communism is the only hope for Africa.

Filmography

Sembene's Films

Borom Sarret (1962), in French
Producers: Les Actualités Françaises/Filmi Doomireew
19 minutes; 35 mm; black & white

Niaye (1964), in French
Producers: Les Actualités Françaises/Filmi Doomireew
35 minutes; 35 mm; black & white

La Noire de (1966), in French
Producers: Les Actualités Françaises/Filmi Doomireew
65 minutes; 35 mm; black & white (some colour sequences)

Le Mandat/Mandabi (1968), in both Wolof and French versions
Producers: Comptoir Français du Film/Filmi Doomireew
French version: 90 minutes; Wolof version 105 minutes; 35 mm; colour

Taaw (1970), in Wolof
Producers: Broadcasting Film Commission, National Council of the Church of Christ
24 minutes; 16 mm; colour

Emitaï (1971), in Diola and French
Producers: Filmi Doomireew
95 minutes; 35 mm; colour

Xala (1974), in Wolof and French
Producers: Filmi Doomireew/Société Nationale de Cinéma (Senegal)
116 minutes; 35 mm; colour

Ceddo (1976), in Wolof
Producers: Filmi Doomireew
120 minutes; 35 mm; colour

Camp de Thiaroye (1988), in French and Wolof
Producers: SNPC (Senegal), ENAPROC (Algeria), SATPEC (Tunisia), and Filmi Doomireew/Filmi Kajoor
147 minutes; 35 mm; colour

Guelwaar (1992), in Wolof and French
Producers: Filmi Doomireew/Galatée Films
107 minutes; 35 mm; colour

Faat Kine (2000), in Wolof and French
Producers: ACCT, Canal & Horizons, EZEF (Germany), Fondation Stanley Thomas
Johnson Stiftung (Switzerland), California Newsreel (USA), Les Films Terre Africaine
(Cameroon), Filmi Doomireew (Senegal)
120 minutes

Availability of Sembene's Films

* Copies of *Borom Sarret, Niaye, La Noire de,* and *Le Mandat* may be viewed at the
  Cinémathèque du Ministère de la Coopération (6, rue Ferrus, 75014 Paris). The
  Cinémathèque also holds a copy of Paulin Soumanou Vieyra's documentary on the
  making of *Ceddo,* entitled *L'Envers du décor* (1980).
* *Xala, Camp de Thiaroye* and *Guelwaar* have all been shown on Channel 4 in recent
  years. *Xala* and *Borom Sarret* are also widely available on video cassette in the BFI's
  African films series.
* The BFI holds a copy of *Ceddo* which may be viewed at their premises in London
  (21 Stephen Street, London W1P 2LN). In France, both *Ceddo* and *Emitaï* are
  distributed by Med Hondo Films (72 bis, rue Philippe de Girard, 75018 Paris), but
  these copies are only available for commercial screenings. I was fortunate to see
  both of these films at a retrospective of Sembene's films at the *Cinéma des cinéastes*
  (7, avenue de Clichy, 75017 Paris), in January 1998.
* I have been unable to trace a copy of *Taaw* either in Britain or in France.

Other Films Cited in this Study

Bathily, Moussa. *Petits Blancs au manioc et à la sauce gombo* (1982)
Buñuel, Luis. *Viridiana* (1961)
Coppola, Francis Ford. *The Godfather* (1972)
Donskoi, Mark. *My Universities* (1941)
Gomes, Flora. *Mortu Nega* (1987)
Hondo, Med. *Sarraounia* (1986)
Khleifi, Michel. *Urs bil Galil* (Wedding in Galilee, 1987)
Kubrick, Stanley. *Paths of Glory* (1957)
Lallaoui, Mehdi. *Les Massacres de Sétif: le 8 mai 1945* (1996)
Mambety, Djibril Diop. *Contras City* (1969)
— *Touki-Bouki* (1973)
— *Hyènes* (1992)
Marker, Chris, and Alain Resnais. *Les Statues meurent aussi* (1953)
Ouédraogo, Idrissa. *Tilaï* (1990)
Pontecorvo, Gillo. *The Battle of Algiers* (1966)
Rocha, Glauber. *Terre em transe* (Land in Anguish, 1967)

Bibliography

Works by Sembene available in English

1. FICTION

A. English Translations
Sembene, Ousmane. *Black Docker*, trans. by Ros Schwartz (London: Heinemann, 1987).
— *God's Bits of Wood*, trans. by Francis Price (London: Heinemann, 1995).
— *Tribal Scars*, trans. by Len Ortzen (London: Heinemann, 1974).
— *The Money Order* with *White Genesis*, trans. by Clive Wake (London: Heinemann, 1972).
— *Xala*, trans. by Clive Wake (London: Heinemann, 1976).
— *The Last of the Empire*, trans. by Adrian Adams (London: Heinemann, 1983).
— *Niiwam* and *Taaw* (London: Heinemann, 1992).

B. Original French Editions
Sembene, Ousmane. *Le Docker noir* (1956; Paris: Présence Africaine, 1973).
— *O Pays, mon beau peuple!* (1957; Paris: Presses Pocket, 1975).
— *Les Bouts de bois de Dieu* (1960; Paris: Presses Pocket, 1971).
— *Voltaïque* (Paris: Présence Africaine, 1962).
— *L'Harmattan* (Paris: Présence Africaine, 1963).
— *Le Mandat* with *Véhi-Ciosane* (Paris: Présence Africaine, 1966).
— *Xala* (Paris: Présence Africaine, 1973).
— *Le Dernier de l'empire* (Paris: L'Harmattan, 1981).
— *Niiwam* and *Taaw* (Paris: Présence Africaine, 1987).
— *Guelwaar* (Paris: Présence Africaine, 1996).

2. NON-FICTION
Sembene, Ousmane. *Man is Culture/L'Homme est culture* (Bloomington, IN: African Studies Program, 1979). The 6th Annual Hans Wolff Memorial Lecture (5 March 1975).

3. INTERVIEWS WITH SEMBENE*
'Le Cahier des textes', *Cahiers du Cinéma*, 170 (September 1965), p. 61 (interview with Sembene and Jean Rouch).

* Sembene has given a large number of interviews during the course of his long artistic career. In order to facilitate the work of the researcher interested in studying these texts, it has been decided to group these interviews together in chronological order of publication. In cases where this method leads to confusion (i.e. two interviews published in the same month, etc.), normal alphabetical rules apply.

Interviews with Sembene

Marcorelles, Louis. 'Ousmane Sembène: romancier, cinéaste, poète', *Les Lettres françaises*, 6–12 April 1967, p. 24.

Morellet, Jean-Claude. 'Cinéma africain: premiers pas en liberté', *Jeune Afrique*, 26 February–3 March 1968, pp. 42–3.

C. V. 'Un Film dont on parle et dont on parlera longtemps: *Le Mandat* de Ousmane Sembene', *Bingo* (April 1969), pp. 41–2.

Hennebelle, Guy. 'Ousmane Sembène: "Pour moi, le cinéma est un moyen d'action politique, mais...'", *L'Afrique littéraire et artistique*, 7 (1969), pp. 73–82.

Prelle, François. 'Ousmane Sembene à bâtons rompus', *Bingo*, 222 (July 1971), pp. 56–60.

Hennebelle, Guy. 'Ousmane Sembène: "En Afrique noire nous sommes gouvernés par des enfants mongoliens du colonialisme"', *Les Lettres françaises*, 6–12 October 1971, p. 16.

Hennebelle, Guy. 'Pour ou contre un cinéma africain engagé?', *L'Afrique littéraire et artistique*, 19 (October 1971), pp. 87–93 (a round table discussion with Sembene, Sarah Moldoror, Youssef Chahine, Timité Bassori, and Sami Nasri).

Diallo, Siradiou. *'Jeune Afrique* fait parler Sembene Ousmane', *Jeune Afrique*, 27 January 1973, pp. 44–9.

Perry, G. M., and Patrick McGilligan. 'Ousmane Sembene: An Interview', *Film Quarterly*, 26, 3 (Spring 1973), pp. 36–42.

'Sembène Ousmane, Cheikh Hamidou Kane, Ousmane Socé, Tchicaya U Tam'si, Camara Laye, Birago Diop, and Abdou Anta Ka', in *African Writers on African Writing*, ed. by G. D. Killam (London: Heinemann, 1973), pp. 148–56 (a round table discussion at the University of Dakar from 1965).

N'Daw, Aly Khary. 'Sembene Ousmane et l'impuissance bourgeoise', *Jeune Afrique*, 27 April 1974, p. 20.

Ndiaye, Ibrahima. 'Entretien avec Ousmane Sembène', in 'La Critique sociale dans l'œuvre littéraire d'Ousmane Sembène, du *Docker noir* à *Xala'* (unpublished master's thesis, University of Dakar, 1974–75), pp. 117–25.

Cheriaa, Tahaar, and Férid Boughedir. *'Jeune Afrique* fait parler Sembene Ousmane', *Jeune Afrique*, 2 April 1976, pp. 54–6.

Ghali, Nourredine. 'Ousmane Sembene: "Le cinéaste, de nos jours, peut remplacer le conteur traditionnel"', *Cinéma*, 208 (April 1976), pp. 83–91.

'The Artist and Revolution', *Positive Review: A Review of Society and Culture in Black Africa*, 1, 2 (1978), pp. 3–7.

Ayari, Farida et al. 'J.A. fait parler Sembène Ousmane: "La Culture est le levain de la politique mais l'intégrisme c'est le fascisme"', *Jeune Afrique*, 19 September 1979, pp. 71–5.

Pfaff, Françoise. 'Entretien avec Ousmane Sembène: à propos de *Ceddo*', *Positif*, 235 (October 1980), pp. 54–7.

Brierre, Jean. 'Sembène Ousmane', *Les Cahiers de l'auditeur*, 12 (January–March 1981), pp. 3–6.

Kane, Mohamadou et al. 'Comme un aveugle qui retrouve la vue', *Le Soleil* [Dakar], 10 July 1981, pp. 1, 4, 5, 6, 7.

Traoré, Biny. 'Entretien de Monsieur Biny Traoré avec le cinéaste Sembène Ousmane', in *Aspects socio-politiques et techniques dans le roman africain d'aujourd'hui: l'exemple de 'Xala' de Sembène Ousmane* (Ouagadougou: [n. pub.], 1981), pp. 169–72.

Bathily, Silman. 'Questionnaire', in 'La Vision marxiste dans *Les Bouts de bois de Dieu* de Ousmane Sembène' (unpublished master's thesis, University of Dakar, 1982), pp. 106–10.

Gabriel, Teshome H. 'Interview with Ousmane Sembene', in *Third Cinema in the Third World* (London: Bowker, 1982), pp. 111–16.

Haffner, Pierre. 'Eléments pour un autoportrait magnétique', *L'Afrique littéraire*, 76 (1985), pp. 20–4 (a compilation of quotes from a number of interviews given by Sembene during a trip to Zaïre in November 1977).

Hennebelle, Guy. 'Sembène parle de ses films', *L'Afrique littéraire*, 76 (1985), pp. 25–9.

Ní Chréacháin, Firinne. 'Si j'étais une femme, je n'épouserais jamais un Africain', *Peuples noirs/Peuples africains*, 14, 8 (March–April 1991), pp. 86–93.

Bibliography

'Cinéma et littérature en Afrique noire: entretien avec Sembène Ousmane', in *Protée noir: essais sur la littérature francophone de l'Afrique noire et des Antilles*, ed. by Peter Hawkins and Annette Lavers (Paris: L'Harmattan, 1992), pp. 204–18.

Ploquin, Françoise. 'Le Remède de l'Afrique est en Afrique: entretien avec Ousmane Sembène', *Diagonales*, 25 (January 1993), pp. 3–5.

'Sembène raconte Paulin', *Sud Quotidien*, 9 November 1993, p. 2.

Diedou, Djib. 'Interview – Sembène entre deux eaux', *Le Soleil* [Dakar], 17 November 1993, pp. 8–10.

'Discussion among the Writers', in *Ousmane Sembène: Dialogues with Critics and Writers*, ed. by Samba Gadjigo et al. (Amherst: University of Massachusetts Press, 1993), pp. 63–80 (a round table discussion with Sembene, Ngugi Wa Thiong'o, John Wideman, Earl Lovelace, and Toni Cade Bambara).

Niang, Sada. 'An Interview with Ousmane Sembène', in *Ousmane Sembène: Dialogues with Critics and Writers*, ed. by Samba Gadjigo et al. (Amherst: University of Massachusetts Press, 1993), pp. 87–108.

'Ousmane Sembène', in *Ousmane Sembène: Dialogues with Critics and Writers*, ed. by Samba Gadjigo et al. (Amherst: University of Massachusetts Press, 1993), pp. 59–62.

'Ousmane Sembène Responds to Questions from the Audience', in *Ousmane Sembène: Dialogues with Critics and Writers*, ed. by Samba Gadjigo et al. (Amherst: University of Massachusetts Press, 1993), pp. 37–44.

'Ousmane Sembène's Remarks after the Showing of his Film, *Camp de Thairoye*', in *Ousmane Sembène: Dialogues with Critics and Writers*, ed. by Samba Gadjigo et al. (Amherst: University of Massachusetts Press, 1993), pp. 81–5.

Kassé, Maguèye, and Anna Ridehalgh. 'Histoire et tradition dans la création artistique: entretien avec Ousmane Sembène', *French Cultural Studies*, 6, 2 (June 1995), pp. 179–96.

Niang, Sada and Samba Gadjigo. 'Interview with Ousmane Sembène', *Research in African Literatures*, 26, 3 (Autumn 1995), pp. 174–8.

'Sembène Ousmane: "Sans la femme, il n'y a plus de vie"', *Amina*, 306 (October 1995), p. 40.

Gadjigo, Samba. 'Ousmane Sembène: les enjeux du cinéma et de la littérature', in *Littérature et cinéma en Afrique francophone: Ousmane Sembène et Assia Djebar*, ed. by Sada Niang (Paris: L'Harmattan, 1996), pp. 110–21 (a biographical article based on a number of interviews with Sembene).

Other Works of Literature

Bâ, Mariama. *Une si longue lettre* (Dakar: Nouvelles Editions Africaines, 1981). English translation by Modupe Bode-Thomas, *So Long a Letter* (London: Heinemann, 1981).

Bebey, Francis. *Le Ministre et le griot* (Paris: Sépia, 1992).

Boto, Eza. *Ville cruelle* (Paris: Présence Africaine, 1954).

Bugul, Ken. *Le Baobab fou* (Dakar: Nouvelles Editions Africaines, 1982).

Césaire, Aimé. *Cahier d'un retour au pays natal* (1939; Paris: Présence Africaine, 1983). English translation by John Berger and Anna Bostock, *Return to my Native Land* (London: Penguin, 1969).

Dadié, Bernard Binlin. *Le Pagne noir* (Paris: Présence Africaine, 1955).

Diagne, Ahmadou Mapaté. *Les Trois volontés de Malic* (1920; Editions Kraus, 1973).

Diallo, Bakary. *Force-Bonté* (1926; Paris: ACCT/Nouvelles Editions Africaines, 1985).

Diop, Birago. *Les Contes d'Amadou Koumba* (1947; Paris: Présence Africaine, 1969). English translation by Dorothy S. Blair, *Tales of Amadou Koumba* (London: Longman, 1985).

Diop, Boubacar Boris. *Le Temps de Tamango* (Paris: L'Harmattan, 1981).

Diop, David. *Coups de pilon* (Paris: Présence Africaine, 1961). English translation by Simon Mpondo and Frank Jones, *Hammer Blows* (London: Heinemann, 1975).

Dongala, Emmanuel. *Jazz et vin de palme* (Paris: Hatier, 1982).

Other Works of Literature

Dürrenmatt, Friedrich. *The Visit*, trans. by Patrick Bowles (London: Cape, 1973).

Genet, Jean. *Les Nègres*, in *Œuvres complètes*, 5 (Paris: Gallimard, 1979).

Hove, Chenjerai. *Shebeen Tales: Messages from Harare* (London: Serif, 1994).

Hudson, Mark. *The Music in my Head* (London: Jonathan Cape, 1998).

Joyce, James. *Ulysses*, ed. by Danis Rose (1922; London: Picador, 1997).

Kane, Cheikh Hamidou. *L'Aventure ambiguë* (1961; Paris: 10/18, 1979). English translation by Katherine Woods, *Ambiguous Adventure* (London: Heinemann, 1972).

Kesteloot, Lilyan and Chérif Mbodj. *Contes et mythes wolof* (Dakar: Nouvelles Editions Africaines, 1983).

Kesteloot, Lilyan and Bassirou Dieng. *Contes et mythes du Sénégal* (Paris: Edicef, 1986).

Kesteloot, Lilyan and Bassirou Dieng. *Du Tieddo au talibé: contes et mythes wolof II* (Paris: Présence Africaine, 1989).

Kourouma, Ahmadou. *Les Soleils des indépendances* (Paris: Seuil, 1968). English translation by Adrian Adams, *The Suns of Independence* (London: Heinemann, 1981).

— *Monnè, outrages et défis* (Paris: Seuil, 1990).

Laferrière, Dany. *Comment faire l'amour avec un nègre sans se fatiguer* (Montreal: VLB, 1985). English translation by David Homel, *How to Make Love to a Negro* (London: Bloomsbury, 1991).

Laye, Camara. *L'Enfant noir* (1953; Paris: Presses Pocket, 1957). English translation by James Kirkup, *The African Child* (London: Fontana, 1959).

— *Le Regard du roi* (Paris: Plon, 1954). English translation by James Kirkup, *The Radiance of the King* (London: Fontana, 1973).

Lopes, Henri. *Tribaliques* (Yaoundé: CLE, 1971). English translation by Andrea Leskes, *Tribaliques* (London: Heinemann, 1987).

McKay, Claude. *Banjo* (1929; New York: Harcourt Brace, 1957).

Malraux, André. *La Condition humaine* (1933; Paris: Gallimard, Collection Folio, 1981). English translation by Alistair MacDonald, *Man's Estate* (London: Penguin, 1972).

Maran, René. *Batouala* (Paris: Albin Michel, 1921). English translation by Barbara Beck and Alexandre Mboukou, *Batouala* (London: Heinemann, 1973).

Martin du Gard, Roger. *Œuvres*, 2 vols (Paris: Gallimard, 1955).

Mudimbe, V. Y. *L'Ecart* (Paris: Présence Africaine, 1979).

Ndao, Cheikh Aliou. *Excellence, vos épouses!* (Dakar: Nouvelles Editions Africaines, 1993).

Niane, Djibril Tamsir. *Soundjata ou l'épopée mandingue* (Paris: Présence Africaine, 1960). English translation by G.D. Pickett, *Sundiata: an epic of old Mali* (London: Longman, 1979).

Okpewho, Isidore. *The Last Duty* (1976; London: Longman African Classic, 1986).

Ouologuem, Yambo. *Le Devoir de violence* (Paris: Seuil, 1968). English translation by Ralph Manheim, *Bound to Violence* (London: Heinemann, 1971).

Oyono, Ferdinand. *Une Vie de boy* (Paris: Presses Pocket, 1956). English translation by John Reed, *Houseboy* (London: Heinemann, 1966).

Roumain, Jacques. *Gouverneurs de la rosée* (1946: Paris: Editions Messidor, 1992). English translation by Langston Hughes and Mercer Cook, *Masters of the Dew* (London: Heinemann, 1978).

Rushdie, Salman. *Midnight's Children* (1981; London: Vintage, 1995).

Sadji, Abdoulaye. *Nini, mulâtresse du Sénégal* (1954; Paris: Présence Africaine, 1988).

Sassine, Williams. *Le Jeune homme de sable* (Paris: Présence Africaine, 1979).

Senghor, Léopold Sédar. *Œuvre poétique* (Paris: Seuil, 1990). Senghor's collected poems have not yet been translated into English but a selection of his poems and essays is to be found in *Léopold Sédar Senghor: Prose and Poetry*, selected and trans. by John Reed and Clive Wake (London: Heinemann, 1976).

Senghor, Léopold Sédar and Abdoulaye Sadji. *La Belle histoire de Leukle lièvre* (1953; London: Harrap, 1965).

Socé, Ousmane. *Karim* (1935; Paris: Nouvelles Editions Latines, 1948).

— *Les Mirages de Paris* (1937; Paris: Nouvelles Editions Latines, 1964).

Sow Fall, Aminata. *La Grève des battù* (Dakar: Nouvelles Editions Africaines, 1979). English translation by Dorothy S. Blair, *The Beggars' Strike* (London: Longman, 1981).

246

Bibliography

— *L'Ex-père de la nation* (Paris: L'Harmattan, 1987).

— *L'Appel des arènes* (Dakar: Nouvelles Editions Africaines, 1993).

Tansi, Sony Labou. *La Vie et demie* (Paris: Seuil, 1979).

— *Les Sept solitudes de Lorsa Lopez* (Paris: Seuil, 1985). English translation by Clive Wake, *The Seven Solitudes of Lorsa Lopez* (London: Heinemann, 1995).

Walker, Alice. *Meridian* (1976; London: Woman's Press, 1982).

Zola, Emile. *Germinal* (1885; Paris: Gallimard, Collection Folio, 1978). English translation by Havelock Ellis and Edith Lees, *Germinal* (London: Everyman, 1996).

Critical Studies: Literature*

Abanime, Emeka P. 'Le Symbolisme de l'impuissance dans *Xala* d'Ousmane Sembene', *Présence Francophone*, 19 (Autumn 1979), pp. 29–35.

Abastado, Claude. '*Les Bouts de bois de Dieu' de Sembène Ousmane* (Abidjan: Nouvelles Editions Africaines, 1984).

Achebe, Chinua. *Morning Yet on Creation Day* (London: Heinemann, 1975).

— 'Le Fardeau de l'écrivain noir', *Présence Africaine*, 59 (3rd quarter 1966), pp. 142–7.

Achiriga, Jingiri J. *La Révolte des romanciers noirs de langue française* (Ottawa: Editions Naaman, 1973).

Ahmad, Aijaz. *In Theory: Classes, Nations, Literatures* (London and New York: Verso, 1992).

Aire, Victor O. 'Affinités électives ou imitation? *Gouverneurs de la rosée* et *O Pays, mon beau peuple!'*, *Présence Francophone*, 15 (Autumn 1977), pp. 3–10.

— 'Didactic Realism in Ousmane Sembene's *Les Bouts de bois de Dieu*', *Canadian Journal of African Studies/La Revue canadienne des études africaines*, 16, 2 (1977), pp. 283–94.

Aje, S. O. 'L'Importance de l'écriture en tant qu'institution sociale dans *L'Argent* (Emile Zola), *Le Roi des Aulnes* (Michel Tournier) et *Le Mandat* (Ousmane Sembene)', *Neohelicon*, 16, 1 (1989), pp. 237–55.

Akpadomyne, Patrick. 'La Parodie et la réécriture chez Sembène Ousmane: problèmes textologiques', *Neohelicon*, 16, 2 (1989), pp. 211–19.

Amela, Amévlavi. 'Littérature africaine et critique traditionnelle', *Présence Africaine*, 139 (3rd quarter 1986), pp. 10–19.

Amuta, Chidi. *The Theory of African Literature: Implications for Practical Criticism* (London and Atlantic Heights, NJ: Zed Books, 1989).

Anozie, Sunday O. *Sociologie du roman africain: réalisme, structure et détermination dans le roman moderne ouest-africain* (Paris: Aubier–Montaigne, 1970).

Arowolo, E. O. 'Problems of Translation in African Writings', *Présence Africaine*, 123 (3rd quarter 1982), pp. 188–94.

Ashcroft, Bill, Gareth Griffiths, and Helen Tiffin, eds. *The Empire Writes Back: Theory and Practice in Post-colonial Literatures* (London and New York: Routledge, 1989).

Ashcroft, Bill, Gareth Griffiths, and Helen Tiffin, eds. *The Post-Colonial Studies Reader* (London and New York: Routledge, 1995).

Badji, Bougoul. '*Le Dernier de l'empire* de Sembène Ousmane', *Présence Africaine*, 123 (3rd quarter 1982), pp. 248–50.

Barker, Francis, Peter Hulme, and Margaret Iversen, eds. *Colonial Discourse/Postcolonial Theory* (Manchester and New York: Manchester University Press, 1994).

Barthes, Roland, *Mythologies* (Paris: Seuil, 1957).

Bathily, Silman. 'La Vision marxiste dans *Les Bouts de bois de Dieu* de Ousmane Sembène' (unpublished master's thesis, University of Dakar, 1982).

Bayo, Ogunjimi. 'Ritual Archetypes – Ousmane's Aesthetic Medium in *Xala*', *Ufahamu* (Journal of

---

* The creation of separate sections for works of literary and cinematic criticism is designed to facilitate the task of the researcher. This classification inevitably gives rise to odd cases of repetition as certain articles and books deal with both of Sembene's chosen media.

the African Activist Association), 14, 3 (1985), pp. 128–38.

Berrian, Brenda F. 'Through her Prism of Social and Political Contexts: Sembène's Female Characters in *Tribal Scars*', in *Ngambika: Studies of Women in African Literature*, ed. by Carol Boyce Davies and Anne Adams Graves (Trenton, New Jersey: Africa World Press, 1986), pp. 195–204.

Berte, Abdoulaye A. *'Le Dernier de l'empire*, par Sembène Ousmane', *Présence Africaine*, 130 (2nd quarter 1984), pp. 170–9.

Bestman, Martin. *Sembène Ousmane et l'esthétique du roman négro-africain* (Sherbrooke, Québec: Editions Naaman, 1981).

— 'L'Esthétique romanesque de Sembène Ousmane', *Etudes Littéraires*, 7, 3 (December 1974), pp. 395–403.

— 'Sembène Ousmane: Social Commitment and the Search for an African Identity', in *A Celebration of Black and African Writing*, ed. by Bruce King and Kolawole Ogungbesan (Zaria, Nigeria: Ahmadu Bello University Press, 1975), pp. 139–49.

— 'L'Univers de *Xala*', *L'Afrique littéraire et artistique*, 48 (1978), pp. 2–19 (also published in *Asemka: A Bilingual Literary Journal of the University of Cape Coast*, 5 (September 1979), pp. 51–62).

— '*Les Bouts de bois de Dieu*: une sollicitation révolutionnaire', *Peuples noirs/Peuples africains*, 7, 40 (July–August 1984), pp. 64–80.

Bhabha, Homi K., ed. *Nation and Narration* (New York and London: Routledge, 1990).

— *The Location of Culture* (New York and London: Routledge, 1994).

— 'The Other Question: Difference, Discrimination and the Discourse of Colonialism', in *Literature, Politics and Theory*, ed. by Francis Barker (New York and London: Methuen, 1986), pp. 148–72.

— 'DissemiNation: Time, Narrative and the Margins of the Modern Nation', in *Nation and Narration*, ed. by Homi K. Bhabha (London and New York: Routledge, 1990), pp. 291–322.

Blair, Dorothy S. *African Literature in French* (Cambridge: Cambridge University Press, 1976).

— *Senegalese Literature: a Critical History* (Boston, MA: Twayne, 1984).

Boafo, Y. S. *'Le Mandat*: critique socio-morale', *Asemka: A Bilingual Literary Journal of the University of Cape Coast*, 3 (September 1975), pp. 35–44.

— '*Voltaïque* d'Ousmane Sembène: commentaires et observations', *Présence Francophone*, 15 (Autumn 1977), pp. 11–30.

Bop, Codou. *'Les Bouts de bois de Dieu*, d'Ousmane Sembene', *Revue africaine de communication*, 5 (March–April 1984), pp. 47–50.

Boyd-Buggs, Debra. 'Marabouts-escrocs: désordre religieux et charlatanisme dans le roman sénégalais', *Présence Francophone*, 32 (1988), pp. 85–101.

Brahimi, Denise. 'L'Anthropologie factice de Sembene Ousmane dans "Le Voltaïque"', in *Images de l'Africain de l'antiquité au vingtième siècle*, ed. by Daniel Droixhe and Klaus Kiefer (Frankfurt: Peter Lang, 1987), pp. 203–9.

Brennan, Tim. 'The National Longing for Form', in *Nation and Narration*, ed. by Homi K. Bhabha (New York and London: Routledge, 1990), pp. 44–70.

Brierre, Jean F. 'Culture sénégalaise', *Revue française de l'élite européenne*, 221 (July 1969), pp. 10–16.

Carassus, Emilien. *Les Grèves imaginaires* (Paris: Editions du CNRS, 1982).

Carpenter, Jeremy. 'Literary Responses to Independence: Recent Developments in the French-African Novel' (unpublished doctoral thesis, Trinity College, Dublin, 1984).

Case, Frederick Ivor. 'Aesthetics, Ideology and Social Commitment in the Prose Fiction of Ousmane Sembène', in *Ousmane Sembène: Dialogues with Critics and Writers*, ed. by Samba Gadjigo et al. (Amherst: University of Massachusetts Press, 1993), pp. 3–13.

— 'Esthétique et discours idéologique dans l'œuvre d'Ousmane Sembène et d'Assia Djebar', in *Littérature et cinéma en Afrique francophone: Ousmane Sembène et Assia Djebar*, ed. by Sada Niang (Paris: L'Harmattan, 1996), pp. 35–49.

Cham, Mbye Boubacar. 'Islam in Senegalese Literature and Film', in *Faces of Islam in African Literature*, ed. by Kenneth W. Harrow (London: James Currey, 1991), pp. 163–86.

Bibliography

Chemain, Roger. *La Ville dans le roman africain* (Paris: L'Harmattan/ACCT, 1981).

— *L'Imaginaire dans le roman africain* (Paris: L'Harmattan, 1986).

Chemain-Degrange, Arlette. *Emancipation féminine et roman africain* (Dakar: Nouvelles Editions Africaines, 1980).

Chevrier, Jacques. *Littérature nègre* (Paris: Armand Colin, 1974).

— 'Kafka au Sénégal', *Le Monde (des Livres)*, 21 February 1970, p. III.

— 'L'Itinéraire de la contestation en Afrique noire', *Le Monde Diplomatique*, 22, 254 (May 1975), p. 25.

— 'Sembène Ousmane, écrivain', *L'Afrique littéraire*, 76 (1985), pp. 12–16.

— 'Roman africain: le temps du doute et des incertitudes', *Jeune Afrique*, 1 March 1989, pp. 62–4.

Chinweizu, ed. *Voices from Twentieth-century Africa: Griots and Towncriers* (London: Faber, 1988).

Chinweizu, Onwuchekwa Jemie and Ihechukwu Madubuike. *Toward the Decolonization of African Literature* (London: Kegan Paul, 1980).

Chrisman, Laura, and Patrick Williams, eds. *Colonial Discourse and Postcolonial Theory* (London: Harvester Wheatsheaf, 1993).

Cissé, Alassane. 'La Fête de l'esprit', *Sud Quotidien*, 18 November 1993, p. 2.

Condé, Maryse. 'Sembene Ousmane: *Xala*', *African Literature Today*, 9 (1978), pp. 97–8.

— 'Négritude Césairienne, Négritude Senghorienne', *Revue de littérature comparée*, 48, 3–4 (July–December 1974), pp. 409–19.

Corcoran, Pat. 'Fathers and Sons in African Fiction', in *Black Accents: Writing in French from Africa, Mauritius and the Caribbean*, ed. by J. P. Little and Roger Little (London: Grant & Cutler, 1997), pp. 83–96.

Cornevin, Robert. *Littérature d'Afrique noire de langue française* (Paris: Presses Universitaires Françaises, 1976).

Le Critique africain et son peuple comme producteur de civilisation (Paris: Présence Africaine, 1977).

Crosta, Suzanne. 'Stratégies de subversion et de libération: l'inscription et les enjeux de l'auditif et du visuel chez Assia Djebar et Ousmane Sembène', in *Littérature et cinéma en Afrique francophone: Ousmane Sembène et Assia Djebar*, ed. by Sada Niang (Paris: L'Harmattan, 1996), pp. 49–81.

Curtius, Anny Dominique and Joseph Paré. '*Le Mandat* de Sembène Ousmane ou la dialectique d'une double herméneutique', in *Littérature et cinéma en Afrique francophone: Ousmane Sembène et Assia Djebar*, ed. by Sada Niang (Paris: L'Harmattan, 1996), pp. 139–48.

Dailly, Christophe. '*L'Harmattan* de Sembène Ousmane', *Annales de l'Université d'Abidjan*, Series D, 3 (1969), pp. 59–61.

Daninos, Guy. 'De l'importance de la littérature orale en Afrique noire et, en particulier, au Congo', *L'Afrique littéraire et artistique*, 48 (1978), pp. 39–48.

Davies, Carol Boyce. 'Introduction: Feminist Consciousness and African Literary Criticism', in *Ngambika: Studies of Women in African Literature*, ed. by Carol Boyce Davies and Anne Adams Graves (Trenton, New Jersey: Africa World Press, 1986), pp. 1–23.

Dehme, Dakha. 'La Transcription du wolof dans l'œuvre d'Ousmane Sembene', *Etudes germano-africaines*, 2–3 (1984/85), pp. 157–61.

Depestre, René. *Bonjour et adieu à la négritude* (Paris: Robert Laffont, 1980).

Désalmond, Paul. *25 Romans clés de la littérature négro-africaine* (Paris: Hatier, 1981).

Diagne, Ismaïla. 'Dramatisation des conflits et mutations dans l'œuvre littéraire de Sembène Ousmane' (unpublished doctoral thesis, University Cheikh Anta Diop of Dakar, 1996).

Diagne, Pathé. 'La Critique littéraire africaine', in *Le Critique africain et son peuple comme producteur de civilisation* (Paris: Présence Africaine, 1977), pp. 429–40.

Diamé, Rokhayatou. 'Ousmane Sembène, peintre des mœurs sénégalaises' (unpublished master's thesis, University of Dakar, 1979).

Dieng, Bassirou. 'La Tradition comme support dramatique dans l'œuvre romanesque de Sembène Ousmane', *Annales de la faculté des lettres et sciences humaines de Dakar*, 15 (1985), pp. 127–43.

Diop, Baba. 'Sembène: enfin prophète chez lui', *Sud Quotidien*, 11 November 1993, p. 2.

— 'Le Sembenomania', *Sud Quotidien*, 8 December 1993, p. 2.

Diop, Mamadou Traoré. 'Ce que je sais d'Ousmane Sembène', *Le Soleil* [Dakar], 10 July 1981, p. 3.

Diop, Papa Samba. *Écriture romanesque et cultures régionales au Sénégal, des origines à 1992: de la lettre à l'allusion* (Frankfurt: IKO, 1995).

— 'La Figure du tirailleur sénégalais dans le roman sénégalais, 1920–1985', in *Tirailleurs Sénégalais*, ed. by János Riesz and Joachim Schultz (Frankfurt: Peter Lang, 1989), pp. 39–56.

Diouf, Bara. 'Ousmane Sembène ou l'itinéraire d'un enfant du siècle', *Le Soleil* [Dakar], 17 November 1993, p. 10.

Diouf, Madior. *Comprendre 'Véhi-Ciosane' et 'Le Mandat' de Sembène Ousmane* (Issy-les-Moulineaux: Editions St. Paul, 1986).

— 'La Composition en abyme dans trois romans sénégalais: *Karim, O Pays, mon beau peuple!* et *Buur Tilleen, roi de la Médina*', *Annales de la faculté des lettres et sciences humaines de Dakar*, 4 (1974), pp. 51–75.

Dorsinville, Roger. 'Des *Bouts de bois de Dieu* à *Véhi-Ciosane*: la création chez Ousmane Sembène', *Le Soleil* [Dakar], 10 July 1981, p. 2.

Dumont, Pierre. 'Le Parler des non-lettrés dans *O Pays, mon beau peuple!* de O. Sembene', *Langas: revue de socio-linguistique*, 22 (1987), pp. 147–57.

Duneton, Claude, and Jean-Pierre Pagliano. *Anti-manuel de français* (Paris: Seuil, 1978).

Elungu, Monique. 'Manuel et Faye: deux héros du développement dans la littérature négro-africaine', *L'Afrique littéraire et artistique*, 46 (4th quarter 1977), pp. 60–9.

Enagnon, Yenoukoumé. 'Sembène Ousmane, la théorie marxiste et le roman', *Peuples noirs/ Peuples africains*, 2, 11 (September–October 1979), pp. 92–127.

Eschemin, Kester. 'Sembène Ousmane et le mythe du peuple messianique', *L'Afrique littéraire et artistique*, 46 (4th quarter 1977), pp. 51–9.

— 'Aspects de la littérature dans le roman africain', *Présence Africaine*, 139 (3rd quarter 1986), pp. 88–114.

Esonwanne, Uzo. 'The Nation as Contested Referent', *Research in African Literatures*, 24, 4 (1993), pp. 49–62.

Fall, Cheikh. 'La Religion dans l'œuvre romanesque de Ousmane Sembène' (unpublished master's thesis, University of Dakar, 1981–82).

Fall, Khady. 'La Recherche d'une voix du salut dans *L'Harmattan* d'O. Sembène et *Das Vorbild* de S. Lenz', *Etudes germano-africaines*, 2–3 (1984–85), pp. 162–72.

Fraser, Robert. 'Sembène Ousmane, *Xala*', *Asemka: A Bilingual Literary Journal of the University of Cape Coast*, 5 (September 1979), pp. 140–1.

Gadjigo, Samba et al., eds. *Ousmane Sembène: Dialogues with Critics and Writers* (Amherst: University of Massachusetts Press, 1993).

Gérard, Albert. *Etudes de littérature africaine francophone* (Dakar: Nouvelles Editions Africaines, 1977).

— *Essais d'histoire littéraire africaine* (Sherbrooke, Québec: Editions Naaman, 1984).

— 'Les Générations dans le roman africain', *Revue générale belge*, 5 (May 1965), pp. 19–33.

— 'Littérature francophone d'Afrique: le temps de la relève', *La Revue Nouvelle*, 25, 49, 2 (February 1969), pp. 198–204.

— 'La Francophonie dans les lettres africaines', *Revue de littérature comparée*, 3–4 (July–December 1974), pp. 371–86.

Gérard, Albert, and Jeannine Laurent. 'Sembene's Progeny: A New Trend in the Senegalese Novel', *Studies in Twentieth Century Literature*, 4, 2 (Spring 1980), pp. 133–45.

Gikandi, Simon. *Reading the African Novel* (London: James Currey, 1987).

Glissant, Edouard. 'Le Romancier noir et son peuple', *Présence Africaine*, 16 (October–November 1957), pp. 26–31.

Gourdeau, Jean-Pierre. *'Les Bouts de bois de Dieu' de Sembène Ousmane* (Paris: Bordas, 1984).

— 'Le Didactisme révolutionnaire des *Bouts de bois de Dieu* de Sembene Ousmane', *Annales de l'Université d'Abidjan*, series D, 8 (1975), pp. 185–201.

Graff, Gerald. 'Co-optation', in *The New Historicism*, ed. by H. Aram Veeser (London: Routledge, 1989), pp. 168–81.

Gugelberger, Georg M., ed. *Marxism and African Literature* (London: James Currey, 1985).

Guibert, Armand. *Léopold Sédar Senghor* (Paris: Seuil, 1969).

Bibliography

Hale, Thomas A. 'Islam and the Griots in West Africa: Bridging the Gap between two Traditions', *Africana Journal*, 13, 1–4 (1982), pp. 84–90.

Hargreaves, Alec G. *The Colonial Experience in French Fiction: A Study of Pierre Loti, Ernest Psichari and Pierre Mille* (London: Macmillan, 1981).

Harris, Rodney. 'Sembene Ousmane', *Dolphin* [University of Aarhus, Denmark], 5 (December 1981), pp. 145–7.

Harrow, Kenneth W., ed. *Faces of Islam in African Literature* (London: James Currey, 1991).

— ed. *The Marabout and the Muse: New Approaches to Islam in African Literature* (London: James Currey, 1996).

— 'Sembene's *Xala*: The Use of Film and Novel as Revolutionary Weapon', *Studies in Twentieth Century Literature*, 4, 2 (Spring 1980), pp. 177–88.

— 'Art and Ideology in *Les Bouts de bois de Dieu*: Realism's Artifices', *French Review*, 62, 3 (February 1989), pp. 483–93.

— 'Introduction: Islam(s) in African Literature', in *Faces of Islam in African Literature*, ed. by Kenneth W. Harrow (London: James Currey, 1991), pp. 3–20.

Havyarimana, Gervais. *Problématique de renaissance et évolution du roman africain de langue française, 1920–1980* (Louvain-la-Neuve: Publications Universitaires de Louvain, 1992).

Hawkins, Peter. 'Marxist Intertext, Islamic Reinscription? Some Common Themes in the Novels of Sembène Ousmane and Aminata Sow Fall', in *African Francophone Writing: A Critical Introduction*, ed. by Laïla Ibnlfassi and Nicki Hitchcott (Oxford: Berg, 1996), pp. 163–9.

Huannou, Adrien. 'Sembene Ousmane, cinéaste et écrivain sénégalais', *L'Afrique littéraire et artistique*, 32, (1974), pp. 35–40, and 33 (1974), pp. 24–8.

— '*Xala*: une satire caustique de la société bourgeoise sénégalaise', *Présence Africaine* (3rd quarter 1977), pp. 145–57.

— 'L'Islam et le christianisme face à la domination coloniale dans *Les Bouts de bois de Dieu* et *L'Harmattan* de Sembène Ousmane', *Nouvelles du sud*, 6–7 (November 1986–April 1987), pp. 41–8.

Hymans, Jacques Louis. *Léopold Sédar Senghor: An Intellectual Biography* (Edinburgh: Edinburgh University Press, 1971).

Ibnlfassi, Laïla, and Nicki Hitchcott, eds. *African Francophone Writing: A Critical Introduction*, (Oxford: Berg, 1996).

Ijere, Muriel I. 'Victime et bourreau, l'Africain de Sembène Ousmane', *Peuples noirs/ Peuples africains*, 6, 35 (September–October 1983), pp. 67–85.

— 'La Condition féminine dans *Xala* de Sembene Ousmane', *L'Afrique littéraire*, 85 (1989), pp. 25–34 (first published in *Revue de littérature et d'esthétique négro-africaines*, 8 (1987), pp. 36–45).

Ikiddeh, Ime. 'Ideology and Revolutionary Action in the Contemporary African Novel', *Présence Africaine*, 139 (3rd quarter 1986), pp. 136–61.

Izevbaye, Dan. 'Reality in the African Novel: its Theory and Practice', *Présence Africaine*, 139 (3rd quarter 1986), pp. 115–35.

Jahn, Janheinz. *Manuel de littérature néo-africaine*, trans. by Gaston Bailly (Paris: Resma, 1969).

Jameson, Fredric. *The Political Unconscious: Narrative as a Socially Symbolic Act* (London: Methuen, 1981).

— 'Third-World Literature in the Era of Multinational Capitalism', *Social Text*, 15 (1986), pp. 65–88.

Jay, Salim. '*Xala*, par Sembène Ousmane', *L'Afrique littéraire*, 73–74 (1984), pp. 122–4.

Johnson, Lemuel A. 'Crescent and Consciousness: Islamic Orthodoxies and the West African Novel', in *Faces of Islam in African Literature*, ed. by Kenneth W. Harrow (London: James Currey, 1991), pp. 239–60.

Jones, Trevor. 'Some intra- and extra-hexagonal attitudes to French', *French Studies Bulletin*, 23 (Summer 1987), pp. 3–5.

Joos, Louis C. D. 'Notes sur la littérature sénégalaise de langue française', *Culture Française*, 12, 4 (1963), pp. 17–22.

Joppa, Francis Anani. *L'Engagement des écrivains africains noirs de langue française: du témoignage au dépassement* (Cape Coast, Ghana: University of Cape Coast; Sherbrooke, Québec: Editions Naaman, 1982).

Julien, Eileen. *African Novels and the Question of Orality* (Bloomington: Indiana University Press, 1992).

Kane, Mohamadou. *Roman africain et tradition* (Dakar: Nouvelles Editions Africaines, 1982).

— 'Sur les "formes traditionnelles" du roman africain', *Revue de littérature comparée*, 3–4 (July–December 1974), pp. 536–68.

— 'Sur la critique de la littérature africaine moderne', in *Le Critique africain et son peuple comme producteur de civilisation* (Paris: Présence Africaine, 1977), pp. 257–75.

— 'Le Féminisme dans le roman africain de langue française', *Le Soleil* [Dakar], 10 July 1981, p. 8.

— 'Les Paradoxes du roman africain', *Présence Africaine*, 139 (3rd quarter 1986), pp. 74–87.

Kassé, Maguèye. 'Sembène Ousmane publié en République Démocratique allemande: affirmation d'une convergence humaniste', *Etudes germano-africaines*, 1 (1983), pp. 119–32.

Katrak, Ketu H. 'Boundaries of Resistance', *Novel*, 24, 2 (Winter 1991), pp. 212–14.

Kesteloot, Lilyan. *Les Ecrivains noirs d'expression française* (1963; Brussels: University of Brussels, 1977). English translation by Ellen Conroy Kennedy, *Black Writers in French* (Philadelphia, PA: Temple University Press, 1974).

Killam, G. D., ed. *African Writers on African Writing* (London: Heinemann, 1973).

Kimoni, Yyay. *Destin de la littérature négro-africaine ou problématique d'une culture* (Sherbrooke, Québec: Editions Naaman; Kinshasa, Zaïre: Presses Universitaires du Zaïre, 1975).

Layoun, Mary N. 'Fictional Formations and Deformations of National Culture', *South Atlantic Quarterly*, 87, 1 (Winter 1988), pp. 53–73.

Lazarus, Neil. *Resistance in Postcolonial African Fiction* (New Haven, CT, and London: Yale University Press, 1990).

— 'Disavowing Decolonization: Fanon, Nationalism and the Problematic of Representation in Current Theories of Colonial Discourse', *Research in African Literatures*, 24, 4 (1993), pp. 69–98.

— 'National Consciousness and the Specificity of (Post)Colonial Intellectualism' in *Colonial Discourse/Postcolonial Theory*, ed. by Francis Barker, Peter Hulme, and Margaret Iversen (Manchester and New York: Manchester University Press, 1994), pp. 197–220.

Lecherbonnier, Bernard. *Initiation à la littérature négro-africaine* (Paris: F. Nathan, 1977).

Lecomte, Nelly. *Le Roman négro-africain des années 50 à 60: temps et acculturation* (Paris: L'Harmattan, 1993).

Lee, Sonia. 'The Awakening of the Self in the Heroines of Sembene Ousmane', *Critique: Studies in Modern Fiction*, 17, 2 (1975), pp. 17–25.

Lenin, V. I. *On Literature and Art* (Moscow: Progress Publishers, 1967).

Lentricchia, Frank. *After the New Criticism* (1980; London: Methuen, 1983).

— 'Foucault's Legacy: A New Historicism?', in *The New Historicism*, ed. by H. Aram Veeser (London: Routledge, 1989), pp. 231–42.

Liakhovskaia, N.D. 'Etude et évaluation de l'œuvre de Sembène Ousmane par la critique soviétique', *Œuvres et critiques*, 3, 2 (Autumn 1979), pp. 167–71.

Little, J. P. *Les Nègres* (London: Grant & Cutler, 1990).

Little, J. P. and Roger Little, eds. *Black Accents: Writing in French from Africa, Mauritius and the Caribbean* (London: Grant & Cutler, 1997).

Little, Kenneth. *The Sociology of Urban Women's Image in African Literature* (London: Macmillan, 1980).

Little, Roger. *Nègres Blancs: représentations de l'autre autre* (Paris: L'Harmattan, 1995).

— 'Sembène and the language dilemma', *French Studies Bulletin*, 25 (Winter 1987/88), pp. 16–17.

— 'Escaping Othello's Shadow: *Un Homme pareil aux autres*, *O Pays, mon beau peuple!* and *Un Chant écarlate*', *ASCALF Yearbook*, 1 (1996), pp. 95–112.

Loutfi, Martine Astier. *Littérature et colonialisme; l'expansion coloniale vue dans la littérature romanesque française, 1871–1914* (Paris and The Hague: Mouton, 1971).

Lubin, Maurice A. '*The Cinema of Ousmane Sembène: A Pioneer of African Film*, by Dr Françoise Pfaff', *Présence Africaine*, 136 (4th quarter 1985), pp. 174–8.

Lüsebrink, Hans-Jurgen. 'De l'incontournabilité de la fiction dans la connaissance historique.

Bibliography

Questionnements théoriques à partir de romans historiques contemporains d'Alejo Carpentier, de Yambo Ouologuem et d'Ousmane Sembène', *Neohelicon*, 14, 2 (1989), pp. 107–28.

Makonda, Antoine. '*Les Bouts de bois de Dieu' de Sembène Ousmane* (Abidjan: Nouvelles Editions Africaines; Paris: F. Nathan, 1985).

Makward, Edris. 'Women, Religion and Tradition in Sembène Ousmane's Work', in *Faces of Islam in African Literature*, ed. by Kenneth W. Harrow (London: James Currey, 1991), pp. 187–99.

Marcato, Franca. 'Introduction à la lecture d'un récit africain d'expression française: *Le Mandat* d'Ousmane Sembene', *Présence Francophone*, 14 (Spring 1977), pp. 73–87.

Mateso, Locha. 'Critique littéraire et ressources de l'oralité', *L'Afrique littéraire et artistique*, 50 (1978), pp. 64–8.

Mathieu, J.-C. *Les Fleurs du Mal de Baudelaire* (Paris: Classiques Hachette, 1972).

Mbelolo Ya Mpiku, Joseph. 'Un Romancier né ex-nihilo: Ousmane Sembene', *Présence Francophone*, 1 (Autumn 1970), pp. 174–90.

Mercier, Roger. 'Les Ecrivains négro-africains d'expression française', *Tendances*, 37 (October 1965), pp. 417–40.

Michel-Mansour, Thérèse. 'Entre l'écrit et l'écran: *Taaw/Tauw* d'Ousmane Sembène', in *Littérature et cinéma en Afrique francophone: Ousmane Sembène et Assia Djebar*, ed. by Sada Niang (Paris: L'Harmattan, 1996), pp. 149–60.

Miller, Christopher L. *Blank Darkness: Africanist Discourse in French* (Chicago: University of Chicago Press, 1985).

— *Theories of Africans: Francophone Literature and Anthropology in Africa* (Chicago and London: University of Chicago Press, 1990).

— 'Francophonie and Independence', in *A New History of French Literature*, ed. by Dennis Hollier et al. (1989; Cambridge, Mass. and London: Harvard University Press, 1994), pp. 1028–34.

— 'Response to Esonwanne: Alien Nation?', *Research in African Literatures*, 24, 4 (1993), pp. 63–8.

Minh-ha, Trinh T. *Woman, Native, Other: Writing, Postcoloniality and Feminism* (Bloomington: Indiana University Press, 1989).

Mohanty, Chandra Talpade. 'Under Western Eyes: Feminist Scholarship and Colonial Discourses', in *Third World Women and the Politics of Feminism*, ed. by Chandra Talpade Mohanty, Ann Russo, and Lourdes Torres (Bloomington: Indiana University Press, 1991), pp. 51–80.

Mongia, Padmini, ed. *Contemporary Postcolonial Theory: A Reader* (London: Arnold, 1996).

Moore, Carrie Dailey. 'Evolution of an African Artist: Social Realism in the Works of Ousmane Sembene' (unpublished doctoral thesis, Indiana University, 1973).

Moriceau, Annie, and Alain Rouch. '*Le Mandat' de Sembène Ousmane: étude critique* (Paris: F. Nathan; Dakar: Nouvelles Editions Africaines, 1983).

Mortimer, Mildred. *Journeys through the French African Novel* (London: James Currey, 1990).

Mouralis, Bernard. *Individu et collectivité dans le roman négro-africain d'expression française* (*Annales de l'Université d'Abidjan*, series D, 2, 1969).

— *Littérature et développement* (Paris: Silex, 1984).

— *L'Europe, l'Afrique et la folie* (Paris: Présence Africaine, 1993).

— '*Voltaïque* (1962) et *Véhi-Ciosane–Le Mandat* (1966) de Sembène Ousmane', *Annales de l'Université d'Abidjan*, series D, 3 (1969), pp. 69–70.

Murphy, David. 'The "architecture secrète" of *Voltaïque*', in *Black Accents: Writing in French from Africa, Mauritius and the Caribbean*, ed. by J. P. Little and Roger Little (London: Grant & Cutler, 1997), pp. 157–69.

— 'Report on the ASCALF Conference, French Institute, London, 29–30 November 1996', *ASCALF Bulletin*, 14 (Spring/Summer 1997), pp. 44–6, 48–53.

— 'Writing a History of Resistance: Sembène's Conception of the *Griot* in *Véhi-Ciosane*', *ASCALF Yearbook*, 3 (1998), pp. 34–42.

— 'Representing Senegal: Narratives and Counter-Narratives of the Nation in the work of Ousmane Sembene and Aminata Sow Fall', *ASCALF Bulletin*, 18 (Spring/Summer 1999), pp. 18–27.

Nantot, Jacques. *Panorama de la littérature noire d'expression française* (Paris: Fayard, 1972).

Critical Studies: Literature

Ndiaye, Ibrahima. 'La Critique sociale dans l'œuvre littéraire d'Ousmane Sembène, du *Docker noir à Xala*' (unpublished master's thesis, University of Dakar, 1974–5).

— 'La Technique romanesque d'Ousmane Sembène' (unpublished master's thesis, University of Dakar, 1981–82).

N'Djore, Tanoh. 'L'Appartenance culturelle dans *Véhi-Ciosane* et *Voltaïque* (Sembène Ousmane)', *Annales de l'Université d'Abidjan*, series D, 3 (1969), pp. 127–9.

Ngara, Emmanuel. *Art and Ideology in the African Novel: a Study of the Influence of Marxism on African Writing* (London: Heinemann, 1985).

Ngugi wa Thiong'o. *Writers in Politics* (London: Heinemann, 1981; Oxford: James Currey, 1997).

— *Decolonising the Mind* (London: Heinemann, 1981; London: James Currey, 1986).

Niang, Sada, ed. *Littérature et cinéma en Afrique francophone: Ousmane Sembène et Assia Djebar* (Paris: L'Harmattan, 1996).

— 'Langue française et écriture romanesque dans les trois premiers romans d'Ousmane Sembène', in *Texte africain et voies/voix critiques*, ed. by Claude Bouygues (Paris: L'Harmattan, 1992), pp. 205–23.

— 'Introduction', in *Littérature et cinéma en Afrique francophone: Ousmane Sembène et Assia Djebar*, ed. by Sada Niang (Paris: L'Harmattan, 1996), pp. 5–13.

— 'Langues, cinéma et création littéraire chez Ousmane Sembène et Assia Djebar', in *Littérature et cinéma en Afrique francophone: Ousmane Sembène et Assia Djebar*, ed. by Sada Niang (Paris: L'Harmattan, 1996), pp. 98–109.

Ní Chréacheáin, Fírinne. 'Sembene Ousmane Incorporated? Bestman's *Sembène Ousmane*: a case-study of hegemonic incorporation in African literary criticism', in *Protée noir: essais sur la littérature francophone de l'Afrique noire et des Antilles*, ed. by Peter Hawkins and Annette Lavers (Paris: L'Harmattan, 1992), pp. 126–40.

Ní Loingsigh, Aedín. 'Exil et perceptions du temps dans *Le Bruit dort* de Mustapha Tlili et *Mirages de Paris* d'Ousmane Socé', *ASCALF Bulletin*, 16–17 (Spring/Summer 1998), pp. 3–21.

Njoroge, Paul Ngigi. *Sembene Ousmane's 'God's Bits of Wood'* (Nairobi: Heinemann, 1984).

Nkashama, Pius Ngandu. 'La Fête et l'extase dans le roman africain de langue française', *L'Afrique littéraire*, 65–66 (1982), pp. 24–36.

N'noruka, Matiu. 'Une lecture de *Xala* de Sembène Ousmane', *Peuples noirs/Peuples africains*, 6, 36 (November–December 1983), pp. 57–75.

— '*Xala* d'Ousmane Sembène à l'heure des émeutes en Afrique: le symbolisme du geste des mendiants', *Peuples noirs/Peuples africains*, 14, 8 (March–April 1991), pp. 94–101.

Nzabatsinda, Anthère. 'La Figure de l'artiste dans le récit d'Ousmane Sembène', *Etudes Françaises*, 31, 1 (Summer 1995), pp. 51–60.

— 'Le Griot dans le récit d'Ousmane Sembène: entre la rupture et la continuité d'une représentation de la parole africaine', *French Review*, 70, 6 (May 1997), pp. 865–72.

— *Normes linguistiques et écriture africaine chez Ousmane Sembène* (Paris: Gref, 1998).

Obielo-Okpala, Louis. 'L'Islam dans l'œuvre littéraire de Sembène Ousmane', *L'Afrique littéraire*, 85 (1989), pp. 14–24.

Ogungbesan, Kolawole. *New West African Literature* (London: Heinemann, 1979).

Ohaegbu, A. U. 'Literature for the People: Two Novels by Sembène Ousmane', *Présence Africaine*, 91 (3rd quarter 1974), pp. 116–31.

Ojo, S. Ade. 'André Malraux et Sembène Ousmane: créateurs de romans prolétariens historiques', *Peuples noirs/Peuples africains*, 3, 17 (September–October 1980), pp. 117–34.

— 'Paul Ngigi Njoroge. *Sembene Ousmane's God's Bits of Wood*', *Research in African Literatures*, 16, 4 (Winter 1985), pp. 593–5.

— 'André Malraux et Sembène Ousmane: peintres du prolétaire', *Neohelicon*, 18, 1 (1991), pp. 117–54.

Ortova, Jarmila. 'Les Femmes dans l'œuvre littéraire d'Ousmane Sembène', *Présence Africaine*, 71 (3rd quarter 1969), pp. 69–77.

Ousmane, Sembène, *O Pays, mon beau peuple!*, ed. by Patrick Corcoran (London: Methuen, 1986).

Pageard, Robert. *Littérature négro-africaine* (1966; Paris: Le Livre africain, 1972).

Bibliography

— 'La Vie traditionnelle dans la littérature de l'Afrique noire d'expression française', *Revue de littéraire comparée*, 3–4 (July-December 1974), pp. 420–54.

— 'L'Evolution de la littérature en Afrique noire: un nouveau manteau d'arlequin', *Lettres Romanes*, 33, 3 (August 1979), pp. 329–33.

Parry, Benita. 'Resistance Theory/Theorising Resistance', in *Colonial Discourse/Postcolonial Theory*, ed. by Francis Barker, Peter Hulme and Margaret Iversen (Manchester and New York: Manchester University Press, 1994), pp. 172–96.

Peters, Jonathan A. 'Sembène Ousmane as Griot: *The Money-Order* with *White-Genesis*', *African Literature Today*, 12 (1982), pp. 88–103.

— 'Madior Diouf. *Comprendre "Véhi-Ciosane" et "Le Mandat" d'Ousmane Sembène*', *Research in African Literatures*, 20, 3 (Fall 1989), pp. 524–6.

Pierre, Michel. 'Vingt auteurs choisis', *Magazine Littéraire*, 195 (May 1983), pp. 32–5.

Pieterse, Cosmo and Donald Munro, eds. *Protest and Conflict in African Literature* (London: Heinemann, 1978).

Ridehalgh, Anna. 'African Literature and Film in French', in *French Cultural Studies: an introduction*, ed. by Jill Forbes and Michael Kelly (Oxford: Oxford University Press, 1995), pp. 135–9.

— 'African Literature and Cinema in French after 1968', in *French Cultural Studies: an introduction*, ed. by Jill Forbes and Michael Kelly (Oxford: Oxford University Press, 1995), pp. 178–85.

— '*Guelwaar*. The Stuff of Legend', in *Black Accents: Writing in French from Africa, Mauritius and the Caribbean*, ed. by J. P. Little and Roger Little (London: Grant & Cutler, 1997), pp. 171–81.

Ricsz, János. 'La "Folie" des Tirailleurs sénégalais: fait historique et thème littéraire de la littérature coloniale à la littérature africaine de langue française', in *Black Accents: Writing in French from Africa, Mauritius and the Caribbean*, ed. by J. P. Little and Roger Little (London: Grant & Cutler, 1997), pp. 139–56.

Rushdie, Salman. *Imaginary Homelands: Essays and Criticism 1981–1991* (London: Granta, 1991).

Sacks, Karen. 'Women and Class Struggle in Sembene's *God's Bits of Wood*', *Signs: Journal of Women in Culture and Society*, 4, 2 (Winter 1978), pp. 363–70.

Said, Edward. *Orientalism* (1978; London: Penguin, 1995).

— *The World, the Text and the Critic* (1983; London: Vintage, 1991).

— *Culture and Imperialism* (1993; London: Vintage, 1994).

Sainville, Léonard. *Anthologie de la littérature négro-africaine: romanciers et conteurs négro-africains*, 1 (Paris: Présence Africaine, 1963).

Sall, Ahmadou Lamine. 'Entre le mythe et la réalité', *Le Soleil* [Dakar], 10 July 1981, p. 3.

Sartre, Jean-Paul. 'Orphée noir', in *Anthologie de la nouvelle poésie nègre et malgache de langue française*, ed. by Léopold Sédar Senghor (1948; Paris: Presses Universitaires Françaises, 1977), pp. ix–xliv.

Savané, Vieux. 'La Femme dans l'univers romanesque de Sembène Ousmane', *Tribune Africaine: revue trimestrielle d'analyse et d'opinion*, 1 (1983), pp. 46–50.

Schipper, Mineke, ed. *Unheard Words: Women and Literature in Africa, the Arab World, Asia, the Caribbean and Latin America*, trans. by Barbara Potter Fasting (London and New York: Allison & Busby, 1985).

Schuerkens, Ulrike. *La Colonisation dans la littérature africaine: essai de reconstruction d'une réalité sociale* (Paris: L'Harmattan, 1994).

Seck, Madické. 'Langue française et réalités africaines dans l'œuvre littéraire d'Ousmane Sembène, du *Docker noir* à *Xala*' (unpublished master's thesis, University of Dakar 1981–82).

Senghor, Léopold Sédar. *Liberté 1: Négritude et humanisme* (Paris: Seuil, 1964).

— *Liberté 3: Négritude et civilisation de l'universel* (Paris: Seuil, 1977).

— *La Poésie de l'action* (Paris: Stock, 1980).

— *Liberté 5: Le Dialogue des cultures* (Paris: Seuil, 1992).

Serceau, Michel. 'De la littérature au cinéma: status de la parole et de l'oralité dans les œuvres cinématographiques de Sembene Ousmane et Pierre Perrault', in *Convergences et divergences dans les littératures francophones* (Paris: L'Harmattan, 1992), pp. 134–41.

Sikoumo, Hilaire. 'Sembène Ousmane, écrivain populaire' (unpublished doctoral thesis, University of Bordeaux III, 1983).

Smith, Esther Y. 'Images of Women in African Literature: Some Examples of Inequality in the Colonial Period', in *Ngambika: Studies of Women in African Literature*, ed. by Carol Boyce Davies and Anne Adams Graves (Trenton, New Jersey: Africa World Press, 1986), pp. 27–44.

Smyley-Wallace, Karen. 'Black Women in Black Francophone Literature: Comparisons of Male and Female Writers', *International Fiction Review*, 11, 2 (Summer 1984), pp. 112–14.

— 'Women and Alienation: Analysis of the Works of Two Francophone African Novelists', in *Ngambika: Studies of Women in African Literature*, ed. by Carol Boyce Davies and Anne Adams Graves (Trenton, New Jersey: Africa World Press, 1986), pp. 63–73.

Soyinka, Wole. *Myth, Literature and the African World* (1976; Cambridge: Cambridge University Press, Canto edition, 1990).

Spivak, Gayatri Chakravorty. *In Other Worlds: Essays in Cultural Politics* (New York and London: Methuen, 1987).

— 'Three Women's Texts and a Critique of Imperialism', *Critical Inquiry*, 12, 1 (1985), pp. 43–61.

— 'Can the Subaltern Speak?', in *Marxism and the Interpretation of Culture*, ed. by Cary Nelson and Lawrence Grossberg (London: Macmillan, 1988), pp. 271–313.

— 'Introduction – Subaltern Studies: Deconstructing Historiography', in *Selected Subaltern Studies*, ed. by Ranajit Guha and Gayatri Chakravorty Spivak (Oxford: Oxford University Press, 1988), pp. 3–32.

Stafford, Andy. 'Work, Racism and Writing in 1950s France', *ASCALF Bulletin*, 12 (Spring/Summer 1996), pp. 3–13.

— '"The Black Atlantic": History, Modernity and Conflict in Sembène Ousmane's "Le Voltaïque"', *ASCALF Yearbook*, 3 (1998), pp. 63–9.

Stringer, Susan. *The Senegalese Novel by Women: Through their own Eyes* (Frankfurt: Peter Lang, 1996).

Suleri, Sara. 'Women Skin Deep: Feminism and the Postcolonial Condition', *Critical Inquiry*, 18, 4 (Summer 1992), pp. 756–69.

Thomas, Dominic. 'Aesthetics and Ideology: The Performance of Nationalism in Recent Literary Productions from the Republic of the Congo', in *Black Accents: Writing in French from Africa, Mauritius and the Caribbean*, ed. by J. P. Little and Roger Little (London: Grant & Cutler, 1997), pp. 128–38.

Tidjani-Serpos, Noureini. *Aspects de la critique africaine*, 1 (Lomé: Editions HAHO; Paris: Editions Silex, 1987).

— 'Roman et société: la femme africaine comme personnage des *Bouts de bois de Dieu* de Sembène Ousmane', *Présence Africaine*, 108 (4th quarter 1978), pp. 122–37.

— 'L'Ecrivain africain, griot contemporain', *Notre Librairie*, 98 (July–September 1989), pp. 63–7.

Tiffin, Chris and Alan Lawson, eds. *De-Scribing Empire: Postcolonialism and Textuality* (London and New York: Routledge, 1994).

Tine, Alioune. 'Etude pragmatique et sémiotique des effets du bilinguisme dans les œuvres romanesques de Ousmane Sembene' (unpublished doctoral thesis, University of Lyon 2, 1981).

— 'Pour une théorie de la littérature africaine écrite', *Présence Africaine*, 133–34 (1st and 2nd quarters 1985), pp. 99–121.

— 'Wolof ou français: le choix de Sembène', *Notre Librairie*, 81 (October–December 1985), pp. 43–50.

— 'La Diglossie linguistique et la diglossie littéraire et leurs effets dans la pratique esthétique d'Ousmane Sembène', in *Littérature et cinéma en Afrique francophone: Ousmane Sembène et Assia Djebar*, ed. by Sada Niang (Paris: L'Harmattan, 1996), pp. 82–97.

Traoré, Biny. *Aspects socio-politiques et techniques dans le roman africain d'aujourd'hui: l'exemple de 'Xala' de Sembène Ousmane* (Ouagadougou: [n. pub.], 1981).

Tsabedze, Clara. *African Independence from Francophone and Anglophone Voices: a Comparative Study of the Post-Independence Novels of Ngugi and Sembène* (Frankfurt: Peter Lang, 1994).

Ugochukwu, Françoise. 'Deux Françaises en Afrique à l'époque coloniale: étude comparée de Sembène Ousmane et de Guy des Cars', *Peuples noirs/Peuples africains*, 9, 51 (May–June 1986), pp. 78–101.

Vaillant, Janet G. *Black, French and African: a life of Léopold Sédar Senghor* (London: Harvard University Press, 1990).

256

Bibliography

Vignal, Daniel. 'Sembène Ousmane nouvelliste', *Peuples noirs/Peuples africains*, 4, 19 (1981), pp. 141–7.

— 'Le Noir et le blanc dans *Voltaïque* de O. Sembène', *Peuples noirs/Peuples africains*, 6, 36 (November–December 1983), pp. 96–115.

Vindt, Gérard, and Nicole Guiraud. *Les grands romans historiques* (Paris: Bordas, 1991).

Wake, Clive. 'Negritude and After: Changing Perspectives in French-language African Fiction', *Third World Quarterly*, 10, 2 (April 1988), pp. 961–5.

— '*O Pays, mon beau peuple!* by Sembène Ousmane, ed. by Patrick Corcoran', *Modern Language Review*, 83, 3 (July 1988), p. 745.

Williams, Raymond. *The Country and the City* (London: Chatto & Windus, 1973).

Wylie, Hal. 'The Political Science of Sembène and Fall: Senghor Revisited', in *Carrefour des cultures*, ed. by Régis Antoine (Tübingen: Narr, 1993), pp. 361–7.

Critical Studies: Cinema

Amenguel, Barthélemy. '*Ceddo* de Sembène Ousmane', *Positif*, 195–6 (July–August 1977), p. 83.

Amiel, Mireille. '*Ceddo* – Ousmane Sembène', *Cinéma*, 249 (September 1979), pp. 92–3.

Andrade-Watkins, Claire. 'Film Production in Francophone Africa 1961–1977: Ousmane Sembène – An Exception', in *Ousmane Sembène: Dialogues with Critics and Writers*, ed. by Samba Gadjigo et al. (Amherst: University of Massachusetts Press, 1993), pp. 29–36.

André, Jacques. '*Mandabi*', *Sénégal d'aujourd'hui*, 3 (December 1968), pp. 36–7.

Armes, Roy. *Third World Film Making and the West* (Berkeley: University of California Press, 1987).

Aumont, Jacques, and Sylvie Pierre. 'Huit fois deux', *Cahiers du Cinéma*, 206 (November 1968), pp. 30–2.

Ayari, Farida. '*Ceddo*: une fable réquisitoire: les hommes du refus', *Jeune Afrique*, 11 July 1979, p. 66.

Barlet, Olivier. *Les Cinémas d'Afrique noire* (Paris: L'Harmattan, 1996).

Bestman, Martin. 'Paulin S. Vieyra, Sembène Ousmane, cinéaste', *Etudes Littéraires*, 7, 3 (December 1974), pp. 495–7.

Billington, Michael. 'All's Welles', *Illustrated London News* (January 1977), p. 49.

Binet, Jacques. 'Classes sociales et cinéma africain', *Positif*, 188 (December 1976), pp. 34–42.

— 'Violence et cinéma africain', *L'Afrique littéraire et artistique*, 44 (1977), pp. 73–80.

— 'Temps et espace dans le cinéma africain', *Positif*, 198 (October 1977), pp. 57–62.

— 'Apport et influence du cinéma négro-africain', *Diogène*, 110 (April–June 1980), pp. 72–89.

— 'Le Sacré dans le cinéma négro-africain', *Positif*, 235 (October 1980), pp. 44–9.

— 'Le Sacré dans le cinéma africain: post-scriptum sur *Ceddo*', *Positif*, 235 (October 1980), p. 53.

Bonitzer, Pascal. 'L'Argent-fantôme', *Cahiers du Cinéma*, 209 (February 1969), pp. 57–8.

Bordwell, David. *Narration in the Fiction Film* (London: Methuen, 1985).

Bordwell, David and Kristin Thompson. *Film Art: An Introduction* (New York and London: McGraw-Hill, 1990).

'*Borom Sarret*: un film de Ousmane Sembène', *L'Avant-Scène Cinéma*, 229 (1 June 1979), pp. 35–42.

Bory, Jean-Louis. 'La Nouvelle arme du tiers monde', *Nouvel Observateur*, 28 October–3 November 1968, pp. 50–1.

— 'L'Annonce faite aux Ouolofs', *Nouvel Observateur*, 2–8 December 1968, pp. 56–7.

— 'Des Regards noirs', *Nouvel Observateur*, 20–26 March 1972, p. 63.

Boughedir, Férid. *Le Cinéma africain de A à Z* (Brussels: OCIC, 1987).

— 'Une parabole des privilégiés', *Jeune Afrique*, 2 April 1976, pp. 56–8.

— 'Qu'on l'admire ou qu'on le dénigre ...', *L'Afrique littéraire*, 76 (1985), p. 4.

Brahimi, Denise. *Cinémas d'Afrique francophone et du Maghreb* (Paris: F. Nathan, 1997).

Braudeau, Michel. 'Lumières sur un massacre: *Camp de Thiaroye*', *Le Monde (des livres)*, 9 September 1988, p. 22.

Brecht, Bertolt. *Brecht on Theatre: The Development of an Aesthetic*, ed. and trans. by John Willett

(London: Eyre Methuen, 1978).

Brière, Eloise. '*Ousmane Sembène: Dialogues with Critics and Writers*, (ed.) Samba Gadjigo et al.', *Research in African Literatures*, 26, 3 (Fall 1995), pp. 198–200.

Capdenac, Michel. 'L'Argent, ou l'idée du bonheur en Afrique', *Les Lettres françaises*, 27 November–3 December 1968, p. 22.

— 'Les Damnés de la terre', *Les Lettres françaises*, 30 September–6 October 1970, pp. 28–9.

Casanova, Marie-Paul. '*Xala*', *La Quinzaine Littéraire*, 16–31 July 1975, p. 10.

Cham, Mbye Boubacar and Claire-Andrade Watkins, eds. *Blackframes: Critical Perspectives on Black Independent Cinema* (Cambridge, Mass., and London: Massachusetts Institute of Technology Press, 1988).

— 'Ousmane Sembene and the Aesthetics of African Oral Traditions', *Africana Journal*, 13, 1–4 (1982), pp. 24–40.

— 'Art and Ideology in the Work of Sembène Ousmane and Hailé Gerima', *Présence Africaine*, 129 (1st quarter 1984), pp. 79–91.

— 'Islam in Senegalese Literature and Film', in *Faces of Islam in African Literature*, ed. by Kenneth W. Harrow (London: James Currey; Portsmouth, NH: Heinemann, 1991), pp. 163–86.

— 'Official History, Popular Memory: Reconfiguration of the African Past in the Films of Ousmane Sembène', in *Ousmane Sembène: Dialogues with Critics and Writers*, ed. by Samba Gadjigo, et al. (Amherst, MA: University of Massachusetts Press, 1993), pp. 22–8.

Cheriaa, Tahaar. *Ecrans d'abondance ou cinéma de libération en Afrique?* (Tunis: SATPEC, 1978).

Ciment, Michel. '*Mandabi* [*Le Mandat*], d'Ousmane Sembene', *Positif*, 100–01 (December 1968 – January 1969), p. 45.

— '*Le Camp de Thiaroye*, de Sembene Ousmane et Thierno Faty Sow', *Positif*, 333 (November 1988), p. 62.

Cohn, Bernard. 'Une Semaine de critique en 1966 à Cannes', *Positif*, 79 (October 1966), p. 96.

Cook, David A. *A History of Narrative Film* (1981; New York and London: Norton, 1990).

Copans, Jean. 'Entre l'Histoire et les mythes', *L'Afrique littéraire*, 76 (1985), pp. 57–9.

Curtius, Anny and Joseph Paré. '*Le Mandat* de Sembène Ousmane ou la dialectique d'une double herméneutique', in *Littérature et cinéma en Afrique francophone*, ed. by Sada Niang (Paris: L'Harmattan, 1996), pp. 139–48.

Daney, Serge. '*Ceddo* (O. Sembene)', *Cahiers du Cinéma*, 304 (October 1979), pp. 51–3.

Desanti, Dominique. 'L'Afrique réelle', *La Quinzaine Littéraire*, 1 May 1966, p. 23.

de Vitry-Maubrey, Luce. 'Pfaff, Françoise: *The Cinema of Ousmane Sembene: A Pioneer of African Film*', *French Review*, 60, 2 (December 1986), pp. 285–6.

Devut, Victor. 'Le Faux-départ du cinéma "bicot-nègre"', *Esprit*, 444 (March 1975), pp. 410–2.

Diawara, Manthia. *African Cinema* (Bloomington: Indiana University Press, 1992).

Diop, Baba. 'L'Année Sembene', *Sud Quotidien*, 24 November 1993, p. 2.

— 'Le Modèle Guélwaar', *Sud Quotidien*, 14 December 1993, p. 2.

Diop, Buuba Babacar. 'Malaise autour de *Ceddo*', *Revue africaine de communication*, 7 (September–October 1984), pp. 45–52.

— 'Littérature et cinéma', *Unir Cinéma*, 19 (August 1985), pp. 4–10.

Diouf, Bara. '*Le Mandat*, film d'Ousmane Sembene', *Dakar-Matin*, 7 December 1968, pp. 1, 8.

Diouf, Mamadou. 'Histoires et actualités dans *Ceddo* d'Ousmane Sembène et *Hyènes* de Djibril Diop Mambety', in *Littérature et cinéma en Afrique francophone*, ed. by Sada Niang (Paris: L'Harmattan, 1996), pp. 15–34.

'Dossier 156/1 – *Guelwaar*', *Unir Cinéma*, 156 (June 1994), pp. 20–6.

Downing, John D. H. *Film and Politics in the Third World* (New York: Autonomedia, 1987).

Dubroux, Danièle. 'Exhibition (*Xala*)', *Cahiers du Cinéma*, 266–7 (May 1976), pp. 72–4.

Eaton, Mick, ed. *Anthropology, Reality, Cinema* (London: British Film Institute, 1979).

El Haj, Bhari Ben, ed. *Une Politique africaine du cinéma* (Paris: Editions Dadci, 1980).

Farès, Tewfik. 'Les gris-gris de Ousmane Sembene', *Jeune Afrique*, 22 July 1972, p. 66.

Gabriel, Teshome H. *Third Cinema in the Third World: the Aesthetics of Liberation* (London: Bowker, 1982).

258

Bibliography

— 'Xala: A Cinema of Wax and Gold', *Présence Africaine*, 116 (4th quarter 1980), pp. 202–14.

Gadjigo, Samba et al., eds. *Ousmane Sembène: Dialogues with Critics and Writers* (Amherst: University of Massachusetts Press, 1993).

Ghali, Noureddine. '*Emitaï*: la vraie nature du colonialisme', *Cinéma*, 208 (April 1976), pp. 94–5.

— 'Xala: histoire symbolique d'une déchéance', *Cinéma*, 208 (April 1976), p. 95.

Gugler, Joseph and Oumar Chérif Diop. 'The Two Incarnations of Ousmane Sembène's *Xala* and Their Audiences', *Research in African Literatures*, 29, 2 (Summer 1998), pp. 147–58.

Haffner, Pierre. *Essai sur les fondements du cinéma africain* (Dakar: Nouvelles Editions Africaines, 1978).

— 'Situation du cinéma négro-africain', *Le Mois en Afrique*, 184–85 (April–May 1981), pp. 127–35.

— 'Le Cinéma, l'argent et les lois: une situation du cinéma sénégalais en 1981', *Le Mois en Afrique*, 198–9 (May–June 1982), pp. 154–66.

— 'Le Cinéma, l'argent et les lois (deuxième partie)', *Le Mois en Afrique*, 203–4 (December 1982–January 1983), pp. 144–54.

— 'Des écrans à la recherche d'une mémoire (des cultures à la recherche d'un miroir)', *Peuples noirs/Peuples africains*, 6, 35 (September–October 1983), pp. 91–102.

— 'Sandy et Bozambo: entretien avec Jean Rouch sur Sembène Ousmane', *L'Afrique littéraire*, 76 (1985), pp. 86–94.

Harrow, Kenneth W., ed. *Research in African Literatures*, 26, 3 (Autumn 1995). Special issue on African Cinema.

— 'Sembene's *Xala*: The Use of Film and Novel as Revolutionary Weapon', *Studies in Twentieth Century Literature*, 4, 2 (Spring 1980), pp. 177–88.

Hennebelle, Monique. '*Sembène Ousmane, cinéaste*: un livre de Paulin Soumanou Vieyra', *L'Afrique littéraire et artistique*, 27 (February 1973), pp. 87–8.

I. R. '*Emitaï* – un film de Sembène Ousmane', *Le Monde Diplomatique*, 24, 279 (June 1977), p. 23.

Iyam, David Uru. 'The Silent Revolutionaries: Ousmane Sembene's *Emitaï, Xala* and *Ceddo*', *African Studies Review*, 29, 4 (December 1986), pp. 79–87.

Jordan, Pierre-L. *Cinéma, Cinema, Kino* (Marseille: Musées de Marseille/Images en Manœuvres Editions, 1992).

Kakou, Antoine. *Emblèmes et métaphores d'un conteur: les bases de l'écriture filmique de Sembène Ousmane* (Abidjan: University of Abidjan, 1980).

— 'Les gris-gris d'un conteur', *L'Afrique littéraire*, 76 (1985), pp. 62–5.

— 'La Thématique', *L'Afrique littéraire*, 76 (1985), pp. 17–19.

Kerr, David. *African Popular Theatre from Pre-colonial Times to the Present Day* (London: James Currey, 1995).

Khatami, Khamaïs. '*Xala*: un catéchisme soporifique', *CinémArabe*, 3 (May–June 1976), p. 40.

Kroll, Jack. 'The World on Film', *Newsweek*, 13 October 1975, pp. 51–2.

Lapsley, Robert and Michael Westlake. *Film Theory: An Introduction* (Manchester: Manchester University Press, 1988).

Larouche, Michel, ed. *Films d'Afrique* (Montréal: Guernica, 1991).

Leahy, James. 'The Language of African Cinema', in *Protée noir: essais sur la littérature francophone de l'Afrique noire et des Antilles*, ed. by Peter Hawkins and Annette Lavers (Paris: L'Harmattan, 1992), pp. 179–202.

Lellis, George. *Bertolt Brecht, 'Cahiers du Cinéma' and Contemporary Film Theory* (London: Bowker, 1982).

Little, Roger, and Nicola Macdonald. 'The Thiaroye Massacre in Word and Image', *ASCALF Bulletin*, 8 (Spring/Summer 1994), pp. 18–37.

Lorenz, Denise. 'Le Cinéma en Afrique noire', *Lendemains*, 19 (1980), pp. 27–43.

Maillat, Philippe. 'Entretien avec Pierre Haffner: "Pourquoi j'ai écrit *Fondements du cinéma africain*"', *L'Afrique littéraire et artistique*, 38 (1975), pp. 106–9.

Malkmus, Lizbeth and Roy Armes. *Arab and African Film Making* (London: Zed Books, 1991).

'*Le Mandat*', *L'Avant-Scène Cinéma*, 90 (March 1969), pp. 147–54.

Marcorelles, Louis. 'Sous l'égide de la Semaine de la critique trois films sénégalais, brésilien et yougoslave présentés à Paris', *Le Monde*, 6 April 1967, p. 17.

— 'Le Mandat', *Les Lettres françaises*, 6–12 November 1968, p. 19.

— 'L'Afrique noire au rendez-vous d'Alger', *Le Monde*, 20 August 1969, p. 10.

— 'Le "ciné-livre" de Sembène Ousmane', *Le Monde*, 6 March 1975, p. 17.

— '*Xala*, de Sembène Ousmane', *Le Monde*, 16 March 1976, p. 33.

— 'Les Vérités premières de Sembène Ousmane', *Le Monde*, 7 May 1977, pp. 1, 33.

— 'L'Avenir du cinéma africain: comment surmonter les mésententes régionales?', *Le Monde Diplomatique*, 32, 376 (July 1985), p. 22.

Maria, Roger. '*Ceddo*', *Raison Présente*, 52 (October-December 1979), pp. 124–5.

Martin, Angela, ed. *African Films: The Context of Production* (London: British Film Institute, 1982).

Masson, Alain. 'Mascarade à Dakar (*Xala*)', *Positif*, 182 (June 1976), pp. 54–6.

Medjigbodo, Nicole. 'Afrique cinématographiée, Afrique cinématographique', *La Revue canadienne des études africaines/Canadian Journal of African Studies*, 13, 3 (1979), pp. 371–87.

Métigeau, Pascal. 'La Chasse aux réalités fuyantes', *Le Monde*, 27 November 1993, p. 20.

Mermin, Elizabeth. 'A Window on Whose Reality? The Emerging Industry of Senegalese Cinema', *Research in African Literatures*, 26, 3 (Autumn 1995), pp. 120–33.

Metz, Christian. *Essais sur la signification au cinéma*, 1 (Paris: Klincksieck, 1975).

Michel-Mansour, Thérèse. 'Entre l'écrit et l'écran: *Taaw/Tauw* d'Ousmane Sembène', in *Littérature et cinéma en Afrique francophone: Ousmane Sembène et Assia Djebar* ed. by Sada Niang (Paris: L'Harmattan, 1996), pp. 149–60).

Minot, Gilbert. 'Toward the African Cinema', *Ufahamu* (Journal of the African Activist Association), 12, 2 (1983), pp. 37–43.

Moitt, Bernard. 'Race, résistance et les tirailleurs sénégalais: une analyse de *Camp de Thiaroye* d'Ousmane Sembène', in *Littérature et cinéma en Afrique francophone: Ousmane Sembène et Assia Djebar*, ed. by Sada Niang (Paris: L'Harmattan, 1996), pp. 122–38.

Monaco, James. *How to Read a Film* (1977; New York and Oxford: Oxford University Press, 1981).

Mortimer, Robert A. 'Ousmane Sembene and the Cinema of Decolonization', *African Arts/Arts d'Afrique*, 5, 3 (Spring 1972), pp. 26, 64–68, 84.

Mpoyi-Buatu, Th. '*Ceddo* de Sembène Ousmane et *West Indies* de Med Hondo', *Présence Africaine*, 119 (3rd trimester 1981), pp. 152–64.

Mulvey, Laura. '*Xala*, Ousmane Sembene 1976: The Carapace that Failed', in *Colonial Discourse and Post-Colonial Theory: A Reader*, ed. by Laura Chrisman and Patrick Williams (London: Harvester Wheatsheaf, 1994), pp. 517–34.

Narboni, Jean. 'Un film sénégalais', *Cahiers du Cinéma*, 190 (May 1967), p. 74.

Niang, Sada, ed. *Littérature et cinéma en Afrique francophone: Ousmane Sembène et Assia Djebar* (Paris: L'Harmattan, 1996).

Niang, Sada. 'Langues, cinéma et création littéraire chez Ousmane Sembène et Assia Djebar', in *Littérature et cinéma en Afrique francophone: Ousmane Sembène et Assia Djebar*, ed. by Sada Niang (Paris: L'Harmattan, 1996), pp. 98–109).

Nichols, Bill. *Ideology and the Image: Social Representation in the Cinema and Other Media* (Bloomington: Indiana University Press, 1981).

— ed. *Movies and Methods* (Berkeley: University of California Press, 1976).

Nicolini, Elisabeth. 'Un Grand débat sur le septième art africain', *Jeune Afrique*, 9 April 1986, p. 64.

Parrain, Philippe. *Regards sur le cinéma indien* (Paris: Le Cerf, 1969), 7, no. 48.

Pearson, Lyle. 'Four Years of African Film', *Film Quarterly*, 26, 3 (Spring 1973), pp. 42–7.

Petty, Sheila, ed. *A Call to Action: The Films of Ousmane Sembene* (Trowbridge: Flick Books, 1996).

Pfaff, Françoise. *The Cinema of Ousmane Sembene: A Pioneer of African Film* (Westport, Connecticut: Greenwood Press, 1984).

— 'The Uniqueness of Ousmane Sembène's Cinema', in *Ousmane Sembène: Dialogues with Critics and Writers*, ed. by Samba Gadjigo et al. (Amherst: University of Massachusetts Press, 1993), pp. 14–21.

Pines, Jim and Paul Willemin, eds. *Questions of Third Cinema* (London: British Film Institute, 1989).

Pommier, Pierre. *Cinéma et développement en Afrique noire francophone* (Paris: A. Pedone, 1974).

Bibliography

Potts, James. 'Is there an International Film Language?', *Sight and Sound*, 48, 2 (Spring 1979), pp. 74–81.

Pouillade, Jean-Luc. 'L'Emblème sur *Ceddo*', *Positif*, 235 (October 1980), pp. 50–3.

Prédal, René. '*La Noire de*: premier long métrage africain', *L'Afrique littéraire*, 76 (1985), pp. 36–9.

'Le Prix Jean Vigo au réalisateur sénégalais Ousmane Sembène', *Le Monde*, 23 March 1966, p. 14.

Ruelle, Catherine. 'La Place de la femme', *L'Afrique littéraire*, 76 (1985), pp. 80–3.

Scheinfeigel, Maxime. '*Borom Sarret*: la fiction documentaire', *L'Afrique littéraire*, 76 (1985), pp. 32–4.

Serceau, Daniel, ed. *L'Afrique littéraire et artistique*, 76 (1985). Special issue on Sembene, focusing mainly on his films.

— '*Ceddo*: la barbarie à visage divin', *L'Afrique littéraire*, 76 (1985), pp. 54–7.

— '*Emitaï*: l'échec d'une transposition dramatique', *L'Afrique littéraire*, 76 (1985), pp. 43–5.

— 'Un "inconnu" nommé Sembène Ousmane ...', *L'Afrique littéraire*, 76 (1985), pp. 5–7.

— 'La Recherche d'une écriture', *L'Afrique littéraire*, 76 (1985), pp. 66–72.

Serceau, Michel. '*Le Mandat*: un film catalyseur des relations sociales', *L'Afrique littéraire*, 76 (1985), pp. 40–2.

— 'Du Masque au mandat: tradition et modernité', *L'Afrique littéraire*, 76 (1985), pp. 72–9.

— '*Niaye*: l'Afrique sans masque', *L'Afrique littéraire*, 76 (1985), p. 35.

— '*Xala*: une fable sur la bourgeoisie africaine', *L'Afrique littéraire*, 76 (1985), pp. 46–50.

— 'De la littérature au cinéma: statut de la parole et de l'oralité dans les œuvres cinématographiques de Sembène Ousmane et Pierre Perrault', in *Convergences et divergences dans les littératures francophones* (Paris: L'Harmattan, 1992), pp. 134–41.

Shaka, Femi Okiremuete. 'Vichy Dakar and the Other Story of French Colonial Stewardship: A Critical Reading of Ousmane Sembène and Thierno Faty Sow's *Camp de Thiaroye*', *Research in African Literatures*, 26, 3 (Fall 1995), pp. 67–77.

Shohat, Ella and Robert Stam. *Unthinking Eurocentrism: Multiculturalism and the Media* (New York and London: Routledge, 1994).

Sokhona, Sidney. 'Notre cinéma', *Cahiers du Cinéma*, 285 (February 1978), pp. 55–7.

Solanas, Fernando and Octavio Getino. 'Towards a Third Cinema', *Afterimage*, 3 (Summer 1971), pp. 16–35.

Songolo, Aliko. 'Vieyra, Paulin Soumanou: *Sembène Ousmane, cinéaste*', *French Review*, 56, 1 (October 1982), pp. 182–3.

Stadler, Eva Maria. 'Francophonie et cinéma: l'exemple de deux cinéastes sénégalais', in *Francographies: création et réalité d'expression française*, ed. by J. Macary (New York: Société des Professeurs Français d'Amérique, 1993), pp. 183–95.

Tarratt, Margaret. '*The Money Order*', *Films and Filming*, 20, 4 (January 1974), pp. 45, 48.

Torok, Jean-Paul. 'Tours: le Trafalgar du court-métrage', *Positif*, 59 (March 1964), p. 45.

Toubiana, Serge. '*Camp de Thiaroye*', *Cahiers du Cinéma*, 412 (October 1988), p. 25.

Traoré, Biny. 'Cinéma africain et développement', *Peuples noirs/Peuples africains*, 6 (May–June 1983), pp. 51–62.

Ukadike, Nwachukwu Frank. *Black African Cinema* (Berkeley and London: University of California Press, 1994).

Un patriote sénégalais S KH SY, '*Ceddo* ou le poids des mystifications en Afrique', *Peuples noirs/Peuples africains*, 2, 12 (November–December 1979), pp. 37–46.

Vieyra, Paulin Soumanou. *Le Cinéma et l'Afrique* (Paris: Présence Africaine, 1970).

— *Sembène Ousmane, cinéaste* (Paris: Présence Africaine, 1972).

— *Le Cinéma africain des origines à 1973* (Paris: Présence Africaine, 1975).

— *Le Cinéma au Sénégal* (Brussels: OCIC/L'Harmattan, 1983).

— 'Le Film africain d'expression française', *African Arts/Arts d'Afrique*, 1, 3 (Spring 1968), pp. 60–9.

— 'Le Cinéma au 1er festival culturel panafricain d'Alger', *Présence Africaine*, 72 (4th quarter 1969), pp. 190–201.

— 'Le Troisième festival panafricain de Ouagadougou', *Présence Africaine*, 82 (2nd quarter 1972), pp. 120–31.

— '6e festival international de films d'expression française', *Présence Africaine*, 92 (4th quarter 1974), pp. 190–5.
— 'Le Deuxième congrès de la FEPACI', *Présence Africaine*, 97 (1st quarter 1976), pp. 165–74.
— 'La Critique et le cinéma en Afrique', in *Le Critique africain et son peuple comme producteur de civilisation* (Paris: Présence Africaine, 1977), pp. 197–209.
— 'Le Cinéma au Sénégal en 1976', *Présence Africaine*, 107 (3rd quarter 1978), pp. 207–16.
— 'Fespaco 1979', *Présence Africaine*, 111 (3rd quarter 1979), pp. 101–6.
— 'Françoise Pfaff, *The Cinema of Ousmane Sembene: A Pioneer of African Film*', *La Revue canadienne des études africaines/ Canadian Journal of African Studies*, 20, 1 (1986), pp. 136–8.
Vitrican, Vincent. '*Guelwaar*', *Cahiers du Cinéma*, 474 (December 1993), p. 81.
Willeumier, Marie-Claire. 'Naissance d'un cinéma', *Esprit*, 362 (July–August 1967), pp. 135–40.
Youssaf, Nahem. 'Sembene Ousmane and "Rhetorical Film Form"', *Wasafiri*, 22 (Autumn 1995), pp. 49–53.
Zacks, Stephen A. 'The Theoretical Construction of African Cinema', *Research in African Literatures*, 26, 3 (Fall 1995), pp. 6–17.
Zimmer, Christian. 'L'Homme enfermé', *Les Temps Modernes*, 31, 360 (July 1976), pp. 2377–94.

Other Secondary Works

Adotévi, Stanislas. *Négritude et négrologues* (Paris: Plon, 1972).
Ageron, Charles Robert. *L'Anti-colonialisme en France de 1871 à 1914* (Paris: Presses Universitaires Françaises, 1973).
Aguessy, Mme. D. 'La Femme dakaroise commerçante au détail sur le marché', in *Dakar en devenir*, ed. by M. Sankalé et al. (Paris: Présence Africaine, 1968), pp. 395–421.
Amin, Samir. *L'Accumulation à l'échelle mondiale: critique de la théorie du sous-développement* (Paris: Anthropos, 1971). English translation by Brian Pearce, *Accumulation on a World Scale: a critique of the theory of underdevelopment* (New York & London: Monthly Review Press, 1974).
— *L'Afrique de l'ouest bloquée* (Paris: Editions de Minuit, 1971).
Anderson, Benedict. *Imagined Communities: Reflections on the Origin and Spread of Nationalism* (London: Verso, 1983).
Appiah, Kwame Anthony. *In My Father's House: Africa in the Philosophy of Culture* (London: Methuen, 1992).
Bâ, Amadou Hampâté. *Aspects de la civilisation africaine* (Paris: Présence Africaine, 1972).
Barratt-Brown, Michael. *After Imperialism* (London: Heinemann, 1963).
Barry, Boubacar. *Le Royaume du Waalo, 1659–1859: le Sénégal avant la conquête* (Paris: Maspéro, 1972).
— 'Neocolonialism and Dependence in Senegal, 1960–1980', in *Decolonization and African Independence: The Transfers of Power 1960–1980*, ed. by Prosser Gifford and Wm. Roger Louis (New Haven, CT, and London: Yale University Press, 1982), pp. 271–94.
— 'Le Renforcement des pouvoirs ceddo aux XVIIe et XVIIIe siècles en Sénégambie', *Revue sénégalaise de philosophie*, 13–14 (1990), pp. 209–19.
Bathily, Abdoulaye. *Mai 68 à Dakar ou la révolte universitaire et la démocratie* (Paris: Editions Chaka, 1992).
Bayart, Jean-François. *L'Etat en Afrique: la politique du ventre* (Paris: Fayard, 1989). English translation: *The State in Africa: the Politics of the Belly* (London: Longman, 1993).
Behrman, Lucy. *Muslim Brotherhoods and Politics in Senegal* (Cambridge, Mass.: Harvard University Press, 1970).
Bernard-Duquenot, Nicole. *Le Sénégal et le Front Populaire* (Paris: L'Harmattan, 1985).
Birmingham, David. *The Decolonization of Africa* (London: University College London Press, 1995).
Boahen, Adu. 'Ghana since Independence', in *Decolonization and African Independence: The Transfers of Power 1960–1980*, ed. by Prosser Gifford and Wm. Roger Louis (New Haven, CT, and London: Yale University Press, 1982), pp. 199–224.

Bibliography

Boilat, Abbé David. *Esquisses sénégalaises* (1853; Paris: Karthala, 1984).

Boulègue, Jean. *Le Grand Jolof (XIIe–XVIe siècle)* (Paris: Editions Façades, Diffusion Karthala, 1987).

Bowao, Charles Z. '"Désethnologiser": Réouverture du débat Hountondji-Diagne', *Bulletin du CODESRIA*, 1 (1995), pp. 15–19.

— 'Mondialité et devenir de l'Afrique', *Démocraties Africaines*, 7 (July–September 1996), pp. 24–8.

Cabral, Amilcar. *Return to the Source: Selected Speeches* (New York and London: Monthly Review Press, 1973).

— *Unity and Struggle: Speeches and Writings* (London: Heinemann, 1980).

Calvet, Louis-Jean. *Les Langues véhiculaires* (Paris: Presses Universitaires Françaises, 1981).

Césaire, Aimé. *Discours sur le colonialisme* (Paris: Présence Africaine, 1955). English translation by Joan Pinkham, *Discourse on Colonialism* (New York: Monthly Review Press, 1972).

Chaliand, Gérard. *Revolution in the Third World: Myths and Prospects* (London: Harvester Press, 1977). Originally published in French as *Mythes révolutionnaires du tiers monde* (Paris: Seuil, 1976).

— 'Frantz Fanon à l'épreuve du temps', in Frantz Fanon, *Les Damnés de la terre* (1961; Paris: Gallimard, Collection Folio, 1991), pp. 7–36.

Chamberlain, Muriel Evelyn. *Decolonization: The Fall of the European Empires* (Oxford: Basil Blackwell, 1985).

Chatterjee, Partha. *Nationalist Thought and the Colonial World: A Derivative Discourse?* (London: Zed Books, 1986).

Chomsky, Noam. *World Order and its Rules: Variations on Some Themes* (Belfast: West Belfast Economic Forum, 1993).

— *World Orders, Old and New* (London: Pluto Press, 1994).

Clegg, Ian. 'Workers and Managers in Algeria', in *Peasants and Proletarians: The Struggles of Third World Workers*, ed. by Robin Cohen, Peter C.W. Gutkind, and Phyllis Brazier (London: Hutchinson, 1979), pp. 223–47.

Copans, Jean, ed. *Anthropologie et impérialisme* (Paris, Maspéro, 1975).

Coquery-Vidrovitch, Catherine. 'The Transfer of Economic Power in French-Speaking West Africa', in *Decolonization and African Independence: The Transfers of Power 1960–1980*, ed. by Prosser Gifford and Wm. Roger Louis (New Haven, CT, and London: Yale University Press, 1982), pp. 105–34.

Coulson, Andrew, ed. *African Socialism in Practice: The Tanzanian Experience* (Nottingham: Spokesman Books, 1979).

Crowder, Michael. *West Africa Under Colonial Rule* (London: Hutchinson, 1968).

Cruise O'Brien, Donal B. *The Mourides of Senegal: The Political and Economic Organization of an Islamic Brotherhood* (Oxford: Oxford University Press, 1971).

— *Saints and Politicians: Essays in the Organization of a Senegalese Peasant Society* (Cambridge: Cambridge University Press, 1975).

Cruise O'Brien, Rita, *White Society in Black Africa: The French in Senegal* (London: Faber & Faber, 1972).

———, ed. *The Political Economy of Underdevelopment: Dependence in Senegal* (Beverly Hills, CA, and London: Sage, 1979).

Curtin, Philip D., ed. *Imperialism* (New York and London: Harper & Row, 1971).

Dadié, Bernard. 'Le Rôle de la légende dans la culture populaire des Noirs d'Afrique', *Présence Africaine*, 14–15 (June–September 1957), pp. 165–74.

Dammann, Ernest. *Les Religions de l'Afrique*, trans. by L. Jospin (Paris: Payot, 1978).

Davidson, Basil. *The Black Man's Burden: Africa and the Curse of the Nation-State* (London: James Currey, 1992).

Davidson, Donald. 'On the Very Idea of a Conceptual Scheme', in *Inquiries into Truth and Interpretation* (Oxford: Clarendon Press, 1984), pp. 183–98.

Davies, Miranda, ed. *Third World – Second Sex: Women's Struggles and National Liberation* (London: Zed Books, 1983).

de Benoist, Joseph-Roger. *La Balkanisation de l'Afrique occidentale française* (Dakar: Nouvelles

Editions Africaines, 1979).

— *L'Afrique occidentale française de Brazzaville (1944) à l'indépendance (1960)* (Dakar: Nouvelles Editions Africaines, 1982).

Decalo, Samuel. *Coups and Army Rule in Africa: Studies in Military Style* (New Haven, CT, and London: Yale University Press, 1976).

Decraene, Philippe. 'Permanence de l'histoire et renouveau politique au Sénégal' *Le Monde Diplomatique*, 32, 326 (May 1981), pp. 8–9.

Delbard, B. 'Les Classes sociales', in *Dakar en devenir*, ed. by M. Sankalé, et al. (Paris: Présence Africaine, 1968), pp. 423–40.

Démb ak tey (Cahiers du mythe), 2–3 (1974). Special issues on Kocc Barma.

Devereux, George. *Ethnopsychoanalysis: Psychoanalysis and Anthropology as Complementary Frames of Reference* (Berkeley and London: University of California Press, 1978).

Dia, Assane. 'Kotch Barma et Socrate: étude comparative de deux philosophes' (unpublished master's thesis, University of Dakar, 1991–92).

Dia, Mamadou. *Mémoires d'un militant du tiers-monde* (Paris: Publisud, 1985).

Diagne, Léon. 'Kotch Barma Fall: un philosophe sénégalais du XVIIe siècle' (unpublished master's thesis, University of Dakar, 1978–79).

Diagne, Pathé. *Langues africaines et impérialisme: africophonie et modernité* (Dakar: IFAN, 1976).

Diagne, Pathé, ed. *Quelle Démocratie pour le Sénégal?* (Dakar: Sankoré, 1984).

Diagne, Souleymane Bachir. 'A partir d'une évidence', in *La Culture du développement*, ed. by Souleymane Bachir Diagne (Dakar: CODESRIA, 1991), pp. 1–5.

— 'L'Avenir de la tradition', in *Sénégal: Trajectoires d'un état*, ed. by Momar Coumba Diop (Dakar: CODESRIA, 1992), pp. 279–98.

Diakhaté, Bassirou Makhoudia. 'Légendes africaines – Kothie Barma', *Paris-Dakar*, 3 September 1955, p. 4.

Diallo, Massaër. 'Tradition orale et autorité', *Revue sénégalaise de philosophie*, 13–14 (1990), pp. 197–208.

Diawara, Mamadou. 'Women, Servitude and History: The Oral Historical Traditions of Women of Servile Condition in the Kingdom of Jaara (Mali) from the fifteenth to the mid-nineteenth century', in *Discourse and its Disguises: The Interpretation of African Oral Texts*, ed. by Karin Barber and P. F. de Moraes Farias (Birmingham: University of Birmingham, Centre for West African Studies, 1989), pp. 109–37.

Dicko, Ahmadou A. *Journal d'une défaite: autour du référendum du 28 septembre 1958 en Afrique noire* (Paris: L'Harmattan, 1992).

Diedhiou, Djib. 'A nos martyres de Thiaroye', *Le Soleil* [Dakar], 1 December 1994, p. 3.

Dieng, Amady Aly. *Classes sociales et mode de production esclavagiste en Afrique de l'ouest* (Paris: Centre d'études et de recherches marxistes, 1974).

— *Hegel, Marx, Engels et les problèmes de l'Afrique noire* (Dakar: Sankoré, 1978).

Diop, Abdoulaye-Bara. *La Société wolof: tradition et changement, les systèmes d'inégalité et de domination* (Paris: Karthala, 1981).

— *La Famille wolof: tradition et changement* (Paris: Karthala, 1985).

— 'L'Organisation de la famille africaine', in *Dakar en devenir*, ed. by M. Sankalé et al. (Paris: Présence Africaine, 1968), pp. 299–313.

Diop, Boubacar. 'L'Autorité des textes religieux dans les batailles politico-idéologiques', *Revue sénégalaise de philosophie*, 13–14 (1990), pp. 221–8.

Diop, M. and H. Collomb. 'Pratiques mythiques et psychopathologie: à propos d'un cas', *Psychopathologie Africaine*, 1, 2 (1965), pp. 304–22.

— 'A propos d'un cas d'impuissance', *Psychopathologie Africaine*, 1, 3 (1965), pp. 487–511.

Diop, Majhemout. *Histoire des classes sociales dans l'Afrique de l'ouest. II: Le Sénégal* (Paris: Maspéro, 1972).

Diop, Momar Coumba and Mamadou Diouf. *Le Sénégal sous Abdou Diouf* (Paris: Karthala, 1990).

Diop, Momar Coumba. 'Introduction: Du "socialisme" au "libéralisme": les légitimités de l'état', in *Sénégal: Trajectoires d'un état*, ed. by Momar Coumba Diop (Dakar: CODESRIA, 1992), pp. 13–38.

Bibliography

Diop, Samba. 'Il y a 50 ans, "Thiaroye 44": une histoire à réhabiliter', *Sud Quotidien*, 1 December 1994, pp. 1, 6.

Diouf, Makhtar. *Sénégal, les ethnies et la nation* (Paris: L'Harmattan, 1994).

Diouf, Mamadou. *Le Kajoor au dix-neuvième siècle: pouvoir ceddo et conquête coloniale* (Paris: Karthala, 1990).

— 'Représentations historiques et légitimités politiques au Sénégal (1960–1987)', *Revue de la Bibliothèque Nationale* [Paris], 34 (1989), pp. 14–23.

— 'Le Clientélisme, la "technocratie", et après?', in *Sénégal: Trajectoires d'un état*, ed. by Momar Coumba Diop (Dakar: CODESRIA, 1992), pp. 233–78.

Dumont, Pierre, *Le français et les langues africaines au Sénégal* (Paris: Karthala, 1983).

— 'L'enseignement du français langue étrangère en Afrique francophone', *Langas: revue de sociolinguistique*, 14 (1983), pp. 41–56.

Dumont, René. *L'Afrique noire est mal partie* (Paris: Seuil, 1962). English translation by Phyllis Nauts Ott, *False Start in Africa* (London: Deutsch, 1966).

— *Pour l'Afrique, j'accuse: le journal d'un agronome au Sahel en voie de destruction* (Paris: Presses Pocket, 1986).

Dyâo, Yoro, and R. Rousseau. 'Le Sénégal d'autrefois. Etude sur le Oualo', *Bulletin du comité d'études historiques et scientifiques de l'A.O.F.*, 12 (1929), pp. 133–211.

— 'Le Sénégal d'autrefois. Etude sur le Cayor', *Bulletin du comité d'études historiques et scientifiques de l'A.O.F.* (1933), pp. 237–98.

Echenberg, Myron J. *Colonial Conscripts: The 'Tirailleurs sénégalais' in French West Africa, 1857–1960* (Portsmouth, N.H.: Heinemann; London: James Currey, 1991).

— 'Tragedy at Thiaroye: The Senegalese Soldiers' Uprising of 1944', in *African Labor History*, ed. by Peter C. W. Gutkind, Robin Cohen, and Jean Copans (Beverly Hills, CA, and London: Sage, 1978), pp. 109–28.

Fall, Mar. *L'Etat et la question syndicale au Sénégal* (Paris: L'Harmattan, 1989).

Fanon, Frantz. *Peau noire, masques blancs* (1952; Paris: Seuil, 1995). English translation by Charles Lam Markmann, *Black Skin, White Masks* (London: Pluto, 1986).

— *Les Damnés de la terre* (1961; Paris: Gallimard, Collection Folio, 1991). English translation by Constance Farrington, *The Wretched of the Earth* (London: Penguin, 1969).

Fieldhouse, D. K. *The Colonial Empires: A Comparative Study from the 18th Century* (1966; Houndmills: Macmillan, 1991).

Foltz, W. J. *From French West Africa to the Mali Federation* (New Haven, CT, and London: Yale University Press, 1965).

Foucault, Michel. *Histoire de la folie à l'âge classique* (1964; Paris: Gallimard, Collection Tel, 1996). English translation by Richard Howard, *Madness and Civilization: a History of Insanity in the Age of Reason* (London: Routledge, 1989).

— *Les Mots et les choses: une archéologie des sciences humaines* (1966; Paris: Gallimard, Collection Tel, 1996). English translation: *The Order of Things: an Archaeology of the Human Sciences* (London: Routledge, 1989).

— *L'Archéologie du savoir* (Paris: Gallimard, 1969). English translation by A. M. Sheridan Smith, *The Archaeology of Knowledge* (London: Tavistock, 1972).

— *Surveiller et punir: naissance de la prison* (1975; Paris: Gallimard, Collection Tel, 1993). English translation by Alan Sheridan, *Discipline and Punish: the Birth of the Prison* (London: Penguin, 1979).

— 'Nietzsche, la généalogie, l'histoire', in *Dits et écrits II: 1970–1975* (Paris: Gallimard, 1994), pp. 136–56. English translation by Donald F. Bouchard and Simon Sherry, 'Nietzsche, Genealogy, History', in *Language, Counter-Memory, Practice: Selected Essays and Interviews*, ed. by Donald F. Bouchard (Oxford: Basil Blackwell, 1977), pp. 139–64.

Fougeyrollas, Pierre. *Où va le Sénégal?* (Dakar: IFAN; Paris: Anthropos, 1970).

— 'Le Devenir des valeurs et des attitudes', in *Dakar en devenir*, ed. by M. Sankalé et al. (Paris: Présence Africaine, 1968), pp. 441–60.

Freud, Sigmund. *The Complete Psychological Works of Sigmund Freud: Five Lectures on Psycho-Analysis,*

Leonardo Da Vinci and Other Works, XI (1957; London: Hogarth Press, 1995).

Frobenius, Léo. *Histoire de la civilisation africaine*, trans. by Dr H. Back and D. Ermont (1936; Monaco: Le Rocher, 1987).

Fukuyama, Francis. *The End of History and the Last Man* (London: Hamish Hamilton, 1992).

Gellar, Sheldon. *Senegal: An African Nation between Islam and the West* (Boulder, CO, Westview Press, 1982).

— *Structural Changes and Colonial Dependency: Senegal 1885–1945* (Beverly Hills, CA, and London: Sage, 1977).

Gifford, Prosser, and Wm. Roger Louis, eds. *France and Britain in Africa: Imperial Rivalry and Colonial Rule* (New Haven, CT, and London: Yale University Press, 1971).

Gifford, Prosser, and Wm. Roger Louis, eds. *Decolonization and African Independence: The Transfers of Power 1960–1980* (New Haven and London: Yale University Press, 1982).

Gilroy, Paul. *The Black Atlantic: Modernity and Double Consciousness* (London and New York: Verso, 1993).

Girard, Jean. *Les Bassari du Sénégal* (Paris: L'Harmattan, 1984).

Girardet, Raoul. *L'Idée coloniale en France, 1871–1962* (Paris: La Table Ronde, 1972).

Gramsci, Antonio. *Selections from the Prison Notebooks of Antonio Gramsci*, ed. and trans. by Quintin Hoare and Geoffrey Nowell Smith (1971; London: Lawrence & Wishart; New York: International Publishers, 1995).

Guidy Wandja, Joséphine. 'Excision? Mutilation sexuelle? Mythe ou réalité?', *Présence Africaine*, 141 (1st quarter 1987), pp. 53–8.

Guissé, Youssouph Mbargane. *Philosophie, culture et devenir social en Afrique noire* (Dakar: Nouvelles Editions Africaines, 1979).

Gutkind, Peter C. W., Robin Cohen, and Jean Copans, eds. *African Labor History* (Beverly Hills, CA, and London: Sage, 1978).

Habermas, Jürgen. *The Philosophical Discourse of Modernity*, trans. by Frederick Lawrence (1985; Oxford: Polity Press, 1987).

Harvey, David. *The Condition of Postmodernity* (1989; Cambridge, MA, and Oxford: Basil Blackwell, 1992).

Hauser, A. 'Les Problèmes du travail', in *Dakar en devenir*, ed. by M. Sankalé et al. (Paris: Présence Africaine, 1968), pp. 359–93.

Hegel, Georg Wilhelm Friedrich. *Lectures on the Philosophy of World History. Introduction: Reason in History*, trans. by H. B. Nesbitt (1830; Cambridge: Cambridge University Press, 1975).

Hobsbawm, Eric. *Nations and Nationalism since 1780* (1990; Cambridge: Cambridge University Press, Revised Canto edition, 1995).

— 'Inventing Traditions', in *The Invention of Tradition*, ed. by Eric Hobsbawm and Terence Ranger (1983; Cambridge: Cambridge University Press, Canto edition, 1992), pp. 1–14.

Hobsbawm, Eric and Terence Ranger, eds. *The Invention of Tradition* (1983; Cambridge: Cambridge University Press, Canto edition, 1992).

Hountondji, Paulin J. *Sur la 'philosophie africaine': critique de l'ethnophilosophie* (Paris: Maspéro, 1977). English translation by Henri Evans with the collaboration of Jonathan Rée, *African Philosophy: Myth and Reality* (London: Hutchinson University Library for Africa, 1983).

— *Les Savoirs endogènes: pistes pour une recherche* (Dakar: CODESRIA, 1994).

— 'Remarques sur la philosophie africaine contemporaine', *Diogène*, 71 (July–September 1970), pp. 120–40.

— 'La Dépendance scientifique, hier et aujourd'hui', *Revue sénégalaise de philosophie*, 13–14 (1990), pp. 17–27.

Hyden, Goran. *Beyond Ujamaa in Tanzania: Underdevelopment and an Uncaptured Peasantry* (London: Heinemann, 1980).

Jablow, Alta. *Yes and No: The Intimate Folklore of Africa* (New York: Horizon Press, 1961).

Jackson, Robert H., and Carl G. Rosberg. *Personal Rule in Black Africa: Prince, Autocrat, Prophet, Tyrant* (Berkeley, Los Angeles, London: University of California Press, 1982).

Jayawardena, Kumari. *Feminism and Nationalism in the Third World* (London: Zed Books, 1986).

Bibliography

Kaba, Lansiné. 'From Colonialism to Autocracy: Guinea Under Sékou Touré', in *Decolonization and African Independence: The Transfers of Power 1960–1980*, ed. by Prosser Gifford and Wm. Roger Louis (New Haven, CT, and London: Yale University Press, 1982), pp. 225–44.

Kabou, Axelle. *Et si l'Afrique refusait le développement?* (Paris: L'Harmattan, 1991).

Kagamé, Alexis. *La Philosophie bantu comparée* (Paris: Présence Africaine, 1976).

Kane, Oumar. 'Samba Gelago-Jegi', *Bulletin de l'IFAN*, series B, 32, 4 (1970), pp. 912–96.

Kiernan, V. G. *The Lords of Human Kind: Black Man, Yellow Man and White Man in an Age of Empire* (1969; London: Hutchinson, 1988).

— *Marxism and Imperialism* (New York: St Martin's Press, 1974).

Klein, Martin A. 'Servitude among the Wolof and Sereer of Senegambia', in *Slavery in Africa: Historical and Anthropological Perspectives*, ed. by Suzanne Miers and Igor Kopytoff (Madison: University of Wisconsin Press, 1977), pp. 335–63.

Kodjo, Edem. *Et demain l'Afrique* (Paris: Stock, 1986).

Laye, Camara. *Le Maître de la parole* (Paris: Plon, 1978). English translation by James Kirkup, *The Guardian of the Word* (London: Fontana, 1980).

Leclerc, Gérard. *Anthropologie et colonialisme* (Paris: Fayard, 1972).

Lévi-Strauss, Claude. *Anthropologie structurale* (Paris: Plon, 1954). English translation by Claire Jacobson and Brooke Grundfest Schoepf, *Structural Anthropology* (London: Penguin, 1968).

Lévy-Bruhl, Lucien. *Les Fonctions mentales dans les sociétés inférieures* (Paris: Alcan, 1910).

Little, Kenneth. *African Women in Towns* (Cambridge: Cambridge University Press, 1973).

Lô, Magatte. *Sénégal: Syndicalisme et participation responsable* (Paris: L'Harmattan, 1987).

Lombard, Maurice. *L'Islam dans sa première grandeur (VIIIe–XIe siècle)* (Paris: Flammarion, 1971).

Lukács, Georg. *History and Class Consciousness*, trans. by Rodney Livingstone (London: Merlin Press, 1971).

McLynn, Frank. *Hearts of Darkness: The European Exploration of Africa* (London: Pimlico, 1992).

MacPherson, Stewart. *Social Policy in the Third World: The Social Dilemmas of Underdevelopment* (Brighton: Wheatsheaf Books, 1982).

Malinowski, Bronislaw. *Sex and Repression in Savage Society* (1927; Cleveland, OH, and New York: World Publishing Co., 1964).

Makhoudia, Bassirou. 'Légendes africaines – Kothie Barma', *Paris–Dakar*, 3 September 1955, p. 4.

Marx, Karl. *Capital*, trans. by Samuel Moore and Edward Aveling (London: Lawrence & Wishart, 1974).

Marx, Karl, and Frederick Engels. *Collected Works*, 6 (London: Lawrence & Wishart, 1976).

Mbodj, I. 'Simplicité et solennité', *Le Soleil* [Dakar], 2 December 1994, p. 2.

Mbow, Lat Soucabé. 'Les Politiques urbaines: gestion et aménagement', in *Sénégal: Trajectoires d'un état*, ed. by Momar Coumba Diop (Dakar: CODESRIA, 1992), pp. 205–31.

Meillassoux, Claude, ed. *L'Esclavage en Afrique précoloniale* (Paris: Maspéro, 1975).

Memmi, Albert. *Le Portrait du colonisé* (1957; Paris: Payot, 1973). English translation by Howard Greenfeld, *The Colonizer and the Colonized* (London: Earthscan, 1990).

Mende, Tibor. *From Aid to Recolonization* (London: Harrap, 1973). Originally published in French as *De l'Aide à la recolonisation* (Paris: Seuil, 1972).

Mernissi, Fatima. *Beyond the Veil: Male-Female Dynamics in Modern Muslim Society* (London: Al Saqi Books, 1985).

Mersadier, Y. 'Les Niveaux de vie', in *Dakar en devenir*, ed. by M. Sankalé et al. (Paris: Présence Africaine, 1968), pp. 247–63.

Meyer, Jean. *Esclaves et négriers* (Paris: Gallimard, 'Découvertes', 1986).

Mies, Maria. *Patriarchy and Accumulation on a World Scale* (London: Zed Books, 1986).

Milliot, Louis and François-Paul Blanc. *Introduction à l'étude du droit musulman* (Paris: Sirey, 1987).

Monteil, Vincent. *L'Islam noir* (1964; Paris: Seuil, 1971).

— *Esquisses sénégalaises* (Dakar: IFAN, 1966).

— 'Lat Dior, Damel du Kayor (1842–1886) et l'Islamisation des Wolof ', *Archives de sociologie des religions*, 16 (1963), pp. 77–104.

Moore, Henrietta L. *Feminism and Anthropology* (Oxford: Polity Press, 1988).

Mudimbe, V. Y. *L'Odeur du père: essai sur les limites de la science et de la vie en Afrique noire* (Paris: Présence Africaine, 1982).

— *The Invention of Africa: Gnosis, Philosophy and the Order of Knowledge* (London: James Currey, 1988).

Ndaw, Alassane. *La Pensée africaine – recherches sur les fondements de la pensée négro-africaine* (Dakar: Nouvelles Editions Africaines, 1983).

Ndiaye, A. Raphaël. *La Place de la femme dans les rites au Sénégal* (Dakar: Nouvelles Editions Africaines, 1986).

Nicolas, Guy. 'Les Transformations de l'Islam en Afrique noire', *Le Monde Diplomatique*, 32, 326 (May 1981), pp. 8–9.

Nolan, Riall W. 'L'Histoire des migrations bassari: influences et perspectives', *Journal des Africanistes*, 42, 2 (1977), pp. 81–101.

— 'Citadins bassari: la révolution tranquille', *Objets et mondes*, 21, 4 (Winter 1981), pp. 155–8.

November, András, *L'Evolution du mouvement syndical en Afrique occidentale* (Paris and The Hague, Mouton, 1965).

Oloruntimehin, B. Olatunji. 'Senegambia – Mahmadou Lamine', in *West African Resistance*, ed. by Michael Crowder (London: Hutchinson, 1971), pp. 80–110.

Ortigues, Marie-Cécile and Edmond. *Œdipe africain* (1966; Paris: Union Générale d'Editions, 1973).

Panter-Brick, Keith. 'Independence French Style', in *Decolonization and African Independence: The Transfers of Power 1960–1980*, ed. by Prosser Gifford and Wm. Roger Louis (New Haven, CT, and London: Yale University Press, 1982), pp. 73–104.

Paulme, Denise. *La Mère dévorante: essai sur la morphologie des contes africains* (Paris: Gallimard, 1976).

Person, Yves. *Samori: une révolution dyula*, 3 vols (Dakar: IFAN, 1968).

— *Samori: la renaissance de l'empire mandingue* (Paris: ABC; Dakar: Nouvelles Editions Africaines, 1976).

Pieterse, Jan Nederveen. *Empire and Emancipation* (London: Pluto Press, 1991).

Piquet, Victor. *Histoire des colonies françaises* (Paris: Payot, 1931).

Rabain, Jacqueline. *L'Enfant du lignage: du sevrage à la classe d'âge chez les Wolof du Sénégal* (Paris: Payot, 1979).

Ranger, Terence. 'The Invention of Tradition in Colonial Africa', in *The Invention of Tradition*, ed. by Eric Hobsbawm and Terence Ranger (1983; Cambridge: Cambridge University Press, Canto edition, 1992), pp. 211–62.

Robinson, David. 'An Approach to Islam in West African History', in *Faces of Islam in African Literature*, ed. by Kenneth W. Harrow (London: James Currey; Portsmouth, NH: Heinemann, 1991), pp. 107–29.

Samb, Amar. 'L'Islam et l'histoire du Sénégal', *Bulletin de l'IFAN*, series B, 33, 3 (1971), pp. 461–507.

Sankalé, M. et al. 'Urbanisation et santé', in *Dakar en devenir*, ed. by M. Sankalé, et al. (Paris: Présence Africaine, 1968), pp. 265–97.

Sankalé, M., et al., eds. *Dakar en devenir* (Paris: Présence Africaine, 1968).

Schenkel, R. 'Le Vécu de la vie sexuelle des Africains acculturés du Sénégal, à partir de notions d'impuissance et de puissance sexuelle', *Psychopathologie Africaine*, 7, 3 (1971), pp. 313–88.

Schipper, Mineke. *Source of all Evil: African Proverbs and Sayings on Women* (London: Allison & Busby, 1991).

Schumacher, Edward J. *Politics, Bureaucracy and Rural Development in Senegal* (Berkeley, Los Angeles and London: University of California Press, 1975).

Seck, Assane. *Dakar: métropole ouest-africaine* (Dakar: IFAN, 1970).

Senghor, Léopold Sédar. *Liberté 2: Nation et voie africaine du socialisme* (Paris: Seuil, 1971).

— *Liberté 4: Socialisme et planification* (Paris: Seuil, 1983).

Simmel, Georg. *The Sociology of Georg Simmel*, trans. and ed. by Kurt H. Wolff (1950; London: Collier-Macmillan, 1964).

Smith, Neil. *Uneven Development: Nature, Capital and the Production of Space* (1984; Oxford and Cambridge, Mass.: Basil Blackwell, 1990).

Bibliography

Sow, Fatou. 'Femmes africaines, emploi et division internationale du travail', *Présence Africaine*, 141 (1st quarter 1987), pp. 195–226.

Suret-Canale, Jean. *Afrique noire occidentale et centrale* (Paris: Editions Sociales, 1958).

— 'L'Almamy Samory Touré', *Recherches Africaines*, 1–4 (1959), pp. 18–22.

— 'The French West African Railway Workers' Strike, 1947–48', in *African Labor History*, ed. by Peter C. W. Gutkind, Robin Cohen, and Jean Copans (Beverly Hills, CA, and London: Sage, 1978), pp. 129–54.

Sy, Cheikh Tidiane. 'Ahmadu Bamba et l'islamisation des Wolof', *Bulletin de l'IFAN*, series B, 32, 2 (1970), pp. 412–33.

Sylla, Assane. *La Philosophie morale des Wolof* (Dakar: Sankoré, 1978).

Tempels, Placide. *Bantu Philosophy*, trans. by Colin King (Paris: Présence Africaine, 1959).

Thiam, Awa. *La Parole aux négresses* (Paris: Denoël, 1978). English translation by Dorothy S. Blair, *Black Sisters, Speak Out* (London: Pluto Press, 1986).

Thiam, Iba Der. *Incidences de l'utilisation des langues nationales sur le fonctionnement des institutions participatives* (Paris: UNESCO, 1983).

— 'L'Evolution politique et syndicale du Sénégal colonial de 1840 à 1936' (unpublished doctoral thesis, University of Paris I, 1983).

— 'Recherches sur les premières manifestations de la conscience syndicale au Sénégal (la période 1936–1937)', *Annales de la Faculté des Lettres et Sciences Humaines de Dakar*, 5 (1975), pp. 235–48.

— 'La Tuerie de Thiès de septembre 1938, essai d'interprétation', *Bulletin de l'IFAN*, series B, 38, 2 (1976), pp. 300–38.

— 'Galandou Diouf et le Front Populaire', *Bulletin de l'IFAN*, series B, 38, 3 (1976), pp. 592–618.

— 'Recherches sur les premières manifestations de la conscience syndicale au Sénégal (l'année 1938)', *Annales de la Faculté des Lettres et Sciences Humaines de Dakar*, 6 (1976), pp. 87–116.

— 'Les Origines du mouvement syndical sénégalais: la grève des cheminots du Dakar-Saint-Louis du 13 au 15 avril 1919', *Annales de la Faculté des Lettres et Sciences Humaines de Dakar*, 7 (1977), pp. 209–39.

Thoré, Luc. 'Mariage et divorce dans la banlieue de Dakar', *Cahiers d'études africaines*, 4, 16 (1964), pp. 479–551.

Towa, Marcien. *Essai sur la problématique philosophique dans l'Afrique actuelle* (Yaoundé: CLE, 1971).

— *Léopold Sédar Senghor: Négritude ou servitude?* (Yaoundé: CLE, 1971).

Uwechue, Ralph, ed. *Africa Today* (London: Africa Books, 1996; third edition).

Vigné d'Octon, Paul. *La Gloire du sabre* (1900; Paris: Quintette, 1984).

Villalón, Leonardo A. *Islamic Society and State Power in Senegal* (Cambridge: Cambridge University Press, 1995).

Wallerstein, Immanuel. *The Capitalist World-Economy* (Cambridge: Cambridge University Press, 1979).

Wauthier, Claude. *L'Afrique des Africains: inventaire de la Négritude* (Paris: Seuil, 1973, second edition). English translation by Shirley Kay, *The Literature and Thought of Modern Africa* (London: Heinemann, 1978).

Werner, Jean-François. *Marges, sexe et drogues à Dakar: enquête ethnographique* (Paris: Karthala/ORSTOM, 1994).

Worseley, Peter. *The Third World* (1964; London: Weidenfeld & Nicolson, 1967).

Young, Crawford. 'The Colonial State and Post-Colonial Crisis', in *Decolonization and African Independence: The Transfers of Power 1960–1980*, ed. by Prosser Gifford and Wm. Roger Louis (New Haven, CT, and London: Yale University Press, 1982), pp. 1–31.

Index

Index

Index

Index

Oyono, Ferdinand
Houseboy, 151

Person, Yves, 25
Pétain, Philippe, 159, 161, 162
Pfaff, Françoise
The Cinema of Ousmane Sembene, 4, 109
polygamy, 104-5, 113, 114, 124, 126, 127, 138,
141-6
Pontecorvo, Gillo
The Battle of Algiers, 151
poststructuralism, 7, 19-20, 21-2, 24-6
Potts, James, 80-1

Ranger, Terence, 16, 22-3
Robinson, David, 174-5
Rocha, Glauber
Terra em transe, 105n
Rouch, Jean, 77-8
Roumain, Jacques
Masters of the Dew, 41n
Rushdie, Salman, 225
Imaginary Homelands, 38
Midnight's Children, 224n

Sadji, Abdoulaye
Nini, mulâtresse du Sénégal, 132
Sassine, Williams, 187
Said, Edward, 11n, 15, 17n, 23, 107, 216
Samb, Amar, 16-17, 18, 174, 223
Schenkel, R., 103-5
Sembene (Ousmane Sembene, Sembene
Ousmane)
biographical information on, 1, 1n, 42-3,
68, 69, 158, 230
concern with form in the work of, 7-8, 40-
65, 73-4, 87-8, 110-12, 122-3, 158, 179-
80, 234, 238-9
critical studies of his work, 3-5, 6, 6n
on *Camp de Thiaroye*, 158, 159, 162-3, 166
on *Ceddo*, 173, 178, 236-7
on cinema, 68-71, 221, 238
on communism, 240
on *Emitaï*, 161, 168-9
on fetishism (animism), 29-30, 99, 108,
122-3, 158
on gender issues, 125, 126, 133-50, 230
on Islam, 30, 138, 172, 175-6
on *Le Mandat/Mandabi*, 74-5, 76-7
on Negritude, 28-9, 31, 52, 58, 197, 232
on role of artist/storyteller, 7-8, 28-9, 35-6,
52-7, 61-6, 162, 225-6
on slave trade, 30, 46, 231-2
on *Xala*, 99-100, 108, 115, 119-20
representation of Africa in the work of, 28-
9, 32-4, 37-8, 39, 43-4, 46-7, 52, 81, 84-

5, 97, 122-3, 133-50, 179-85, 215-16,
224-5, 232, 235-6
work on *Kaddu* (Wolof-language newspaper), 119, 119n, 173, 236-7
Senegal
caste system in, 54-5
cinema in, 66, 69-70, 69n, 98-9, 99n
ethnic groups in, 54-5, 168-9, 174, 175,
176, 205n, 235-6
French colonisation of, 2, 151-72, 203, 237
history of, 1-2, 16-18, 23, 33, 48, 151-84,
203, 231, 237
Islam in, 16-18, 172-84, 237
literature of, 1, 2-3, 2n, 12-14, 225-6
neo-colonialism in, 9, 75, 110, 110n, 112,
188, 192-204
polygamy in, 141-2
politics in, 1, 6, 12-14, 26, 36-8, 52, 54, 56,
56n, 81-5, 110, 110n, 112, 129, 167-8,
172-3, 192-204, 222, 225-6, 236-7
studies of impotence in, 103-5
urbanisation in, 82-3
Senghor, Léopold Sédar, 1, 2, 5, 12-14, 15, 15n,
37n, 44, 52, 56, 65n, 74, 76, 81, 82, 83, 84,
86n, 112, 112n, 130, 131, 132-3, 135-6,
173-4, 188, 192-9, 204, 205, 206, 225, 226,
236
Sierra Leone, 203
Simmel, Georg, 87n
slave trade, 29-30, 46-7, 47n, 50, 172, 175-6,
176n, 180-1, 184, 232
Socé, Ousmane, 2
Karim, 54, 132
Sokhona, Sidney, 71n
Solanas, Fernando, 79
Somalia, 19, 203
Sow Fall, Aminata
L'Appel des arènes, 25n, 140-1
The Beggars' Strike, 121n
L'Ex-père de la nation, 197n
Soyinka, Wole,
Myth, Literature and the African World, 14-15,
15n, 32, 34, 34n
Spivak, Gayatri Chakravorty, 5, 19, 125
Stafford, Andy, 6n, 46n
Suleri, Sara, 126
Sylla, Assane, 23n, 175, 223

Taaw (film), 3, 3n, 65n, 66, 219
Taaw (novella), 3, 65n, 135, 144n, 145-6, 150,
230
Tansi, Sony Labou, 187
The Seven Solitudes of Lorsa Lopez, 224n
Tanzania, 191-2
Thiam, Awa, 129, 138, 138n
Thiam, Habib, 54

274

Index